# Conflict,
# Cooperation,
# and Justice

Barbara Benedict Bunker
Jeffrey Z. Rubin
and Associates

· · · · · · · · · · · · · · · · · · · · · · · · · · · · · ·

Foreword by Stuart Oskamp

# Conflict, Cooperation, and Justice

Essays Inspired by the Work of Morton Deutsch

Jossey-Bass Publishers
San Francisco

Substantial discounts on bulk quantities of Jossey-Bass books are available to corporations, professional associations, and other organizations. For details and discount information, contact the special sales department at Jossey-Bass Inc., Publishers. (415) 433–1740; Fax (800) 605–2665.

For sales outside the United States, please contact your local Paramount Publishing International office.

 Manufactured in the United States of America on Lyons Falls Pathfinder Tradebook. This paper is acid-free and 100 percent totally chlorine-free.

**Library of Congress Cataloging-in-Publication Data**

Conflict, cooperation, and justice : essays inspired by the work of
  Morton Deutsch / [edited by] Barbara Benedict Bunker, Jeffrey Z.
  Rubin. — 1st ed.
     p.   cm. — (The Jossey-Bass management series)
  Includes index.
  ISBN 0–7879–0069–9 (acid-free paper)
   1. Deutsch, Morton, date.  2. Social justice.  3. Social
conflict.  I. Deutsch, Morton, date.  II. Bunker, Barbara
Benedict.  III. Rubin, Jeffrey Z.  IV. Series.
HM216.C657   1995
303—dc20
                                      94–46743

FIRST EDITION
HB *Printing*     10 9 8 7 6 5 4 3 2 1

# Conflict, Cooperation, and Justice

Essays Inspired by the Work of
Morton Deutsch

Jossey-Bass Publishers
San Francisco

Substantial discounts on bulk quantities of Jossey-Bass books are available to corporations, professional associations, and other organizations. For details and discount information, contact the special sales department at Jossey-Bass Inc., Publishers. (415) 433–1740; Fax (800) 605–2665.

For sales outside the United States, please contact your local Paramount Publishing International office.

 Manufactured in the United States of America on Lyons Falls Pathfinder Tradebook. This paper is acid-free and 100 percent totally chlorine-free.

**Library of Congress Cataloging-in-Publication Data**

Conflict, cooperation, and justice : essays inspired by the work of
  Morton Deutsch / [edited by] Barbara Benedict Bunker, Jeffrey Z.
  Rubin. — 1st ed.
     p.    cm. — (The Jossey-Bass management series)
   Includes index.
   ISBN 0–7879–0069–9 (acid-free paper)
   1. Deutsch, Morton, date.  2. Social justice.  3. Social
conflict.  I. Deutsch, Morton, date.  II. Bunker, Barbara
Benedict.  III. Rubin, Jeffrey Z.  IV. Series.
HM216.C657    1995
303—dc20                                                           94–46743

FIRST EDITION
HB Printing          10 9 8 7 6 5 4 3 2 1

The Jossey-Bass Conflict Resolution Series

• • • • • • • • • • • • • • • • • • • • • • • • • • • • • • • •

Consulting Editor
Jeffrey Z. Rubin
*Tufts University*

Sponsored by the
Society for the
Psychological Study of Social Issues

# Contents

· · · · · · · · · · · · · · · · · · · · · · · · · · · · · · ·

## Part One: Conflict

# Foreword

Conflict, cooperation, and justice—in the 1990s these concepts are central both in international affairs and in people's personal lives. This book aims to expand our knowledge of these crucial topics, just as its inspiration, Morton Deutsch, has been doing during his fifty-year career as a social psychologist.

These topics are also central to the mission of the Society for the Psychological Study of Social Issues (SPSSI). SPSSI was formed in 1936 with the goal of bringing psychological theory and practice together to help resolve human problems of groups, communities, and nations. It seeks to follow the dictum of one of its founders, Kurt Lewin, that "there is nothing so practical as a good theory." Therefore, SPSSI is delighted and proud to sponsor this book in honor of Morton Deutsch, who was one of Lewin's students and who has notably advanced Lewin's efforts toward resolving social conflicts.

In an article in the *Journal of Social Issues* in 1992, Deutsch described what it was like to be in the pioneering group of social psychologists that formed around Lewin in the 1940s. Since those early days, Mort's research and theoretical writings have made him the preeminent authority on the dynamics of conflict, cooperation, and justice. During his more than twenty-five years of leadership of the social psychology program at Teachers College, Columbia University, Mort served as mentor and friend to countless social scientists. Within SPSSI, he also took a vital leadership role, serving as president in 1960–61 and receiving SPSSI's highest research honor, the Kurt Lewin Memorial Award, in 1968.

This book not only honors the work of Morton Deutsch but, as its editors indicate, it aspires to present new cutting-edge ideas and perspectives on the topics that have been central in Mort's research career. The editors and authors have written provocative chapters that press the frontiers of our current knowledge and suggest issues and paths that require future concentrated attention. The result is a very stimulating collection of papers that should be of wide general interest, with special importance for the key social issues at the heart of SPSSI's mission.

My role as an officer of SPSSI is to launch this volume and to say "well done!" On behalf of readers and colleagues everywhere, thanks go to Mort Deutsch for his lifetime of dedication to central issues of human interaction and his commitment to helping improve social problems. And thanks to the authors and editors of this book for following Mort's example in offering their devoted concentration and thoughtful insights on the ways in which justice in human affairs can be advanced or inhibited by processes of cooperation or competition.

*Claremont, California*                                   Stuart Oskamp
*March 1995*                                     *SPSSI president 1993–94*

# About the Book

. . . . . . . . . . . . . . . . . . . . . . . . . . . . . . . . .

This book honors and, we hope, extends the intellectual contribution that Morton Deutsch has made to understanding conflict, cooperation, and justice. As editors, we want to describe how this book came to be and also to comment on the quality of the mentoring relationships that Mort has had over the years, not only with those of us whom he trained but also with many others in the field.

We were students in the early days of the social psychology program that Deutsch founded in 1963 at Teachers College, Columbia University. While seminar encounters were formative for all of us, the informal faculty-student lunches at the Interchurch Center, where we discussed the relationship of social psychology to everything from civil rights to urban anomie, linger in our memories. The Lewinian tradition of social concern and social relevance—the intimate linkage of theory and practice—was key in our training.

In 1990, some of the students Mort had trained in his twenty-five-plus years at Teachers College gathered with faculty and friends to celebrate his seventieth birthday and "retirement" from the college. (Deutsch-style retirement consists of maintaining an office at the college, while continuing to write and do research at an only slightly less intense pace.)

During the celebration, we had a series of conversations about what could be done to honor the contribution that Morton Deutsch has made to social psychology. Festchrifts were out, and besides they were usually boring. You don't honor someone who has been an endless source of interesting ideas with a boring book!

Motivated to do something but still at a loss, we decided to get together with Mort and talk about his career. We made a date when we were all in New York and had a long and leisurely lunch at a favorite cafe on Broadway. We talked of the early days of social psychology, of life around Lewin, of Mort's first meeting with him at the Edison Hotel. We talked about the different stages in the development of Mort's work. We ran out of time and scheduled another lunch. Three lunches later, we had developed an idea that we really liked so we tested it out with Mort.

What if we took the three major areas of work where Mort had made a distinguished contribution—conflict, cooperation, and justice—and tried to identify some of the still unresolved issues and questions in each area? Then we would ask scholars in the field to address these unanswered questions. We loved our idea, and so did Mort. It felt like a really different kind of book, one that we would all enjoy bringing to life.

We interviewed Mort in depth about unresolved issues, first in conflict, then in cooperation, and then in justice. We reacted, we clarified, we felt completely engaged. By this time we were "doing" Sunday mornings at his upper–West Side apartment and taking Lydia Deutsch with us to lunch. Finally, we left Mort alone and sat down to write a prospectus and think about possible contributors to this venture.

Encouraged by Bill Hicks at Jossey-Bass, we began to approach authors; to our delight, the response was overwhelmingly positive and enthusiastic. The authors of *Conflict, Cooperation, and Justice* are all authorities in their field. They are Mort's colleagues, students, grand-students, admirers, loyal opposition, and friends. At the same time, we began talking with the Society for the Psychological Study of Social Issues (SPSSI) about the possibility of sponsoring the book. SPSSI's answer was immediate and enthusiastic, a fitting response for an organization with which Mort has had long ties, including service as SPSSI's president and as recipient of SPSSI's prestigious Lewin Award.

As our dialogue with authors began, it occurred to us that readers might enjoy Mort's own responses and reactions to the chapters we had solicited. We asked him if he would comment on each of the sections after he had had a chance to read and digest the papers, and Mort quickly agreed. Throughout the process, working with Mort has been a delight. We hope that the book itself, as well as the process that created it, will be as satisfying to him as it has been to us.

Also in the first order of acknowledgments must be the women and men who authored chapters in this book. Their willing and enthusiastic agreement to our initial request to participate in this venture, along with their good-humored response to several rounds of feedback and revisions, have made the process of completing this project more pleasurable and less painful.

Bill Hicks and Cedric Crocker at Jossey-Bass shepherded this book at every step along the way. They encouraged us to take intellectual chances and to experiment; they have been a source of wise counsel throughout. We are also indebted to Mary Garrett for her careful copyediting of the final manuscript.

This has not been one of those enterprises where we must thank our families for forsaking vacations and putting up with bad temper, unusual stress, or total unavailability. Rather, we have done this work along with the busy rest of our lives. It has been a pleasure to have a joint project that provided opportunities to talk and to work together.

*Cruz Bay, Saint John*　　　　　　　　　Barbara Benedict Bunker
*U.S. Virgin Islands*　　　　　　　　　　　Jeffrey Z. Rubin
*March 1995*

Steve Manville

# About Morton Deutsch

· · · · · · · · · · · · · · · · · · · · · · · · · · · · · · · · · · · · · · · ·

The American Psychological Association's Distinguished Scientific Contribution Award citation (1987) to Morton Deutsch
begins: "For rigorous scientific study of significant social problems."

Morton Deutsch's life and career have been characterized by an
abiding concern for social justice and the welfare of humanity. Born
in New York City in 1920, he grew up in a home alive with conversation and debate about socialism and Marxism. A precocious
child, Deutsch skipped several grades in school. By high school, he
was reading Freud and was intrigued with those new ideas, as well
as the writings of Fromm and Horney. As a fifteen-year-old student
entering the City College of New York in the 1930s, he lived with
an acute awareness of the Nazi menace and the grave inequities
between social classes, which were made vivid by the Depression.
Then came the barbarism of World War II and the atomic bomb,
the knowledge that we can destroy ourselves or work together to
create a harmonious world.

At first, Deutsch headed toward a clinical career, receiving a
master's degree (1940) in clinical psychology from the University
of Pennsylvania. This was followed by a rotating internship in several New York State institutions that enriched his clinical training.
In 1942, he entered the air force, where he saw active duty as a nav-
igator until the war's end. Then, the GI Bill made returning to graduate school a reasonable next step. He was interested in the work

of Carl Rogers at the University of Chicago, Clark Hull and his followers at Yale, and Kurt Lewin at the Massachusetts Institute of Technology (MIT). Increasingly, during the war, Deutsch had been impressed by the importance of social factors in human life, and his interests began to shift from clinical to social psychology. His first meeting with Kurt Lewin was a breakfast at the Hotel Edison in New York in September 1945. He remembers that Lewin arrived late, jacketless and bursting with enthusiasm. It was Lewin's energetic determination to be at the leading edge of pressing scientific and social issues that captured Deutsch's imagination and led him to decide in favor of MIT.

The Center for Group Dynamics at MIT in the mid 1940s attracted a formidable array of notable names in social psychology. Kurt Back, Alex Bavelas, Dorwin Cartwright, Leon Festinger, John R. P. French, Murray Horwitz, Harold Kelley, Ronald Lippitt, Albert Pepitone, Stanley Schachter, John Thibaut, and Alvin Zander became, with Deutsch, the creative group that led social psychology for several generations.

In this stimulating milieu, research and social concerns were closely interwoven. When Deutsch began to develop his own dissertation, his early attraction to research on group size and task structure faded as he realized that he wanted to engage in intellectual work that was both theoretically and socially significant. When he began to consider cooperation and competition, he realized that this was, indeed, an area where people often had impassioned beliefs, but no one had really tried to carefully understand the underlying structure, antecedents, and consequences of these two types of social interdependence. His dissertation was the first major theme in Deutsch's intellectual career: the work on cooperation. His classic study on the effects of cooperation and competition laid the groundwork for hundreds of other studies, although he himself did not linger long in this area.

A deeply rooted New Yorker who has never lost his love of walking the city streets, Deutsch's early career at New York University and the New School for Social Research led him to study issues of intergroup prejudice and discrimination. He also coauthored one of the first texts on research methods. Then, in 1956, he was invited to join a newly formed basic research group at Bell Laboratories, across the river from his beloved New York. His work there with Robert Krauss aided him in devising new methods for studying interpersonal bargaining in situations of potential conflict. Deutsch has always drawn on his life experience to stimulate and inform his intellectual ideas; in this case, a summer drive down a one-lane section of the Amalfi Coast Road in a Volkswagen with poor brakes became the inspiration for the Acme Bolt Trucking Game.

When Deutsch accepted the invitation to start a new doctoral program in social psychology at Teachers College, Columbia University, in 1963, his New Jersey commuting days ended, but his work on conflict resolution took on new energy. He continued to see a few patients each week in his psychoanalytic practice and to apply ideas drawn from intrapsychic conflict to his laboratory studies of interpersonal and intergroup conflict. He also engaged his students in lunchtime discussions of current social issues (of which there were many in the protest-filled 1960s), as well as of ways of applying social psychology to help create a better world. For a period of close to fifteen years, Deutsch and his students studied a broad spectrum of conflict themes that are well summarized in *The Resolution of Conflict* (1973).

The third phase of Deutsch's intellectual career began when Mel Lerner invited him to write a paper for a conference on injustice in North America, and, shortly thereafter, another one for *The Journal of Social Issues*. The result was two innovative and provocative papers: "Awakening the Sense of Injustice" and "Equity, Equality, and Need." The papers sparked a new research development that began in the late 1970s and continues to this day. At the same time, the papers continued a theme in Deutsch's work that harks back to his dissertation concern with mixed-motive situations and the conditions under which one can obtain a fair and just agreement. Much of the work of Deutsch and his students in this area has been published in his book *Distributive Justice* (1985).

In 1990, Deutsch officially retired and became the E. L. Thorndike Professor Emeritus of Psychology and Education at Teachers College. However, he has continued as director of the International Center for Cooperation and Conflict Resolution (ICCCR), where he and his students have done research on the effects of training in cooperation and conflict resolution on students in an alternative high school. Along with Ellen Raider, he has recently initiated a new graduate studies program in conflict resolution and mediation at Teachers College.

In a field that sometimes sees quick shifts in researcher interests, Morton Deutsch's career has had a focus and a unity that marks it clearly. Deutsch has been recognized by peers with numerous honors: The American Association for the Advancement of Science Sociopsychological Prize, the G. W. Allport Award, the Kurt Lewin Award, the Nevitt Sanford Award, the Distinguished Scientist Award of the Society of Experimental Social Psychology, and the American Psychological Association Distinguished Scientific Contribution Award, as well as the presidencies of several scientific societies.

From the beginning, Morton Deutsch's interests and research goals have been deeply and consciously affected by his profound social concerns. His unshakable conviction that social science can make a major contribution to the betterment of humanity has struck a resonant chord in the minds and hearts of Morton Deutsch's many students and admirers.

## Students Whose Doctoral Dissertations Were Conducted with Morton Deutsch as Principal Advisor

### New York University

| Name | Date of Degree |
| --- | --- |
| Harold Proshansky | 1952 |
| Seymour Levy | 1953 |

| | |
|---|---|
| Joseph B. Margolin | 1954 |
| Harold Yuker | 1954 |
| Leonard Solomon | 1957 |
| James L. Loomis | 1957 |
| Robert M. Krauss | 1964 |

## Teachers College, Columbia University

| Name | Date of Degree |
|---|---|
| Harvey A. Hornstein | 1964 |
| David W. Johnson | 1966 |
| Stephen Thayer | 1966 |
| Bert Brown | 1967 |
| Peter Gumpert | 1967 |
| Abaineh Workie | 1967 |
| Yakov M. Epstein | 1968 |
| Miriam G. Keiffer | 1968 |
| Roy J. Lewicki | 1968 |
| Jeffrey Z. Rubin | 1968 |
| Donnah Canavan | 1969 |
| Barbara B. Bunker | 1970 |
| Mary Chase | 1971 |
| Ella Lasky | 1971 |
| Lois Biener | 1972 |
| Madeleine E. Heilman | 1972 |
| Lida Orzeck | 1973 |
| Kenneth Kressel | 1973 |
| Lorenz J. Finison | 1973 |
| Rebecca C. Curtis | 1973 |

| | |
|---|---|
| Antonietta Graciano | 1974 |
| Barbara J. Stembridge | 1974 |
| Charles M. Judd, Jr. | 1975 |
| Sharon P. Kaplan | 1975 |
| Joyce Slochhower | 1976 |
| Nancy L. Hedlund | 1977 |
| Janice Steil | 1979 |
| Michelle Fine | 1980 |
| Sherry Deren | 1980 |
| William A. Wenck, Jr. | 1981 |
| Cilio R. Ziviani | 1981 |
| Dolores Mei | 1981 |
| Shula Shichman | 1982 |
| Bruce Tuckman | 1982 |
| Ivan Lansberg | 1983 |
| Louis Medvene | 1983 |
| Janet Weinglass | 1983 |
| Susan Boardman | 1984 |
| Ellen Cooper | 1984 |
| Nefertari Crummey | 1984 |
| Sandra Horowitz | 1984 |
| Lorinda Arella | 1985 |
| Eric Marcus | 1985 |
| Rachel Solomon-Ravich | 1985 |
| Susan Opotow | 1986 |
| Rony I. Rinat | 1987 |
| Marilyn Seiler | 1987 |
| Cathie M. Currie | 1989 |

| | |
|---|---|
| Jorge da Silva Ribeiro | 1990 |
| Nisha Advani | 1991 |
| Curtis Dolezal | 1991 |
| Adrienne Asch | 1992 |
| Lela Tepavac | 1992 |
| Quanwu Zhang | 1992 |
| Martha Gephart | 1993 |
| Judith K. Herschlag | 1993 |
| Nidhi Khattri | 1993 |
| Eben Weitzman | 1993 |

# About the Authors

. . . . . . . . . . . . . . . . . . . . . . . . . . . . . . .

## The Editors

*Barbara Benedict Bunker* received her training in social psychology with Morton Deutsch at Teachers College, Columbia University, where she received her Ph.D. degree (1970) in social psychology. Her doctoral dissertation explored the impact of self-disclosure on the development of trust in cooperative and conflictful situations.

For the past twenty-five years, she has worked as a professor in the Department of Psychology at the State University of New York, Buffalo, where at various times she has been head of the Social Psychology Doctoral Program, director of graduate studies, and has trained many students in organizational psychology and consultation. In 1984 and 1991 she held Fulbright Lectureships in Japan, first at Keio University and later at Kobe University.

Bunker's interest in the applications of social psychology to social issues has been expressed in her research and writing about organizational change processes, small and large group dynamics, gender in work organizations, theory of practice, and commuting couples. She is the author of numerous articles and books on these topics, including *Social Intervention* (1971, with H. Hornstein and others) and *Mutual Criticism* (1975, with M. Levine).

She is an internationally known organizational development consultant to a variety of clients. She has taught in executive development programs at Columbia and Harvard and is an often-invited presenter at national conferences on change. She served for seven years on the board of directors of NTL Institute (Washington, D.C.), including three years as chairperson.

Bunker's professional life is renewed in international travel, with her twelve grandchildren, and at the new house in the country.

*Jeffrey Z. Rubin* received his Ph.D. degree (1968) in social psychology from Teachers College, Columbia University. Morton Deutsch was his major professor and mentor for a study of the effects of competitive or cooperative motivation and relative power on behavior in four-person groups. Twenty-five years later, all of it spent in Boston, Rubin is professor of psychology at Tufts University, senior fellow and former executive director of the Program on Negotiation at the Harvard Law School, and professor of diplomacy at the Fletcher School of Law and Diplomacy, Tufts University.

An internationally recognized scholar in bargaining and negotiation, Rubin has also served as a negotiation consultant and trainer at workshops for universities here and abroad, Fortune 500 companies, nonprofit organizations, and the U.N. He has authored numerous books and articles, most recently *Social Conflict* (1994, with D. G. Pruitt and S. H. Kim), *Culture and Negotiation* (1993, with G. O. Faure), *Mediation in International Relations* (1992, with J. Bercovitch), and *Negotiation Theory and Practice* (1991, with W. Breslin). He is the editor of *Negotiation Journal* and consulting editor for the Jossey-Bass conflict resolution series.

Rubin is a recipient of Guggenheim and Fulbright fellowships, a fellow of three divisions of the American Psychological Association, and a fellow of the American Psychological Society. He was president of the Society for the Psychological Study of Social Issues during 1987–88.

Rubin considers himself most fortunate to have ended up doing the things he loves the best: teaching, writing, traveling, and collaborating with friends on book projects like this one.

# The Contributors

*Maura A. Belliveau* is assistant professor of organizational behavior at the Fuqua School of Business, Duke University. She expects to receive her Ph.D. degree in organizational behavior from the University of California, Berkeley, in May 1995. Belliveau's research addresses procedural fairness in organizations. Her recent work examines how human resource policy implementation, procedural fairness judgments, and career outcomes influence employee attitudes toward affirmative action.

*Robert T. Buttram* is a doctoral candidate in organizational behavior at the A. B. Freeman School of Business, Tulane University. He received his M.S. degree (1990) in social psychology from Purdue University. His research interests include organizational justice, contingent employment, organizational wrongdoing, and collective motivation.

*Guy Olivier Faure* is associate professor of sociology at the Sorbonne University, Paris, where he teaches international negotiation. His major research interests are in business negotiations, especially with China and Asian countries, and in developing interdisciplinary approaches. He has coauthored several books, including *Culture and Negotiation* (1993, with J. Rubin).

*Michelle Fine* is professor of psychology at the City University of New York, Graduate Center, and senior consultant at the Philadelphia Schools Collaborative. She received her Ph.D. degree (1980) in social psychology from Teachers College, Columbia University. Her recent publications include *Chartering Urban School Reform: Reflections on Public High Schools in the Midst of Change* (1994), *Beyond Silenced Voices: Class, Race, and Gender in American Schools* (1992), *Disruptive Voices: The Transgressive Possibilities of Feminist Research* (1992), and *Framing Dropouts: Notes on the Politics of an Urban High School* (1991).

*Robert Folger* is professor of organizational behavior and Freeman Professor of Doctoral Studies and Research at the A. B. Freeman School of Business at Tulane University. He received his Ph.D. degree (1975) in social psychology from the University of North Carolina, Chapel Hill. He is a Fellow in Divisions 8 and 14 of the American Psychological Association. He has been widely published and has taught students and faculty from more than a dozen countries. His interests include organizational fairness, work-team motivation, and total quality management.

*David W. Johnson* is professor of educational psychology at the University of Minnesota, where he holds the Emma M. Birkmaier Professorship in Educational Leadership and is co-director of the Cooperative Learning Center. He received his Ph.D. degree (1966) in social psychology from Teachers College, Columbia University. He has published over three hundred research articles and book chapters and has authored over forty books. Johnson has received numerous awards for outstanding research and teaching. For the past thirty years, he has served as an organizational consultant to schools and businesses in many parts of the world.

*Roger T. Johnson* is professor of curriculum and instruction at the University of Minnesota, where he is co-director of the Cooperative Learning Center. He received his Ph.D. degree (1969) in educational psychology from the University of California, Berkeley. He has consulted with schools throughout the United States and Canada, Panama, England, Germany, Norway, Sweden, Finland, and New Zealand. He has received many awards and is the author of numerous research articles, book chapters, and books. Nationally, Johnson is a leading authority on inquiry teaching and science education.

*George Levinger* is emeritus professor of psychology at the University of Massachusetts, Amherst. He received his Ph.D. degree

(1955) in social psychology from the University of Michigan. He has authored many papers concerning close relationships and interpersonal and group behavior. He is coauthor of *Close Relationships* (1983, with H. Raush and others) and an editor of *Close Relationships* (1977) and *Divorce and Separation* (1979, with O. Moles).

*Roy J. Lewicki* is professor of management and human resources at the Max M. Fisher College of Business, The Ohio State University. Lewicki received his Ph.D. degree (1969) in social psychology from Teachers College, Columbia University. He is the author of numerous books and articles in the fields of negotiation, dispute resolution, organizational justice, and organizational behavior.

*Paul V. Olczak* is professor of psychology at the State University of New York, Geneseo. He received his Ph.D. degree (1972) from Northern Illinois University, with training in both social and clinical psychology. Olczak is a licensed clinical psychologist and has coauthored one book and published more than forty book chapters and articles on a variety of topics, including psychology and the law, interpersonal psychiatry, individual differences, behavior modification, and conflict resolution.

*Susan Opotow* is an independent scholar affiliated with Teachers College, Columbia University. She received her Ph.D. degree (1987) in social and organizational psychology from Teachers College, Columbia University. She is an active member of the Society for the Psychological Study of Social Issues (SPSSI), serving on its council and on the editorial board for the *Journal of Social Issues*. She is also editor-in-chief of the *SPSSI Newsletter*. Her research examines exclusion from the scope of justice, particularly its application to everyday life and to educational and environmental issues.

*Dean G. Pruitt* is distinguished professor in the psychology department at the State University of New York, Buffalo. He received his Ph.D. degree (1957) in psychology from Yale University. He is author, coauthor, editor, or coeditor of many books, including *Theory and Research on the Causes of War* (1969, with R. C. Snyder). He is the 1992 winner of the Harold D. Lasswell Award for Distinguished Scientific Contribution to Political Psychology from the International Society of Political Psychology and the 1994 winner of the award for Significant Contribution to Conflict Management Literature of the *International Journal of Conflict Management*.

*Ellen Raider* is training director of the research-based International Center for Cooperation and Conflict Resolution at Teachers College, Columbia University, where she conducts workshops in conflict resolution and mediation for educators, serves as mediator for school disputes, and currently teaches two interdisciplinary practica as part of the newly created graduate studies in conflict resolution program. Raider received her M.Ed. degree (1968) in educational psychology from Temple University. As a management consultant, she has taught international and cross-cultural negotiation skills to corporate executives, diplomats, and nonprofit managers.

*Blair H. Sheppard* is professor of management and associate dean, executive education, at the Fuqua School of Business, Duke University. He received his Ph.D. degree (1980) in social and organizational psychology from the University of Illinois. Sheppard's research focuses on the broad topic of managing relations within and between organizations, including conflict management, negotiation, alliances, organizational justice, and firm restructuring. He has published articles on all of these topics in a range of business and psychology journals and is coeditor of an annual series entitled *Research on Negotiation in Organizations*.

*Tom R. Tyler* is professor of psychology at the University of California, Berkeley. He received his Ph.D. degree (1978) in social psychology from the University of California, Los Angeles. His research interests include social justice, legal psychology, and organizational behavior. Tyler is coauthor (1988, with A. Lind) of *The Social Psychology of Procedural Justice* and author of *Why People Obey the Law* (1990).

*Virginia J. Vanderslice* is founder and president of Praxis Associates, a Philadelphia consulting firm specializing in assisting employee-owned companies. She is also a member of the faculty at the University of Pennsylvania, where she is a lecturer in the dynamics of organization graduate program. She received her Ph.D. degree (1986) in social psychology from the State University of New York, Buffalo.

*L. Mun Wong* is a doctoral candidate in social-personality psychology at the City University of New York, Graduate Center, where he is completing his dissertation on the subjectivity of poor women in the welfare state. His works encompass critical psychological, feminist, race, and queer theories, the politics of methodology, and issues of injustice.

# Conflict, Cooperation, and Justice

# Introduction

## Conflict, Cooperation, and Justice

### Barbara Benedict Bunker, Jeffrey Z. Rubin

Conflict, cooperation, and justice are urgently important topics in today's world. We live at the end of the twentieth century (and a second millennium) in a time when there has been "peace," meaning no world war, for fifty years. Yet, in the wake of our optimism about the decrease in tensions between the former U.S.S.R. and the West, there is a disturbing resurgence of ethnic and political conflict at new levels of intensity in Bosnia-Croatia, Rwanda, and Haiti. There are still unresolved and threatening issues of nuclear capability, now in North Korea, tomorrow somewhere else. And old, deep conflicts continue in places such as Cyprus.

Within our own country, violent crime is increasing. There is also a widening chasm dividing those who can live the good life from those who cannot. Conflict at the societal level is mirrored by conflicts at the intergroup and individual levels: the increasing numbers of hate crimes toward Jews, the shooting of the person who took your parking place, or the doctor who was willing to perform abortions.

Acknowledging the complexity of factors that create these conflicts does little to resolve them. These are times when social scientists need to actively collaborate with others, contributing what they know to understanding and resolving these conflicts.

Morton Deutsch, whose fifty-year career as a social psychologist began shortly after the end of World War II, has focused his work

1

on the three separate but very much linked topics of this book: conflict, cooperation, and justice. His was a generation of social psychologists—led by his teacher and the founder of social psychology, Kurt Lewin—that was intensely interested in bringing research to bear on the pressing and perplexing social issues of the time. Mort's deep commitment to the theoretical understanding of conflict processes and the development of resolution strategies inspired the development of this book. Conflict, cooperation, and justice are the three conceptual pillars that mark off Deutsch's intellectual work.

Deutsch's early work compared the learning outcomes of competition to cooperation and advanced a series of key ideas about the structure of cooperation. If competition is a motivation that creates a "win-lose" world and separates people into different sides, cooperation is a motivation that acknowledges interdependence, a state in which people work with and can count on each other. Although there are certainly times when competition can be energizing and productive, the "fixed camps" that often emerge tend to rigidify and deplete creative possibilities. In the United States, competition is a dominant modality in many work and educational institutions. Critics from without and within have decried this situation over the years. Yet only recently, as we have become global citizens, has this critique commanded attention. Now we can see how adversarial relationships between labor and management, for example, keep organizations from devoting energy to increasing productivity. In education, we are beginning to understand how important cooperation can be for learning.

This, then, is a time when cooperation is coming into its own. Rather than seeing Japan and other collectivist societies in which working together is important as peculiar, we are now willing to learn about the benefits of more cooperative relationships. Business institutions are increasingly organizing in teams in order to create better products and services. Employees are buying bankrupt airlines and creating new cooperative structures for work. The complexity of modern social, medical, and organizational problems can no longer be treated by single specialties; interdisciplinary teams are necessary for a full-scale assault. It appears that we are only at the leading edge of developments that require a renewed understanding of cooperation.

In this world of conflict and collaboration, an overarching concern of human beings is that they be treated fairly. Justice is a topic that is as old as civilization and as recent as the morning newspaper. There are many places at home and abroad where people suffer injustice. Although we do not fully understand how justice is perceived from culture to culture and we suspect that there are real differences, all societies have standards for behavior and acceptable practice. We need a fuller understanding of how people make judgments of whether they were fairly treated and what the consequences are if they believe that justice has been denied. Exploring this area can lead to a deeper understanding of what supports and what wounds the human psyche, as well as why injustice is allowed to prevail.

Conflict, cooperation, and justice—three key topics for our time—form the subject matter of this book. We identified some of the troubling and still unresolved questions in each area. Then we asked scholars in the field to write provocative chapters about these unanswered questions. Why are they so difficult? Why has research faltered or the area been ignored? What needs to happen to move the issue forward? This, then, is not the usual social science edited volume of reports on the latest research in each area. Rather, we encouraged authors, each of whom is an authority in his or her area, to take risks and venture beyond what we now know. Our intention is to push the field, to make a real contribution to thinking by identifying and exploring issues that need attention. Some of the issues are theoretical, some quite practical and applied. The tension in Lewin's well-known dictum that nothing is so practical as a good theory is well represented in this book, with some chapters more theoretical and some intensely practical. Our general request to all authors, however, was to write a provocative chapter. As we describe the organization of the book, we will indicate briefly the issue or questions the authors were asked to address.

## Conflict

We begin the book with conflict because it represents the heart of Morton Deutsch's contribution to knowledge and his most extensive theoretical and research area. Conflict occurs, according to Deutsch, when two or more people perceive there to be divergent interests that they wish to pursue and believe that these interests cannot both be realized. Conflict can exist, escalate, de-escalate, and finally, either be settled or resolved. If it is settled, the parties reach some kind of agreement through such processes as negotiation, domination, capitulation, withdrawal, or third-party intervention. Whatever the process, behavior changes and the parties consider the conflict to be ended, at least for that moment. If the conflict is resolved, however, attitudes as well as behavior change, and there is a greater probability that conflict will not reemerge.

Despite the rather large literature on conflict, not only in social psychology but in many other disciplines, such as political science, sociology, and economics, many issues are still unresolved or unattended.

In the first chapter in the conflict section, Jeffrey Z. Rubin and George Levinger explore the question of whether principles generated at one level of analysis, for example, the interpersonal level, can usefully be generalized to another level, say the international level. Much of the work by Deutsch and other conflict theorists assumes that work done at one level is generalizable to other levels. We asked Rubin and Levinger to think more carefully about that issue. To what extent is this really an appropriate assumption? Do principles of conflict really operate the same way at different levels of complexity? Using interpersonal and international conflict as contrasts, they present an analysis of the similarities and very real differences between conflicts at these two levels.

The second chapter, by Guy Olivier Faure, also deals with the issue of generalizability, but this time the question is "How much of what we know about conflict is so closely tied to the cultural tradition of North America that to assume it will generalize is dangerous?" In a series of powerful examples, Faure shows us how conflict, negotiation, peace, and aggression are defined differently in different cultures, how even the way we frame the issues is culture bound. He then goes on to propose a plan for pursuing an intercultural approach. It is clear from Faure's chapter that there is a long way to go before conflict studies are free of Western domination and conflict theory is truly universal.

We asked Dean G. Pruitt and Paul V. Olczak to address the issue of intractable conflict. Are some conflicts so severe that they are really intractable and beyond hope of resolution or settlement? How do we know when conflict has reached this state? What can be done to intervene in conflicts at this level? Pruitt and Olczak present a new model for understanding and differentiating highly escalated conflict from more moderate conflict. They draw the ideas for their model from the interpersonal level—from the marital conflict literature—and go on to apply the model to international conflict. They propose that highly escalated conflict may not be susceptible to the usual interventions—such as mediation or negotiation—useful in more moderate conflict. Then they develop seven intervention modules for escalated conflict and suggest how to diagnose and sequence them.

In the final chapter in the conflict section we asked Ellen Raider to address the rapid development of conflict resolution training in schools. What are its objectives? Is it effective? This chapter is but one example of the interesting applications currently emerging of conflict principles to the real world. Raider presents both the successes and failures and offers a useful model for thinking about the issues surrounding the translation of conflict theory into applied skills.

## Cooperation

In his dissertation, Deutsch described the differences among three fundamental orientations: competitive, cooperative, and individualistic motivations. His groundbreaking work elaborated the structure of cooperation. Cooperative relationships are characterized by trust and trustworthiness, the willingness to accept influence from one another, and the ability to help move one another toward shared goals. A large body of experimental research and conceptual analysis has been given over to the conditions that promote cooperative relations. In addition, as Deutsch's original dissertation research made clear, cooperation and competition have distinctly different consequences for individual functioning. An interest in stimulating cooperative relationships has been especially evident in education, where, building on Deutsch's work, programs designed to heighten learning by structuring the classroom cooperatively have taken root.

Many scholars and practitioners believe that it is easier to move from cooperation to competition than to do the reverse. Less clear, however, is precisely why this should be so. It has been suggested that cooperation is fragile, easily disrupted. Is this the case? In the first chapter in this section, Roy J. Lewicki and Barbara Benedict Bunker deal with this issue by focusing on a key factor in cooperation: trust. They examine the relationship of cooperation and trust, describe an original three-stage model of trust development in cooperative relationships, and then describe what happens when trust that has been established is broken. Lewicki and Bunker take us from a unidimensional notion of trust to different forms of trust in the development of relationships and propose that the fragility of trust is related to the stage of development.

If cooperation is potentially difficult to maintain, is there such a thing as too much cooperation? Deutsch suggested that this could be so and proposed that three "pathologies of cooperation"—overconformity, nepotism, and vested interest—flow from three structural characteristics of cooperation. Little work has been done to establish whether excessive cooperation is a problem that actually occurs in cooperatively structured organizations. We turned to Virginia J. Vanderslice, whose career has focused on studying and consulting to worker cooperatives, for an analysis of this question. In the second chapter in this section, Vanderslice looks for each of the pathologies in four worker cooperatives she has studied. As she reports her findings, she also describes other threats to cooperation in organizations structured on cooperative principles and makes a number of useful suggestions for ameliorating these difficulties.

For any who find social psychology not interested enough in practical application, the effects of cooperation is an area where theory has been clearly translated into practice and extensively studied. The final chapter in the cooperation section, by David W. and Roger T. Johnson—founding authorities in the field of cooperative education—deals with the impact of cooperative learning on education and on its future. The Johnsons review the theory and research on social interdependence and then turn to the translation of these Deutschian principles in education. They detail the successes and dilemmas of cooperative education in a largely competitive educational system. Their chapter ends optimistically by describing the potential applications of cooperative learning to educational issues like diversity, globalization, and social and psychological health and development.

## Justice

In 1975, Morton Deutsch wrote a paper about equity theory that broke new ground for the field. In it he suggested that equity is not the only motivation that may be involved in the pursuit of justice. He proposed that equality and need are sometimes justice principles as well. This stimulated many investigations in what has come to be known as justice research.

How do people assess the fairness or unfairness of the situation in which they find themselves? Robert Folger, Blair H. Sheppard, and Robert T. Buttram explore what underlies the selection of the three modes of thought represented by the three justice principles: equity, equality, and need. At three levels—organizational/societal, interpersonal, and individual—they find that remarkably similar principles evolve. They then wonder whether other principles of justice conform to this same pattern and turn to procedural justice for an analysis that for the most part appears to support their ideas. In the intriguing final section of their chapter, they analyze complex situations such as layoffs or apologies, where a policy is dictated by one justice principle but where flexibility in implementation could allow for other principles to come into play.

The second chapter in this section follows nicely from the first. Tom R. Tyler and Maura A. Belliveau begin with Deutsch's 1975 proposal that norms of equity foster productivity while norms of equality foster harmony, thus posing a dilemma of how to maximize both productivity and harmony in organizational life. Since Deutsch's original work, a substantial literature has explored distributive justice and, more recently, proposed other justice principles, especially procedural justice. Distributive justice is "whether I got my fair share," and procedural justice is whether the process by which the decision was made was fair. In their provocative chapter, Tyler and Belliveau suggest that there are ways to maintain social order and support individual self-image by using distributive principles to make decisions and procedural principles to implement them. This work suggests the possibility of bridging differences of interests and values in such difficult contemporary issues as downsizing. It also makes salient the importance of individual identity as a key factor in the justice equation.

We asked Michelle Fine and L. Mun Wong to take on the important and much debated topic of perceived justice. In their chapter, they address this question: if perceived injustice leads people to act to restore justice and thus stimulates social change, what are the effects of perceived justice? Does it lead to stable arrangements that are fair, or can it promote exploitation? As we hoped they would, Fine and Wong begin with an exploration of the psychology of victimization. They explore conditions of injustice when people do and do not see their situation as unjust. Then they look at conditions under which victims of injustice are willing to grieve their situation. Their discussion of the subtle ways institutions silence critiques is telling and sobering. In the end, they call for courageous research to explicate more of the picture and for the creation of organizational safe places where critical talk can percolate and one can begin the work of transformation.

The justice section ends with Susan Opotow's chapter. We asked Opotow to consider the psychological mechanisms that make it possible for people to draw the line between notions of justice as applied to self and as applied to others. She took up the challenge and begins by asking how genocide can occur. The answer emerges in the process we use to determine "the scope of justice," which is affected, research demonstrates, by utility, similarity, and particularly by conflict. Opotow describes a cycle of exclusion that occurs and suggests ways to interrupt the cycle and draw the circle wider.

At the end of each of the three major parts of the book, we present Morton Deutsch's thoughts and reactions to the ideas developed in the chapters in that section. We asked him to respond in whatever way he saw fit, challenging, supporting, elaborating. We know that readers will appreciate hearing from our mentor directly. We kept Mort waiting quite a while before we would give him the final chapters. One of our delights in doing this project was the eagerness with which he kept asking when the manuscript would be ready to read. He was as curious and excited to see what our authors would make of these unresolved issues as we were!

As editors, we have set before you a considerable feast. We expect you, our readers, to partake as you wish. As the hosts, who planned the meal and hovered over the stove, however, we want to bring the project full circle and record our own thoughts and reactions to what has been served up. So we end the book with a chapter of our own.

# Part I

............................

## Conflict

# 1

# Levels of Analysis

## In Search of Generalizable Knowledge

### Jeffrey Z. Rubin, George Levinger

W hen scholars and practitioners first began writing about conflict as a topic of inquiry in its own right, there was little intercourse among the many relevant disciplines. Mathematicians and economists tended to understand conflict through the prism of game and utility theory. Political scientists used the lens of power, while sociologists relied on notions of group and organizational structure. Psychologists used ideas drawn from decision theory and cognition, while international relations scholars organized their conflict analysis around the concept of the state. It was only when important books such as Schelling's *The Strategy of Conflict* (1960), Boulding's *Conflict and Defense* (1962), and Deutsch's *The Resolution of Conflict* (1973) appeared that it became fashionable to regard conflict processes as fundamentally alike from one setting to the next.

Such an emphasis served a useful practical end, since it helped enable a genuine interdisciplinary field of conflict and negotiation studies to emerge.[1] Scholars from different backgrounds could gather together, exchange views on a common set of problems and processes, and marvel at the areas of overlap among their contrasting approaches. The view that conflicts are fundamentally alike

*Note:* We gratefully acknowledge the helpful comments of the following graduate students at the Fletcher School of Law and Diplomacy: Betsy Block, Fadi Esta, Geoffrey D. Fink, Daniel Lieberfeld, Joshua Lincoln, Maria Baute Stewart, and Heinz Waelchli.

allowed people to come together in pursuit of an Esperanto of sorts, a shared language for describing concepts heretofore understood mainly within the confines of singular disciplinary fiefdoms.

The weakness of such a universalistic perspective, however, is that it ignores differentiation in its quest for universality. If there really *are* important differences among conflicts at various levels of complexity, then it is well to understand them. In attempting to do so in this chapter, we hope to improve our grasp of how conflicts at different levels are connected or divided by conceptual bridges and barriers.

Other authors (for example, Bonham, 1971; Deutsch, 1973; Druckman, 1990; Druckman & Mahoney, 1977; Galtung, 1968; Guetzkow, 1968; Keohane & Nye, 1977; Singer & Ray, 1966; and Strauss, 1978) have considered the issue of generalizability from micro to macro levels of analysis, and have for the most part ended by cautioning against generalization. Our approach differs in our emphasis on both similarities and differences from one level to the next—with our ultimate interest in knowing whether these areas of similarity and difference make a difference.

While our final goal is to help reexamine the parallels among interpersonal, intergroup, interorganizational, and international levels of conflict, we have elected to concentrate primarily on the first and last of these levels in this chapter. Lying at opposite ends of a number of continua, interpersonal and international conflict afford a good starting place in our analysis. Moreover, many of the features of intergroup and interorganizational conflict are embedded in the complexities of international relations. Although the following analysis focuses on similarities and differences in interpersonal and international conflict, we will add observations about the other two levels where appropriate.

## Similarities Between Interpersonal and International Conflict

Across different levels of analysis, conflict has a number of similar properties, six of which we consider particularly striking (see also Deutsch, 1973; Rubin, Pruitt, & Kim, 1994). All social conflict

1. Derives from perceived divergence of interest

2. Can be addressed in a relatively small number of ways

3. Contains a mixture of motives

4. Can be ended through either behavior or attitude change

5. Leads to outcomes that range from purely destructive to
   purely constructive

6. Stems from a broad variety of causal antecedents

## Definition of Conflict

Every form of social conflict implies a perception of divergent interests—whether or not they are divergent in reality. Whether these
differences occur between individuals or between states, between
groups or between organizations, any conflict signifies some degree
of perceived incompatibility between the parties' goals or between
their preferred means of achieving similar goals.

Conflicts may derive from competition for scarce resources, differences in values or beliefs, or the parties' differing definitions of
their relationship (see Deutsch, 1973, pp. 15–17). For example, a
husband and wife may disagree about how much each spouse will
use the couple's car (a resource), whether they want to have children (values and beliefs), or how good it is for one spouse to be
highly dependent on the other (their relationship definition). Similarly, neighboring states may disagree about who should be allowed
to fish in their coastal waters (a resource), the desire for free trade
between them (values and beliefs), or whether one nation should
give emergency aid to its neighbor in time of crisis (their relationship definition).

Note further that, regardless of level of analysis, the parties
involved often misperceive their mutual problem. A couple may
think they disagree only about a procedure for paying their bills,
whereas the conflict really represents a more fundamental difference
about how husband and wife construe the meaning of money and
possessions in general. Or they may argue about how he talks about

her mother, while ignoring his feeling of being neglected when his wife leaves home to spend large chunks of time at work. Similarly, the member states of the European Community may act as if a conflict over European auto emission standards is an isolated source of difficulty, whereas it actually bears on the broader question of how decisions are to be made and control exercised in the unified Europe of the future. In other words, conflict over one set of issues is often confounded with, or obscured by, conflict over issues at a different level, and this is true in international as well as in interpersonal relations. The same phenomenon can be observed in intergroup and interorganizational relations, where the text and subtext of conflict may be widely divergent.

## Ways of Responding to Conflict

When a conflict exists between two or more parties—whether they are individuals, groups, organizations, or states—a rather limited number of ways exists for dealing with it (Rubin et al., 1994).

### Domination

Domination occurs when one side attempts to impose its will through physical or psychological means. Between individuals, it may be one spouse physically abusing the other or making the other feel guilty. Between states, it may be a trade embargo, blockade, or all-out war. Between groups it may take the form of excluding the other group from one's own prized preserve, and between organizations it may be driving another firm out of business.

### Capitulation

Capitulation is one side unilaterally ceding to the other whatever the latter demands or expects. A husband may decide to give in to his wife's demands for a two-week vacation next summer, or the French may decide to yield to American economic pressure concerning subsidies for dairy farmers. Capitulation may result from the belief that decision makers have little choice, or it may derive from more instrumental motives (for example, the belief that the other party can be induced to yield later on a different issue). Note that yielding to the other out of love may occur between spouses, but never between states!

## Withdrawal

When one side abandons the conflict, refusing to be a party to it any longer, that side has withdrawn. An angry marriage partner may choose to walk out of the house in a huff, and a state may decide to break off all ties (including diplomatic recognition) with another— as in the case of the United States and the People's Republic of China some years ago.

## Inaction

Inaction is when one side deliberately does nothing in the hope that the passage of time will favorably change the situation. It may be a child conveniently forgetting to clean up her room, in the hope that her parents will also forget. It may be the upstream interest in a river dispute electing to do nothing to stop the industrial pollution. Or it may be a minority population willing to delay efforts to wrest control from the majority, confident that demographic changes will turn the minority into the majority before long.

## Negotiation

When two or more interdependent parties use the give-and-take of offers and counteroffers in an effort to build a mutually acceptable settlement, negotiation occurs. Illustrations are countless, of course, be it a husband and wife deciding how to spend an evening together when they have conflicting preferences or the United States, Canada, and Mexico reconciling their differences over trade arrangements by devising the North American Free Trade Agreement.

## Third-Party Intervention

This method of addressing conflict is when an individual or group that stands apart from a particular dispute helps the parties to the conflict to identify issues and move toward settlement. Illustrations of third-party actions abound in interpersonal and international relations, from a neighbor intervening in a dispute between two others to the United Nations attempting to mediate conflict in the former Yugoslavia.

To recapitulate, there are a limited number of ways of addressing conflict, and these approaches can be found wherever conflict arises. As we will subsequently argue, however, there may be important differences in the accessibility of these approaches; withdrawal is probably far easier to pursue in interpersonal than in international conflict, while inaction is a more accessible option in international than in interpersonal relations.

### Mixture of Underlying Motives

As Deutsch (1960) observed years ago, all conflicts are driven by one or more of three underlying motives: competition, cooperation, and individualism. In its purest form, a competitive motive invokes the wish to do well at another party's expense. It is the "I swim, you sink" mentality that is characteristic of zero-sum relationships. In contrast, pure cooperation invokes the norm of sinking or swimming together; each party's objective is not only to do well for itself but to make sure that its counterpart also does as well as possible. Finally, an individualistic motive drives the decision maker to largely ignore the other side in the pursuit of its own objectives. Interested neither in helping nor hindering the other party, the individualist simply tries to do as well for itself as possible.

Rarely are conflicts, at any level of analysis, characterized by pure competition, cooperation, or individualism. Instead, most are mixed-motive arrangements, especially those conflicts characterized by interdependence. If two people have something that the other wants or needs, then some degree of cooperation will be required—even if it is allowing each to attempt to do better than the other. I may wish to use negotiation to conclude a deal more favorable to me, but I need your agreement if I am to get anything at all. Lax and Sebenius (1986) describe this as the tension in negotiation between creating value (expanding the pertinent resource pie) and claiming value (dividing the pie between the disputants). In order for one side to lay claim to the larger piece of pie, it makes sense to first work cooperatively with the other in order to make sure that the resource pie is as large as possible.

## Settlement Versus Resolution

Conflicts at every level can lead to one of two broad kinds of solutions: settlement and resolution. *Settlement* refers to behavioral change, as when two sides find a way to reach agreement but their basic attitudinal opposition remains largely unchanged. *Resolution* implies not only a change in behavior but also a convergence in underlying attitudes.

Behavior change without corresponding attitude change often occurs when one party (a timorous spouse or a weak state) acquiesces to the other's demands, but does so resentfully and while feeling coerced. Such settlements usually depend on the more powerful party's presence or surveillance and are, therefore, rarely durable; when the stronger party is absent or not paying attention, the weaker party has little reason to continue its prior compliance (French & Raven, 1959; Kelman, 1958; and chap. 5 in this book by Lewicki & Bunker). Such settlements tend not to endure.[2]

In contrast, conflict resolution usually entails mutual attitude change so that both parties internalize new patterns of interaction. Behavior changes not because another party forces such change but because the disputants' attitudes have shifted. As a result, whatever causes led to the conflict in the first place are now less likely to arise, and behavior change is likely to persist.

Two people in the throes of an angry exchange may be induced by a third party to stop fighting, but unless they have come to understand *why* the angry exchange erupted in the first place, their cease-fire is likely to be short lived. In international relations, compare the armistice agreement between the allies and the Axis powers that ended World War I (an agreement that affected behavior only, with no apparent consequences for underlying attitudes) to the emergence of the European Community in the aftermath of World War II (an arrangement that led the member states to think very differently about their interdependent relations with one another). Obviously, we can also find illustrations in intergroup and interorganizational relations.

### Destructive Versus Constructive Conflict

All conflicts exist on a continuum ranging from totally destructive (relationship damaging) to totally constructive (relationship enhancing). At the most destructive pole, imagine a duel between crack shots fought with pistols at thirty paces, where both combatants are likely to suffer injury or death. Its international analogue is a nuclear war between two equally powerful states. Destructive conflict ends with both combatants gravely weakened.

Yet not all conflict has negative outcomes. In constructive conflict, relationships actually improve after differences are confronted (Coser, 1956). As a result of each party voicing its own views and basic interests, it becomes possible to find solutions that benefit both parties (Fisher, Ury, & Patton, 1991). Such benefits may arise from the immediate outcome, for example, enjoying a talk with one's partner and discovering hitherto unexperienced areas of commonality. Or they may result from a long-term improvement of the relationship and an enhanced ability to communicate.

That conflict can have both constructive and destructive consequences is evident at all levels. A husband and wife may find themselves using conflict as a means of building an even stronger relationship; adversity may provide them with new experiences that bring the couple closer together. On the other hand, words exchanged in the heat of an angry marital squabble may have destructive, lasting consequences, as when one person says particularly hateful things to the other that will not soon be forgotten.

In international relations, there is surely no shortage of destructive conflict; the history of carnage through the ages speaks for itself. But as the European Community illustrates, conflict can also become the basis of a transcendent agreement. Out of the ashes of World War II have come new patterns of economic, military, and political interdependence among the nations of Western Europe that make the specter of another war there unlikely. Similarly, the pending Mercosur Agreement among Argentina, Brazil, Paraguay, and Uruguay illustrates a constructive solution to conflict that, under other circumstances, could have had very different consequences.

### Antecedents

All conflicts can be understood in terms of a broad array of antecedent conditions, each of which has rather predictable consequences. Students of conflict and its management through negotiation and third-party intervention (Pruitt, 1981; Pruitt & Carnevale, 1993; Rubin & Brown, 1975; Rubin et al., 1994) have documented this litany of independent variables and have demonstrated their effects empirically. In summary, the antecedent conditions that affect conflict include factors that bear on the *physical context* of conflict (site location, communication opportunities, time limits), its *social context* (number of disputants, openness of the conflict site to various observers or third-party intervenors, aspects of the disputants' relationship, individual expectations, personality considerations), and its *issue context* (the number of issues in dispute, their sequencing and packaging). Each of these many independent variables has been found to have a consistent impact on how conflict is managed.

Two conceptual illustrations may suffice to make our point. First, a frequent source of conflict is a party's misconstrual of others' intentions. An action that A sees as harmless or even beneficial to B may be perceived by B as interfering, constraining, or even insulting. For example, a boss may intend her detailed advice on how her employee should do a job as helpful, while he sees it as controlling and demeaning. Or Country A may justify its desire to add a new clause to a trade treaty as strengthening the treaty, whereas Country B regards it as self-aggrandizing trickery.

Second, observing audiences (whether onlookers in a workplace squabble or the media in an international dispute) have the effect of leading disputants to take tough and extreme positions from which they are subsequently reluctant to budge. People who in private might be willing to make concessions in order to settle a conflict are likely, in the presence of observing audiences, to experience intensified concerns about face management. They will be reluctant to give up anything to the other side, lest they be regarded as weak and thus prone to subsequent exploitation.

There are many areas of similarity between interpersonal and international conflict—and, though we have said less about them, between intergroup and interorganizational conflict. These parallels are pervasive and are at the core of efforts over the last several decades to argue for the fundamental resemblance among conflicts at different levels. But now let us turn to the less obvious, and certainly less studied, side of the story: the areas of dissimilarity and discontinuity.

## Differences Between Interpersonal and International Conflict

While we acknowledge that the following listing is perhaps incomplete, we have identified eleven key differences.

### Number of Parties

Many interpersonal conflicts involve two people. In international relations, however, where there are often more than two parties to a dispute, the situation is more complex. Even when there are only two sides, there are often allies and adversaries with an interest in the proceedings. As the number of parties increases, it becomes more difficult to reach agreement, simply because there are now more preferences and expectations to coordinate.

On the other hand, as Pruitt (1981) and others have observed, as the number of parties to a conflict increases (as in international relations), so does the availability of additional resources (in the form of money, new ideas, and so on) that additional participants may bring with them to the table. These make various "pie-expanding" solutions more likely. Moreover, as Rubin et al. (1994) point out, the chances of reaching agreement are enhanced in multiparty arrangements because of the increased opportunities for developing cross-cutting ties among the disputants. It may be very difficult to persuade the member states in the European Community to agree on a single course of action, but the group does contain the resources necessary to expand the pie, as necessary, and to create various coalitions among member states that may make it possible to assemble an overall agreement.

Further complicating the settlement of international conflict is the fact that there are not only a larger number of parties but the parties themselves are typically nonhomogeneous; each side may contain both hawks and doves who are themselves in conflict with each other. Conflict between groups is characterized by the presence of multiple roles and functions among the membership, and relations between organizations are similarly complicated by the existence of hierarchies that sort members into different statuses. Since international relations, in turn, is almost always conducted by the groups and organizations that comprise the entity known as "the state," it stands to reason that such relations will be conducted by complex, nonhomogeneous parties. (Summit conferences between national leaders are an exception, but even these are usually complicated by the bureaucratic structures in which leadership is embedded.)

A striking example of the difficulties introduced into international relations by the presence of multiple, nonhomogeneous parties can be seen in the ongoing effort by the European Community to form a united Europe. Tensions continue to exist among the twelve member states over a variety of issues, including the fundamental desirability of a united Europe. Some states, such as England, have been reluctant participants from the very beginning. Others, such as France, Germany, and Italy, have consistently supported the vision of a united Europe. But even among these three stalwarts, relations have been far from equal, with Germany able to get what it wants much of the time (Hoffman, 1993). Further complicating matters are the internal conflicts between the European Community's institutions and national institutions, and also the internal disarray found in countries such as Italy.

## Number of Issues

Perhaps because "the state" is a more complex and differentiated entity than an individual, the international arena contains more conflicts than are possible in the interpersonal relationship. As with more parties, more issues mean greater difficulty because there is now more to coordinate. On the other hand, more issues also imply additional opportunities for assembling packages, which increases the possibilities for one party to trade concessions on issues to which it is largely indifferent for another party's concessions on issues that matter to the first party (Pruitt, 1981). For example, during the Law of the Sea negotiations several years ago, there were so many issues under discussion that there were always opportunities for tradeoffs— although reaching agreement was a painfully difficult process. Landlocked states (such as Nepal, Paraguay, and Afghanistan) were able to exchange their support for a proposal concerning access to strategic waterways (of concern to nations such as Egypt and Turkey) for the latter countries' support of proposals concerning the distribution of wealth resulting from deep sea mining activities in the future.

## Exit

As we commented earlier, withdrawal is a possible solution to conflicts at all levels of analysis. Even so, we also noted that it is easier to withdraw from interpersonal than from international relations. If you are sufficiently angry or disappointed with your spouse, you can walk out, sue for divorce, and perhaps never have to deal with the other person again.

But what does it mean to walk out in international relations? What is the international equivalent of suing for divorce? There is no "helluva good universe next door" (Cummings, 1944) for states to escape to. One side can withdraw in international conflict, but such withdrawal is temporary at most. In international conflict, there ultimately is no exit.

It was Jean-Paul Sartre (1955) who observed in his play *No Exit* that if you cannot leave the scene, conflict becomes more intense. Given great intensity of conflict, there should be increased pressure to cope with the conflicts that arise. And if one cannot resort to withdrawal, then other solutions become more likely, including (as the history of warfare makes clear) efforts at domination through armed force.

## Power Asymmetry

For interpersonal relationships to be stable, the parties must be roughly equal in power. If not, the more powerful party will attempt to exploit its less powerful counterpart; in turn, the latter will attempt to withdraw from the relationship (though in some interpersonal relationships withdrawal is not immediately available). There are often inequalities in power between parents and children, between teachers and students, as well as between various groups and organizations. Over time these inequalities typically diminish as children grow into adults, students acquire much of their teachers' expertise, and groups or organizations move toward symmetry (possibly when the less powerful entities move away). In most voluntary interpersonal relationships (and, we suspect, in many intergroup and interorganizational relations), power is either roughly symmetrical or moves over time toward symmetry.

In international relations, however, power symmetry is more the exception than the rule. There is a vast inequality between the United States and Bali, between Nepal and France. Resources are dramatically asymmetrical among states; moreover, those with greater power behave in ways that cause them to become even more powerful, while their less fortunate counterparts tend to be locked into less favorable positions. In effect, the rich get richer, while the poor remain the same. One consequence of such power asymmetry is that the more powerful states are likely simply to impose their will on their less powerful counterparts, while the latter have little choice but to accept such imposition or to resist through armed warfare. The Cold War was characterized by the perverse symmetry of mutually assured destruction. The Cold War's demise has, if anything, increased the tendency of states to use power asymmetry to their advantage; witness, for instance, the conflicts in the former Yugoslavia and elsewhere in Eastern Europe.

### Enforceability of Agreements

In interpersonal, intergroup, and interorganizational relations, there is usually a powerful authority that can ensure that conflicts are settled and remain settled. Indeed, societies create laws for the preservation of interpersonal stability and set up institutions—such as the courts and the police—to make sure that agreements are not violated. Similarly, groups adhere to codes of conduct, and organizations have penalties for failure to follow standard operating procedures.

In international relations the picture is far more complex. Although an International Court of Justice exists and hands down decisions based on international law and the United Nations exists to prevent war and maintain international peace, the world's nations do largely as they please. As one of the world's most powerful nations, the United States abides by the decrees of the International Court of Justice when it so chooses—and flouts its decisions on other occasions.

### Effective Third-Party Intervention

In international relations there are few opportunities for effective intervention by third parties—except by the most powerful actors, those in a position to coerce agreements through threats or to buy agreements by lavishing rewards; witness Saudi Arabia and the United States in this regard.

Interpersonal, intergroup, and interorganizational relations provide a far broader range of intervention opportunities and methods. Indeed, as documented by scholars such as Bercovitch and Rubin (1992), Kressel and Pruitt (1989), and others, there are numerous third-party roles in the settlement of conflict (ranging from mediation to arbitration, fact-finding to conciliation). But whereas quarreling individuals, groups, or organizations may be persuaded to settle their differences if an older, stronger, respected third party urges them to do so, there are few equivalents in international relations. The secretary-general of the United Nations is rarely effective on the world stage; the only effective third parties are typically representatives of resource-rich nations.[3]

## Audiences

Groups (and, to a lesser extent, organizations) can conduct their business with some semblance of privacy. A husband and wife can close their bedroom door and argue (or abuse each other) in private. There is no equivalent in the international arena. Every act, either immediately or potentially, occurs in full view of a world of onlookers. International negotiators may speak to each other secretly, but their discussions must typically be reported to their superiors. This makes eventual leaks to the media more likely. As research has documented (Pruitt, 1981; Rubin & Brown, 1975), negotiators are likely to take tougher, more extreme positions in the presence of observing audiences than they do under conditions of privacy.

Moreover, once they have taken these extreme positions, negotiators are likely to be slow to yield. One of the reasons for this is psychological entrapment (Brockner & Rubin, 1985), the tendency of decision makers to become overcommitted to a course of action in which they believe they have invested a great deal. Having committed themselves to extreme positions of intransigence, negotiators may come to believe they have too much invested to change.

### Representative Negotiation

In interpersonal conflict, the disputants typically represent themselves. In relations between groups, organizations, and nations, the situation is very different; groups typically relate to each other through spokespersons. Organizations often arrange for contact between individuals who are at comparable levels in their respective hierarchies. In international relations—as conducted through the groups and organizations that comprise "the state"—there are *always* representatives. Even heads of state speak for others as much as for themselves. Representatives serve as agents for their superiors or their constituencies, meet with their counterparts, and then make recommendations concerning settlement of conflict to those to whom they are responsible.

The introduction of representatives into the conflict settlement process clearly changes things compared to the simpler situation where people represent themselves (Rubin & Sander, 1988). Extra "moving parts" are introduced, which may be a source both of greater difficulty and of greater opportunity (in the form of the representatives' special expertise). More elements are now susceptible to disruption, including the representatives themselves, who often serve limited terms or may be replaced. Thus, the relationship that two representatives develop or the agreements they reach may be jeopardized if one or both representatives is supplanted. For example, a routine problem in American foreign policy occurs every four or eight years, when a new presidential administration assumes office; ambassadorships and other senior foreign policy posts are typically turned over by the new administration, which results in shifting policies toward other countries that are as much a function of changing representatives as of systematic adjustments in foreign policy.

### Information About One's Counterpart

If two friends have a quarrel, they can deal directly with each other—at the same place and time—in an effort to understand the issues and concerns at stake. International relations, however, is conducted through a mix of groups and organizations holding opposing ideas and goals. As Allison (1971) observes, what may look like a unitary position of the other side in an international conflict may actually be the resultant of a complex clash of internal forces and vectors. Add to this cultural differences that may make it difficult to understand the meaning of the other side's moves and gestures. Physical distances and time zone differences further complicate matters; even such communication advances as fax machines, e-mail, and teleconferencing do not succeed in placing international negotiators in the same place at the same time.

The upshot of all this is that international conflict is more susceptible to selective perception and other forms of cognitive distortion than interpersonal, intergroup, and interorganizational relations. It is generally more difficult to pinpoint the other party's preferences, intentions, and expectations.

## Trust

Given less reliable information about the other party in international conflicts, as well as the other obstacles noted earlier, international conflicts appear far less conducive to trust and empathy than interpersonal ones (with intergroup and interorganizational conflicts lying somewhere in between). According to studies of close relationships, interpersonal trust begins with one side's perception that the other is predictable, followed by information that the other is highly dependable, followed by the development of a mutual attachment that is accompanied by faith in the other's responsiveness to one's needs (Holmes, 1991; Rempel, Holmes, & Zanna, 1985). Trust is an individuating process that develops from a lengthy series of mutually positive experiences. For example, spouses-to-be may gradually, from their very first meeting, build a mutual chain of predictability, dependability, and attachment as a result of direct and repeated contact.

It is far easier to experience such contact in the interpersonal realm. International relations, for example, are fraught with informational uncertainty, extra actors, and the tendency for individuals to keep each other guessing in order to maintain negotiating freedom or competitive advantage. And, as noted above, when international conflict is confounded with intercultural differences it may prove all but impossible to convince another party of one's own trustworthiness (see chap. 2, by Faure, in this book).

### Institutions and Bureaucracies

Unlike individuals and groups, organizations and states tend to develop powerful institutional structures—such as armies or intelligence agencies—that may benefit from the perpetuation of conflict and mistrust. For example, as recent U.S. Senate testimony confirmed, American intelligence estimates regularly inflated Soviet defense capabilities and derogated corresponding U.S. capabilities in order to justify enormous increases in the U.S. military budget during the Cold War.

Furthermore, as we have seen during the last few years, military and intelligence institutions strongly resist attempts to reduce their power after the need for them is much diminished. We find no parallel for this at the interpersonal level.

To frame these observations more broadly, it is clear that states are characterized by organizational structures—institutions and bureaucracies—that help give the state a life of its own quite independent of the proclivities of individual actors. As Allison (1971) observed in his analysis of the 1962 Cuban missile crisis, bureaucracies have inertia. They are slow to be set in motion and are also slow to change direction. When such bureaucracies and institutions operate in the service of international cooperation, so much the better for prospects of conflict settlement. But if those structures serve the purposes of escalation (as is often the case), then conflict reduction will prove to be far more difficult.

## Lessons for International Conflict Settlement

From the preceding analysis, it becomes clear why international conflict is so formidable. The presence of multiple parties, as well as the tendency of the parties to be heterogeneous, makes the task of developing agreements that all sides find acceptable unusually difficult. So does the abundance of issues on the table. Observing audiences abound, making it more likely that disputants will take extreme positions from which they refuse to budge lest they risk losing face. The fact that exit is not really a viable option in international conflict increases the pressure on the parties to settle their differences by other means, notably through efforts at domination. The temptation to solve conflict through domination is given further impetus by the likelihood of power asymmetry in international relations. And if one is fortunate enough to be the more powerful party in this asymmetrical relationship, *tant mieux*; what could be easier than settling one's conflict by simply taking what one wants from the other side?

Because there are typically multiple parties involved, because confrontations typically involve representatives rather than the principals themselves, because official state policy often belies the internal tumult behind a unified position, and because international conflicts are typically extended over distances of space, time, and especially culture, it is exceedingly difficult in the international arena to obtain reliable information about one's counterparts. The presence of additional moving parts—including the bureaucracies in each state—makes a Murphy's Law scenario all the more likely: if things can go wrong, they will! Selective perception is likely to dominate the proceedings, as each side forms distorted impressions of the other based on partial information skewed in the direction of one's biased hypotheses. Under these conditions, trust in another nation's reliability will indeed be difficult to achieve and maintain.

Further complicating matters is the fact that the agreements parties reach in international relations are not easily enforceable. There are neither other parties with sufficient power nor third parties with sufficient credibility and legitimacy to guarantee that such agreements will be honored. For instance, as powerful as the United States continues to be, even it is limited in its ability to monitor conflict and impose agreements as part of a Pax Americana.

What the international arena often offers, then, is a Greek tragedy, with escalation all but inevitable. Conflicts are driven in an escalatory direction by the temptation to prevail through domination, by the absence of social and structural constraints against such behavior, and by the prevalence of distorted information. Small wonder that so many international conflicts end up in armed warfare and prove so resistant to outside intervention.

And yet this picture is not entirely bleak; there is a rosier aspect to be considered. For when we examine the similarities among conflict at different levels, there is evidence of flexibility, of a system that may be more malleable than is commonly assumed. Consider: we have argued that conflict is driven more by the *perception* of divergence of interest than by the reality of such divergence. Thus, by framing the way in which parties see the conflict and one another, it should be possible to modify the experience of conflict.

Second, the fact that a limited number of ways exists for solving conflict (domination, capitulation, inaction, withdrawal, negotiation, and third-party intervention) invites the possibility of influencing the disputants toward one approach over the others. As Rubin et al. (1994) point out, by influencing each side's aspiration level and its perceived willingness to make concessions from those aspirations, it is possible to turn from one solution to another.

Third, the fact that conflicts at all levels are characterized by mixed motives (by a mix of cooperativeness and competitiveness, in particular) invites the possibility that an analyst or activist can fiddle with this mixture, to carburet it so that the parties are moved from competition to cooperation, from positions to interests, from distributive agreements to integrative mutual gains solutions.

Fourth, the fact that the outcome of successful conflict management is either settlement (when behavior alone has changed) or resolution (when attitudes have changed as well) suggests that the intervenor can operate at multiple levels; the conflict can perhaps be addressed through behavior change first and attitude change later on.

Fifth, we have argued that all conflicts are located on a continuum ranging from destructive to constructive. Regarding conflicts in this fashion leads to the conclusion that there is nothing inherently wrong with conflict and invites the possibility of changing the structure of the conflict in ways that make it more constructive.

Finally, we have argued for the presence of a large and diverse—but also fixed—number of antecedent variables that affect the course of all conflict. If this array of independent variables is finite in number and has effects that are predictable and consistent, the lessons we learn from one setting will carry over to other settings.

Add to this mix the fact that the same bureaucratic structures that help to perpetuate an existing international conflict also offer a potentially valuable buffer in the service of conflict settlement. If bureaucracies could be established to serve the purposes of international harmony, they could conceivably lend stability to peaceful relations despite the vagaries of leadership. The United Nations is an example of such a bureaucracy. Moreover, the very inertia of bureaucracies could serve the purpose of conflict settlement.

In summary, we find that the differences between international and interpersonal conflict are nontrivial. They are a reminder of the many ways in which international conflict is more likely to escalate and resist de-escalation than interpersonal, intergroup, and interorganizational conflicts. At the same time, we find that the similarities among conflicts at different levels are also nontrivial. The most destructive aspects of conflict are often the result of seeing conflict in particular ways. The very fact that conflict can be construed differently invites the intervenor to shift the parties' construction so as to make dispute settlement a more likely outcome.

## Conclusion

Many scholars have considered the generalizability of concepts from interpersonal relations to the international, intergroup, or interorganizational arena. It is extremely tempting to draw lessons from relations between individuals to relations between states. Our examination of the problem has looked most closely at the similarities and differences between interpersonal and international relations, with an occasional glance at the intergroup and interorganizational levels. Our perhaps predictable conclusion is that one must extrapolate from one level to another with caution.

To understand how careful the analyst must really be, imagine that one were asked to advise international specialists about ways of settling conflict on the basis of what is already known about interpersonal conflict, for example, among school children.[4] Drawing from current knowledge of schoolyard quarrels, one would advise nations to "fight fair" with one another. According to one recent booklet on children's "creative conflict solving" (Schmidt & Friedman, 1985), to fight fair means you should (1) identify the problem; (2) focus on the problem, not on other issues; (3) attack the *problem*, not the other person; (4) listen with an open mind; (5) treat the other's feelings with respect; and (6) take responsibility for your own actions.

Although all these suggestions are sensible, how applicable are they to the international realm? Regarding suggestions 1 through 3, even the most talented international representatives will have great difficulty identifying "the" problem between their respective nations or separating it from the sociocultural identities of their people. In reality, they deal with a layered multiplicity of issues, compounded by their people's different interpretations of meanings and priorities. The negotiators may try to follow suggestions 4 through 6, but how well can they carry out those aims when both countries' media regularly attack the other country, distort its policies and actions, and blame the entire dispute on the *other's* previous and present behavior?

Nor does the international scene contain adequate enforcement authority for preventing internation conflicts from escalating beyond control. Whereas children who beat up their playmates are likely to get into trouble, nations who bully their weaker neighbors are much more apt to escape censure. Furthermore, while it makes sense to advise quarreling children to take turns, share, and apologize, giving sovereign nations such advice seems ludicrous. Finally, getting help from third parties (such as peers or authority figures) is far more difficult for nations, where choosing a mutually acceptable judge or mediator becomes a major political issue.

The literature on marital conflict management (Hendrick & Hendrick, 1992; Peterson, 1983) does not offer much more by way of guidance. It suggests that partners should confront each other directly, listen to each other nonjudgmentally, focus on each other's behavior rather than on their personality, and consider the possibility of separation if the conflict appears irreconcilable. And there is at least one other important contrast: two spouses are part of the same unit, so that the impact of any single disagreement is weighed against a long history of mutual caring. Two contentious nations are generally not.

Clearly, the conceptual path from interpersonal to international—or to intergroup or interorganizational—conflict is a rocky one. But although one cannot easily move from one plane to another, a comparative appraisal of conditions at each level can improve our understanding of conflict.

In this chapter we have emphasized taxonomy over theory, focusing on issues to be faced if one is to generalize from one to another level of conflict. We have tried to clarify why so many international conflicts prove so pernicious, as well as illustrate ways in which they may be amenable to intervention. Whereas conflict theory in earlier decades gained greatly from bridging levels of analysis, we suggest that, in future years, we will also have much to gain from differentiating among levels of analysis.

## Notes

1. For example, the Program of Negotiation at Harvard Law School (with which the first author has been affiliated since the early 1980s) is comprised of scholars from a wide variety of disciplines

who all share the view that conflicts at different levels of analysis obey a standard set of principles and lend themselves to a standard set of interventions.

2. One of our students has noted that settlement may occur for reasons other than the more powerful party's coercion. She gives the example of one spouse agreeing to curb an action the other finds annoying because that action, or changing it, is far less important than the relationship as a whole. Settlement here would be exactly the right response.

3. Norway's mediation of the PLO-Israeli conflict in 1993, Algeria's mediation of the Iranian hostage crisis, and Switzerland's mediation of the ongoing conflict between the United States and Cuba are striking precisely because these mediation efforts have been exceptions to the usual rule.

4. Some practitioners are ready to do precisely this, that is, to use research on interpersonal relations to offer advice to practitioners in the international arena. We have grave reservations about the wisdom of offering such advice.

## References

Allison, G. T. (1971). *Essence of decision: Explaining the Cuban missile crisis*. Boston: Little, Brown.

Bercovitch, J., & Rubin, J. Z. (Eds.). (1992). *Mediation in international relations: Multiple approaches to conflict management*. New York: St. Martin's Press.

Bonham, G. M. (1971). Simulating international disarmament negotiations. *Journal of Conflict Resolution, 15*, 299–315.

Boulding, K. E. (1962). *Conflict and defense: A general theory*. New York: Harper-Collins.

Brockner, J., & Rubin, J. Z. (1985). *Entrapment in escalating conflicts: A social psychological analysis*. New York: Springer-Verlag.

Coser, L. A. (1956). *The functions of social conflict*. New York: Free Press.

Cummings, E. E. (1944). *I x I*. Orlando, FL: Harcourt Brace.

Deutsch, M. (1960). The effect of motivational orientation on trust and suspicion. *Human Relations, 13*, 123–139.

Deutsch, M. (1973). *The resolution of conflict: Constructive and destructive processes*. New Haven, CT: Yale University Press.

Druckman, D. (1990). The social psychology of arms control and reciprocation. *Political Psychology, 11*, 553–581.

Druckman, D., & Mahoney, R. (1977). Processes and consequences of international negotiations. *Journal of Social Issues, 33*, 60–87.

Fisher, R., Ury, W. L., & Patton, B. M. (1991). *Getting to yes: Negotiating agreement without giving in* (2nd ed.). New York: Penguin.

French, J. R. P., Jr., & Raven, B. H. (1959). The bases of social power. In D. Cartwright (Ed.), *Studies in social power* (pp. 150–167). Ann Arbor, MI: Institute for Social Research.

Galtung, J. (1968). Small group theory and the theory of international relations: A study of isomorphism. In M. A. Kaplan (Ed.), *New approaches to international relations* (pp. 270–302). New York: St. Martin's Press.

Guetzkow, H. (1968). Some correspondences between simulations and "realities" in international relations. In M. A. Kaplan (Ed.), *New approaches to international relations* (pp. 202–269). New York: St. Martin's Press.

Hendrick, C., & Hendrick, S. S. (1992). *Liking, loving, and relating* (2nd ed.). Pacific Grove, CA: Brooks/Cole.

Holmes, J. G. (1991). Trust and the appraisal process in close relationships. In W. H. Jones & D. Perlman (Eds.), *Advances in personal relationships* (Vol. 2, pp. 57–104). London: J. Kingsley.

Kelman, H. C. (1958). Compliance, identification, and internationalization: Three processes of attitude change. *Journal of Conflict Resolution, 2*, 51–60.

Keohane, R. O., & Nye, J. S. (1977). *Power and interdependence*. Boston: Little, Brown.

Kressel, K., & Pruitt, D. G. (1989). *Mediation research: The process and effectiveness of third-party intervention*. San Francisco: Jossey-Bass.

Lax, D. A., & Sebenius, J. K. (1986). *The manager as negotiator: Bargaining for cooperation and competitive gain*. New York: Free Press.

Peterson, D. R. (1983). Conflict. In H. H. Kelley, E. Berscheid, A. Christensen, J. H. Harvey, T. L. Huston, G. Levinger, E. McClintock, L. A. Peplau, & D. R. Peterson (Eds.), *Close relationships* (pp. 360–396). New York: W. H. Freeman.

Pruitt, D. G. (1981). *Negotiation behavior*. San Diego: Academic Press.

Pruitt, D. G., & Carnevale, P. J. (1993). *Negotiation in social conflict*. Pacific Grove, CA: Brooks/Cole.

Rempel, J. K., Holmes, J. G., & Zanna, M. P. (1985). Trust in close relationships. *Journal of Personality and Social Psychology, 49*, 95–112.

Rubin, J. Z., & Brown, B. R. (1975). *The social psychology of bargaining and negotiation*. San Diego: Academic Press.

Rubin, J. Z., Pruitt, D. G., & Kim, S. H. (1994). *Social conflict: Escalation, stale-mate, and settlement* (2nd ed.). New York: McGraw-Hill.

Rubin, J. Z., & Sander, F. E. A. (1988). When should we use agents? Direct v. representative negotiation. *Negotiation Journal, 4,* 395–401.

Sartre, J. P. (1955). *No exit and three other plays.* New York: Random House.

Schelling, T. C. (1960). *The strategy of conflict.* Cambridge, MA: Harvard University Press.

Schmidt, F., & Friedman, A. (1985). *Creative conflict solving for kids.* Miami: Peaceworks.

Singer, J. D., & Ray, P. (1966). Decision making in conflict: From interpersonal to international relations. *Menninger Clinical Bulletin, 30,* 300–312.

Strauss, A. (1978). *Negotiations: Varieties, contexts, processes, and social order.* San Francisco: Jossey-Bass.

# 2

# Conflict Formulation

## Going Beyond Culture-Bound Views of Conflict

### Guy Olivier Faure

The question I ask in this chapter is whether we can analyze a social event that takes place in Manhattan and one that happens in Timbuctu with the same scientific, conceptual, and methodological means we possess today. In other words, are existing theories universally valid? Are they completely acultural? For example, if a human population were discovered on Antares, could we accurately study its methods of conflict resolution using the intellectual approaches that have been devised here on earth during the past three decades?

Sociologists and ethnologists (Cook & Hegtvedt, 1983; Nader & Todd, 1978) have demonstrated that methods for solving conflicts vary considerably from one society to another. One essential reason for these differences is the way conflict is perceived, defined, and finally, as a consequence, dealt with. Practical and theoretical thinking on conflict are similar in that they also are, to some extent, culturally rooted. This remains a major obstacle to the development of science and a real challenge for the future. In his time, Voltaire, a French philosopher, was already questioning the universal validity of the concepts he was using.

I contend that the analytical frameworks developed in North America during the last decades have enabled researchers to make major progress in theorizing conflict. But for this intellectual legacy to become a universal instrument, it must undergo considerable cultural adaptation. In this chapter I investigate the nature of the problem, establish a causal diagnosis, and suggest orientations leading to solutions.

## Establishing the Facts

"What is it that cannot quite be seen but follows us around constantly? And what is it that remains when all else is forgotten . . . culture" (Faure & Rubin, 1993, p. xi). In this way culture hides itself in the most unsuspected places and leaves its invisible trail. This is as true for a complex intellectual construct as it is for the naming of the most simple objects. Let us take the example of the octopus. Cultures name it differently according to the dominant way each one perceives the creature. In the Anglo-Saxon and the French cultures, the octopus is described by its shape: "eight feet" and "many feet." So it is with the Chinese culture: the "spider with long legs." Germans and Swedes focus on one of its functions: "ink fish," the fish that produces ink. Finally, this same animal may also be named according to a behavioral characteristic; in dialectical Arabic, the octopus is "the cunning," and in colloquial German, it is "the one that grasps."

From this one example, we draw an obvious conclusion: names arise from perceptions, which can be significantly different. The intellectual capture of the octopus is a work of selection and interpretation that testifies to the presence and the role of culture.

The cultural dimension is critical to the field of behavioral sciences. Individuals do not passively reflect an external environment; they are active creators of their environment. A number of authors have observed the absence of culture in social psychological theories and have questioned the cross-cultural generalizability of such theories (Pepitone & Triandis, 1987; Bond, 1988). Others have commented that what cross-cultural research does exist lacks theoretical focus and has done little to substantially integrate the concept of culture with mainstream psychology (Betancourt & Lopez,

1993). My purpose in this chapter is not to debate such topics but to examine the specific area of conflict and conflict resolution.

## Concepts

The words used to formulate facts and behaviors referring to conflict—"conflict," "aggression," "peace," "time," "negotiation"—present two types of problems, given the present state of their development. They do not reflect the same content from one culture to another, and they are not value-free, which means that they carry judgments with them that may orient their use in certain ways.

### Conflict

Deutsch (1973, p. 10) writes that "a conflict exists whenever incompatible activities occur. . . . An action that is incompatible with another action . . . in some way makes the latter less likely or less effective." Pruitt and Rubin (1986, p. 4) adopt a more restrictive meaning of conflict as a "perceived divergence of interest or a belief that the parties' current aspirations cannot be achieved simultaneously." Both of these Anglo-Saxon definitions are part of the same approach, that is, to identify as conflictual any situation in which one actor is perceived as not able to reach his or her goals because of another.

Hubert Touzard (1977, p. 51), reflecting French culture, gives a different meaning to conflict. For him, conflict is a situation in which total control of another's behavior is either the goal or a chosen means to attain a goal, as well as a situation in which actors aim at goals that are different, supporting contradictory values. There is, in this understanding of conflict, a necessary degree of antagonism between actors that is much higher than in the Anglo-Saxon concept. A French reference dictionary (*Le Robert*) confirms this view, defining conflict as a "war, an encounter between contrary elements that oppose each other." In French culture, "to oppose" is a strong term, conveying powerful antagonism; it is the opposite of "to compromise" or "to come to terms."

The Chinese have a similar understanding of conflict, which is usually translated as "fighting" or "struggling." It is clear that the concept of conflict includes quite distinctive meanings. As a consequence, it is a concept laden with cultural bias.

Conflict resolution raises similar issues; it can be viewed as a cultural indicator of the way a society looks at conflict in order to deal with it. If we consider how American society handles conflict—through elements such as the number of firearms kept by people or the number of lawyers—we may draw some conclusions concerning the dominant values of the society. Now if we look at China it is exactly the opposite; both weapons and lawyers are very few. Thus, both societies have very different views on conflict resolution. The differences might be explained by how each society defines conflict.

The American approach to resolving conflicts expresses an underlying value. Salem (1993, p. 364) argues that "western conflict resolution relies heavily on the assumption that pain is bad and pleasure or comfort is good." Again such an assumption is not value-free and introduces cultural biases into the understanding of conflict.

### Aggression

Aggression poses a similar problem in terms of values. As a learnable behavior, it is a cultural product with attendant judgments and emotions that can be quite strong in some societies. A major difficulty concerns this concept's definition and its scope. Aggression, usually defined as intentionally hurting another person, is a reflection of norms of conduct; what hurts in one society may not be what hurts in another society. Indicators of aggression may then vary, as well as the degree to which people tolerate aggression. As a consequence it becomes impossible to capture aggression in a homogeneous way and to develop a truly cross-cultural approach.

For instance, in the Middle East a direct refusal is considered a hostile gesture. One must always be careful never to say no to an offer, even if the offer is rejected. In other cultures, raising an objection is a customary, well-accepted way to behave and is everyone's basic right. In China, during a discussion around a cup of tea, if the spout of the teapot is pointed toward a person, it means that the presence of this person is challenged and that he or she should leave. In Western cultures, the position of the teapot on the table would never be understood as a sign of hostility. Such differences in the nature and measurement of the indicators of aggressive behavior are a major obstacle to the development of universally valid cross-cultural approaches based on observations or experiments.

## Peace

The term *peace*, as the crystallization of various implicit values, has the same difficulties. In Western cultures, peace is thought of as the absence of conflict. In Chinese culture, a peaceful situation is one characterized by additional traits, such as the prominence of a principle of harmony and the establishment of a balanced relational system. A Westerner may perceive the successful restoration of peace; a Chinese may see a situation of non-open aggression.

From an Arab viewpoint, Salem (1993, p. 362) contends that the "concept of peace itself has a particular and positive cultural valuation in the West." He attributes this bias—seeing peace as a positive state and war as a negative one—to Christian influence and points out that the desirability of peace might be questionable in other cultural contexts.

## Time

People's perceptions of time influence social processes, including conflict. Durkheim considered time a social construct that varies according to the socioeconomic conditions of a society. The distinction between duration and sequential succession may be just a Western interpretation and sophistication of a reality expressing itself traditionally through the movement of the seasons. The Chinese concept of time aggregates these two distinctive elements. One might be surprised to learn that the French use the same word to express time and weather.

Sometimes it is difficult to know if an actor is referring to the past, the present, or the future. Some societies do not make such time distinctions, and it becomes quite challenging to understand people's behavior and perceptions through categories that have no relevance for them.

### Negotiation

In the West, negotiation is defined as a way of accommodating divergent interests. Thus bargaining is viewed as a very broad activity, ranging from such issues as what a family might do on the next weekend or how to share a cake among the children, to freeing hostages or bringing an end to a war. From cooperative activities to highly conflictual interactions, the concept of negotiation encompasses many activities.

Chinese culture has a radically different view. It links negotiation to a much narrower and more specialized understanding—that of conflict settlement. To capture the precise content of negotiation, we must distinguish it from the idea of discussion, which is its cooperative aspect. Literally speaking, in the Chinese language "to negotiate" (*tan pan*) is the combination of two ideas: "talking and making judgment." The global orientation is basically conflictual. "To discuss" (*tao lun*) connects two activities—"searching and exposing"— and is first of all a communication exercise to achieve a cooperative end. In discussion, harmony, a central value in Chinese culture, is never challenged, while it is broken in the case of a negotiation. The Chinese concept of negotiation includes the content of its Western equivalent but is also heavily value laden. This may preclude its study by any Western approach conceived as scientific.

In the Arabic language, the number of ways to express negotiation gives evidence of a semantic dysjunction between the Arabic and the Western concepts, as well as showing a significant split in the corresponding ways of understanding negotiation in its context. For instance, negotiating in the marketplace has nothing to do with negotiating within the family, and each activity is expressed with distinctive words.

Does Western culture enable researchers to conceptualize negotiation as it is understood and practiced all over the world? Is Western culture able—and entitled—to do the job alone? Here again the matter is not merely a language convention, a misfit between concepts that have to be clarified, for the underlying meaning is provided by culture. Syntax alone cannot yield semantics, and a concept—a tool for a theory that originates in a particular culture—cannot a priori be operationalized into a conceptual equivalent within another cultural setting. To name, to designate negotiation, is a transcultural exercise that has not yet been achieved. The quest for universality is still in progress.

## Problematiques

Ways of understanding logics are culturally rooted. For instance, Greek thinking developed the art of proving; other cultures were content to observe and establish facts. Individuals think through categories, using them as analytical tools to question social facts and human activity. In this way, concepts are elaborated and ideas and questions are put forth. Such a process advances through the system of questions, which commands and organizes the answers ("if your only tool is a hammer, then every problem is a nail"). But if specific questions are not asked, answers in a certain domain are not provided. In the same way that space influences colors, context has an effect on the object itself.

Culture affects both perception and understanding. Social concerns, for instance, orient and—to a certain extent—govern research developments. Jahoda (1979) argues that dominant theories in social psychology are the product of a particular cultural milieu. They may carry hidden assumptions, social presuppositions that are not pertinent in other societies. The question of the conditions under which a theory transfer can be achieved, or a reformulation made in a relevant way, has then to be raised.

Cases drawn from anthropology show how important this issue is and how real and concrete the problem remains. The cultural context of the example that follows is that of the southern Madang region in New Guinea, where in the years 1940 and 1950 a strange religious belief called the Cargo Cult experienced a strong revival (Lawrence, 1964). According to this belief, all the wealth of the world promised to the natives—the Cargo—was diverted on its way to them by white people before it could reach its final destination. A number of rituals need to be accomplished to enable the natives to get back what is rightfully theirs, but this information is kept secret by the white people. Some Australian missionaries unsuccessfully tried to convince the cult followers that this explanation made no sense. The missionaries invited one of the main apostles of this cult—a man named Yali—to pay a visit to what he thought of as the paradise, the place where the cargo was stored, the Australian city of Sydney. So Yali spent several weeks in Sydney, getting acquainted with the industrial, materialistic, and rational civilization.

However, the result was not what the missionaries expected. Yali, far from changing his system of beliefs when confronted with the objective truth, came away from his visit with his initial beliefs reinforced. For example, the totems, both animals and plants, that were so vigorously denounced as superstition by the missionaries were seen by Yali as carefully kept in the homes in the form of flower bouquets on tables. Animals were accommodated in many houses, some of them being kept in places especially designed for them—such as cages in zoos—so that they would not escape and deprive the people of their beneficial influence. The nice words pronounced by the whites had only one goal: to hide the real importance of the totems, thus enabling them to keep all the cargo for themselves.

The Cargo Cult example shows the difficulty of moving from one culture to another, that is, from one system of beliefs with its hidden assumptions to another. This story may appear a little ridiculous or amusing to some, but it accurately illustrates what happens when one analyzes events of a society with the help of categories belonging to another society. To a certain extent, the way that Western cultures scrutinize social phenomena of other cultures is not very different from Yali's approach.

I now examine two aspects of social psychological research: first, its origins (cultural, intellectual, or social) and second, its consequences in terms of thinking and of action.

## On Origins and Related Effects

Mainstream social psychology is characterized by cultural insularity. A content analysis performed by Gabrenya (1988) on 3,305 journal references in the *Journal of Personality and Social Psychology* (*JPSP*), the *Journal of Cross-Cultural Psychology*, the *American Anthropologist*, the *American Sociological Review*, and *Ethos* indicates that *JPSP* has an extremely low percentage of foreign journals cited (3 percent); none of the other journals exceeds 10 percent.

Such insularity finds its origin in the history of the social and behavioral sciences in North America. As a consequence of its success, social psychology has tended to isolate itself from outside contributions. Thus it has grown from an Anglo-Saxon cultural base, on North American questionings, and on Western human and social values.

Difficulties do not just crop up when social psychological theories deal with non-Western issues; they occur across Western cultures. French ways of framing problems are sometimes quite different from those used in the United States. In France, the system of questioning that governs the way to think about a topic is called a *problematique*. There is no equivalent in the English language, only imperfect approximations such as "intellectual perspective," "scientific issue," "organization of questioning," "problem area," and so on. But in fact, to set a *problematique* is not only to raise a question within an intellectual perspective. It is also to structure the intellectual domain in such a way that the questioning attains a meaningful relevance. Thus a *problematique* may concern a conceptual problem that is then applied to some substantive issues or real-world cases. French culture provides an appropriate way of dealing with these types of issues and has specific words to name the process, like the twenty words available to Eskimos to name the different types of snow they may come across.

France is one of the very few countries, if not the only one, where the study of philosophy is compulsory in the middle schools. In the same way, the French have developed analytical tools to deal with abstractions and process them. There is no concrete way to represent these concepts and tools, and this is why it can be so difficult to transfer them to a culture where semantics are more related to concrete action. The issue is how cultures deal with and process abstractions. What may intellectually rebuff an American researcher will not upset a French scholar.

There are many intellectual approaches to thinking, elaborating, and constructing a question. The point is not only a matter of accurate translation but of organizing the questioning, which governs the potential answers, which, in turn, has important consequences for the nature and orientation of knowledge.

Being a non-American can provide some cultural distance, but this does not substantially help the scholar. In research work one always starts from what exists, what is readily available—which is American knowledge. This leaves people outside the United States—in France or elsewhere—to use perspectives and analytical categories developed in the United States by American researchers to structure a problem, define it, and organize it. Consequences of such a North American anchoring are multiple and significant. Most research in social psychology uses one category of subjects— the American undergraduate student—and one category of issues—

those that relate to dominant social concerns in that part of the world. Should we consider American students as perfectly representing the human species, including natives from New Guinea and those from Timbuctu? When cross-cultural approaches are used in social psychology, most of the time they consist of simply plugging the rest of the world into theoretical models developed from North American *problematiques*.

Concepts, models, and paradigms of the behavioral sciences largely focus on the autonomous actor. Such an approach already reveals a choice of values. Sarason (1981) notes that the psychology created in the United States by and for Americans has made up its own subject matter: the self-contained individual. As a consequence, conflict is widely perceived and studied as an outcome of activities among individuals. One may assume that the intellectual capture of the problem has gone through a process of psychologization. This founding ethnocentrism, this parochialism, raises questions about a science that has largely ignored culture, history, and society, which could have enabled it to develop as a science constructed on a true epistemology. This construction—based on American values and concerns such as the individual subject, social intervention, efficiency, and adjustment—drives the research in an ideological direction.

Another key issue is the generalizability of research findings. The instrumental categories that provide for understanding American society are not necessarily the most appropriate to capture what goes on in China, for instance, for what is meaningful in the United States in terms of research questions may not be relevant over there. Thus, research can transform reality in surreptitious ways, through manipulation of the subjects along cultural lines (including cross-cultural studies within which implicitly or explicitly the non-American is compared to the American reference) and of course with the help of American analytical categories.

The use of the Kelley (1966) pay-off matrix illustrates the difficulty. Negotiators from twelve different cultures are used as experimental subjects—all under similar conditions—and their performances compared. The intent is praiseworthy, and the comparative approach useful. However, similarity is not neutrality. If every group—Japanese, German, Chinese, American, and so on—is dealt with in an identical way, it results in a fictitious equality because the experiment is designed using the tools of only one culture. It is similar to testing subjects' ability to eat by providing them with a bowl of rice and a pair of chopsticks.

How meaningful can social psychological categories be when applied to Russian culture, which has no verb "to be" or "to have"? How useful in terms of knowledge can a comparative approach be that compares radically different systems of thinking? The Vienna Congress (1814–1815), one of the most remarkable international negotiations ever, gathered representatives of the European powers of that time to examine national borders to ensure equilibrium. The meetings were held in French, the diplomatic language of that time. Would the results have been different if the negotiation had been carried out in English? Such a question—one with no answer—still makes sense.

Thinking in general—and scientific elaboration in particular—base their development on metaphors, which are analogical substitutes, transfers of signification orienting the reasoning and structuring the available answers. Thus, sociology borrowed from mechanistic metaphors to describe the functioning of a society. In a similar way the systems approach has taken most of its characteristics from biological metaphors; liberal economics borrowed from Newtonian physics.

Metaphors are not culturally independent. For instance, American metaphors of conflict mainly refer to games, whereas Chinese metaphors equate conflict with war. The conceptual capture of situations, as well as subsequent reasoning, are then caught within particular logics, conscious or unconscious ones, that orient the results.

The concept of negotiation leads to similar observations. The Chinese metaphors of negotiation are of two different forms, as is true of the concept itself. Antagonistic negotiation (*tan pan*) is compared to a chess game, whereas cooperative negotiation (*tao lun*) is viewed as a duet, as a concert with two instruments. Chess implies, in its Chinese version as in its international version, the idea of fight, a duel aiming at producing a winner and a loser. A duet, on the contrary, excludes any idea of opposition and conveys the image of a joint project that needs both parties. This image fits the social ideal of Chinese tradition: the quest for a stable, balanced order, in other words, the search for harmony. Thus, in the underlying metaphors of conflict and negotiation are embedded cultural meanings that make them express the values, visions, and concerns specific to a society. The behavioral sciences perpetuate the ideology that gave birth to them.

Behavioral sciences vary considerably from one culture to another. American culture tends to promote research leading to practical consequences, concrete applications, which is not true in every culture. This is why the U.S. conflict resolution approach has no real equivalent in France, where research would rather deal with what is called *polemology* (the study of conflicts). In the United States, the final purpose is usefulness, in the form of an intervention; in France, the observations are made to feed knowledge. The consequences of the different approaches are at the same time scientific and practical. In the United States, we see the development of the behavioral sciences and the creation of organizations such as peace institutes. This contrasts with what can be observed in France, for example. The point here is not to decide who is right and who is wrong but simply to underline the differences, which make all efforts toward any generalization more difficult to undertake.

## An Intercultural Approach

Science as a form of knowledge always develops within a society. Paradigms are socially rooted because researchers work according to the a priori ideas they carry with them about the world and the relations between people. Only numbers can be considered spontaneous universal concepts. The point then is not to reject culture, an act that would make no more sense than rejecting humans from the behavioral sciences, but to cope with it. So, if no concept is spontaneously intercultural, we must work to produce some that are.

We need to work on the two major difficulties I have outlined: the non-neutral, value-laden approaches and the generalizability of research findings. Neither of these tasks are, strictly speaking, insurmountable. To some extent, the situation is comparable to the study of the boiling point of water, when researchers realized that water does not boil everywhere at the same temperature. But wherever water is studied, it always does boil, and—on this earth—it will never be above or below a certain temperature.

According to Karl Popper, science produces only questionable assumptions. What escapes from the possibility of refutation belongs to the world of mysticism or magic, not to the domain of science. Max Weber (1949) also emphasized the open-ended nature of science. A concept is never a final account of reality but rather a heuristic device. Starting research within one culture is a necessary step and using experimental tools can be convincing to some extent. But one should do this while considering the next steps to be taken.

Cultural metaphors must first be understood in terms of what culturally shapes them. For instance, to be relevant, negotiation metaphors must integrate the cultural dimension and express facts that can be understood as such in the culture of the actor. To this end, the researcher has to identify a paradigm that belongs to a specific culture or resort to a more universal tool, proving that it has the necessary external validity. An example that expresses the necessary cultural dimensions explains the Chinese approach to negotiation with the help of a metaphor drawn from the Chinese context: riding a bicycle in Beijing. This metaphor, which expresses the tacit coordination and negotiation that occurs as thousands of Chinese bicycle around the city, reveals a number of the main characteristics of the Chinese way of negotiating (Faure, 1995).

In studying conflict, the point is to carefully distinguish the context of discovery from the context of justification. This is the raison d'être of cross-cultural research and why it is essential to orient research in this direction. Studying conflict and conflict resolution should not be an introduction to American culture and society; neither should it be "an American export commodity that commenced virtually to flood the world market" (Koch, 1985, p. 25). Methodology and instruments must be devised that take into account new concerns. One might give up some of the "existing instruments" that, according to Brislin (1986, p. 139), are measures that were developed and standardized in one culture, in spite of the fact that use of these measures provides many facilities for collecting data and publishing research. A very significant example of one such measure, according to Brislin, is provided by intelligence tests constructed in the United States. These tests, even once methodologically "purified" (that is, when items with a low total correlation are discarded) are culture bound. Brislin adds that psychology's history does include cross-cultural use of IQ tests to rank cultures on intelligence (p. 139). This is precisely the type of instrument that must be completely reconsidered, in its present form and even in principle.

## Options for Moving Ahead

There are several ways to promote a higher degree of research generalizability. First, we must emphasize data from parts of the world where values such as the "self-contained individualist" do not prevail in order to broaden the validity of existing theories. Second, we should start from the beginning, avoiding from the very start the domination of American perspectives. Fundamentally we should assume that culture is not a variable in the methodology of conflict studies but rather the law of variation of this methodology.

The point is not just to include culture as one among other components of the situations—as it is done, for instance, in the Sawyer and Guetzkow model (1965)—but to assume that all factors in the model are culturally driven and, as a consequence, potentially different from one culture to another. One, then, could speak of culturalized variations of a formal hypothetical model.

Substantial results have already been achieved in examining distributive justice in a broader way. Deutsch (1975) relates allocation rules and social values that people try to achieve: equity is preferred when the goal is to increase productivity; equality is preferred when the goal is to improve social relations; and the needs rule is preferred when the goal is to foster personal development. Empirical work with American and Korean subjects (Leung & Park, 1986; Stake, 1983) has confirmed the two first propositions. It would be quite interesting to test Deutsch's third rule of allocation. Before beginning, however, researchers should question individuals from various cultures on their understanding of the three rules and their associated content. In other words, it is essential to know if concepts such as equity or equality carry the same meanings in Manhattan and in Timbuctu.

Other ways of developing research could be considered, such as (1) integrating transcultural perspectives at the beginning of the methodological process, at the very first stage of the work; (2) constructing nonverbal tools, concepts expressed using figures instead of words; or (3) carrying out a "re-problematization" of the concepts before any theoretical work is done. Integrating transculturality at the very first stage of research supposes resorting to culture-aware approaches. It can be done, for instance, by organizing work teams made up of individuals from various cultures and elaborating together concepts and intellectual approaches. A researcher working alone must have sufficient experience of other cultures. One has to be, as well, extremely aware of social values that belong to his or her culture and result in hidden assumptions.

Resorting to nonverbal intercultural concepts means producing descriptive and analytical concepts not as texts but as symbolic figures that express similar meanings in various cultures. This method is especially appropriate for cultures where evocative expressions, concrete thinking, or symbolic signs play an important role. A major advantage of such an approach is avoiding the use of verbatim, which can be influenced by the culture of the scholar or by the one in which the theory was born. My work (1993) on Sino-French bicultural constructs on negotiation theory provides an example. I presented during training sessions some analytical concepts to various publics in the two cultures, knowing that the Chinese have a strong liking for metaphors and images and that the French are inclined to choose a more abstract approach. The concepts— process, structure, and their interrelations—were presented in a pictorial mode.

As previously mentioned, another means of exploring new avenues for interculturality consists in reformulating concepts after building up new *problematiques* and then applying them to the theoretical field. The main purpose of a "re-problematization" is to enable the scholar to avoid the initial system of questioning that produced those basic concepts, thus reducing the influence of the involved culture. Intervention at the very beginning of the process ensures a higher degree of neutrality of the concept to be used as a tool. First, the concept is selected, depending on the goals to be reached, then re-problematized, then re-constructed with a new definition, and lastly subjected to cultural testing.

Introducing more value neutrality and striving to achieve a higher degree of generalizability are projects that any researcher concerned with the behavioral sciences may consider a major goal for the near future.

## References

Betancourt, H., & Lopez, S. R. (1993). The study of culture, ethnicity, and race in American psychology. *American Psychologist, 48*(6).

Bond, M. (Ed.). (1988). *The cross-cultural challenge to social psychology.* Newbury Park, CA: Sage.

Brislin, R. (1986). The wording and translation of research instruments. In W. Lonner & J. Berry (Eds.), *Field methods in cross-cultural research.* Newbury Park, CA: Sage.

Cook, K. S., & Hegtvedt, K. A. (1983). Distributive justice, equity, and equality. *Annual Review of Sociology, 9,* 217–241.

Deutsch, M. (1973). *The resolution of conflict: Constructive and destructive processes.* New Haven, CT: Yale University Press.

Deutsch, M. (1975). Equity, equality, and need: What determines which value will be used as the basis of distributive justice? *Journal of Social Issues, 31,* 137–149.

Faure, G. O. (1993). Negotiation concepts across cultures. *Negotiation Journal, 9*(4), 355–359.

Faure, G. O. (1995). Nonverbal negotiation in China: Cycling in Beijing. *Negotiation Journal, 11*(1), 11–17.

Faure, G. O., & Rubin, J. Z. (Eds.). (1993). *Culture and negotiation.* Newbury Park, CA: Sage.

Gabrenya, W. K. (1988). *Social science and social psychology: The cross-cultural challenge to social psychology.* Newbury Park, CA: Sage.

Jahoda, G. (1979). A cross-cultural perspective on experimental social psychology. *Personality and Social Psychology Bulletin, 5,* 142–148.

Kelley, H. H. (1966). A classroom study of the dilemmas in interpersonal negotiations. In K. Archibald (Ed.), *Strategic interaction and conflict.* Berkeley: Institute of International Studies, University of California.

Koch, S. (1985). Wundt's creature at age zero—and as centenarian. In S. Koch & D. E. Leary (Eds.), *A century of psychology as a science.* New York: McGraw-Hill.

Lawrence, P. (1964). *Road belong Cargo: A study of the Cargo movement in the southern Madang district, New Guinea.* Manchester, England: University of Manchester.

Leung, K., & Park, H. J. (1986). Effects of interactional goal on choice of allocation rule: A cross-national study. *Organizational Behavior and Human Decision Processes, 37,* 111–120.

Nader, L., & Todd, H. F. (1978). *The disputing process: Law in ten societies.* New York: Columbia University Press.

Pepitone, A., & Triandis, H. (1987). On the universality of social psychological theories. *Journal of Cross-Cultural Psychology, 18,* 471–498.

Pruitt, D. G., & Rubin, J. Z. (1986). *Social conflict: Escalation, stalemate, and settlement.* New York: Random House.

Salem, P. (1993). A critique of Western conflict resolution from a non-Western perspective. *Negotiation Journal, 9*(4), 361–369.

Sarason, S. B. (1981). An asocial psychology and a misdirected clinical psychology. *American Psychologist, 36,* 827–836.

Sawyer, J., & Guetzkow, H. (1965). Bargaining and negotiation in international relations. In H. C. Kelman (Ed.), *International behavior: A social psychological analysis*. Troy, MO: Holt, Rinehart & Winston.

Stake, J. E. (1983). Factors in reward distribution: Allocator motive, gender, and Protestant ethic endorsement. *Journal of Personality and Social Psychology*, *44*, 410–418.

Touzard, H. (1977). *La médiation et la résolution des conflits*. Paris: Presses Universitaires de France.

Weber, M. (1949). *The methodology of the social sciences*. New York: Free Press.

# 3

# Beyond Hope

## Approaches to Resolving
## Seemingly Intractable Conflict

### Dean G. Pruitt, Paul V. Olczak

In this chapter we examine the resolution or amelioration of severe, seemingly intractable conflicts—the kind that grind on and on. Every day there are fresh reports of military actions in Bosnia or political murders in the Middle East; rival gangs keep Los Angeles regularly on edge; and the people downstairs never stop yelling at each other. Such conflicts often seem hopeless. Yet most of them are eventually resolved or at least greatly ameliorated: to name but a few, the sixty-year controversy between England and its North American colonies, which produced the American Revolution and the War of 1812; the forty-five years of the Cold War between the United States and the Soviet Union; and the thirty-year struggle between Israel and the Palestine Liberation Organization. How do conflicts of this kind get resolved? What must be done to resolve them?

We are in a period of competing singular remedies for social conflict. Each group of scholars or practitioners advocates a different line of attack, and there are debates between opposing schools. One group champions principled negotiation (Fisher, Ury, & Patton, 1991). Others are enthusiasts for induced cooperation (Johnson,

*Note:* We wish to thank Barbara B. Bunker, Douglas E. Calvin, Joseph M. Mikolic, John C. Parker, France J. Pruitt, Jeffrey Z. Rubin, and I. William Zartman for helpful comments on earlier drafts. We owe a special debt to Kenneth Kressel, who provided a full written critique of the manuscript.

Johnson, & Maruyama, 1984; Sherif, Harvey, White, Hood, & Sherif, 1961), "ripeness" (Zartman & Aurik, 1991), or unilateral tension-reducing initiatives (Osgood, 1962; Lindskold, 1986). A social movement has grown up around the virtues of mediation (Duffy, Grosch, & Olczak, 1991; Kressel & Pruitt, 1989). Advocates of problem-solving workshops (Burton, 1969; Kelman, 1993) argue vigorously with advocates of traditional diplomacy (Zartman & Berman, 1982).

Virtually all of these approaches are supported by some evidence, suggesting that they are of value. But there is not yet a synthesis that shows the conditions under which each of them is useful or how they relate to each other.

There is another field of scholarship and practice—just emerging from a similar period of disarray—that may provide a model for the field of conflict management: the treatment of psychological disorders. For years, psychotherapy and behavior modification were hampered by what Kiesler (1966) calls the "uniformity assumption myth," the belief that all patients are alike and that, therefore, there is only one correct therapy. In a humorous critique of this myth, Lazarus (1976, p. 11) observes: "How nice if insight alone or a soul-searching scream could pave the way to mental health. How simple and convenient for countless addicts if aversion therapy afforded long-lasting results. And what a boon to phobic sufferers if their morbid fears were enduringly assuaged by systematic desensitization and assertive training methods."

The modern approach to treating psychological disorders is one of technical eclecticism. Lazarus (1976), the originator of this approach, views the human personality as an interaction among seven systems or modalities, which spell out the acronym BASIC ID. These are behavior, affect, sensation, imagery, cognition, interpersonal relations, and a physiological or biological substrate that he calls "drugs." There are disorders and remedies specific to each of these modalities. Hence, it is necessary to engage in careful diagnosis and choice among methods of treatment.

Another tenet of the modern approach to psychological problems is that these modalities are interrelated, so more than one modality is likely to be deficient. This means that in serious disorders, there is a danger of relapse if only one modality is treated, even if the treatment is highly successful. The relatively unchanged structures in the other modalities will eventually overwhelm whatever progress has been made. The answer to this problem is a broad-spectrum or multimodal approach, involving the diagnosis and treatment of several modalities. Indeed, Lazarus (1976) believes that any lasting change is in direct proportion to the number of modalities treated.

There are signs that the treatment of social conflict may also be moving in an eclectic and multimodal direction. Peterson (1983, p. 395), for example, comments that "different strategies and tactics will be required for different patterns of conflict." Marital therapists (who are often psychotherapists by training) have produced several modules for treating different aspects of marital disorder (Baucom & Epstein, 1990; Jacobson & Addis, 1993). Recent research has shown that the most effective mediators are highly flexible, using different strategies at different times or in different situations (Carnevale, Lim, & McLaughlin, 1989; Donohue, 1989). And Fisher and Keashly (1990) have presented a contingency model (described below) that prescribes different forms of third-party intervention for different levels of conflict escalation. But these are only isolated trends in a field whose practitioners are still mainly advocates of singular remedies.

In our view, an eclectic and multimodal approach is essential to further progress in the field of conflict management. Such an approach must be grounded in a broad-gauged theory of the dynamics of conflict—built on the foundations erected by Deutsch (1973) and others—so that it rises above the intuitive maxims that characterize much of the field today (Pruitt, 1986).

This chapter is an effort to further such an enterprise. We first present a systems model, which traces social conflict to changes in five modes of human experience. We then discuss seven classes of remedies that alter one or another of the five underlying modes, thus helping to ameliorate conflict. Finally, we examine how and when these remedies should be invoked, in a discussion of diagnosis, sequencing, and synergy. Most of our points are illustrated by examples from two realms of theory and practice where the literature is particularly rich: marital conflict and international conflict.

While we are mainly concerned with the most severe conflicts—those involving heavily escalated relationships between the parties—our model deals with conflict in general and is applicable to milder forms of conflict as well. For the sake of simplicity, we talk in terms of two parties to conflict. But our analysis can be applied to multilateral conflict as well.

## The MACBE Model: A Systems Approach

Adapting a model of psychological disorder developed by Carson and Butcher (1992), we propose that each party to a conflict be represented by a conglomerate of five interdependent modes or subsystems that can be targeted for therapeutic attention: motivation (M), affect (A), cognition (C), behavior (B), and the surrounding social environment (E).[1] We call this the MACBE model, an acronym composed of the first letters of the names of these modes.

### Systems Theory and Circular Causality

We assume that the modes in the MACBE model are parts of a conflict system. According to von Bertalanffy (1973), a system can be defined as a group of elements and the relationships among them. The elements in our proposed system (M, A, C, B, and E) are not linearly related but interact according to a holistic principle of circular causality; each influences and is in turn influenced by the others.

Heavily escalated relationships usually entail hostile elements in all five components of the MACBE model, in contrast to mildly escalated relationships, where the problem will often be more localized. Motives (the M component) are likely to involve winning and hurting or even destroying the other. Each party has hostile feelings toward the other (the A component) and harbors negative perceptions of the other, including a large measure of distrust (the C component). Hostile and maladaptive behavioral sequences (the B component) are also common in such relationships and are what we mean by severe conflict. Furthermore, community polarization is often found, which means that the social environment surrounding each party (the E component) supports hostility toward the other side.

Circular causality means that these hostile motives, feelings, cognitions, behaviors, and social environments tend to reinforce each other (Rubin, Pruitt, & Kim, 1994). Uncomplimentary perceptions of the other party (cognitions) tend to validate hostile feelings, and hostile feelings make uncomplimentary perceptions seem right. Furthermore, perceptions and feelings are likely to color interpretations of events, producing new grievances that reinforce the perceptions and feelings. For example, a wife who distrusts her husband may misinterpret his coming home late from work as evidence of an outside romantic involvement, reinforcing her distrust.

Perceptions and feelings also induce motives and behavior, which tend to validate these perceptions and feelings. Thus, the same wife may speak harshly to her husband about his lateness, acting on and hence reinforcing the negative perceptions that gave rise to her grievance. In addition, people tend to seek the company of others who share their perceptions, feelings, and motives—for example, other women with similar grievances against their husbands—producing a social environment that reinforces these mental structures.

The two parties to a heavily escalated conflict may be regarded as subsystems in an overall system, in which each party's behavior reinforces the hostile processes on the other side, in a never ending circle. Thus, the wife's criticism may encourage her husband to view her as unreasonable, contributing to his already unfavorable image of her and legitimizing additional punitive behavior on his part. This behavior is likely to further encourage the wife's distrust, making her even more critical, and so on and on. Circular processes of this kind are called "conflict spirals" (Rubin et al., 1994, p. 67).

Because of conflict spirals, new grievances are constantly being added to the original set of issues, producing what McEwen and Milburn (1993, p. 67) call a "metadispute." As these grievances mount up, they contribute to a belief that the other party's faults are stable and global, which leads to a sense of hopelessness about reforming the other's thinking and motivation. As a result, it seems even more necessary to employ heavy-handed tactics aimed at changing the other party's behavior.

### Implications for Treatment

The previous discussion has implications for conflict resolution. Assuming that the problems in mildly escalated relationships are narrowly localized, major improvements can be made by changing one or two key parts of the system. Because all parts of the system are interrelated, a "ripple effect" (deShazer, 1985) will then resolve any minor difficulties that may exist in other parts.

But in heavily escalated relationships, a broad assault on all parts of the system is needed to prevent relapse. This is because there are durable conflict-inducing structures throughout. Changes at only one or two locations are likely to be reversed in the long run because other unchanged structures will eventually reassert the original pattern. In short, the most severe conflicts require a multimodal approach.

### Relevance to Intergroup Conflict

Our analysis so far has focused on interpersonal conflict, but the MACBE model also applies, with some modification, to conflict between groups. By group we mean any collective that is capable of coordinated action, including families, organizations, legislatures, and nations. When groups are involved, cognitions and feelings are still properties of individuals, but they are affected by group norms, which make them fairly uniform across group members. Groups also have motives (group goals) that produce group behavior. The social environment for a group consists of other comparable groups, for example, during the Cold War, the Western Alliance for the United States and the Warsaw Pact for the Soviet Union.

Groups differ from individuals in two seemingly contradictory ways. On the one hand, there is evidence that conflict between groups is more likely to escalate and to produce strained relations than conflict between individuals (McCallum et al., 1985; Komorita & Lapworth, 1982; Lindskold, McElwain, & Wayner, 1977; Pruitt, Mikolic, Eberle, Parker, & Peirce, 1993; Tajfel, Flament, Billig, & Bundy, 1971). This is because groups are more competitive and less trusting of each other than individuals and because attitudes become more extreme as a result of group discussion. On the other hand, it can be argued that groups are more capable of escaping severe conflict when there are compelling reasons for doing so. This is because even in the darkest of conflicts, groups usually contain dovish factions that are working toward peace with the adversary. If escalation becomes costly and unworkable, such factions tend to gain political strength, bringing with them a peaceful agenda and a set of relevant contacts. A fuller discussion of similarities and differences between interpersonal and intergroup conflict is found in the chapter by Rubin and Levinger in this volume.

## Changes in the Components of the MACBE Model

In this section, we discuss seven conditions and procedures that ameliorate conflict by producing changes in one or another of the five components of the MACBE model. Most of these conditions and procedures were originally championed as singular remedies capable of curing all conflicts. We treat them instead as modules that can be employed selectively after diagnosis or combined with each other to form a logical sequence.

The list starts with the best known procedures, negotiation and mediation, which aim at reaching agreements that alter the parties' behavior. The other six topics are presented in a "discovery" order, each being shown to remedy defects in the prior procedure or set of procedures. For example, negotiation and mediation are only workable if the parties are motivated to escape conflict. Hence, our second topic is this motive (which, if it exists on both sides, is called "ripeness") and its antecedents. People will often not act on the motive to escape conflict unless they believe that the other side is also so motivated. Therefore, our third topic is trust, the perception that the other side is also motivated to escape the conflict. All the motivation and trust in the world cannot make negotiation succeed if people lack problem-solving skills and fail to understand the conflict that divides them. Hence, our fourth and fifth topics are problem-solving training (a form of behavioral intervention) and analysis of the cognitive, emotional, and motivational dynamics of the conflict. Furthermore, negotiation by the most skillful and knowledgeable practitioners will seldom solve all problems. Therefore, the parties must be encouraged to reduce their aspirations (another aspect of motivation) on issues that cannot be resolved— our sixth topic. Finally, the best agreements in the world may be subverted when the parties reenter their prior social environments and encounter people who are still hostile to the adversary. Hence, it is often useful to restructure the social environment, moving the parties away from divisive affiliations and toward integrative ones. This is our seventh and last topic.

Though far-reaching, the seven conditions and procedures just listed are only a sample of the many routes to conflict resolution. For instance, a good case can be made for the effectiveness, under some circumstances, of equal status contact (Deutsch & Collins, 1951) and cooperation on common goals (Johnson et al., 1984; Sherif et al., 1961). What distinguishes our seven topics is that they pertain in one way or another to success in negotiation and mediation.

## Negotiation and Mediation: Altering Behavior

Negotiation, which can be defined as discussion aimed at reaching an agreement that changes behavior on one or both sides, is the most popular approach to conflict resolution (Peirce, Pruitt, & Czaja, 1993). Conflict is often resolved, or at least diminished, through negotiation.

Negotiation is a mixed-motive enterprise, in the sense of involving both cooperation and competition. Negotiators compete with each other in an effort to influence the terms of the agreement; yet they must also cooperate in an effort to reach agreement.

There are two ways to cooperate in negotiation: concession making and problem solving. The latter approach tries to locate an option that appeals to both sides, a so-called win-win agreement. Win-win agreements can be reached in three basic ways (Pruitt & Carnevale, 1993):

- Expanding the pie by increasing the available resources so that both sides can get what they want.

- Exchanging concessions on different issues so that each side wins on its issues of highest priority. This includes making side payments to the other party in exchange for concessions.

- Analyzing the underpinnings of the parties' positions in an effort to find a new approach. Some underpinnings are motivational, involving needs, goals, and values. Others are cognitive, involving assumptions about the nature of reality.

When negotiation is unproductive, third parties often help the negotiators reach agreement. This is mediation, which must be distinguished from arbitration, in which third parties make a decision about the issues. An example of mediation is the role of the United States in helping Israel and Egypt reach a negotiated agreement at

Camp David in 1978. The mediator was President Carter (and his aides), who shuttled back and forth between President Begin of Israel and President Sadat of Egypt. The result was an agreement that required Israel to give back the Sinai Peninsula, which it had occupied during a war, in return for full normalization of relations between the countries.

There are hundreds of mediator tactics, each designed to deal with a different impediment to successful negotiation (Bercovitch, 1992; Kressel & Pruitt, 1989). For example, mediators can provide a sympathetic view of the other party's motives in an effort to allay fears, devise a possible win-win agreement when the parties lack an overview of the conflict, or present a party's new proposal as their own when there is a danger that the other party will devalue it or view it with suspicion.

Negotiation and mediation are often successful in regulating or resolving conflict. But they are not panaceas. Sometimes the parties will not deal with each other or with a mediator, preferring to continue efforts to defeat the other side. In other cases, negotiation fails to produce an agreement or the parties fail to comply with the agreement, a problem of relapse. These difficulties often reflect insufficient motivation to escape the conflict, the topic to which we now turn.

### Ripeness: The Motivation to Escape Conflict

When both sides are motivated to escape conflict, the situation is said to be "ripe" for resolution, a term employed by scholars in the field of international relations (Kriesberg, 1991; Rubin, 1991; Zartman, 1989).

#### Sources of Ripeness

Ripeness often results from one or more of the following circumstances, which have been best described by Zartman and Aurik (1991):

• The parties perceive that they are in a *hurting stalemate*, suffering costs in a struggle they cannot win. Many Americans who protested the Vietnam War regarded it just this way; winning the war seemed hopeless, and it was bleeding the United States of valuable resources.

• The parties have experienced á *recent catastrophe* or *near catastrophe* associated with the conflict, a precipice they fell over or nearly fell over. For Sadat at Camp David, the Yom Kippur War was a recent catastrophe that drove home the urgency of preventing a new round of escalation. The Cuban missile crisis of 1963 was a near catastrophe that encouraged awareness of the dangers of nuclear war in both the United States and the Soviet Union, motivating a series of successful efforts to regulate the conflict between these countries (Hopmann, 1991; Hurwitz, 1991).

• The parties become conscious of an *impending catastrophe* or *deteriorating position* associated with the conflict. For Gorbachev, economic and military failure were impending catastrophes that drove him to search for peace. For both Arafat and his Israeli counterparts, the rise of militant Islamism posed a future threat they could face only if they resolved the conflict between them.

• The parties perceive an *enticing opportunity*, that is, the possibility of finding a peaceful solution to the conflict that preserves essential values.

In addition, third parties can encourage ripeness. Ripeness may result from third-party pressure or enticements for conflict resolution. Thus, for both Israel and Egypt in the late 1970s, the motivation to resolve their conflict was partly produced by American pressure and the promise of increased American aid (Hurwitz, 1991). Third parties may also produce ripeness by means of power balancing—coming to the rescue of the weaker disputant or failing to support further escalation by the stronger one. Such actions produce a hurting stalemate or impending catastrophe for the stronger party (Zartman & Aurik, 1991). In addition, the availability of a competent mediator contributes to a sense of enticing opportunity and hence to ripeness because it begins to seem possible to find an acceptable solution to the conflict (Rubin, 1991).

### A Perspective on Ripeness

Ripeness is usually described as a bilateral state of affairs, affecting both parties for the same reasons. For example, Zartman and Aurik (1991, p. 155) speak of a "mutually hurting stalemate" and Zartman (1989, p. 233) of a "catastrophe . . . into which the parties are . . . sinking deeper and deeper." But we think it is useful to do a separate analysis of the motivation on each side. This allows for the possibility that the situation will be ripe for different reasons on each side. Thus, the negotiations that ended the Vietnam War appear to have been primarily motivated by a sense of hurting stalemate in the United States and a sense of enticing opportunity in North Vietnam, the latter resulting from American signals of a readiness to make substantial concessions.

Such a separate analysis also encourages attention to situations involving unequal readiness to settle, where one party is anxious to escape the conflict and the other is unmotivated to do so. For example, after Stalin's death in 1953, Soviet leaders sent signals of an interest in de-escalating the Cold War by signing a peace treaty with Austria. But these signals were of little interest to the United States, which was preoccupied with developing a series of alliances to resist "Godless communism."

Though technically unripe, situations involving unequal readiness for settlement are by no means always as hopeless as in this example from early in the Cold War. They sometimes provoke a series of events that strengthen the laggard party's motivation to settle to a point where the conflict can be resolved. The first step in this series often occurs when the party who is motivated to de-escalate begins to gather information about its adversary. For instance, toward the end of the Cold War, Gorbachev, convinced of the need for peace to repair the Soviet economy, turned for advice to individuals and institutes familiar with the United States. Such information gathering is likely to produce a more complex picture of the adversary, revealing divisions between hawks and doves and raising the possibility that one's own behavior toward the adversary is part of the problem. The result may be a reconceptualization of the nature of the challenge.

This reconceptualization may then lead to a new strategy, such as seeking negotiation or taking unilateral conciliatory initiatives. In 1977, Egypt's President Sadat, convinced that the controversy with Israel was a conflict spiral, made a surprise trip to Jerusalem to raise the level of trust and thus cut off the escalation. The end result of this trip was the Camp David negotiation. Similarly, the Soviet Union—under Gorbachev—withdrew from Afghanistan and made unilateral armament cuts, thereby vastly improving relations with the West. Both are examples of unilateral conciliatory initiatives.

In a more pessimistic vein, it is important to note that situations that are ripe, with a strong motive to de-escalate on both sides, do not always end in conflict resolution. When the relationship between the parties has severely deteriorated, progress may still be blocked by distrust, lack of problem-solving skills, absence of insight into the other party, or a divisive social environment. In other words, ripe moments will often be frittered away unless these problems are solved. We turn now to these additional requirements.

## The Development of Trust: A Type of Cognition

Trust, in its most general sense, is a belief that another party can be relied on in a situation where that party controls one's outcomes (Deutsch, 1973). However, we use the term more narrowly here to refer to a belief that one's adversary is motivated to resolve the conflict—that the situation is, in a manner of speaking, ripe for the other side. Trust is clearly a cognition, though it is often influenced by other components of the MACBE model, such as affect.

Trust is often the missing component that blocks a ripe situation from moving toward agreement. Both sides want to escape the conflict, but neither believes that the other side is so motivated. Hence, neither is willing to take a first conciliatory step for fear of looking weak if the other fails to reciprocate. Something like this was happening between Egypt and Israel in 1977 before Sadat's dramatic trust-building trip. If Egypt had been led by a different ruler, one less willing to take risks, this trip would probably not have been made, and the period of ripeness might well have been squandered.

When coupled with the motive to escape conflict, trust is an important antecedent of conflict resolution (Pruitt & Kimmel, 1977). Trust means we believe that the other party will reciprocate rather than exploit our concessions. This makes it easier to concede, thereby moving toward agreement. In addition, a trusted other is viewed as likely to search hard for a mutually acceptable agreement and to adhere to this agreement once reached. Hence, it seems safer to enter negotiation, engage in joint problem solving, and conclude an agreement (Kimmel, Pruitt, Magenau, Konar-Goldband, & Carnevale, 1980; Lindskold & Han, 1988).

A party can engender trust by taking unilateral conciliatory initiatives, such as Sadat's trip to Jerusalem, which produced a dramatic rise in Israeli readiness to trust Egypt (Kelman, 1985). Such initiatives are likely to be especially effective if they fulfill three conditions: (1) they are unexpected, so that they provoke thought; (2) they weaken or are costly to their originator, so that they cannot easily be dismissed as a trick; and (3) their originator has equal or greater power than their target, so that they cannot easily be written off as a sign of weakness (Mitchell, 1991; Pruitt & Carnevale, 1993). Sadat's initiative fulfilled all of these conditions.

There are many other sources of trust, including a perception that the other party is humble and self-effacing, is a member of our group, or is dependent on ourselves (Pruitt, 1981). Third parties can encourage trust by asserting that the adversary is genuinely interested in settling the conflict and is willing to make reasonable concessions in search of settlement.

In addition, third parties sometimes provide substitutes for trust, employing tactics that move the situation toward agreement when trust is low. For example, mediators often engineer simultaneous concessions so that it is not necessary for each side to rely on the other's willingness to reciprocate. Furthermore, they commonly engage in problem-solving discussions with each party separately, increasing the likelihood of locating win-win agreements (Welton, Pruitt, McGillicuddy, Ippolito, & Zubek, 1992).

## Problem-Solving Training: Developing Negotiator Skills

An example of problem-solving training is that developed by marital therapists to combat the problem of relapse (Baucom & Epstein, 1990; Jacobson & Margolin, 1979). Relapse was common in the early days of behavioral marital therapy, which were dominated by efforts to establish agreements to regulate behavior between spouses, with the therapist as mediator. These "marital contracts" were found not to last, often ceasing to be followed after the termination of therapy (Jacobson, 1984). New issues typically arose that were not covered by the agreement, and the parties returned to their prior pattern of squabbling. One solution to this difficulty became training the parties in problem solving, teaching them how to locate creative solutions to future issues.

Problem-solving training now supplements the mediation of contracts in most marital therapy. Husband and wife are taught skills of listening, communicating clearly, avoiding efforts to pin blame on the other, posing issues that involve both parties' needs, reconceptualizing these issues if they are unproductively framed, and brainstorming for solutions to issues. In addition to developing individual skills, spouses learn to interact productively with each other. Under the watchful eyes of the therapist, they practice a coordinated joint routine and develop a nonprovocative, common vocabulary with a shared set of meanings.

Research shows that a combination of marital contracting and problem-solving training is more successful in the long run than either method used separately (Jacobson, Schmaling, & Holtzworth-Munroe, 1987).

Similar training procedures have been developed in a number of other realms (Donohue & Kolt, 1992; Fisher et al., 1991; Fisher, 1994; Johnson & Johnson, 1994; Katz & Lawyer, 1985). A thorough discussion of problem-solving training in the public schools is found in the chapter by Raider in the current volume.

Problem-solving training is useful in intergroup as well as interpersonal realms, and it can be argued that all group representatives should receive problem-solving training. However, this training can often be abbreviated when larger groups (such as nations) are involved, since it is usually possible to find some group members who are already good at problem solving. In such cases, the challenge is to get these people involved in the negotiation and to help them communicate effectively with each other (Kelman, 1993).

Assertiveness training (Hollon & Beck, 1986) can be helpful as a supplement to problem-solving training if one disputant in interpersonal conflict is too timid or fearful to present its own needs effectively. Training in the control of expressed anger (Hankins, 1988; Novaco, 1975) may be useful for other types of disputants. This is not to say that anger should never be expressed. Occasional mild displays can be beneficial, alerting the adversary to one's core needs and values, which must be satisfied in any comprehensive settlement.[2] However, regular outbursts of anger are destructive of relationships and impede effective problem solving.

### Analyzing Basic Conflict Dynamics: Cognitions, Feelings, and Motives

Problem solving is usually designed to solve a narrow set of concrete issues that are front and center for the involved parties: custody of the children in a failed marriage, a wage rate in labor-management negotiation, the location of a boundary in negotiations to end a war. However, it is often necessary to analyze the conflict more deeply, looking for its basic dynamics (Fisher, 1994). The presenting issues may be expressions of more fundamental needs and principles that are being frustrated. Severe relationship problems may be at the root of the conflict, for example, distrust and persistent anger or a desire to defeat or harm the other. Or there may be repetitive cycles of conflict, with the same issue or sequence of issues recurring again and again.

Lack of attention to basic dynamics may make it hard to reach agreement or may produce superficial contracts without lasting value. For example, in a study of community mediation, which usually focuses on an immediate issue, short-term success and long-term success were found to be unrelated (Pruitt, Peirce, McGillicuddy, Welton, & Castrianno, 1993). This means that many good agreements, ones that solved immediate problems and satisfied the disputants, were followed by a reassertion of preexisting problems in the relationship. Further issues quickly arose, and the parties resumed their quarrel. By contrast, in a study of custody mediation, mediators who sought to analyze the dynamics of the conflict achieved more durable agreements than those who only sought to solve the presenting problems (Kressel, Frontera, Forlenza, Butler, & Fish, 1994).

Modern marital therapists usually try to help their clients understand the basic dynamics of their conflict. Particular emphasis is usually placed on the role of negative affect in generating conflict behavior. Baucom and Epstein (1990) have developed a method of "emotional expressiveness training," which is designed to help couples understand and cope with their own and the other parties' feelings, and Greenberg and Johnson (1988) have developed a similar "emotionally focused couples therapy." The latter has been shown to be effective in two evaluation studies (James, 1991; Johnson & Greenberg, 1985).

In these therapies, each party is urged to reveal how he or she felt in reaction to concrete instances of the other's behavior. Special emphasis is placed on repetitive sequences of behavior, for example, the common pursuit-withdrawal pattern, in which the wife feels neglected and seeks attention from the husband, and the husband feels under attack and withdraws further into his shell. Each party is also urged to acknowledge the feelings that are revealed by the other and to accept them as a necessary part of the problem to be solved. This allows the spouses to reconceptualize the issues in a productive fashion.

In addition to analyzing emotional dynamics, it is useful for the parties to explore their perceptions of each other and the attributions (explanations) they make for the other's behavior. For example, in the pursuit-withdrawal pattern, the wife often erroneously attributes the husband's behavior to lack of love or an uncaring disposition.

Motivation also needs to be examined. The strong feelings found in severe conflict typically arise from the frustration of basic human needs (Burton, 1990; Fisher, 1994) or the perception that fundamental principles of justice have been violated. Examples are the need for status or freedom of action, and the principle that benefits received should be proportional to sacrifices made. Such needs and principles have universal appeal and are often easy to understand when they are revealed by the adversary. Understanding them makes it easier to tolerate the adversary's behavior and allows one to act in ways that are less annoying to the adversary. Furthermore, showing that one understands the motives underlying the adversary's feelings helps to build trust in the adversary's mind. One appears to be an empathic human being who is trying to grasp what is happening.

Analysis of basic conflict dynamics is useful in relations between organizations or nations as well as in interpersonal relations. For example, it seems reasonable to assume that such conversations took place between the United States and the Soviet Union as the Cold War wound down in the 1980s. During this period, Gorbachev exhibited what looked like a detailed understanding of Western perceptions of Soviet intentions and of those Soviet actions that were especially alarming and enraging to the West. One can guess that this resulted from the thousands of conversations that had taken place over the prior decade in such gatherings as the Dartmouth Conference (Kettering Foundation, 1988), where the relationship between the countries was analyzed in depth.

Emotionally focused marital therapy has a parallel in a tradition of problem-solving workshops for dealing with international conflict that has grown up over the past twenty-five years (Burton, 1969; Fisher & Keashly, 1988; Kelman, 1993). Such workshops are a form of private diplomacy. Well-placed individuals from both sides meet for a week or more to explore the conflict. A major aim is to help each side understand the other side's motives, perceptions, and feelings as they impact the conflict. Incidents that occur within these sessions are often analyzed as fresh examples of the dynamics of the controversy. It seems likely that the end product of such workshops is a greater understanding of one's own and the other party's behavior in the conflict.[3]

These and similar procedures should have a number of positive benefits, including the following:

- Improvement of problem solving by helping the parties grasp underlying issues, thereby encouraging the development of lasting agreements.

- Enhancement of trust by making the adversary seem less malevolent. An understanding of the other party's true motives is often reassuring because it reveals that there are limits to that party's behavior.

- Enhancement of trust by allowing the adversary to show that it understands the motives and principles underlying one's behavior.

- Reduction of anger and hostility by making the adversary's aversive behavior seem less arbitrary.

- Elimination of actions that unwittingly annoy each other.

## Reducing Aspirations: Motivation Revisited

While problem solving is a useful skill, its importance for conflict management has probably been overemphasized in recent years. Win-win solutions are not always available, and a meeting of minds is not always possible. Research on marital satisfaction (Fitzpatrick, 1988; Gottman, 1993; Raush, Barry, Hertel, & Swain, 1974) reveals that problem solving is only one of several successful approaches to conflict. Many happily married couples have adopted another, very different style that involves studied avoidance of conflict. This requires the two individuals to fend for themselves whenever possible rather than depend on each other. It also requires scaling down aspirations to fit what is available in the relationship. If the wife is not warm, the husband learns to aspire to less affection. If the husband spends money easily, the wife comes to accept a lower standard of living. Each party accommodates to what is available rather than endlessly trying to reform the other.

Jacobson (1992) recommends a combination of problem solving and conflict avoidance for married couples who are trying to resolve deep-seated conflict. Spouses should strive to solve those problems that can be solved and learn to live with those that cannot. Jacobson has designed "acceptance therapy" as an adjunct to the development of marital contracts and problem-solving training. The goal is to help people accept what cannot be changed in the other party's character and behavior. Such training seems applicable to all conflict settings.

Acceptance may be difficult because of the competitive stance that so often develops in conflict. Self-esteem becomes bound up in winning every contest; people act as if they believe Vince Lombardi's quip, "Winning isn't everything, it's the only thing." It is hard to back down because it seems to imply that the adversary is right and the party retreating is wrong. Yet some concessions are almost always needed for conflict to be resolved.

It is easier to reduce aspirations if the other party does so too.

For example, after the Cuban missile crisis, both the United States and the Soviet Union were careful not to challenge each other's spheres of influence, in what amounted to an undeclared treaty. This was hard for many in the United States because it meant abandoning their goal of liberating Eastern Europe from Soviet domination. But most people who thought about it were willing to allow this concession because it reduced the chances of violent confrontation between the superpowers and because the Soviet Union reciprocated.

## Restructuring the Social Environment

It is hard to resolve a conflict between parties whose allies keep pulling them apart. Hence, a comprehensive therapy for conflict often must deal with the social environment. For example, two neighbors observed by one of the authors during a mediation session discovered that friends were pushing them into conflict with each other; hence they decided not to discuss their controversy with these friends. Some troubled marriages can be improved by disregarding the views of in-laws.

Another example comes from organizational development workshops that are aimed at teaching co-workers to deal more effectively with each other. Relapse is often a problem when small groups of co-workers are trained because at the end of training they return to the same social environment from which they came. To remedy this problem, it is now common to bring large parts of an organization into training at the same time.

In Western countries, it is conventional for mediators to concentrate their attention on the disputing parties, ignoring the social milieu in which these parties are imbedded—and thus running the risk of relapse. But this is by no means a universal tradition. In the People's Republic of China, for instance, the mediator consults with neighbors, relatives, and associates of conflicting parties in an effort to put together an integrated solution (Wall & Blum, 1991). Whole communities are involved in mediation efforts in many nonindus-

trial societies (Gulliver, 1979; Merry, 1989). Such mediation practices seem more likely to produce lasting change because the social
environment is restructured along with the disputants.

In restructuring the social environment, it is wise to think ahead
to conflicts that may develop in the future. Ury, Brett, and Goldberg (1988) have put forward a series of principles for constructing
conflict management systems in communities. They recommend
that potentially conflicting groups appoint and give authority to
negotiators, who then meet and get to know each other so that they
can communicate on short notice if a crisis develops. Active mediators who seek out conflicts and offer their services should also be
available, and an early warning system should be installed to sum-
mon these mediators.

An early warning system has recently been instituted in South
Africa by the National Peace Secretariat. This consists of a network
of local dispute resolution committees and international monitors
that seek to detect conflict when it is first brewing and to intervene
rapidly. According to *The Washington Post*, "Some of their work has
been heroic, and much of it has paid off" (Taylor, 1993, p. A34).

## Diagnosis, Sequencing, and Synergy

We have just presented seven broad modules, consisting of conditions and procedures that contribute to conflict resolution by changing one or another component of the MACBE model. The question
we address in this section is how people who are trying to resolve
conflict (whether third parties or the disputants themselves) should
choose among these modules.

As mentioned earlier, if there is moderate escalation, changes
are likely to be needed in only one or two key realms. A new behavioral agreement is negotiated, and labor and management get back
to work. A critical motive or misperception is changed, and colleagues are again able to coordinate. A divisive parent moves to a
retirement community, and husband and wife become reconciled.
In short, the issue in moderate conflict is one of diagnosis and "sur-

gical" treatment, to locate and then alter the offending element(s) of the system.

But when escalation is severe and conflict seems intractable, a multimodal approach is needed. There is no magic bullet; most or all of the modules must be involved. The parties must become motivated to escape their conflict, trust must develop, problem-solving skills must be honed, perceptions and feelings must be uncovered and dealt with, unrealistic aspirations must be modified, divisive alliances must be eliminated, and the parties must negotiate a new mode of dealing with each other. Failing to deal with any part of the conflict system runs the risk that the old pattern will eventually reassert itself. The message is not either-or, but all.[4]

Having said this, two issues remain. First is the question of sequencing: in what order should the modules be invoked? Second is the issue of synergy or potentiation: do some of the modules interact so that when they are combined, the effect is greater than or different from the sum of its parts?

## Sequencing

Fisher and Keashly (1990) have provided an initial answer to the question of sequencing in the form of a contingency model of third-party intervention. They argue that the type of intervention should depend on the level of escalation in the relationship, and they identify four levels (which they call "stages") of escalation (p. 236):

- Discussion, in which "perceptions are still accurate, commitment to the relationship strong, and belief in possible joint gain predominant"

- Polarization, in which "trust and respect are threatened, and distorted perceptions and simplified stereotypes emerge"

- Segregation, in which "competition and hostility are the basic themes and the conflict is now perceived as threatening basic needs"

- Destruction, in which "the primary intent of the parties is to destroy or at least subjugate each other through the use of violence"

The third party's goal at higher levels of escalation should be to de-escalate the conflict to the next lower level, continuing on down to the discussion level, where conflict can be most easily resolved. If we translate Fisher and Keashly's points into the terms used in our analysis, they recommend the following.

At the lowest level of escalation—the discussion level—the parties need to engage in negotiation, in search of a win-win solution. The third party should act as a mediator, facilitating communication between the parties while intruding as little as possible into their dialog.[5]

At the second level—polarization—the third party needs to engage in "consultation," helping the parties understand the dynamics of their conflict—the perceptions and motives that must be addressed for a lasting solution to be accomplished. One goal of consultation is to encourage a reconciliation between the parties, allowing them to move into productive negotiation. Another goal is to provide the information they need to negotiate lasting agreements.

At the third level—segregation—the third party needs to employ incentives in an effort to discourage the parties from taking hostile actions and encourage them to reach some basic agreements that will "demonstrate to the parties that agreement is still possible on substantive issues" (p. 237). This requires that the third party be more powerful than at the lower two levels. However, the goal is not to arbitrate the entire controversy but only to push the parties into exploring the dynamics of their conflict and engaging in effective negotiation.

At the fourth level—destruction—the third party becomes a peacekeeper seeking to "forcefully separate the parties and control escalating violence" (p. 237). Once this goal is accomplished, it should be possible to move to the more creative roles of consultation and mediation.

There are points of similarity and difference between Fisher and Keashly's contingency model and our own approach. The theories are similar in their recognition that highly escalated conflicts require a broad set of interventions. They differ in that the contingency model prescribes negotiation and mediation for mildly escalated relationships, whereas our approach holds that different procedures may be appropriate depending on the diagnosis.

## Analysis Before Negotiation

The most interesting contribution of the contingency model is found in two of its assumptions about the order in which changes must take place in heavily escalated relationships. The first assumption is that analysis of the dynamics of the conflict should precede negotiation. This point is also endorsed by Kelman (1993; Rouhana & Kelman, 1994), who observes that in problem-solving workshops, much time must be spent on conflict analysis before effective negotiation is possible. Another way of putting this is that instant diplomacy between confirmed antagonists is usually destined for failure.

## Primacy of Motivation

The second (and somewhat hidden) assumption in the contingency model concerns the primacy of motivation in combating heavily escalated conflict. In other words, the initial step must be the development of motivation to escape the conflict—in our terms, the development of ripeness. This point can be inferred from Fisher and Keashly's conclusion that third parties must employ incentives at the segregation level of escalation to move the disputants into negotiation. It is also implied by their recommendation for peacekeeping at the destruction level of escalation. By preventing violent struggle, the third party forces the disputants to seek a different strategy, which will often involve negotiation.

We agree about the primacy of motivation for the resolution of severely escalated *interpersonal* disputes. In the absence of motivation to escape the conflict, one cannot expect people to engage in creative conflict analysis or problem solving.

When there is mild escalation, people are likely to be sufficiently alarmed that they develop the motivation to escape conflict. But paradoxically, when escalation is severe, such motivation is likely to dry up. This is because each party tends to feel that the other is the source of the problem and therefore has sole responsibility for its solution. It is also because distrust and other negative perceptions make it seem impossible to escape from the conflict.

Of course, third-party intervention is not the only source of motivation to escape conflict. As mentioned previously, such motivation may also derive from hurting stalemates, impending catastrophes, and the like. Furthermore, motivation to escape conflict must usually be supplemented by trust—a belief that the other party is also motivated to escape the conflict.

The primacy of motivation is not so clear in severe *intergroup* (including international) conflict. In such conflict, it is often possible for a few doves or "realists" on each side to begin analyzing the basic conflict, even though there is no groupwide motivation to end the conflict. This is the function of events like the Dartmouth Conferences, problem-solving workshops, and other examples of private diplomacy by individual citizens. The understanding and contacts developed by individuals at such events become a basis for effective negotiation if and when motivation develops at the group level. In other words, private diplomacy produces a resource that can be accessed when the ripe moment arrives.

Private diplomacy, in which the roots of the conflict are analyzed in off-the-record unofficial meetings, may seem disheartening in its small initial payoff. In the Dartmouth Conferences, Soviet and American citizens met biyearly over a twenty-six-year period without apparent success in ending the Cold War (Kettering Foundation, 1988). Yet they were laying the foundation for effective de-escalation when Soviet leaders began to realize the danger and futility of continuing the Cold War. Without this basis, and the groundwork produced by other private contacts, it seems unlikely that Gorbachev would have known how to execute the smooth set of de-escalatory moves he accomplished or that negotiation between the countries would have moved ahead so rapidly. The period of ripeness might well have been wasted without this foundation.

Similar contacts between Israelis and members of the Palestine Liberation Organization, which took place secretly in Norway, were responsible for the Middle East breakthrough of 1993 (Haberman, 1993).

### Synergy

Synergy refers to an interaction among several causal forces such that their joint impact is greater than or different from the sum of their individual impacts. Synergistic effects are sometimes called "martini" or "cocktail" effects, on the assumption that the combination of gin and vermouth produces a greater psychopharmacological effect than the sum of the effects of the two drinks separately.

Synergistic effects have been found in the treatment of psychological disorders (Polfai & Jankiewicz, 1991). For example, individual psychotherapy on hospitalized schizophrenics is usually ineffective, but it is beneficial when combined with the use of a psychotropic drug (Klerman, 1986). Likewise, in research on marital conflict, Jacobson and his colleagues (Jacobson et al., 1987) show that a combination of marital contracting (negotiation) and problem-solving training is more successful in the long run than either procedure used separately.

It seems probable that there are many synergistic effects among the seven modules described earlier. For instance, we have hypothesized that mutual ripeness is much more likely to lead to effective negotiation if combined with mutual trust and an understanding of the basic conflict dynamics between the parties. However, there is little hard evidence as yet about such effects.

## Conclusions

We have described an eclectic approach to conflict resolution, which contrasts sharply with the usual emphasis on singular remedies. This approach is based on the MACBE model, which explains conflict in terms of five modes or components of the human makeup: motivation, affect, cognition, behavior, and the social environment. We have also presented seven broad modules for combating conflict by means of various changes in these modes. We hypothesize that mild conflicts often result from pathology in a single mode and can be treated by intervening in that mode. But severe, seemingly intractable conflicts require multimodal change; the entire system must be fundamentally altered in order to avoid relapse.

The precise changes needed and their proper order of occurrence differ somewhat from conflict to conflict. But there is a logical sequence among the seven broad modules for dealing with severely escalated interpersonal relationships, as in marital therapy. Ripeness—that is, the sense of developing motivation to escape the conflict on both sides—appears to be preliminary. Following this, trust must be built, in the sense of convincing each side that the other is motivated to escape the conflict. This allows the parties to begin analysis of the dynamics of the conflict, preliminary to negotiation of a behavioral agreement. Behavioral agreements may well involve a restructuring of the social environment. Following that, the parties are well advised to reduce their aspirations on issues that do not yield to negotiation. The seventh module, problem-solving training, can probably best be accomplished in conjunction with analysis of the dynamics of the conflict. Such a rigid sequence may not be essential in all cases of severe interpersonal conflict, but it has its logic.

The order of events appears to be somewhat less uniform for severe intergroup (including international) conflict, since dovish minorities engaging in private diplomacy may begin to analyze the dynamics of the conflict well in advance of ripeness on the part of the groups as a whole. Such activities may seem minor at the time but often are of great ultimate importance when majority ripeness finally arrives, because the doves can provide leadership, information, and trust-laden contacts with the other side. Problem-solving training would appear to be less significant in intergroup than in interpersonal conflict. But it is important for third parties to identify and try to recruit good problem solvers on each side and to help them learn how to communicate with each other.

There is clearly a research frontier in this area. Heretofore, most theoretical thinking and empirical research have dealt with singular remedies, and little attention has been paid to how these remedies fit together. Research is particularly needed on sequencing and the synergistic effect of various combinations of remedies.

## Notes

1. We use the simpler term "mode" where Lazarus uses "modality."

2. In a survey of people who had been targets of angry displays (Averill, 1983), 76 percent reported that they had realized their own faults and 48 percent that their relationship with the angry person was strengthened.

3. Other possible end products of such workshops are a common, non-provocative vocabulary and a set of new ideas about how to solve the conflict (Kelman, 1993).

4. Kenneth Kressel (personal communication, June 1993) suggests that this position is too strong because "there are some severe conflicts whose severity is primarily the function of one profound issue or cause (for example, in divorce mediation we often found that one of the parents was severely out of touch with reality because of psychopathology, narcissistic preoccupations, or substance abuse)." It follows that "an approach which is multimodal might lead to a neglect of the central focus that is necessary in addressing the root cause of the problem." We agree that one spouse's psychopathology is sometimes the root cause of marital dysfunction, but we believe that our position is not too strong when applied to conflict between normal individuals or between groups.

5. Evidence that intrusive mediation is counterproductive under such circumstances can be seen in a study by Donohue (1989).

## References

Averill, J. R. (1983). Studies on anger and aggression: Implications for theories of emotions. *American Psychologist, 38,* 1145–1160.

Baucom, D. H., & Epstein, N. (1990). *Cognitive-behavioral marital therapy*. New York: Brunner/Mazel.

Bercovitch, J. (1992). The structure and diversity of mediation in international relations. In J. Bercovitch & J. Z. Rubin (Eds.), *Mediation in international relations: Multiple approaches to conflict management* (pp. 1–29). New York: St. Martin's Press.

Burton, J. W. (1969). *Conflict and communication: The use of controlled communication in international relations*. London: Macmillan.

Burton, J. W. (1990). *Human needs theory*. New York: St. Martin's Press.

Carnevale, P. J., Lim, R. G., & McLaughlin, M. E. (1989). Contingent mediator behavior and its effectiveness. In K. Kressel and D. G. Pruitt, *Mediation research: The process and effectiveness of third-party intervention* (pp. 213–240). San Francisco: Jossey-Bass.

Carson, R. C., & Butcher, J. N. (1992). *Abnormal psychology and modern life* (9th ed.). New York: HarperCollins.

deShazer, S. (1985). *Keys to solutions in brief therapy*. New York: W. W. Norton.

Deutsch, M. (1973). *The resolution of conflict: Constructive and destructive processes*. New Haven, CT: Yale University Press.

Deutsch, M., & Collins, M. E. (1951). *Interracial housing: A psychological evaluation of a social experiment*. Minneapolis: University of Minnesota Press.

Donohue, W. A. (1989). Communicative competence in mediators. In K. Kressel & D. G. Pruitt (Eds.), *Mediation research: The process and effectiveness of third-party intervention* (pp. 322–343). San Francisco: Jossey-Bass.

Donohue, W. A., & Kolt, R. (1992). *Managing interpersonal conflict*. Newbury Park, CA: Sage.

Duffy, K. G., Grosch, J. W., & Olczak, P. V. (Eds.) (1991). *Community mediation: A handbook for practitioners and researchers*. New York: Guilford.

Fisher, R., Ury, W. L., & Patton, B. M. (1991). *Getting to yes: Negotiating agreement without giving in* (2nd ed.). New York: Penguin.

Fisher, R. J. (1994). Generic principles for resolving intergroup conflict. *Journal of Social Issues, 50*, 47–66.

Fisher, R. J., & Keashly, L. (1988). Third-party interventions in intergroup conflict: Consultation is not mediation. *Negotiation Journal, 4*, 381–393.

Fisher, R. J., & Keashly, L. (1990). A contingency approach to third-party intervention. In R. J. Fisher (Ed.), *The social psychology of intergroup and international conflict resolution* (pp. 234–238). New York: Springer-Verlag.

Fitzpatrick, M. A. (1988). *Between husbands and wives: Communication in marriage*. Newbury Park, CA: Sage.

Gottman, J. M. (1993). The roles of conflict engagement, escalation, and avoidance in marital interaction: A longitudinal view of five types of couples. *Journal of Consulting and Clinical Psychology, 61*(1), 6–15.

Greenberg, L. S., & Johnson, S. M. (1988). *Emotionally focused therapy for couples.* New York: Guilford.

Gulliver, P. H. (1979). *Disputes and negotiations: A cross-cultural perspective.* San Diego: Academic Press.

Haberman, C. (1993, September 5). How the Oslo connection led to the Mideast pact. *The New York Times,* p. 1.

Hankins, G. (1988). *Prescription for anger: Coping with angry feelings and angry people.* New York: Warner.

Hollon, S. D., & Beck, A. T. (1986). Cognitive and cognitive-behavioral therapies. In S. L. Garfield & A. E. Bergin (Eds.), *Handbook of psychotherapy and behavior change* (3rd ed., pp. 443–482). New York: Wiley.

Hopmann, P. T. (1991). The changing international environment and the resolution of international conflicts: Negotiations on security and arms control in Europe. In L. Kriesberg & S. J. Thorson (Eds.), *Timing the de-escalation of international conflicts* (pp. 31–57). Syracuse, NY: Syracuse University Press.

Hurwitz, R. (1991). Up the down staircase? A practical theory of de-escalation. In L. Kriesberg & S. J. Thorson (Eds.), *Timing the de-escalation of international conflicts* (pp. 123–151). Syracuse, NY: Syracuse University Press.

Jacobson, N. S. (1984). A component analysis of behavioral marital therapy: The relative effectiveness of behavior exchange and communication/problem-solving training. *Journal of Consulting and Clinical Psychology, 52,* 295–305.

Jacobson, N. S. (1992). Behavioral couple therapy: A new beginning. *Behavior Therapy, 23,* 493–506.

Jacobson, N. S., & Addis, M. E. (1993). Research on couples and couple therapy: What do we know? Where are we going? *Journal of Consulting and Clinical Psychology, 61,* 85–93.

Jacobson, N. S., & Margolin, G. (1979). *Marital therapy: Strategies based on social learning and behavior exchange principles.* New York: Brunner/Mazel.

Jacobson, N. S., Schmaling, K. B., & Holtzworth-Munroe, A. (1987). Component analysis of behavioral marital therapy: Two-year follow-up and prediction of relapse. *Journal of Marital and Family Therapy, 13,* 187–195.

James, P. S. (1991). Effects of a communication training component added to an emotionally focused couples therapy. *Journal of Marital and Family Therapy, 17,* 263–276.

Johnson, D. W., & Johnson, R. T. (1994). Constructive conflict in the schools. *Journal of Social Issues, 50,* 117–137.

Johnson, D. W., Johnson, R., & Maruyama, G. (1984). Goal interdependence and interpersonal attraction in heterogeneous classrooms: A metanalysis. In N. Miller & M. B. Brewer (Eds.), *Groups in contact: The psychology of desegregation* (pp. 187–212). San Diego: Academic Press.

Johnson, S. M., & Greenberg, L. S. (1985). Differential effects of experiential and problem-solving interventions in resolving marital conflict. *Journal of Consulting and Clinical Psychology, 53,* 175–184.

Katz, N. H., & Lawyer, J. W. (1985). *Communication and conflict resolution skills.* Dubuque, IA: Kendall/Hunt.

Kelman, H. C. (1985). Overcoming the psychological barrier: An analysis of the Egyptian-Israeli peace process. *Negotiation Journal, 1,* 213–234.

Kelman, H. C. (1993). Coalitions across conflict lines: The interplay of conflicts within and between the Israeli and Palestinian communities. In S. Worchel & J. A. Simpson (Eds.), *Conflict between people and groups: Causes, processes, and resolutions* (pp. 236–258). Chicago: Nelson-Hall.

Kettering Foundation (1988). *Dartmouth Conference XVI: A Soviet-American dialogue April 24–May 7, 1988.* Kettering Foundation.

Kiesler, D. J. (1966). Some myths of psychotherapy research and the search for a paradigm. *Psychological Bulletin, 65,* 110–136.

Kimmel, M., Pruitt, D. G., Magenau, J., Konar-Goldband, E., & Carnevale, P. J. (1980). The effects of trust, aspiration, and gender on negotiation tactics. *Journal of Personality and Social Psychology, 38,* 9–23.

Klerman, G. L. (1986). Drugs and psychotherapy. In S. L. Garfield and A. E. Bergin (Eds.), *Handbook of psychotherapy and behavior change* (pp. 777–812). New York: Wiley.

Komorita, S. S., & Lapworth, C. W. (1982). Cooperative choice among individuals versus groups in an n-person dilemma situation. *Journal of Personality and Social Psychology, 42,* 487–496.

Kressel, K., Frontera, E. A., Forlenza, S., Butler, F., & Fish, L. (1994). The settlement-orientation versus the problem-solving style in custody mediation. *Journal of Social Issues, 50,* 67–84.

Kressel, K., & Pruitt, D. G. (1989). Conclusion: A research perspective on the mediation of social conflict. In K. Kressel & D. G. Pruitt (Eds.), *Mediation research: The process and effectiveness of third-party intervention* (pp. 394–435). San Francisco: Jossey-Bass.

Kriesberg, L. (1991). Introduction: Timing conditions, strategies, and errors. In L. Kriesberg & S. J. Thorson (Eds.), *Timing the de-escalation of international conflicts* (pp. 1–24). Syracuse, NY: Syracuse University Press.

Lazarus, A. A. (1976). *Multimodal behavior therapy*. New York: Springer.

Lindskold, S. (1986). GRIT: Reducing distrust through carefully introduced conciliation. In S. Worchel & W. G. Austin (Eds.), *Psychology of intergroup relations*. Chicago: Nelson-Hall.

Lindskold, S., & Han, G. (1988). GRIT as a foundation for integrative bargaining. *Personality and Social Psychology Bulletin, 14*, 335–345.

Lindskold, S., McElwain, D. C., & Wayner, M. (1977). Cooperation and the use of coercion by groups and by individuals. *Journal of Conflict Resolution, 21*, 531–550.

McCallum, D. M., Harring, K., Gilmore, R., Drenan, S., Chase, J. P., Insko, C. A., & Thibaut, J. (1985). Competition and cooperation between groups and between individuals. *Journal of Experimental Social Psychology, 21*, 301–320.

McEwen, C. A., & Milburn, T. W. (1993). Explaining the paradox of mediation. *Negotiation Journal, 9*, 23–36.

Merry, S. E. (1989). Mediation in nonindustrial societies. In K. Kressel & D. G. Pruitt (Eds.), *Mediation research: The process and effectiveness of third-party intervention* (pp. 68–90). San Francisco: Jossey-Bass.

Mitchell, C. R. (1991). A willingness to talk: Conciliatory gestures and de-escalation. *Negotiation Journal, 7*, 405–430.

Novaco, R. W. (1975). *Anger control: The development of an experimental treatment*. Lexington, KY: Lexington.

Osgood, C. E. (1962). *An alternative to war or surrender*. Urbana: University of Illinois Press.

Peirce, R. S., Pruitt, D. G., & Czaja, S. J. (1993). Complainant-respondent differences in procedural choice. *International Journal of Conflict Management, 4*, 199–222.

Peterson, D. R. (1983). Conflict. In H. H. Kelley and Associates, *Close relationships* (pp. 360–396). New York: W. H. Freeman.

Polfai, T., & Jankiewicz, H. (1991). *Drugs and human behavior*. Dubuque, IA: Brown.

Pruitt, D. G. (1981). *Negotiation behavior*. San Diego: Academic Press.

Pruitt, D. G. (1986). Trends in the scientific study of negotiation and mediation. *Negotiation Journal, 2*, 237–244.

Pruitt, D. G., & Carnevale, P. J. (1993). *Negotiation in social conflict*. Pacific Grove, CA: Brooks/Cole.

Pruitt, D. G., & Kimmel, M. J. (1977). Twenty years of experimental gaming: Critique, synthesis, and suggestions for the future. *Annual Review of Psychology, 28*, 363–392.

Pruitt, D. G., Mikolic, J. M., Eberle, R., Parker, J. C., & Peirce, R. S. (1993,

June). *The escalation of conflict: Group versus individual response to persistent annoyance*. Paper presented at the Sixth Annual Conference of the International Association for Conflict Management, Houthalen, Belgium.

Pruitt, D. G., Peirce, R. S., McGillicuddy, N. B., Welton, G. L., & Castrianno, L. M. (1993). Long-term success in mediation. *Law and Human Behavior, 17*, 313–330.

Raush, H. L., Barry, W. A., Hertel, R. K., & Swain, M. A. (1974). *Communication conflict and marriage*. San Francisco: Jossey-Bass.

Rouhana, N. N., & Kelman, H. C. (1994). Promoting joint thinking in international conflict: An Israeli-Palestinian continuing workshop. *Journal of Social Issues, 50*, 157–178.

Rubin, J. Z. (1991). The timing of ripeness and the ripeness of timing. In L. Kriesberg & S. J. Thorson (Eds.), *Timing the de-escalation of international conflicts* (pp. 237–246). Syracuse, NY: Syracuse University Press.

Rubin, J. Z., Pruitt, D. G., & Kim, S. H. (1994). *Social conflict: Escalation, stalemate, and settlement* (2nd ed.). New York: McGraw-Hill.

Sherif, M., Harvey, O. J., White, G. J., Hood, W. R., & Sherif, C. W. (1961). *Intergroup conflict and cooperation: The robbers cave experiment*. Norman, OK: Institute of Group Relations.

Tajfel, H., Flament, C., Billig, M. G., & Bundy, R. F. (1971). Social categorization and intergroup behavior. *European Journal of Social Psychology, 1*, 149–177.

Taylor, P. (1993, May 28). South African woman bears fresh scars from township violence. *The Washington Post*, p. A34.

Ury, W. L., Brett, J. M., & Goldberg, S. (1988). *Getting disputes resolved: Designing systems to cut the costs of conflict*. San Francisco: Jossey-Bass.

von Bertalanffy, L. (1973). *General systems theory*. New York: Braziller.

Wall, J. A., Jr., & Blum, M. (1991). Community mediation in the People's Republic of China. *Journal of Conflict Resolution, 35*, 3–20.

Welton, G. L., Pruitt, D. G., McGillicuddy, N. B., Ippolito, C. A., & Zubek, J. M. (1992). Antecedents and characteristics of caucusing in community mediation. *International Journal of Conflict Management, 3*, 303–317.

Zartman, I. W. (1989). *Ripe for resolution: Conflict resolution in Africa* (2nd ed.). New York: Oxford.

Zartman, I. W., & Aurik, J. (1991). Power strategies in de-escalation. In L. Kriesberg & S. J. Thorson (Eds.), *Timing the de-escalation of international conflicts* (pp. 152–181). Syracuse, NY: Syracuse University Press.

Zartman, I. W., & Berman, M. R. (1982). *The practical negotiator*. New Haven, CT: Yale University Press.

# 4

# Conflict Resolution Training in Schools

## Translating Theory into Applied Skills

### Ellen Raider

Conflict resolution training has increased dramatically in educational, industrial, and community settings over the past two decades. Despite this activity, the gap between where our society needs to be and where we are now in our ability to handle conflict constructively is still quite large. My focus in this chapter is on the critical role of schools in closing this gap and on what can be done to institutionalize the concepts and skills of constructive conflict resolution within the educational system. First I provide an historical context by briefly describing the current state of conflict resolution training in industry and in local communities. Then, turning to education, I examine four training interventions currently used in schools. Second, I identify issues in teaching conflict resolution to educators, including the implications of viewing cooperative negotiation as a social skill. Finally, I reflect on the difficulties involved in incorporating skills learned in a training environment to people's real lives—and what society as a whole needs to do to ensure the spread and success of these programs and skills.

The term *conflict resolution training* is used generically in this paper to describe negotiation and mediation training. In some school-based programs, conflict resolution is used to describe the

*Note:* I would like to thank Rachel Burd, Sandy Snyder, and Sarah Towle for their research and editorial assistance.

basic negotiation process. The term *negotiation* seems to be negatively associated with the formal contentious process often experienced in union/management bargaining. This term needs to be de-stigmatized to enable educators and others to fully appreciate cooperative negotiation and access the literature on integrative bargaining (Rubin, Pruitt, & Kim, 1994).

## Brief Overview of Conflict Resolution Training

Training in negotiation skills has been emphasized in industry based on the assumption that parties need to work out their conflicts directly with one another. In contrast, the emphasis in community dispute resolution centers has been on training in mediation to establish a volunteer cadre of third-party neutrals. This approach assumes that conflicting parties who come to these centers either do not know how or are not willing to negotiate directly with one another and need help to resolve their conflict. Mediation training has dominated the conflict resolution training movement in schools; however, recently schools are adding negotiation skills training as part of their conflict resolution program, recognizing that negotiation is the more basic of the two processes because it teaches the parties to solve their conflicts themselves, without dependency on a third party. I discuss these training trends in more detail below.

### Industry

The past two decades have seen the institutionalization of negotiation skills training in industry. According to *Training Magazine's Industry Report* (1992), 49 percent of all firms with one hundred or more employees are now offering negotiation skills training to their employees. In larger firms the percentage is even higher. In firms with ten thousand or more employees, 75 percent offer such courses.

Corporations use negotiation skills training to enhance relationships and achieve creative solutions to external as well as internal conflicts. In particular, as international market shares of U.S. firms are challenged by increased global competition, many firms want their negotiators to be sensitive and responsive to the needs and cultures of their clients. Internally, many firms are teaching negotiation skills to managers as a way of handling the inevitable conflicts that arise within and between work units.

The typical training program lasts from two to five consecutive days. Because of the proprietary nature of the training materials used by various consulting firms, it is difficult to summarize what is being taught in these programs. Weiss-Wik (1983), however, reviewed six of the most popular books on the art of negotiation and summarized their common guidelines. They include prescriptions to "adopt a win-win outlook, prepare for the negotiation, concentrate on negotiators' needs, consider sources of power and implement appropriate tactics, endeavor to communicate adroitly, monitor the other negotiator's behavior, demonstrate willingness to cooperate and adapt, and finalize agreements clearly, definitely and by your own hand whenever possible" (pp. 715–716).

From my experience as a corporate trainer I can confirm that these prescriptions are more or less the common content base of many programs. However, training programs vary enormously as to the methodology used and the relative emphasis on skills as opposed to content objectives.

## Community Settings

The last decade has seen the growth of community mediation centers throughout the country. According to the National Institute for Dispute Resolution in Washington, D.C., there were 79 community mediation centers in operation in the United States in 1980 and between 250 and 300 in 1990 (C. Colosi, personal communication, 1991). These centers were largely established due to the court system's inability to handle the increasing backlog of cases. Courts are now referring more and more cases that they consider resolvable by mediation to community mediation centers rather than using the judicial process. Community mediation centers are staffed by volunteers who receive twenty to thirty hours of mediation skills training and supervision. This has resulted in the training of literally thousands of people throughout the country who view themselves as practitioners in the alternative dispute resolution movement.

## Schools

In schools, two kinds of training fall under the rubric of conflict resolution and are often confused. One type focuses on identifying the destructive aspects of conflict—its causes, phases, and consequences—and on immediate crisis intervention techniques to prevent conflict escalation and violence. This *violence prevention* or *crisis management* approach can be contrasted with training that focuses on the constructive aspects of conflict by teaching long-term positive resolution methods such as negotiation and mediation.

Both serve important functions. Violence prevention training teaches students to identify and disengage from potentially life-threatening situations and to deal productively with anger (Prothrow-Stith, 1987). Crisis intervention training for educators shows them how to intervene safely and humanely during a physical fight between students (Rekoske & Wyka, 1990). Negotiation and mediation skills training goes further, however, in empowering students and adults to know that they can handle conflict through positive means. I focus on these latter skills in this chapter.

It is possible to select from four levels of training intervention when bringing constructive conflict resolution concepts and skills into a school or district. The easiest intervention to accomplish is at Level 1—*Discipline*. Interventions at Level 2—*Curriculum* and Level 3—*Pedagogy* are progressively more difficult but have the potential to reach more students. The intervention at Level 4—*School Culture* is the most complex. It is therefore the most neglected level of intervention, but I believe the most essential both for institutionalizing conflict resolution programs at the first three levels as well as providing a fundamental tool for school reform.

## Level 1—Discipline

Peer mediation programs are typically brought into a school as part of the overall disciplinary system. Spurred on by the success of community-based programs, two mediation centers—The Community Board on the West coast in 1982 and Victim Services Agency in the East in 1983—began offering training programs and services to schools in an attempt to set up similar programs to handle student conflicts. The executive director of the National Association for Mediation in Education (NAME), in Amherst, Massachusetts, guesstimates that five thousand schools now have peer mediation or conflict resolution programs (personal communication).

Mediation training for students consists of ten to fifteen hours of initial concept and skill training with subsequent follow-up supervision as they begin to mediate. Mediation training teaches students the steps of mediation, including setting the ground rules, hearing each disputant's perspective, helping disputants walk in each other's shoes (perspective taking), brainstorming solutions, and writing the resolution contract. While an adult coordinator is always within hearing distance, the students conduct mediations themselves, either singly or in pairs as co-mediators. Students as young as in the third grade are working as playground mediators to handle on-the-spot disputes. At the middle and high school levels, formal mediation centers receive referrals from deans as well as students. Most centers handle student/student conflicts exclusively, while a small percentage deal with teacher/student conflicts as well (using both a teacher and a student as co-mediators).

Word-of-mouth accounts of effective peer mediation efforts have stimulated interest in these programs. However, with few exceptions (see Lam's review of the research, 1989), little research has been conducted on the magnitude and direction of the impact of school mediation programs, according to Daniel Kmitta, coordinator of the NAME Research Network (personal communication).

## Level 2—Curriculum

Some schools and districts have brought conflict resolution skills into the curriculum, either as a stand-alone course or as units within existing programs. This is easier to accomplish at the elementary level due to the flexibility of its scheduling; it is more difficult at the secondary level due to curricular mandates at the state level. The Children's Creative Response to Conflict, of Quaker-Friends origin, first introduced general conflict resolution concepts and skills into the classroom in 1972 (Prutzman, Burger, Bodenhamer, & Stern, 1978). More recently, Educators for Social Responsibility, The Community Board Program (1987), and David and Roger Johnson, to name a few, have developed curriculum and training programs in this area.

NAME publishes and updates an annotated bibliography of books and curriculum materials available for use in the classroom. These curricula provide lessons and activities grouped under such themes as understanding conflict, communications, dealing with anger, cooperation, affirmation, bias awareness, cultural diversity, conflict resolution, and peacemaking. Teachers may choose lessons to meet individual class needs.

There are also few studies documenting the *effects* of training in conflict resolution in schools (Lam, 1989). Among those that do exist, the majority are atheoretical and lack sophisticated research designs. An exception is a two-year longitudinal study by Deutsch (1993a) of the International Center for Cooperation and Conflict Resolution (ICCCR). This study generated hypotheses based on Deutsch's theoretical framework. Through both quantitative and qualitative data, the study showed that at-risk students from an alternative urban high school who received training in conflict resolution or cooperative learning exhibited improvement in the management of personal conflicts, experienced increased social support, and felt less victimized by others. Enhanced relationships with others led to increased self-esteem and more frequent positive feelings of well-being among these students, as well as a decrease in feelings of anxiety and depression. Higher self-esteem, in turn, produced a greater sense of personal control over their own lives and futures. The increase in their sense of personal control and their positive feelings of well-being led to higher academic performance.

### Level 3—Pedagogy

In addition to learning conflict resolution skills in specific units or courses, students can be exposed to and practice these skills in their regular subject areas with the appropriate pedagogical methods. Two such teaching strategies—cooperative learning and academic controversy—require students to practice conflict resolution skills to complete school tasks.

Cooperative learning already has a large national following within the educational community as well as a considerable research base supporting its efficacy (Johnson, Johnson, & Holubec, 1993). Many teachers have been trained in this method, but most would require additional training in the specifics of conflict resolution to maximize its pedagogical potential for building negotiation and mediation skills. In a cooperative learning environment, students accomplish academic tasks together in small interdependent work groups. They often find themselves in conflict with teammates. In addition to being concerned with academic mastery, therefore, the teacher must aid students in learning social skills such as listening, affirming, and accepting others' points of view; each may be seen as a separate component skill within the negotiation or mediation skill set.

Academic controversy (Johnson & Johnson 1987, 1991) is yet another valuable pedagogical technique. It is, however, less widely known and therefore underutilized at this time. With this method, students take opposing points of view on controversial issues. They must hear the other side's perspective, reverse roles, and finally come to a collaborative synthesis.

It takes three to five years for a trained teacher to achieve mastery and sustained use of the above techniques. These techniques have the potential to bring about needed change in the school environment, both by revolutionizing teaching practices as well as by providing a vehicle for infusing the skills of conflict resolution into any curricular area.

### Level 4—School Culture

To ensure the institutionalization of conflict resolution skills in a school or district, it is imperative that teachers, administrators, parents, and school boards both learn and use cooperative negotiation and mediation techniques with each other as well as with students. At a recent national meeting of a large educational organization, I conducted an informal survey of one hundred participants on the conflict resolution strategy used by their schools and districts. Most said their schools and districts operated competitively, not cooperatively. Conflicts were either avoided or handled by the imposition of positional power.

The school improvement literature is filled with evidence of the difficulty in changing school culture (Fullan, 1993; Glasser, 1992; Louis & Miles, 1990; Sarason, 1982). Restructuring initiatives such as site-based management (SBM) and shared decision making (SDM) are designed to increase participation at the local school level among all stakeholders, including administrators, teachers, parents, students, and the community. Early research on these efforts indicates that interpersonal and intergroup conflicts are one of the major obstacles inhibiting their successful implementation (Leiberman, Darling-Hammond, & Zuckerman, 1991). Such restructuring efforts will not have the intended impact on fundamental systemic change without specific training in cooperative conflict resolution and problem solving, one important way of over-coming the competitive aspects of the current school culture.

Unfortunately, most conflict resolution programs throughout the country focus primarily on children. This approach denies the reality that most adults in schools (as well as in other bureaucracies) have had little preparation, training, or encouragement to manage their own conflicts cooperatively, let alone teach these skills to others. Those in low power positions tend to avoid conflict or say yes to placate their superiors. They then close their doors and do what they intended anyway—and the system does not change. Many in positions of power still use out-of-date authoritarian or boss styles of management to achieve compliance (Glasser, 1992). Teachers then mirror this top-down approach in their interactions with students. Fundamental changes in students' abilities to handle conflict and reduce the risk of violence must go hand-in-hand with fundamental change in the culture of schools.

The problem is that current in-service teachers and administrators lack the knowledge and experience both to use and teach constructive conflict resolution skills effectively. Moreover, colleges of education have neither programs nor standards for pre-service certification of school-based conflict resolution specialists or generalists. Action must be taken now to remedy this situation. A sustained joint effort of the conflict resolution community, researchers and trainers, as well as the educational establishment, school districts, policy makers, foundations, and colleges of education is imperative to meet this challenge.

Some beginning efforts are under way to address this need. The International Center for Cooperation and Conflict Resolution (ICCCR) at Teachers College, Columbia University, conducts workshops and mediations for school boards, administrators, teachers, and parents who are bringing SBM and SDM into their schools or districts. A joint venture between the Washington, D.C.–based National Institute for Dispute Resolution (NIDR) and the National

Association for Mediation in Education (NAME) seeks to bring curriculum material to colleges of education so that conflict resolution concepts and skills are incorporated into the training of teachers, administrators, and counselors as part of pre-service certification. The Association for Supervision and Curriculum Development (ASCD), a large professional educational association, has produced an introductory video program entitled *Adult Conflict Resolution* (1993) intended to increase awareness that conflict resolution is not just for kids.

## Teaching Conflict Resolution to Educators

There is an extensive theoretical and empirical literature on the nature of conflict and the processes of negotiation and mediation (Deutsch, 1977, 1985; Fisher, Ury, & Patton, 1991; Lewicki & Litterer, 1985; Lewicki, Weiss, & Lewin, 1992; Rubin, Pruitt & Kim, 1994; Rubin & Brown, 1975; Folberg & Taylor, 1984; Ury, 1993). Considerable attention is being paid to conflict resolution applications in diplomacy, business, and labor relations. There is, however, very little systematic research on the pedagogy of conflict resolution, the models and methods used to teach these skills to adult or student learners.

In order to foster more dialogue among training practitioners, educators, and researchers, I detail here what a conflict resolution practitioner considers during the design, delivery, and implementation of a conflict resolution program. I focus primarily on teaching negotiation skills to adults but similar considerations apply to the teaching of mediation. I start with an exploration of the knowledge, skills, and attitude objectives of a skills-based negotiation training. I then examine the nature of social skills training and the school's role in this effort. I end with a survey describing what goes into a training design. This section is based on my own reflections as a trainer as well as on theoretical insights from the fields of mental health and education.

**Learning Objectives of a Negotiation Skills Training Program**

Professional trainers distinguish among three different kinds of learning objectives: knowledge, skills, and attitude. Depending on the time allotted for the training program, the trainer will select several specific objectives within these key areas that can be effectively accomplished in the training framework.

*Knowledge* objectives are designed to give the trainee new information or elicit previously known information. Examples of knowledge components in a negotiation training may include the extent to which participants will be able to:

- Identify the difference between cooperative and competitive negotiations

- Identify the difference between needs and positions

- Identify five conflict resolution behavioral styles

- Discuss how culture can impact the negotiation process

*Skills* objectives are designed to help participants acquire new skills or reinforce old ones. Examples include:

- Practicing active listening skills

- Asking open-ended questions to probe for underlying needs

- Reframing conflicting interests into a joint problem to be solved

- Diffusing anger

*Attitude* objectives encourage trainees to adopt a different view regarding the skills and concepts being learned. *Attitude* examples might include:

- Valuing cooperation

- Wishing to continue to improve conflict resolution skills

- Appreciating and respecting cultural differences in conflict resolution styles

Deutsch (1993b, pp. 511–515) offers guidelines for designers of conflict resolution training programs. As the result of a comprehensive program, participants should:

- Know what type of conflict they are involved in.

- Be aware of the causes and consequences of violence and of the alternatives to violence, even when very angry.

- Face conflict rather than avoid it.

- Respect oneself and one's own interests; respect the other and his or her interests.

- Avoid ethnocentrism; understand and accept the reality of cultural difference.

- Distinguish clearly between "interests" and "positions."

- Explore one's interests and the other's interests to identify the common and compatible interests of both.

- Define the conflicting interests between oneself and the other as a mutual problem to be solved cooperatively.

- Listen attentively and speak so as to be understood when communicating with the other.

- Be alert to the natural tendencies toward bias, misperceptions, misjudgments, and stereotypical thinking that commonly occur during heated conflict.

- Develop skills for dealing with difficult conflict so that one is neither helpless nor hopeless when confronting those who are more powerful, those who don't want to engage in constructive conflict resolution, or those who use dirty tricks.

- Know oneself and how one typically responds in different kinds of conflict situations.

The interdisciplinary knowledge base and attitudinal frame of mind implied above are not currently a regular part of teacher education. But even with a good grasp of theory and a desire to change, the average adult needs considerable practice, feedback, and coaching at a behavioral level in order to put these skills into his or her active repertoire. My experience as a trainer convinces me that for many adults learning cooperative negotiation is equivalent to acquiring a new social skill. Although there is systematic research on social skills development in marital conflicts, along with numerous popular books that prescribe specific behavioral skills for conflict resolvers, research on social skills acquisition seems to be neglected in the conflict resolution literature.

## Issues in Teaching Social Skills

What are social skills? How are they taught?

Experimental psychology has studied the principles that govern skills performance in both laboratory and field settings. The bulk of the work has focused on the learning and performance of perceptual and motor skills. The principles underlying skills performance on these kinds of tasks can be applied to social skills as well (Trower, Bryant, & Argyle, 1978).

Social skills are learned behaviors that individuals use in interpersonal situations to get their needs met; these skills function like behavioral pathways or avenues to an individual's goals (Kelly,

1982). Social skills can be observed and described in an objective manner; the verbal and nonverbal elements of social behavior have been identified by researchers. Specific skills such as conversational skills, dating skills, job interviewing skills, assertiveness skills, and children's pro-social play skills have been analyzed. For example, the researched components of the much-studied "refusal assertion skill" include *non-verbal* behaviors—such as eye contact, appropriate affect, speech loudness, and physical gestures—and *verbal* behaviors—such as an understanding statement of the problem, request for new behaviors, proposal of solutions, and noncompliance (Trower et al., 1978).

Further, as in the case of motor skills, social skills are hierarchically organized; larger units such as interviews are composed of smaller units—answering questions—and single behaviors—like smiles and head nods (Trower et al., 1978). In learning a new social skill, it is necessary to break a larger unit (the skill set) down into its component parts to learn each behavior individually.

The point I am making here is that the component parts of the negotiation and mediation skill sets need to be identified for the purpose of teaching these skills to others. Trainers have already done some work in this area, but more systematic efforts are required. For example, the Huthwaite Research Group (Rackham, 1993), a British training organization using an observational technique known as behavioral analysis, studied the behavior of successful negotiators. Subjects were rated successful by their peers, had a track record of success as negotiators, and experienced low rates of implementation failure. The Huthwaite Group found that skilled negotiators spend less time defending their position or attacking their opponents; they use fewer irritators, spend more time testing and understanding the other side's position and needs, and ask more questions than the average negotiator. With this information, the Group was able to diagnose the pre-training behaviors of their corporate trainees and work with them, both conceptually and behaviorally, to improve their skills in appropriate areas.

## Role of Schools in Teaching Social Skills

Students, their teachers, and administrators come into the school setting with habitual methods of handling conflict. Some avoid it; others use verbal attacks, threats, or the power of their positions or physical size to get their own way. Some resort to physical violence, while others are skilled as cooperative negotiators. Assuming that most of these approaches are undesirable, as they neither produce positive outcomes nor build relationships, we must accept that many adults and children in our society have poor constructive conflict resolution skills.

Unproductive behavior is learned by each individual in the way all social behavior is learned: through observation, feedback, and reinforcement. Before new conflict resolution skills may be acquired, one must be motivated to do so. This requires (1) an individual's awareness that he or she does not possess good conflict resolution skills, (2) the desire to have such skills, and (3) assurance of support from the environment as the individual tries to change behavior (Schein & Bennis, 1965). There are, however, significant obstacles to this motivational process, especially for young males in a culture that glorifies and reinforces violence (Miedzian, 1991).

Some argue that teaching social skills is the responsibility of parents, not of the schools. Unfortunately, many adults have poor conflict resolution skills, which makes it unlikely that children will learn these skills at home. While training activities in industry and community-based programs will certainly enhance some adults' abilities, these programs are not widespread enough to change the cultural norms and values that support avoiding conflict and destructive responses to conflict (Miedzian, 1991). In addition, there is no quick fix to this problem. If, as a society, we want a more cooperative response to conflict, schools will have to play a large part in the re-socialization effort by integrating these important social skills into the curriculum—from kindergarten to high school.

A more radical perspective argues that needed social change can only occur through power politics. Individuals who hold this view challenge the conflict resolution movement, saying that it preserves the status quo. While conflict resolution training alone cannot address the structural violence in our society nor the "savage inequality" in our schools (Kozol, 1991), it can help individuals and groups deal productively with many kinds of conflict in their lives. It is important to know when conflict lends itself to cooperative approaches and when other means are necessary to bring about social justice. A dispute between two neighbors about a noisy record player or a parking space should be treated differently than social injustices such as apartheid. The first is negotiable; the second was not negotiable until blacks built up a power base to challenge an intractable white minority.

### Methods of Teaching Social Skills

The process of teaching conflict resolution and negotiation as a skill—what is being done now and what is working—is not well studied. The conflict resolution teaching models currently used in schools need to be fully articulated, researched, tested, and compared. There have been investigations of skills training in related areas, however, particularly in therapy (Trower et al., 1978; Kelly, 1982) and in other areas of teaching (Marzano 1992; Joyce & Showers, 1980, 1982, 1983; Showers, 1942). These models are useful and applicable to our current discussion.

Several steps are involved in teaching social skills to individuals in a clinical setting: assessing current performance to analyze troublesome behavior; providing instruction, coaching, and a rationale for changing behavior in a specific way; modeling the new behavior; giving feedback and reinforcement of the new behavior during training; and last, following up and supporting the behavior in its transfer to the natural environment (Kelly, 1982).

The International Center for Cooperation and Conflict Resolution (ICCCR) (with which I am associated) uses a similar methodology in large group trainings (twenty to thirty persons) for educators. We find it necessary to pay particular attention to unfreezing the old, less effective behaviors when working with adults (Lewin, 1951). We do this by videotaping a diagnostic exercise at the beginning of each training. Participants receive feedback on their current behaviors and are usually shocked by the amount of attacking and blaming behaviors they exhibit. Because the taping is done in small groups, participants are able to receive this information in a friendly, supportive environment. After the first shock, there is usually a lot of laughter. We have found that this unfreezing of old behaviors in small peer groups begins to motivate trainees to learn new behaviors.

Early in the training process, participants need to see cooperative negotiation modeled by skilled individuals. This modeling can be done live or through prerecorded videotapes. The situations modeled should seem realistic to the viewing audience, and the person doing the modeling should be as much like the participants as possible.

A number of studies have investigated the circumstances under which modeled learning is most likely to be imitated and exhibited by the observer (Bandura, 1985). Some of the factors that appear to facilitate this observational learning process include: (1) age of the model, (2) sex of the model, (3) likability of the model, (4) perceived similarity to the observer, (5) observed consequence to the model when the model engages in the social behavior being learned, and (6) the observer's own direct learning history for engaging in the same or similar social behavior as exhibited by the model (Kelly, 1982). This research has important implications both for student and adult training. In order to reach students, teachers will need videos of skilled students of various ages from diverse cultural backgrounds and trained young people who can assist in teaching these skills to their peers.

Marzano (1992) outlines a method for teaching procedural knowledge, that is, teaching how to do something as contrasted to imparting information. This approach has three phases: constructing models, shaping, and internalizing. These lend themselves to conflict resolution training, as is illustrated below.

### Constructing Models

Marzano argues that procedural learning models can take several forms: a series of steps performed in a specific order (algorithms); general rules providing a general order of application (tactical models); or a general set of rules or heuristics that are not specific to one task (strategic models).

While the step-by-step, algorithmic approach is not useful in conflict resolution training (it is too rigid to allow for human behavior), tactical and strategic learning models have been constructed to teach the negotiation process. An example of a tactical model is our Bare Bones Negotiation Model (Raider & Coleman, 1992), which allows learners to rehearse cognitively a fairly complex unresolved work conflict of their own choosing (see Exhibit 4.1).

The bare-bones technique is a mental map or outline. It does not model real-time conversation but provides the trainee with a road map through the often complex and circuitous territory of negotiation. This model integrates two component parts of our overall negotiation model: one focusing on need versus positions, the other focusing on specific negotiating behavior, that is, informing, opening, and uniting.

### Shaping

After the model has been constructed, the next step is to shape and modify the performance of a skill or process as it is being learned. According to Marzano (1992), this is the most important step in developing procedural expertise because this is the phase where systematic errors can creep in and where learners develop their conceptual understanding of a skill or process. Marzano believes that those who do not complete this stage use their learning in shallow and ineffective ways; understanding the steps in a math problem does not imply that a student can interpret the concepts behind those steps, for example.

Exhibit 4.1.  The Ten-Step Bare Bones Negotiation Model.

*Step 1:*  A and B engage in ritual sharing (a type of **uniting** behavior).

*Step 2:*  A expresses his or her *position* using **informing** behavior.

*Step 3:*  B inquires about the underlying *needs* of A using **opening** behavior.

*Step 4:*  A responds with information about his or her underlying *needs* using **informing** behavior.

*Step 5:*  B uses **opening** behavior by paraphrasing the *need* expressed by A in order to check his or her understanding of the *need*.

*Step 6:*  A inquires as to B's concerns using **opening** behavior, for example, "How do you feel about this proposal?"

(Repeat Steps 2–5, starting with B.)

*Step 7:*  A and B now work together to develop a *reframing* question (a type of **uniting** behavior), which combines the needs of A and B into a joint problem to be solved.

*Step 8:*  A and B work together to develop several possible solutions (**uniting**). Brainstorming might be a good way to come up with possible *alternatives*.

*Step 9:*  A and B pick the solution that works best for the two of them (**uniting**).

*Step 10:*  Either A or B, or both, summarize what they have agreed to.

*Source:* Raider and Coleman, 1992. © Ellen Raider and Susan W. Coleman, 1992. All rights reserved.

The shaping phase of building negotiation skills can be accomplished through video and audio feedback of actual performance. During ICCCR training with educators, participants audiotape and videotape their performances during all role-play practice sessions. In addition, each time trainees listen or view their own performances, they are given specific observational protocols so they can monitor their own behaviors and receive directed feedback from fellow trainees and trainers. The specific skills that need improvement—as indicated by the performance tapes—are then worked on in skills practice sessions.

When the practiced behavior is put back into real-time negotiation, errors occur that require attention. That is why coaching and feedback are so important in this shaping stage. It is similar to learning a sport like tennis. The coach can isolate a poor backhand; the student can practice it in isolation and begin to see improvement. However, in the heat of the game, the old behavior (poor backhand) may reemerge.

### Internalizing

Last, Marzano asserts that internalizing is the process that creates an automatic phenomenon—such as brushing one's teeth. This internalization is essential for successful negotiation training and needs, in my experience, considerable follow-up support. This is much easier in schools and districts committed to the institutionalization of cooperative behavioral strategies throughout the system. Putting a trained individual back into a setting that reinforces old behaviors is likely to negate most of the benefits of the training.

### Design Decisions in Conflict Resolution Training

A training design is a particular scope and sequence of activities that the trainer believes will help participants acquire the learning objectives of the particular training program. In addition to employing specific learning objectives to meet the needs of the participants, the trainer must consider a number of factors, including time frame, pacing, choice of methods, and the learning styles and cultural background of the audience.

## Time Frame

Current workshops in conflict resolution for educators can vary in length from several hours to a full-year practicum as part of a degree program. While shorter training programs offer awareness of concepts and skills and are usually experiential, they cannot build the skill base necessary for competent implementation. School systems are naive in their belief that they can send a staff member to a one- to three-day training program and expect that staff member to be able to teach these skills to others. It is analogous to teaching someone a few finger positions on a violin and immediately expecting that person to play first chair in an orchestra. Given the level of knowledge and skill of most adults in our competitive society, only programs of a longer duration coupled with follow-up support should be used for skills development.

## Methods

Conflict resolution training methods range along a continuum from lecture and discussion to more experiential types. Methods used include role-play simulations, cooperative reading, discussions, practice dyads, controlled pace (fishbowl) negotiations with trainer feedback, questionnaires, readings, lectures, demonstrations, performance of what has been learned, journal writing, and videotape and audiotape recording of role plays. A trainer picks the methods that best fit the particular training objective and varies methods to reach all participants' learning styles. If the goal of the training is awareness building, then lecture and discussion can be the vehicles. If training objectives are skills oriented, the methodology must give the trainees an opportunity to practice these social skills and receive feedback about the quality of that practice. For example, in order to teach active listening skills, the sequence might start with a demonstration and discussion of good and poor listening habits, followed by a small group discussion of participants' own listening behaviors (described by peers through a questionnaire circulated before the course began). Then small groups of three participants would practice active listening and receive feedback on their performance. The final exercise in the sequence might be a negotiation role play where participants could practice skills in an extended conflict situation. They would then receive feedback from fellow trainees and the trainer while watching the videotape of their negotiation. Teaching one skill of the complex negotiation skill set can take many hours and still requires follow-up support.

### Cultural Differences

There are both individual and cultural differences in learning styles (Bennett, 1990). Since most teaching is done in group settings, it is important that teachers be aware of the different ways individuals learn so that the same concepts and skills can be delivered in various ways to reach all learners.

Research has shown that the more control a society or culture exercises over its children in the socialization process, the more field dependent they become; the less control, the more field independent (Bennett, 1990). Field-dependent learners are aware of and attuned to their environment and have highly developed social skills; they are global learners who may prefer to see a video or live demonstration of a real-life negotiation to get a feel for process before trying to deal with any of its parts. Field-independent learners tend to be more individualistic and less sensitive to the emotions of others, with poorly developed social skills; they are analytical learners who may appreciate logical, sequential models that walk them through the negotiation process step by step.

Culture not only affects an individual's learning style but also the way an individual views the educational process itself

(Hofstede, 1986). For example, in cultures that accept a high degree of inequality in status as natural, one would not publicly disagree with an authority figure such as a teacher or administrator. Neither would one question a decision that an authority figure made about a child's education. Parents from such a "high power distance culture" (Hofstede, 1986) might find themselves in conflict if a teacher or principal from a "low power distance culture"—in which status differences are minimized—asked them to come to school to collaboratively discuss a problem their child was having. The parents would assume this decision to be the sole responsibility of the school authorities. The administrator or teacher might then make the erroneous assumption that the parents did not care about the child's poor performance. It is incumbent on educators to be sensitive to and knowledgeable about these critical cross-cultural value differences toward education and to anticipate these potential intercultural conflicts when working with parents, especially newly arrived immigrants.

Culture also affects the way individuals and groups conceptualize and deal with conflict (Weiss & Stripp, 1985; Kochman, 1981; Faure's chapter in this volume). It is normative in some cultures for individuals to be highly emotional and to demonstrate passionate support for their point of view. If they are not emotional, their reactions are not trusted as sincere. In other cultures, people are expected to demonstrate nonemotional rationality when dealing with contentious issues. Imagine the perceptions of people with these two differing orientations during a conflict at a board of education meeting. They would each miss the original issue under discussion, reacting instead to each other's culturally based conflict style. A mediator skilled in cross-cultural processes can often be helpful to both parties by understanding and clarifying these style issues. Experienced international negotiators sensitive to such issues modify their behavior in order to be appropriate to their counterparts' expectations or structure the negotiation process itself to deal with cultural differences.

## Transfer of Training

Currently, most evaluation efforts of conflict resolution programs in schools measure satisfaction with the programs or are individual self-assessments rather than independent measures of behavioral change. Does training actually translate into changed behavior in the classroom, at home, or on the streets? Too little consideration has been paid to the transfer issue.

From industry (Broad & Newstrom, 1992) we learn that some of the major factors that inhibit the success of training and its transfer are:

- Lack of involvement by top management in the behavior change process
- Unrealistic expectations of the training program: too much is expected too soon
- Lack of reinforcement on the job
- Discomfort on the part of trainees with the efforts that must be made to accomplish change
- Peer pressure to resist change

The transfer record of staff development efforts in schools is equally disappointing. In addition to the lack of administrative support, many training programs do not provide for sufficient demonstration, practice, feedback, and on-the-job coaching (Joyce & Showers, 1982, 1983; Showers, 1942). Teachers need fifteen to twenty demonstrations during a training sequence and a dozen or more opportunities to practice in order to learn a new teaching strategy (Joyce & Showers, 1983). Furthermore, research shows that information or theory-only trainings have minimal effect on teachers' attitudes, knowledge, and skills, as well as on the transfer of the new pedagogical techniques to the teacher's active repertoire. The combination of theory, demonstration, practice, and feedback has meaningful effects on skills acquisition but minimal impact on transfer of training. The addition of on-site coaching to these four elements significantly increases the utilization of newly learned skills and strategies in classroom instruction (Bennett, 1987). While this information is known in educational circles, many districts have not modified their staff development programs accordingly.

What are the implications for bringing conflict resolution concepts and skills into the classroom? Some teachers come to conflict resolution training with knowledge and skill of competitive (not cooperative) negotiation techniques. Others come with the belief that their behavior is cooperative and find with feedback that this is not so. Still others come with good intuitive skills but lack the analytic understanding of the process that would enable them to teach these skills to others. Trainers have in their classes a heterogeneous mix of skill levels. Some educators require a 180° turnaround while others need only a gentle nudge in the cooperative direction.

In all cases, two distinct kinds of coaching are required for educators during and after training: one to learn the actual skills for resolving personal and professional conflicts; the other to learn how to teach these same skills to others—both adults and children. Conflict resolution training for teachers is doubly complex because it involves learning or refining personal skills and learning new strategies to teach and support the learning of social skills by others. Many teachers have little experience teaching social skills; most of their training has taught them to deliver content knowledge. Therefore, in addition to learning the concepts and skills of conflict resolution, teachers need a fully articulated pedagogy to diagnose and teach students at various skill levels (Brion-Meisels & Selman, 1992).

## Future Challenges for Conflict Resolution Programs in Education

Through its ongoing exploration of cooperative strategies for resolving conflict, society has indicated its dissatisfaction with the traditional conflict resolution methods of violence and aggression, on the one hand, and avoidance, on the other. The question remaining is whether or not society—in general—and the educational system—in particular—are willing to commit resources to fully explore and institutionalize alternative conflict resolution techniques. Necessary efforts include the following:

- Schools must be considered essential sites for conflict resolution training, and training must be provided for children (K–12) as well as included in staff development programs.

- Colleges of education must teach constructive conflict resolution as part of pre-service certification so that future teachers may take these concepts and skills directly into the school environment.

- Researchers, educators, and conflict resolution practitioners must work more closely in order that teaching models may be articulated, tested, and improved.

This work must begin now if the promise of the conflict resolution movement is to have an impact on future generations.

## References

Association for Supervision and Curriculum Development. (1993). *Adult conflict resolution* (Videotape). Alexandria, VA: Author.

Bandura, A. (1985). *Social foundations of thought and action: A social cognitive theory*. Englewood Cliffs, NJ: Prentice-Hall.

Bennett, B. B. (1987). *The effectiveness of staff development training practices: A meta-analysis*. Unpublished doctoral dissertation, University of Oregon, Eugene.

Bennett, C. J. (1990). *Comprehensive multicultural education: Theory and practice*. Needham Heights, MA: Allyn & Bacon.

Brion-Meisels, S., & Selman, R. L. (1992). *Fight, flight, or collaboration? Individual and institutional development in the school*. Unpublished manuscript.

Broad, M. L., & Newstrom J. W. (1992). *Transfer of training*. Reading MA: Addison-Wesley.

Community Board Program, Inc. (1987). *Conflict resolution: A secondary school curriculum*. San Francisco: Conflict Resolution Resources for Schools and Youth.

Deutsch, M. (1977). *The resolution of conflict: Constructive and destructive processes*. New Haven, CT: Yale University Press.

Deutsch, M. (1985). *Distributive justice: A social psychological perspective*. New Haven, CT: Yale University Press.

Deutsch, M. (1993a). Conflict resolution and cooperative learning in an alternative high school. *Cooperative Learning, 13*(4).

Deutsch, M. (1993b). Educating for a peaceful world. *American Psychologist, 49*(5), 510–517.

Fisher, R., Ury, W. L., & Patton, B. M. (1991). *Getting to yes: Negotiating agreement without giving in* (2nd ed.). New York: Penguin.

Folberg, J., & Taylor, A. (1984). *Mediation: A comprehensive guide to resolving conflicts without litigation*. San Francisco: Jossey-Bass.

Fullan, M. (1993). *Change forces: Probing the depths of educational reform*. London: Falmer Press.

Glasser, W. (1992). *The quality school*. New York: HarperCollins.

Hofstede, G. (1986). Cultural differences in teaching and learning. *International Journal of Intercultural Relations, 10*, 301–320.

Johnson, D. W., & Johnson, R. T. (1987). *Creative conflict*. Edina, MN: Interaction.

Johnson, D. W., & Johnson, R. T. (1991). *Teaching students to be peacemakers*. Edina, MN: Interaction.

Johnson, D. W., Johnson, R. T., & Holubec, E. (1993). *Circles of learning: Cooperation in the classroom* (3rd ed.). Edina, MN: Interaction.

Joyce, B., & Showers, B. (1980). Improving in-service training. *Educational Leadership, 37*, 379–385.

Joyce, B., & Showers, B. (1982). The coaching of teaching. *Educational Leadership, 40*, 4–10.

Joyce, B., & Showers, B. (1983). *Power in staff development through research on training*. Alexandria, VA: Association for Supervision and Curriculum Development.

Kelly, J. (1982). *Social-skills training: A practical guide for interventions*. New York: Springer.

Kochman, T. (1981). *Black and white styles in conflict*. Chicago: University of Chicago Press.

Kozol, J. (1991). *Savage inequalities: Children in America's schools*. New York: Crown.

Lam, J. A. (1989). *The impact of conflict resolution programs on schools: A review and synthesis of the evidence* (2nd ed.). Amherst: University of Massachusetts.

Leiberman, A., Darling-Hammond, L., & Zuckerman, D. (1991). *Early lessons in restructuring schools*. New York: National Center for Restructuring Education, Schools, and Teaching, Teachers College, Columbia University.

Lewicki, R. J., & Litterer, J. A. (1985). *Negotiation*. Homewood, IL: Dow Jones-Irwin.

Lewicki, R. J., Weiss, S. E., & Lewin, D. (1992). Models of conflict negotiation and third-party intervention: A review and synthesis. *Journal of Organizational Behavior, 13,* 209–252.

Lewin, K. (1951). Frontiers in group dynamics. In *Field theory in social science.* New York: HarperCollins.

Louis, K. S., & Miles, M. B. (1990). *Improving the urban high school: What works and why.* New York: Teachers College Press.

Marzano, R. J. (1992). *A different kind of classroom: Teaching with dimensions of learning.* Alexandria, VA: Association for Supervision and Curriculum Development.

Miedzian, M. (1991). *Boys will be boys: Breaking the link between masculinity and violence.* New York: Doubleday.

Prothrow-Stith, D. (1987). *Violence prevention curriculum for adolescents.* Newton, MA: Education Development Center.

Prutzman, P., Burger, M. L., Bodenhamer, G., & Stern, L. (1978). *The friendly classroom for a small planet: A handbook on creative approaches to living and problem solving for children.* Wayne, NJ: Avery.

Rackham, N. (1993). The behavior of successful negotiators: Huthwaite Research Group, 1980. In R. Lewicki, J. Litterer, D. Saunders, & J. Minton (Eds.), *Negotiation Readings, Exercises, and Cases.* Homewood, IL.: Dow Jones-Irwin.

Raider, E., & Coleman, S. (1992). *School change by agreement.* New Paltz, NY: Ellen Raider International.

Rekoske, D., & Wyka, G. T. (1990). *Breaking up fights: How to safely defuse explosive conflicts.* Brookfield, WI: National Crisis Prevention Institute.

Rubin, J. Z., & Brown, B. R. (1975). *The social psychology of bargaining and negotiation.* San Diego: Academic Press.

Rubin, J. Z., Pruitt, D. G., & Kim, S. H. (1994). *Social conflict: Escalation, stalemate, and settlement* (2nd ed.). New York: McGraw-Hill.

Sarason, S. B. (1982). *The culture of the school and the problem of change.* Needham Heights, MA: Allyn & Bacon.

Schein, E. H., & Bennis, W. G. (1965). *Personal and organizational change through group methods: The laboratory approach*. New York: Wiley.

Showers, B. (1942). Teachers coaching teachers. *Educational Leadership, 42,* 43–48.

*Training Magazine's industry report*. (1992). Minneapolis: Lakewood Press.

Trower, P., Bryant, B., & Argyle, M. (1978). *Social skills and mental health*. Pittsburgh: University of Pittsburgh Press.

Ury, W. L. (1993). *Getting past no*. New York: Bantam Books.

Weiss, S. E., & Stripp, W. (1985). *Negotiating with foreign businesspersons: An introduction for Americans with propositions on six cultures*. Unpublished manuscript, New York University Graduate School of Business Management, International Business Department, New York.

Weiss-Wik, S. (1983). Enhancing negotiators' successfulness. *Journal of Conflict Resolution, 27*(2), 706–739.

# Commentary

. . . . . . . . . . . . . . . . . . . . . . . . . . . . . . .

# The Constructive Management of Conflict

## Developing the Knowledge and Crafting the Practice

### Morton Deutsch

Let me begin by indicating how pleased and excited I was to read the four chapters in this part. They are superb! They deal with fundamental questions in an original, thoughtful way and provide new insights into the issues they discuss.

The chapters by Rubin and Levinger and by Faure examine issues fundamental to both theory and practice in the area of conflict. Each chapter addresses different facets of the question, *how far can we generalize?* Rubin and Levinger focus on the social actors—the individual, the group, the organization, and the nation. They raise the issue of how and when it is appropriate to generalize from theoretical and empirical research on interpersonal conflict to international conflict (and vice versa). Faure is concerned with a similar question: how appropriate is it to generalize across cultures? Until recently, the field of conflict resolution has been largely a product of Western scholars. Are theory and practice in this area so influenced by implicit Western values—ways of knowing, social norms—that they do not have applicability in other cultures?

In the course I have been teaching in conflict resolution for many years, I deal with the issue of generalizability in the following way. I tell my students that there are two kinds of theorists: the *picayune* and the *grandiose*. The picayune mainly does not generalize beyond the data, so his or her generalizations are very limited; they are likely to be valid but not very useful. I identify myself as a grandiose theorist, one brashly seeking to develop ideas that apply from cave people to space people, from interpersonal to international conflict, from the aborigines in Kakadu to the sophisticates on Park Avenue. This is grandiose indeed!

I also tell my students that one advantage of a grandiose approach to theorizing is that other scholars will be quite happy to indicate the areas in which these generalizations are inappropriate. Unfortunately, this has not been quite true in the field of conflict resolution. For the most part, as Rubin and Levinger indicate, it has been assumed that the same intellectual framework and the same concepts apply with different kinds of social actors and in different cultures. Rubin and Levinger and Faure, in their respective chapters, challenge this assumption.

Rubin and Levinger, in their pathbreaking essay, do more than challenge this assumption; they describe a number of ideas that seem applicable across different types of social actors and some that do not. Their analysis provides a valuable model for scholars who wish to identify further similarities and differences with regard to conflict processes across various kinds of social actors. It also provides important cautions for those who seek to generalize from one substantive area to another.

Faure raises fundamental questions about the field of conflict. He makes the case that the concepts of this field primarily reflect the culture of North American scholars, who have been its predominant theorists and researchers. With convincing examples, he illustrates how the concepts employed in the study of conflict do not mean the same from one culture to another and are not value-free. Faure is not pessimistic about the possibilities of developing the study of conflict so that it has more universality, and he outlines several approaches for doing so. One such approach involves generalizing "symbolic figures" that express similar meanings in various cultures as a way of creating intercultural concepts. This point needs further elaboration.

In the language of the philosophy of science, Faure appears to be suggesting (and I strongly agree) the need for the development of an abstract language of *constructs* whose meanings are partly determined by their relationships with other constructs and partly by rules of correspondence that link some of the theoretical constructs to the concrete data of observation and experiment. In Lewinian terminology, constructs are like genotypes, and the observational data are similar to phenotypes. A given genotype can be expressed in many different types of phenotypes (for example, the color of two genotypically identical hydrangeas will differ as a function of the acidity of the soils in which they are planted), and a given construct (for example, aggression) can be manifested in many ways depending on the environment as well as the state of the other constructs with which it is interrelated.

My brand of grandiosity is at the level of constructs, not at the level of phenomena. It is my hope that our field can develop constructs and then be able to specify the relationships among them so that they are applicable across cultures and time, and to different types of social actions. The phenomena to which one would relate the underlying constructs ("interdependence," "trust," "hostility," "influence," "goal," "cooperation," "competition," "conflict") would vary considerably from culture to culture, from one type of social actor to another, from one situation to another.[1] Thus, hostility would be manifested differently in Japan than in the United States and would be expressed differently between nations than between people. But presumably hostility would have the same basic relation to the other constructs in the theory in the various contexts.

For example, in my most peacockish moments, I consider that the ideas in my theories of cooperation, competition, and conflict resolution are universally applicable. Thus, I speculate that it is useful to think that *promotively or contriently* interdependent relations can exist in different cultures and in the relations between nations, as well as between people. It is also useful to theorize that these two types of relationships have different antecedents and consequences but that the relationship between the type of interdependence and its antecedents and consequences are structurally analogous in different social contexts. My theories are neither rigorous nor complete, so it is difficult to be truly serious about their universal applicability. What I mean to propose here is an aspiration that, as a field, we should be bold enough to strive for even if it turns out to be unattainable.

The Pruitt and Olczak essay is a brilliant exposition of a multifaceted approach to intractable conflicts and also to what I have termed *malignant conflicts* (Deutsch, 1983). They are the first to articulate so fully and clearly a comprehensive approach to these difficult disputes.

My own approach to such conflict was less explicitly articulated. It arose from dual careers as a social psychologist and psychoanalyst. I have tried to combine in my practice as a therapist—as well as in my theoretical and experimental work—the knowledge and insights that come from each of these areas. My work on conflict resolution as a social psychologist was strongly influenced by images of marital couples in conflict, and my therapeutic work was influenced by our studies of conflict, bargaining, and negotiation as well as by psychoanalytic models of intrapsychic conflict. Although in my practice I often had to deal with "intractable" conflicts, my social psychology work was not specifically directed toward such conflicts. However, I have written several essays—three in relation to the Cold War (Deutsch, 1961, 1962, 1983), one in connection with the Arab-Israeli conflicts (Deutsch, 1988), and one general essay (Deutsch, 1994)—that directly relate to these matters. Research by several of my former students (Kressel, 1985; Gephart, 1993; Herschlag, 1993) also are concerned with the processes involved in escalating and de-escalating conflicts in the marital context.

The approach of my students and myself has been more limited than that of Pruitt and Olczak. Our emphases are on the factors contributing to the escalation of conflicts and the social psychological processes involved in their persistence and destructiveness.

Our suggestions for intervention in such conflicts borrow heavily from a therapeutic model. Pruitt and Olczak are also indebted to the insights to be gained from therapy in their multimodal approach, but they provide a very useful organizing heuristic in their MACBE model, which should be of enormous value to anyone seeking to understand or intervene in intractable conflicts.

There is one point about such disputes that I would stress somewhat more than they do. The dynamics of a malignant conflict have the inherent quality of a folie à deux, where the self-fulfilling prophecies of each side mutually reinforce one another. Each side blames the other for its own malevolent actions. Each comes to believe that its own hostility, its own aggressive and defensive behaviors toward the other result from the other's provocative, dangerous, and untrustworthy actions. In an intractable conflict, these perceptions become reality. After a while, it is not a distortion or a misperception for each side to see the other as having malevolent intentions, as being potentially dangerous and untrustworthy. The conflict process has made the perceptions become reality. As a result, both sides are right to think that the other is hostile.

The blaming and denunciation of the other, which are so unhelpful but so common in this kind of conflict, may come to be grounded in accurate perceptions of the other's behavior, but they are based on an incorrect causal attribution. Neither side recognizes its own part in maintaining the malignant relations nor understands how these hostile actions result from the mutually reinforcing self-fulfilling prophecies derived from the conflict process in which they are enmeshed. An important early strategic objective of an intervention is to help the conflicting parties understand the nature of this vicious circle so they can stop the blaming and begin the problem-solving process. Pruitt and Olczak's multimodal approach suggests various avenues of approach for achieving this objective.

The chapter by Ellen Raider is a gem. Not only does it give a fine overview of the current status of conflict resolution training in the United States, it also provides a framework for thinking about the major issues pertinent to such training—particularly in the schools. Raider does a masterful job in raising questions related to training that should pique the interest of theorists and researchers— as well as practitioners—in this area.

Very much stimulated by discussions I have had with Ellen Raider, I have begun to do some thinking about some of the social psychological issues that relate to training (Deutsch, 1994). There appear to be some important differences between social skills and skills that can be employed without taking into account the others with whom you are interdependent. Social problem solving may utilize the skills involved in individual problem solving, but more is required if one is to be effective in the social situation. There is a valuable summary in Raider's chapter of the methods that are used in teaching skills, nonsocial as well as social. However, it is evident from her discussion that there are basic theoretical as well as applied research questions that need to be asked and answered before we have a good characterization of the nature of social skills. Clarification here would be enormously helpful to those who are training practitioners.

Also, it is apparent from Raider's chapter that there is an appalling lack of research on the various aspects of training in the field of conflict resolution. We haven't begun to collect the data that are needed to begin to answer such questions as: *who* benefits and *how* (including how much and for how long), through what mediating processes, as a result of receiving *what type of training*, for *how long*, by what kind of *trainers and training*, in what *sorts of circumstances*. This incomplete outline is an illustration of the many different kinds of questions that need research before training in this area is well grounded.

Many of us entered the field of conflict resolution because we wanted to participate in developing the knowledge and practice that could contribute to the prevention or "pacification" of the types of destructive conflicts so prevalent in the world today at the interpersonal, intergroup, and international levels. Development of the knowledge, professional skills, and appropriate organizations to educate children and adults to manage conflicts more constructively would be an important contribution to making our world more humane.

## Note

1. Ideally the constructs would not be labeled with words from any existing language. Currently, terms tend to introduce the cultural biases implicit in the language used. However, until the study of conflict is much further advanced, the advantages of employing a widely used language to label constructs outweigh its disadvantages.

## References

Deutsch, M. (1961). Some considerations relevant to national policy. *Journal of Social Issues, 17*, 57–68.

Deutsch, M. (1962). A psychological basis for peace. In Q. Wright, W. M. Evan, & M. Deutsch (Eds.), *Preventing World War III: Some proposals* (pp. 369–392). New York: Simon & Schuster.

Deutsch, M. (1983). Preventing World War III: A psychological perspective. *Political Psychology, 3*, 3–31.

Deutsch, M. (1988). Negotiating the non-negotiable. In B. Kellerman & J. Z. Rubin (Eds.), *Leadership and negotiation in the Middle East* (pp. 248–263). New York: Praeger.

Deutsch, M. (1994). Constructive conflict management for the world today. *International Journal of Conflict Management, 5*, 111–129.

Gephart, M. A. (1993). *The escalation of marital conflict.* Unpublished doctoral dissertation, Teachers College, Columbia University, New York.

Herschlag, J. K. (1993). *The characteristics and processes of tractable and intractable conflicts as they occur between spouses in stepfamilies.* Unpublished doctoral dissertation, Teachers College, Columbia University, New York.

Kressel, K. (1985). *The process of divorce.* New York: Basic Books.

# Part II

Cooperation

# 5

Trust in Relationships

## A Model of Development and Decline

### Roy J. Lewicki, Barbara Benedict Bunker

I s trust easier to destroy than it is to build? The presumption that the answer to this question is a resounding yes has been prevalent in cooperation and conflict management research for over thirty years. Observation of the relationship development process between subjects in simple experimental research game paradigms (for example, Prisoner's Dilemma or Acme-Bolt) shows that cooperative behavior can be developed over a long series of predictable moves by the parties. But this cooperation can be rapidly destroyed if one party decides to defect—if the defection violates the expectations of the other—and can be even more destructive if the defection occurs after the parties have made some explicit agreement to coordinate their moves (Deutsch, 1958; Deutsch & Krauss, 1962). Similarly, friends, spouses, and business partners may take months or years to learn how to cooperate with each other; yet the foundations of their cooperation can be destroyed in a heartbeat if one party engages in behavior destructive to that cooperation (Lorenz, 1988).

In spite of the presumption that cooperation is easier to destroy than to build, a systematic examination of how and why this might be true has not occurred. There are several reasons why. First,

*Note:* We are indebted to Blair Sheppard for several discussions about the concepts in this chapter and for comments on earlier drafts.

existing theories of the structure, nature, and dynamics of trust are fragmented and simplistic. Second, in order to understand the dynamics of the creation and destruction of trust, we also need a model of relationships—how relationships develop or deteriorate over time. Until recently, almost all conflict and negotiation research focused on the dynamics of static, transactional exchanges between parties, rather than on the development of cooperation and the management of conflict in the context of complex, multi-faceted relationships. Finally, it has been assumed that trust only develops in partnership with cooperation; thus, as trust increases, so does cooperation. While we will argue that cooperative processes facilitate trust, some of the types of trust we propose can exist in competitive relationships as well.

Our premise in this chapter is that the answer to our question—is trust easier to destroy than to build—must be rooted in an understanding of how trust develops and how trust development is linked to processes of relationship development. Our intent is first to briefly review the existing literature on trust. We will examine existing definitions and models of trust to ascertain whether these models proceed beyond static definitions of trust and effectively account for both the development and decline of trust. Finding most models wanting (especially in describing the decline of trust), we then select what we believe to be the most promising models of trust and build on them to explore the dynamics of trust escalation and de-escalation in relationships. We then turn to the task of grounding this model of trust in a broader paradigm of relationships and their development. Finally, we examine situations where trust is violated or disconfirmed and return to our key question: is trust fragile?

## Current Definitions and Research Approaches

Trust is a concept that has received attention from several of the social sciences—psychology, sociology, political science, economics, anthropology, history, and sociobiology (Gambetta, 1988). As can be expected, each field has approached the problem with its own disciplinary lens and filters. Thus, economists suggest that trust is a form of implicit contracting (Arrow, 1974; Achian & Demsetz, 1972). Sociologists such as Schutz (1967) describe trust as "the taken-for-granted world in common" that makes social life possible. Psychologists such as Rotter (1967, 1971) approach trust as the generalized expectation of an individual that the promise or statement of another individual can be consistently relied on.

Given the level of interest in trust across the disciplines, one might be tempted to assume that a coherent and integrated literature exists. Unfortunately, nothing could be further from the truth. As noted by several critics (Lewis & Weigert, 1985; Worchel, 1979), the different approaches to trust derive from the different theoretical orientations and research interests of those studying the process. Each discipline assumes its own frame and perspective on the phenomenon without effectively articulating the parameters of that frame; each is a blind man describing his own small piece of the elephant. There has been remarkably little effort to integrate these different perspectives or articulate the key role that trust plays in critical social processes (for example, cooperation, coordination, and performance).

Worchel (1979) proposes that these different perspectives fall into at least three different groups. First are *personality theorists*, who have focused on individual personality differences in the readiness to trust and on the specific developmental and social contextual factors that shape this readiness. At this level, trust is conceptualized as a belief, expectancy, or feeling that is deeply rooted in the personality, with its origins in the individual's early psychosocial development. Rotter (1971), for example, defined trust as a generalized expectancy that the word, promise, or verbal or written statement of another individual is reliable. According to Rotter, trust is a generalized response derived from the reinforcement history of previous social interactions.

Several researchers see trust as a faith in humanity and have developed self-report inventories to measure the strength of this faith (Wrightsman, 1966, 1972; Sato, 1988, 1989; Yamagishi & Sato, 1986). Wrightsman (1966, 1972), in his articulation of philosophies of human nature, states that people develop a personal philosophy about how other people will behave. The first element in this personal philosophy is one's view on trust—that is, whether people are basically honest or basically immoral and irresponsible.

Erikson (1963) and Bowlby (1973) proposed basic models of personality development that stressed trust development—the reliance on another's integrity, as when the infant with unmet needs comes to trust his or her world to provide for those needs—as a core personality characteristic and as a foundation of healthy personality development. Trust is shaped by the early relationship between the individual and the caregiver; the adequacy of this relationship dictates whether an individual develops a core orientation that others can or cannot be trusted, thus affecting his or her overall "readiness to trust" in interpersonal relationships (Ainsworth, Blehar, Waters, & Wall, 1978).

Other researchers have focused on those life events that affect and shape an individual's predisposition to trust, such as cultural and socioeconomic differences in child-rearing practices (Erikson, 1963, 1968), group membership (Kramer & Brewer, 1984), similarity of another to oneself (Apfelbaum, 1974), or other mechanisms that produce a perceived similarity between self and others in attitudes and behaviors (Pruitt & Carnevale, 1993).

Worchel's second group consists of *sociologists and economists*, who have focused on trust as an institutional phenomenon. At this level, trust can be conceptualized both as a phenomenon within and between institutions and as the trust individuals put in those institutions. Neu (1991) has noted the difference between trust in individuals and trust in institutions. One can have trust in particular people (personal trust) and trust in organized systems (institutional trust) (see also Zucker, 1986). Personal trust develops through repeated interactions with others and is based on familiarity, interdependence, and continuity in relationships (Granovetter, 1985; Shapiro, 1987). In this view, personal trust develops to meet an individual's need to reduce uncertainty in regularized social interactions; in short, people will buy from, sell to, and work with those whom they trust. Institutional trust develops when individuals must generalize their personal trust to large organizations made up of individuals with whom they have low familiarity, low interdependence, and low continuity of interaction.

Problems develop when this trust is inappropriately generalized or is violated. For example, Flacks (1969, p. 132), in discussing the erosion of the perceived legitimacy of authority, suggests that trust is the "perception that those in authority are not biased against one, that the working of the system does not result in special costs for oneself or one's group." Developing and sustaining institutional trust is dependent on factors such as the openness of the political system to citizen participation, the objectivity of the authorities in handling disputes, and the degree to which the administration of law enforcement is perceived as fair and evenhanded (Tyler, 1990). (See also Sheppard, Lewicki, & Minton, 1992, for a discussion of the fairness factors that lead individuals to trust a system).

*Social psychologists*—the last of Worchel's three groups—focus on the transactions between individuals that create or destroy trust at the interpersonal and group levels, unlike the personality construct approaches that focus on how early life experiences impact trust development. Trust has been defined as a relatively simple expectation of the other party in a transaction—that the other will behave in a certain way (Pearce, Branyiczki, & Bakasci, 1994), be cooperative or uncooperative (Pruitt & Carnevale, 1993), have a differential readiness for coordination (Pruitt, 1981; Pruitt & Kimmel, 1977), or be exploitative or accommodative (Hovland, Janis, & Kelley, 1953). Others, such as Deutsch (1958, p. 266), view trust as an expectation of interpersonal *events*, not people: "An individual may be said to have trust in the occurrence of an event if he expects its occurrence and the expectations lead to behavior which he perceives to have greater negative motivational consequence if the expectation is not confirmed than positive motivational consequence if it is confirmed."

However, trust is more than simple expectations; as social psychologists note, expectations are set within particular contextual parameters and constraints. For example, Lewis and Weigert (1985) argue that trust is not mere predictability, but confidence in the face of risk (a contextual variable that is central to most social psychological definitions). Deutsch (1973) notes the different ways trust can be interpreted in the context of evaluating the positive and negative consequences of a trusting act. Kahneman, Knetsch, and Thaler (1986) observe that in the absence of enforcement mechanisms, trust is faith that others "will not cheat with impunity." Similarly, Zand (1972, p. 230) defines trust as "actions which increase one's vulnerability to another whose behavior is not under one's control in a situation in which the penalty one suffers, if the other abuses that vulnerability, is greater than the benefit one gains if the other does not abuse that vulnerability."

Many definitions move beyond expectations to specify the key situational parameters that describe or define situational risk. Deutsch (1960) suggests that a decision to trust is made in situations in which the following situational parameters exist: a course of future action that is ambiguous, outcomes that depend on the behavior of others, and greater consequences of a harmful event than of a beneficial event. In a subsequent article, Deutsch (1973) refines his position into a series of hypotheses about the conditions under which trusting choices will be made. Similarly, Schlenker, Helm, and Tedeschi (1973, p. 419) define trust as the "reliance upon information received from another person about uncertain environmental states and their accompanying outcomes in a risky situation." In order for trust to be demonstrated, they argue that the situation must contain: ambiguity about the future; cues, such as the communication of another's intentions, that provide some information as to the probability of certain states occurring; and the resulting behavior of the person demonstrating reliance on this uncertain information.

In this chapter, we adopt the definition of trust proposed by Boon and Holmes (1991, p. 194); they define trust as "a state involving confident positive expectations about another's motives with respect to oneself in situations entailing risk." Boon and Holmes's definition of trust is based on three elements: an individual's *chronic disposition* toward trust (see our previous discussion of personality), situational *parameters*, and the *history of the relationship*. We now turn to the relationship dimension of trust.

## Trust in Intimate and Professional Relationships

Much of the earlier work we have cited assumes that "interpersonal trust" and "relationship" are synonymous and interchangeable. More recent work attempts to separate the two, although the separation may be indiscernible because many of these studies (Rempel, Holmes, & Zanna, 1985; Holmes, 1991; Boon & Holmes, 1991) focus on trust development only in the context of a close, personal relationship (a romantic one, for example). Yet trust occurs in business, professional, and working relationships as well. It is beyond the scope of our chapter to put forward a comprehensive model of relationships and relationship development (for efforts in this direction, see Duck, 1993a, 1993b; Sheppard, in press; Greenhalgh & Chapman, 1994a, 1994b). Yet some framework is necessary in order to properly ground our discussion of the evolution and devolution of trust.

Relationships have at a minimum a structural component and an affective one. Deutsch's description of cooperation and "promotive interdependence" (1949) suggests that situations of promotive interdependence include substitutability (the degree to which one party's actions can substitute for the other), inducibility (the degree to which one party can influence the other), and positive cathexis (a positive attitude or disposition toward the other). These elements provide the structural parameters that permit cooperation, that is, long-term relationships. Kelley's theory of interdependence of relationships (1979) includes two of Deutsch's components: outcome correspondence and mutual dependence. (Kelley is interested in specifying degrees of interdependence, not defining cooperation.) He adds "basis of dependence," or the kind of behavior control in the relationship, and "degree of dependence," or alternatives available in other relationships, as additional key factors. He omits affect, positive cathexis, and substitutability as factors of interest. Thus, there seems to be some agreement that people get together in some context with aspirations (goals) for their respective outcomes. The nature of these goals, and how the goals and context are structured, define the dependence/interdependence dimension of the relationship.

Because we have embraced Boon and Holmes's definition of trust, we will first explain how they propose that trust develops in the context of a romantic relationship. We then turn to the development of trust in nonromantic relationships and propose a more complex model of trust that better accounts for the evolution and devolution dynamics.

## Trust in Intimate Relationships

Boon and Holmes (1991), in their research on romantic relationships, suggest that romantic relationships move through developmental stages or phases. This developmental sequence is shown across the rows of Table 5.1. As the relationship moves from the romantic to the evaluative and then to the accommodative stage, the parties engage in fundamentally different behaviors. These behaviors are necessary both to develop and sustain their relationship. More important, however, Boon and Holmes suggest that the dynamics of trust are different at each of the three stages. This is a fundamentally different perspective on trust from the ones we have explored thus far. In this view, the essence of trust cannot be

Table 5.1. Boon and Holmes's Stages of Relationships and Trust.

| Relationship Stage | Primary Dynamics | Trust Development |
|---|---|---|
| Romantic Love | Surge of positive feelings. Idealization of the partner. Expectations enhanced by projection on the other. | Trust and love tend to be undifferentiable. Hope that the relationship will work overshadows fear that it may not. |
| Evaluative Stage | Close contact reveals imperfections in the other, leading to "step back and evaluate." Pros and cons of relationship are debated. Effort to get to know the other better—motives, intentions, predispositions, realities. | "Real" trust takes root. Parties engage in risk—reciprocal self-disclosure of thoughts and feelings, responding to other's thoughts and feelings. Determine whether other's responsiveness is genuine or pretentious—is there real "caring"? |
| Accommodative Stage | Negotiation of conflicting needs and expectations; deal with incompatibilities surfaced in previous stage. Develop confidence in future of the relationship. | Solidification of trust. "Leap of faith" that one can never know everything about the other, but that the relationship can sustain the threat of large differences or incompatibilities. |

Source: Adapted from Boon and Holmes, 1991.

captured by a single, static definition of its key elements and attributes. Trust is a dynamic phenomenon that takes on a different character in the early, developing, and mature stages of a relationship.

## Trust in Professional Relationships

An effort to link trust development and relationship development in a business context was recently undertaken by Shapiro, Sheppard, and Cheraskin (1992). These authors suggest that three types of trust operate in the development of a business relationship: deterrence-based trust, knowledge-based trust, and identification-based trust.

Deterrence-based trust is based on consistency of behavior—that people will do what they say they are going to do. Behavioral consistency is sustained by the threat of punishment if consistency is not maintained. A boy can be trusted to come home for dinner at 6:00 because he knows what his mother will do if he doesn't. Trust based on consistency alone, and grounded in punishment for inconsistency, is deterrence based.

The second type of trust is knowledge-based trust. This type of trust is grounded in behavioral predictability—a judgment of the probability of the other's likely choice of behaviors. Knowledge-based trust occurs when one has enough information about others to understand them and to accurately predict their likely behavior. While deterrence-based trust is based on the creation of a sufficient level of punishment to ensure fear (and create deterrence), knowledge-based trust is more sophisticated. In this second form of trust, we come to understand the decision maker's actions, thoughts, and intentions well enough to effectively predict what he or she will do. Thus, in the case of a husband and wife, the wife "trusts" that the husband will take out the trash because he is a very neat, organized person who likes a clean apartment and hates the odor of garbage.

The third type of trust is called identification-based trust and is based on a full internalization of the other party's desires and intentions. At this level, trust exists because each party effectively understands, agrees with, empathizes with, and endorses what the other wants, and can act for the other. Identification-based trust thus permits one to act as an agent for the other, substituting for the other in interpersonal transactions. One can be confident that the other will not act harmfully, will protect and defend one's own interests, and that no surveillance of the other is required. In this form of trust, the boy returns for dinner on time because he identifies with the family unit, whose expectations are that all family members are home for dinner by 6:00. Moreover, the boy's mother, who identifies with her son's love of baseball, cheerfully tells his coach that she will make sure dinner is served promptly at 6:00 so he can be ready for his 7:00 game.

### Comparison with Boon and Holmes's Approach

In both models, trust is fundamentally different at different stages of the relationship. The difference between the Boon and Holmes approach to trust and the Shapiro et al. approach is that in the former model, the early driver of the relationship is the emotional, romantic attraction for the other. As Boon and Holmes note, "trust and love tend to be strongly related at this stage, even though a fragile expression of hope may be the only basis for this sense of trust. Any doubts or fears regarding trust tend simply to be denied importance, drowned amidst a sea of positive feelings" (1991, pp. 201–202). As the initial infatuation begins to fade and the parties stand back and evaluate the relationship with regard to risk and vulnerability, the first "real" trust is initiated. In contrast, in the Shapiro et al. model of the business (or nonromantic) relationship, trust first develops on a calculative basis, as the parties attempt to determine the nature of their interdependence, what they will get from the relationship and give to it, and what their risks and vulnerabilities are. Trust is strengthened as knowledge about the other is gained and eventually solidified if identification with the other develops. Thus, trust is a core issue from the beginning of a business relationship, while a secondary one at the beginning of a romantic relationship.

Ultimately, in both models, emotional involvement and inter-dependence become intertwined. In a business relationship, as the parties develop their interdependence around joint outcomes, they may grow to like each other and develop strong friendships, cama-raderie, or even romantic attachments.

## Types of Trust

The three types of trust proposed by Shapiro et al. (1992) offer a considerably more sophisticated and multidimensional approach to trust than previous models. Different types of trust are predicated on different levels of understanding of and control over the other. We propose to expand and extend this work in several ways:

• The three types of trust are probably linked and sequential. Shapiro et al. propose the three as simply different types of trust, perhaps separate and independent. We suggest that they are linked in a sequential iteration in which achievement of trust at one level enables the development of trust at the next level.

• The development of these three types of trust may suggest something more basic about the development of relationships in which trust is a central element. By understanding how trust changes, grows, and declines, we may also understand how rela-tionships change, grow, and decline.

• Articulating a model of transitional stages in trust develop-ment creates the groundwork necessary to be more precise about those factors necessary to sustain and cultivate trust at each level. It also allows for a determination of whether those same factors (perhaps in different forms) contribute to trust deterioration and decline. We thus are able to create a framework that permits us to return to our original question: is it easier to destroy trust than it is to build it?

We now turn back to consider the three types of trust in more detail, expanding on the earlier descriptions of Shapiro et al. (1992)

and suggesting the linkages and progressions between the types. We propose that these types of trust can be effectively applied to both intimate and professional relationships.

## Calculus-Based Trust

Recall that the first kind of trust was deterrence-based trust: individuals will do what they say because they fear the consequences of not doing what they say. Like any behavior based on a theory of deterrence, trust is sustained to the degree that the deterrent (punishment) is clear, possible, and likely to occur if the trust is violated. Thus, the threat of punishment is likely to be a more significant motivator than the promise of reward.

A broader view of deterrence-based trust is that this form is grounded not only in the fear of punishment for violating the trust but also in the rewards to be derived from preserving it. At this level, trust is an ongoing, market-oriented, economic calculation whose value is derived by comparing the outcomes resulting from creating and sustaining the relationship to the costs of maintaining or severing it. This transactional view of trust is based on concepts used to describe the economic behavior of actors in a firm (Williamson, 1975, 1981), only applied at the interpersonal transaction level. Based on these concepts, calculus-based trust in any given transaction with another may be derived by determining:

- Benefits to be derived from staying in the relationship

- Benefits to be derived from cheating on the relationship

- Costs of staying in the relationship

- Costs of breaking the relationship

For multiple transactions in a relationship—more typical of human interaction—we may develop a broader set of calculations that includes the number of different types of interdependence, the costs and benefits derived from cheating (breaking those interdependencies), and the associated costs and benefits of seeking other relationships.[1] A comparable calculative model was proposed by Deutsch (1973) based on simple subjective utility calculations (Edwards, 1954). Deutsch proposed that decisions to act trustingly could be accounted for by understanding the relative strengths of positive and negative "motivational consequences" (outcomes) that would derive from choices in an ambiguous situation and the subjective probabilities that those consequences would actually occur. Individuals make a trusting choice when they confront an ambiguous choice situation in which the negative consequences are stronger than the positive consequences, but the individual believes that the probability of the positive consequences outweighs the probability of the negative ones. Deutsch's model also attempts to account for different motivations and intentions in trusting choices, particularly ones that can account for altruistic behavior, reliable interpersonal exchanges between parties, and power differences between the parties.

While calculus-based trust may equally be driven by the value of benefits or the costs of cheating, we argue that Shapiro et al. were correct in their original formulation of this type of trust as deterrence based; the deterrent elements are a more dominant motivator than the benefit-seeking elements. Punishment for nonconsistency is more likely to produce this type of trust than rewards or incentives derived from maintaining the trust. The "trust calculus" is made effective, therefore, by the adequacy and costs of deterrence. "Deterrence-based trust exists when the potential costs of discontinuing the relationship or the likelihood of retributive action outweigh the short-term advantage of acting in a distrustful way" (Shapiro et al., 1992, p. 366). The authors propose three vehicles by which continued trust is ensured through deterrence:

- Possible defections from trust can be sustained if the parties have *repeated interactions*, in which each single transaction contains some of the elements of benefit that the parties gain from each other. As parties grow to trust each other, their interdependence becomes multifaceted. If the relationship is broken off, the parties also have multiple ways to hurt each other; therefore, any single destructive incident today can play itself out over future interactions in the relationship, which may in themselves hold the relationship together. Trust violations jeopardize the relationship and undermine the future interdependencies of the parties.

- The second way that calculus-based trust is ensured is through the *degree of interdependence and alternative relationships*. Complex relationships are built on many points of simultaneous or closely connected contact. Parties may share interests, own common property, and be entwined in complex, binding legal and financial arrangements. Just as a distrustful interaction in the current situation can jeopardize future interactions, it can also spread from one aspect of a multifaceted relationship to another. If one has multiple interdependencies with others, this may preclude interdependencies outside the relationship. As the number of interdependencies increases inside a relationship, the number of interdependencies outside the relationship decreases. Thus, trust erosion can affect not only concurrent transactions with the other but also one's ability to have needs met externally. (In the parlance of Fisher, Ury, and Patton, 1991, the party loses his or her Best Alternative.) Suppose A and B are close friends and have lots of interdependencies; A has few other close friends, while B has several. If A and B have a fight and decide to break off the relationship, A may suffer higher costs because A has no other friends to whom she may turn.

- The third vehicle is *personal reputation as a hostage*; if trust is violated, an individual's reputation can be tarnished throughout his or her network of friends and associates. In a business relationship, the professional reputation of the other side serves as a hostage. If one party begins to violate the other's trust, the violated party quickly lets it be known, throughout the accused's network of friends, colleagues, and associates, that the other is a disreputable individual. "People invest resources for the purpose of building a reputation for honesty" (Dasgupta, 1988, p. 70). Even for a dishonest person, a reputation for honesty (or trustworthiness) is a valuable asset, one a businessperson wants to maintain. So, even if there are opportunities to be dishonest (or untrustworthy), any short-term gains from untrustworthy acts must be balanced (in a calculus-based way) against the longer run gains of maintaining a good reputation. Gossip is a form of social deterrence; the victim hopes to gain some sympathy and public support and also to damage the credibility of the other in future interactions. A trusted auto mechanic in a small town might be severely hurt if an unsatisfied customer begins to talk about the poor service and price gouging he recently experienced at the mechanic's garage.

Hostages can also be used more directly, as parties use their network of relationships to threaten to harm someone the other cares about. In a marriage, children often serve as potential hostages if one spouse does not follow the other's requests. (See Deutsch, 1973, for a discussion of the role of hostages as a signal of commitment to carry out an exchange.)

In summary, for the threat of deterrence to be effective, the following conditions must exist:

• The potential loss of future interaction with the other must outweigh the profit potential that comes from defecting from the relationship. The short-term temptation to cheat, and the gains accruing from such behavior, must be overshadowed by the long-term costs if one is caught.

• Deterrence requires monitoring to work; the parties must monitor each other and be willing to tell each other when a trust violation has been noted.

• An injured party must be willing to withdraw benefits from— or harm—the person acting distrustfully. In short, threats must be credible and must be executed, even if their execution destroys the relationship. The stresses and strains of executing such threats is reflected in the remarks of the parent who is about to spank a child: "this is going to hurt me more than it hurts you."

- Finally, the calculations of calculus-based trust may be shaped by the actor's orientation toward risk. While Williamson's model assumes that trust actions are rational and aim to maximize outcomes, economic rationality is often influenced by orientation to risk (Bazerman, 1994). In assessing the benefits of interdependence, the costs of cheating, and the associated probabilities, an actor's perceptions are shaped by risk biases that predispose either party toward being exploited (we are naive and risk seeking, trusting those who do not deserve to be trusted) or toward being suspicious (we are cautious and risk averse, not trusting those who deserve to be trusted). In the former case, our naiveté leads us to be "taken" by those who exploit our trust; in the later case, our suspicion leads us to avoid potentially valued relationships with others because we fear the possibility of their exploitative action.

## Knowledge-Based Trust

The second form of trust is knowledge-based trust. This form of trust is grounded in the other's predictability; we can anticipate his or her behavior. Knowledge-based trust relies on information rather than deterrence. The better we know the other individual, the more accurately we can predict what he or she will do; as long as the other remains predictable (that is, confirming our knowledge and acting consistently with that knowledge), trust will endure.

There are several dimensions to this knowledge-based trust (Shapiro et al., 1992). First, and most simple, information contributes to predictability of the other, which contributes to trust. The better I know the other, the better I can trust what the other will do because I can accurately predict how they will respond in most situations (see also Kelley & Stahelski, 1970).

Second, predictability enhances trust even if the other is predictably untrustworthy because we can predict the ways that the other will violate the trust. Brothers who are always competing with each other learn to anticipate the other's tactics so well that they can predict exactly how one will attempt to cheat and therefore take measures to ensure that cheating isn't attempted.

Third, accurate prediction requires an understanding that develops over repeated interactions in multidimensional relationships (similar to calculus-based trust) plus two additional factors: regular communication and courtship (Shapiro et al., 1992). Regular communication puts a party in constant contact with the other, which allows for exchanging information about wants, preferences, and approaches to problems. Regular communication enhances our ability to understand the way the other approaches the world and allows us to compare it with our own. Without regular communication, we lose touch with each other—not only emotionally but in our ability to think like and react like the other. Courtship is behavior specifically directed at relationship development, at learning more about a possible partner. Courtship is conducted by "interviewing" the other, watching the other perform in social situations, experiencing the other in a variety of emotional states, and learning how other people view the other's behavior. Courtship permits actors to gain enough information to determine whether the parties can work together well, whether compatibility in style, approach, and preferences exist. For example, Shapiro et al. describe the differences in the practice of business relationship courtship between Americans and Japanese. Representatives of Asian firms usually prefer to conduct long courtships of potential business partners, in which much time is spent up front getting to know their American counterparts before substantive business issues are discussed. This reflects the widely held—outside of the United States—cultural assumption that personal relationships are central to good business relationships. If the courtship is deemed successful, a variety of business transactions may ensue. In contrast, in North America—where work and social relationships are mostly separate—this process is frequently viewed by Americans as tedious and time consuming, since Americans tend to view business deals as short-term, limited, finite transactions. In short, Americans tend to construe business deals as a series of one-time dates, while Japanese are likely to view them as similar to marriage.

### Identification-Based Trust

The third type of trust is based on identification, that is, a full internalization of the other's desires and intentions. At this third level, trust exists because the parties effectively understand, agree with, and endorse each other's wants; this mutual understanding is developed to the point that each can effectively act for the other. Identification-based trust thus permits a party to serve as the other's agent and to substitute for the other in interpersonal transactions. The other can be confident that his or her interests will be fully defended and protected, without surveillance or monitoring of the actor. A true affirmation of the strength of identification-based trust between parties is found when one party acts for the other even more zealously than the other might. For example, if party A is hesitant to defend himself against criticism from an outsider but Party B is willing to take on the outsider and aggressively protect A, A's trust in B may be affirmed and enhanced by B's willingness to do for A what A could not do for himself. Interestingly, however, if B makes claims about A that exceed even what A might say about himself, A could lose some trust in B because B's exaggeration may lack credibility. In identification, B must act like A but not overreact on behalf of A.

A corollary of this acting for each other in identification-based trust is that as both knowledge and identification develop, a party not only knows and identifies with the other but comes to understand what the party herself must do to sustain the other's trust. This process might be described as second-order learning. A learns what really matters to B and comes to place the same importance on those behaviors as B does. For example, Spouse A comes to learn how critical Spouse B believes it is to pick up the children from day care at the appointed hour. Spouse B is concerned for the children, who have been at day care all day, and also has high empathy for the teachers in the day-care center, who want to go home on time. Spouse A knows that if he is late, Spouse B will become very angry and take this lateness as evidence that Spouse A can't be trusted to pick up the children on time. Thus, Spouse A has internalized the same sense of urgency as Spouse B and regularly makes sure that he is not late to pick up the children. If A is late, even though the children are not in danger, B loses trust in A.

Many of the same activities that build and strengthen calculus-based and knowledge-based trust also serve to develop identification-based trust. In addition to those already mentioned, Shapiro et al. (1992) discuss four types:

- *Commonalty in name* (collective identity). One vehicle to create common identification is a joint name or identity. Mergers, strategic alliances, and joint ventures create new company names and identities—buildings, logos, mission statements, slogans, trademarks, colors, and so on—to constantly remind themselves and others of their collective intentions. Married partners take on each other's name, or combine their names, to form a common identity.

- *Colocation.* A second way to create a common identification is to colocate—the same city, same building, same room—or to share some linking vehicle, such as a communication tool, work flow system, meeting structure, or even bathroom or coffee pot. Colocation constantly bring parties into regular and consistent contact with each other and permits them to affirm their identity. Boeing Corporation colocated engineers and assemblers for the 777 aircraft in order to increase interaction between the two groups and speed the new model into the marketplace.

- *Creation of joint products and goals.* When people work to create joint products and goals, they strengthen their identification with each other. For example, in the well-known Robbers' Cave experiment (Sherif, 1967), when competing groups in the summer camp worked together on joint projects and activities, their competitiveness was reduced and cooperation increased.

- *Shared values.* Finally, over time, the parties can actually come to believe in and stand for the same core values, beliefs, and concerns. To the degree that this actually happens, one partner can effectively stand in for the other. By being able to substitute for each other in transactions, the parties' joint goals and interests can be effectively leveraged and enhanced. Members who identify with the firm can speak for the firm, can be given authority, and can use that authority to enhance the firm's interests.

## Dynamics of Trust Development

Having identified the three different types of trust, we now explore two additional features. First, we have implied, but not clearly stated, that the three types of trust are related to each other in some manner. In this section, we compare the three bases, particularly calculus-based to knowledge-based and knowledge-based to identification-based trust. Second, we argue that the development of trust proceeds through these three stages and describe this stage-wise progression.

### Comparison of Calculus-Based and Knowledge-Based Trust

Calculus-based trust is founded on consistency and on deterrence— ensuring the other's consistency through costs for inconsistency. Behavior *control* is central to this form of trust; actions are designed to get the other to do what the actor wants. Knowledge-based trust is founded on *information*, not control. While calculus-based trust is essentially an effort to curtail individual differences and uniqueness, knowledge-based trust embraces such differences. In the former case, "I trust you because I can control what I want you to do and eliminate the risk of your unpredictability"; in the later case, "I trust you because I know enough about you to know what you will do, even if I can or will not try to control it."

As a developmental process, we believe that the appropriate metaphor for the growth of calculus-based trust (CBT) is tactical climbing (as with ladders or mountains). The parties attempt to coordinate their actions as they move on to increasing levels of risk and vulnerability with each other, testing consistency, calculating costs, and exercising deterrence as necessary. As the parties reach higher levels, serious acts of inconsistency create disruption for one or both parties; this disruption may be sufficient to topple the ladder, destroy the trust, and crumble the relationship. Perhaps a more complete metaphor can be derived from the children's board game "Chutes and Ladders." Progress is made by dice throws that permit the player to move ahead in a stepwise fashion; however, if one lands on a chute, the player is quickly dropped back a number of steps. In calculus-based trust, forward progress is made by ladder climbing in a slow, stepwise fashion; however, a single event of inconsistency may "chute" the individual back several steps—or in the worst case, back to square one. At this early stage, trust is partial and quite fragile.

In comparison, the development of knowledge-based trust (KBT) is a fundamentally different process of relationship building and testing. The more appropriate metaphor is from agriculture: KBT development is like gardening—tilling the soil year after year to understand it, to know the sandy and moist sections, the shady and sunlit sections, and to know what will grow in what locations. This knowledge comes by experimenting with a series of different crops over the years and building on that experience. Parties cultivate their knowledge of each other by gathering data, seeing each other in different contexts, experiencing each other's range. At this level, trust is not necessarily broken by inconsistent behavior. As long as I believe that I can adequately explain or understand your behavior, I am willing to accept it (even if it has created costs for me), forgive you, and move on in the relationship. Consider the example of two friends who agree to meet at a restaurant at 6:00. Person A fails to show up until 6:30, and B is kept waiting. To the degree that their friendship is founded simply on calculus-based trust, B will be angry at the high costs she incurs for being stood up, be upset at A's unreliability, and may be angry enough to terminate the relationship. If they are operating more on knowledge-based trust, however, B will tolerate A's behavior to the degree that she can muster some adequate explanation for B's behavior—"he must have gotten stuck at work," or "he is caught in heavy downtown traffic," or "he is always running behind and that doesn't bother me because I know he'll get here eventually."

## Comparison of Knowledge-Based and Identification-Based Trust

Development of knowledge-based trust requires information about the other, in order to learn as much as possible about the other. The greater the variety of shared experiences, the greater the generated knowledge base and the more an individual's behavior becomes predictable and confirmable. In contrast, identification-based trust (IBT) develops as one not only knows and predicts the other's needs, choices, and preferences but also shares those same needs, choices, and preferences. Increased identification enables us to think like the other, feel like the other, and respond like the other. In cases of complete identification, we may in fact substitute or even lose parts of our own identity (needs, preferences, thoughts, and behavior patterns) as we take on the other's identity and a collective identity develops. While the appropriate metaphor for KBT development is gardening, the most suitable metaphor for IBT is a musical one such as harmonizing. The parties know each other well enough that they begin to see themselves as a collective identity, learning how to use their voices to sing a collective melody that is integrated and complex. Each knows the other's range and pitch, each knows when to lead and follow, each knows how to play off the other to maximize their strengths, compensate for each other's weaknesses, and create a joint product that is much greater than the sum of its parts. The unverbalized, synchronous chemistry of a capella choirs, string quartets, highly skilled interactive work groups, or mature basketball teams in a championship game provide excellent examples of this trust in action.

## Stage-Wise Evolution of Trust

In addition to the differences between CBT and KBT, and between KBT and IBT, our description implies a stage-wise development from one to another. We want to point out, however, that ours is not a normative model. The three stages are very different, but one is not necessarily better than the others. Most people want—and have—relationships in each stage because relationships have different purposes. For example, many business and legal relationships begin and end in CBT.

We now lay out the fundamental premises of the developmental process. A primitive representation of the overlap and evolution of these three stages appears in Figure 5.1. How does trust develop over time in this model? We propose the following steps:

1. Trust evolves and changes. If a relationship goes through its full development into maturation, the movement is from CBT to KBT to IBT. However, not all relationships develop fully; as a result, trust may not develop past the first or second stage.

Figure 5.1. The Stages of Trust Development.

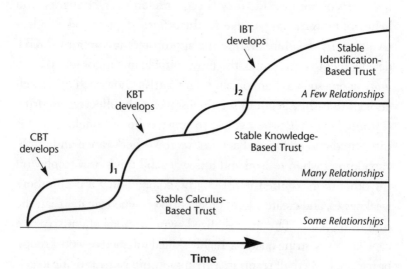

$J_1$ At this juncture, some CBT relationships become KBT relationships.
$J_2$ At this juncture, a few KBT relationships where positive affect is present go on to become IBT relationships.

2. Relationship building begins with the development of calculus-based trust activities. If these activities develop in a manner that confirms the validity of the trust (the other party is consistent, and deterrence is not frequently required), the parties will also begin developing a knowledge base about the other's needs, preferences, and priorities. This information about the other creates the foundation for knowledge-based trust and occurs at point $J_1$ in Figure 5.1. However, the parties may *not* move past calculus-based trust, for many reasons. For example:

- The relationship does not necessitate more than business or arms-length transactions. In other words, the parties are only interested in establishing sufficient trust to effectively transact exchanges of information or goods and services.

- The interdependence between the parties is heavily bounded and regulated. The parties might like to move beyond calculus-based trust, but formal, legal, or organizational arrangements preclude it from happening.

- The parties have already gained enough information about each other to know that any further information gathering (development of KBT) is unnecessary or likely to be unproductive. Models of acquaintance and friendship suggest that the development of these relationships is predicated on identifying similarities and commonalities. If the parties know they have little in common or are repulsed by what they have already learned, it is unlikely that the relationship will develop further.

- The calculus-based trust already in place has been violated one or more times. These violations make one or both parties leery of developing the relationship further.

3.  If the parties move into knowledge-based trust, they engage in the activities previously described. Some significant percentage of relationships move on to this level. In fact, it is possible for some aspects of a relationship to be in CBT while others are in KBT. The movement from knowledge-based trust to identification-based trust occurs in a similar manner and begins at point $J_2$ in Figure 5.1. As the parties come to learn more about each other, they may also begin to internalize the other's needs, preferences, and priorities, eventually coming to see them as their own. Internalization leads to a search for more information, which creates a broader foundation for knowledge-based trust and more dimensions on which the parties may identify with each other. Our discussion thus implies that the stages overlap, in that the development of KBT begins while the parties are primarily at the CBT stage and that the development of IBT begins while the parties may still be primarily at the KBT stage. However, if a relationship moves to KBT, it may also remain there. In KBT, the parties gain information about each other that permits them to know each other well. However, the relationship may not move on to IBT, for the following reasons:

- The parties lack the time or energy to invest beyond the KBT level. Because parties can only sustain a few very strong personal relationships, sheer availability of time and energy may preclude the relationship from going forward.

- The parties may have no desire to identify with each other. Identification implies the development of some affect, moving beyond the cognitive acquisition of information. The parties may not want to develop an attachment: one party doesn't want to "get involved" or the relationship may jeopardize another relationship.

- Developing knowledge about the other may lead one individual to not identify with the other. For example,

if gaining information about a new business partner
leads one to find that the partner has been involved in
many shady business practices, the party may decide
that further relationship development is unwise.

- The information gained about the other may not lead
  to effective understanding of the other or prediction of
  his or her behavior. Either one cannot comprehend the
  other well or knowledge and prediction are consistently
  disconfirmed.

4. The movement from one stage to another may not be smooth
and linear; it may require a "frame change" in the relationship—that
is, a fundamental shift in the dominant perceptual paradigm (Gersick, 1989). In the first case—movement from CBT to KBT—the
frame change is a fundamental shift from a perceptual sensitivity to
*contrasts* (differences) between self and the other to a perceptual sensitivity to *assimilation* (similarities) between self and the other. We
represent this as a transitional slope in Figure 5.1, indicating that
the frame change is not a simple linear increase but requires an
accelerated momentum to move up onto the next plateau. Similarly,
when the parties are working at the KBT level, detection of large
differences between the self and the other, or accumulation of many
small differences, may be sufficient to tip the balance and send the
relationship back "down the chute" to CBT. When one reaches the
KBT level, differences between self and the other are minimized to
the degree that they can be explained by what one has learned about
the other; any suitable explanation for unpredictable behavior will
be seen as adequate, and trust will be sustained. Only when the
other's behavior is sufficiently extreme as to be unexplainable and
unpredictable or destructive of the underlying foundation of CBT
will it threaten the trust between the parties.

A similar frame change occurs in the evolution from KBT to
IBT. In this case, the shift is from simply extending one's knowledge

about the other to a more personal *identification* with the other. To the degree that this shift is mutual, the parties begin to take on each other's identity and also to develop a shared identity that represents their complex collaborative interface. They may agree to take the same name, wear the same clothes or uniforms, represent each other's interests in events that affect their relationship, commit to a joint statement of principles and values, and consult each other on every decision affecting them jointly.

5. What about the further development of the relationship beyond identification-based trust? There are at least two possible submodels to explain these dynamics. The first is submodel A (the less likely). Given the massive complexity of humans, the changing dynamics of their needs, desires, and wants, and stimuli from the external world, the parties simply remain at the third level as each learns more about the other, learns how to understand and predict the other's behavior, and comes to internalize these patterns more into their own actions.

Submodel B is the more likely scenario. There is a cycling back and forth between KBT and IBT. As the parties come to identify with each other, they begin to naturally substitute for each other's actions; they can anticipate the other, know the other's strengths and weaknesses, and begin to compensate for the other. For example, if one is good at bookkeeping while the other is good at cooking, one will keep the books and records while the other prepares the meals. But they also function in a complex, dynamic, and highly stimulating world; their own maturation also leads their interests, experiences, and worlds to change. Because B cooks for A, it does not mean that A has more time to spend in bookkeeping—or wants to spend more time in bookkeeping. Instead, A may decide that he has time to go back to school and get a master's degree, or he may go out and learn to play golf. These activities take A away from B and create new experiences for A; now B must learn more about A's new interest and how to assimilate it into knowledge about A. A may find that he truly enjoys playing golf and spends a great deal of time at this new activity. These changes may be new, unexpected, or even disconfirming to B in her knowledge about A. She may also try learning golf—to understand why A likes it so much and whether she might like it as well. She may decide that she does like it, and the two play a lot of golf together, which forms another dimension on which A and B solidify and broaden their base of both knowledge-based and identification-based trust. In contrast, B may decide she hates golf, but A's time playing golf creates a time for her to pursue a hobby she never had time for—rock climbing. A never knew that B wanted to rock climb and knows he would not like it himself. As the parties now pursue their individual hobbies, they spend less time with each other; the basis for their identification with each other may erode, as each tries to understand why the other person is "so crazy about that stupid hobby." Increased pursuits of very different interests shrink the knowledge and identification bases on which trust is built and sustained.

## What Causes Trust to Decline?

As we have already seen, our question—is trust fragile?—is answered in part by the kind of trust that develops at a particular stage. In common parlance, however, the question usually implies that a violation has occurred. Some types of violation destroy in one stroke the trust that has been built so painstakingly. In other words, trust is fragile because it takes time to build up and no time to destroy.

Before we can fully examine the fragility issue, we need a model to describe what happens when trust is violated. Our model (see Figure 5.2) presents the point of view of the person who experiences the trust violation.

We begin with a relationship in which mutual trust has become established and where the parties have achieved an equilibrium. One of the parties is perceived by the other as acting in such a way that this mutual trust is violated. This creates instability and upsets

Figure 5.2. Dynamics of Trust Violation As Seen by the Violated Person.

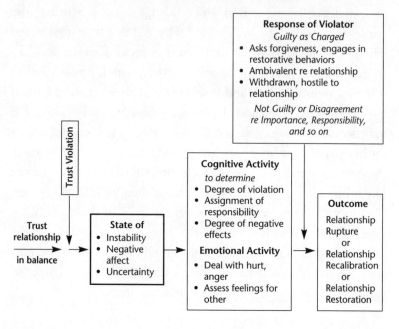

the recipient, who then assesses the situation at a cognitive and emotional level. Cognitively, the individual thinks about how important the situation is, where the responsibility for it lies, and draws the implications for herself and others. Emotionally, she experiences strong feelings of anger, hurt, fear, and frustration; her reactions lead her to reassess how she feels about the other.

While all of these thoughts and feelings are occurring, she is probably still interacting with the party who violated the trust, and who may respond in a number of ways. On the one hand, the violator may accept or deny the other's reactions, while at the same time indicating how he feels about continuing the relationship. This behavior becomes a factor in the response of the recipient, leading her to pursue one of three outcomes: terminating the relationship, renegotiating the relationship and encouraging it to develop on a different basis, or restoring the relationship to its former state.

Although we may use the same words—"my trust was violated"—to describe many different types of situations, we believe that examining the nature of a violation in each stage helps to clarify what leads to a relationship's decline or disruption.

## Violations of Calculus-Based Trust

Hirschman (1984) points out that trust is a peculiar resource, one that is increased rather than depleted through use. At the beginning of relationships, trust is very fragile, for there is no history to rely on. Relationships founded on CBT are one way of dealing with the lack of trust when parties first get together. In these relationships, parties are careful about the degree of risk and build in safeguards to protect themselves. If there is a violation, the relationship can quickly drop down the chute back to zero. CBT relationships may be either short term or long term. The parties stay in them as long as the mutual payoffs are satisfactory and the rewards and sanctions produce consistent behavior. If one party violates the trust, the other is likely either to renegotiate the contract, to better ensure the desired outcomes, or to seek another relationship. In CBT, trust is indeed fragile and easy to destroy.

However, it is also probably true that the parties do not have any long-term expectations for the relationship or do not have any specific agreements to formally bind their trust in legal, contractual form. While they may be disappointed, they will not feel deeply aggrieved if trust is broken. The tone might be, "you win some, you lose some." Hopefully, the parties have not overinvested in the relationship and can stand to lose what they have invested or have also established legal safeguards to protect that investment.

## Violations of Knowledge-Based Trust

In our model of trust development (Figure 5.1), knowledge of the other develops in low-risk situations. Over time, enough information about the other is gathered so that behavior becomes predictable. In KBT, the other is trusted because his or her behavior is predictable, based on prior experiences. Contracts, penalties, and legal arrangements are replaced with a willingness to trust based on more direct knowledge of the other's behavior.

What happens when the other violates the trust? The disconfirmation of expectations is unsettling, not only because the other fails to act as expected but because the failure raises questions about the perceptual capacity of the observer. Here the considerable literature on causal attribution (Ross, 1977) helps us to predict that the behavior will be viewed as situationally determined, rather than personally determined. Trust is violated when the person is perceived as acting freely. When situational factors are perceived to control behavior (and the other can clearly make this attribution) or causal accounts can be made to this end (Bies, 1987, 1989), trust is less likely to be disrupted and no violation may be perceived.

If the violation is one that appears to be the choice of the other, the actor must reorganize his or her knowledge base and perceptions in the face of the unexpected or disconfirming event. If the event is unpredictable based on what the actor knows about the other, the actor may be bewildered: "I don't know you any more." This experience of estrangement is strongly related to a diminished willingness to trust. We would expect an active cognitive and emotional reassessment to occur in an effort to both incorporate this information into the actor's understanding of the other person and to redefine the relationship in light of this event (see Figure 5.2). If the event cannot be dismissed as an aberration, then the actor develops a revised knowledge base and perceptual set of the other. In the same way that initial trust took time to develop, this perceptual and knowledge-based recalibration probably takes some time. A certain tentativeness, characteristic of new relationships, may be reintroduced for a time. If the new perception solidifies, the relationship will restore itself on this new ground. However, it is also possible that the new information may turn out to be so disconfirming of the actor's prior image, or conflict so strongly with the actor's personal values, or cause such personal harm that the sense of not knowing the other will be difficult to overcome. If this is the case, the trust in the relationship may be permanently destabilized.

It is important to point out that if the parties develop a strong

knowledge-based trust, the relationship may be able to sustain challenges to the calculus-based trust that might have been damaging
if KBT had not developed. For example, an elderly gentleman rents
out several rooms in his house to a college student. As a landlord,
the elderly gentleman asks the student to sign a rental agreement
that specifies that if the rent is not paid within ten days of the due
date, a late fee will be assessed. The rental agreement is the formal
document that binds the calculus-based trust. If the elderly gentleman and the student never see each other and know very little
about each other, the landlord might impose the late fee when the
student fails to pay the rent on time. In contrast, if the gentleman
and student get to know one another, if the student does yard work
for free, and if they spend a lot of time talking sports every weekend, the student's failure to pay the rent on time is more likely to
lead to a conversation about the problem—initiated by either one
of them—than the immediate imposition of any late fee.

## Violations of Identification-Based Trust

Finally, in IBT relationships, violations of trust can be major
relationship-transforming events. Violations of trust in IBT involve
more than unpredictability, more than forgetting to bring home the
milk, pick up the dry cleaning, or pay the household bills. Since
trust at this level is based on identification, trust violations challenge the underlying similarities and commonalities. They are
actions that go against common interests or agreements. They tap
into values that underlie the relationship and create a sense of moral
violation. They rend the fabric of the relationship, and like reweav-
ing, the relationship may never be quite the same.

This kind of trust violation can be asymmetrical. It only requires
one person to experience a "moral" violation, a challenge to one's
core values or to the very basis of one's identification with the other.
We propose that achieving the next level of trust can modify reactions to violations at lower levels. Furthermore, we see in this example how trust occurs at several levels at once.

Comparably, relationships characterized by strong identification-based trust may be able to sustain rather strong challenges to both calculus-based and knowledge-based trust. The capacity of the relationship to sustain CBT and KBT disruptions is determined, in part, by factors such as the magnitude of the disconfirmation at these levels and the dynamics of the cognitive and emotional evaluation that goes on after the disconfirming events. We all know people who appear to sustain trust in someone with whom they closely identify—a spouse, a child, or a hero figure—in the face of massive evidence (to others) that the individual's devious or despicable conduct no longer warrants that trust. To an objective observer, the individual cannot be trusted, but that judgment is based on CBT or KBT grounds. To the person with a strong foundation of IBT trust, the same evidence may not be as compelling. However, we should also recognize that for the actor to accept the invalidating information, he or she must be willing to acknowledge that the decision to trust the other was erroneous and ill considered. Such dissonant cognitions may be rejected out of hand as a form of self-preservation; accepting them requires a willingness to see oneself as a fool for trusting, which is a self-image most would prefer to reject if alternative cognitions and interpretations can be found.

The work of Gottman (1993) on long-term voluntary relationships is relevant as we consider trust violations in the IBT stage. Gottman is interested in characteristics of relationships that predict the dissolution of the relationship. In analyses of interactions between married couples, he identifies stable and unstable relationships. The key variable is the way negative affect is managed. In stable relationships, there are different patterns of managing negative affect; however, all stable (balanced) relationships are characterized by a 5:1 ratio of positive to negative affect exchange. Unstable (unbalanced) relationships have a much higher ratio of negative affect.

Gottman's work calls our attention to the absence of discussions of feelings and affect in much of the trust literature. Trust violations are negative events that undoubtedly create both dissonant cognitions and negative feelings. It seems clear that violations of IBT, especially in relationships in which people have strong investments for the long term, can undermine the relationship. This undermining is likely to lead to a significant increase in the volume of negative affect, which will change the balance of affective communication in the relationship. While research has yet to show the explicit causal links between IBT violations, patterns of cognitive and emotional responses, and the eventual dissolution of relationships, it is clear that the elements are interrelated and require further study.

## Summary

We began this chapter with an apparently rather simple theoretical question: is trust fragile? The presumed answer—yes—was based on many years of observing subjects in laboratory-based research on negotiation, conflict, and the development of cooperation. We thought we could affirm our answer by examining the trust literature directly, showing how trust building was "ladder climbing" and trust fragility was a simple but dangerous "chute."

Our investigation of contemporary theory development on trust and relationship development has yielded a much more complex but (we believe) realistic answer to our original question. The answer is, it depends. This answer reflects the following premises:

- Trust is not a unidimensional concept, as many earlier theories suggested. These approaches simply tried to differentiate trust depending on the level of analysis (intrapersonal, interpersonal, or institutional). Instead, within the interpersonal framework, trust changes character and texture as a relationship develops.

- The three different types of trust are discernibly different but are linked and build on each other as a relationship develops.

- Depending on the types and levels of trust operational in any given relationship, certain types of actions may or may not be sufficient to destroy the trust and the relationship. Thus, if trust has only developed to the calculus-based stage, actions that threaten the transactions between the parties may be sufficient to destroy the trust and render the relationship irreparable. However, if trust has developed to the identification-based stage, the same actions may have a negligible impact, one easily repaired through the strong bonds that the parties have built with each other.

In closing, we return to our original question with a significantly enhanced perspective, including an appreciation of the complex nature of trust. The simple answer yes was probably derived from the manner in which negotiation and conflict paradigms have approached the study of trust. Most of these studies used simple economic games, involving low-stakes outcomes, with subjects who had no relationship prior to the study nor any anticipation of one afterwards (see Greenhalgh, in press, and Greenhalgh & Chapman, 1994b, for critiques of this paradigm). As such, the relationship developed between subjects in these games reflected, at best, minimal levels of calculus-based trust, a type of trust that would definitely be fragile in these circumstances. In contrast, when these scenarios have been enacted with parties who had prior knowledge of—and relationship with—their partner, different results appear to occur (see Valley, Neale, & Mannix, in press, for one review). Future research on the development and management of trust in existing relationships will probably lead to new conclusions about trust and its fragility.

## Note

1. For those who are quantitatively inclined, the value of cheating behavior in a calculus-based trust relationship can be quantitatively represented. To do so, first compute

   • The number of different types of interdependence actor has with the other

   • The benefits to actor that are derived from those interdependencies

- The benefits to actor derived from cheating on or breaking those interdependencies

- The costs to actor of getting caught while cheating

- The costs of breaking those interdependencies and having them satisfied elsewhere

In quantitative form, then,

**Value of cheating = [(benefits from cheating) x (probability of cheating successfully)] − [(probability of losing the benefits derived from current interdependencies) x (value of those benefits)]**

## References

Achian, A., & Demsetz, H. (1972). Production, information costs, and economic organization. *American Economic Review, 62*(5), 777–795.

Ainsworth, M.D.S., Blehar, M. C., Waters, E., & Wall, E. (1978). *Patterns of attachment: A psychological study of state development.* Hillsdale, NJ: Erlbaum.

Apfelbaum, E. (1974). On conflicts and bargaining. In L. Berkowitz (Ed.), *Advances in experimental social psychology* (Vol. 7). San Diego: Academic Press.

Arrow, K. (1974). *The limits of organization.* New York: W. W. Norton.

Bazerman, M. (1994). *Judgment in managerial decision making.* New York: Wiley.

Bies, R. J. (1987). The predicament of injustice: The management of moral outrage. In L. L. Cummings & B. M. Staw (Eds.), *Research in organizational behavior* (Vol. 9, pp. 289–319). Greenwich, CT: JAI Press.

Bies, R. J. (1989). Managing conflict before it happens: The role of accounts. In M. A. Rahim (Ed.), *Managing conflict: An interdisciplinary approach* (pp. 83–91). New York: Praeger.

Boon, S. D., & Holmes, J. G. (1991). The dynamics of interpersonal trust: Resolving uncertainty in the face of risk. In R. A. Hinde & J. Groebel (Eds.), *Cooperation and prosocial behavior* (pp. 190–211). Cambridge, England: Cambridge University Press.

Bowlby, J. (1973). *Attachment and loss: Vol. 2. Separation: Anxiety and anger.* London, England: Hogarth Press.

Dasgupta, P. (1988). In D. Gambetta (Ed.), *Trust: Making and breaking cooperative relations* (pp. 47–72). Cambridge, MA: Blackwell.

Deutsch, M. (1949). A theory of cooperation and competition. *Human Relations, 2,* 129–151.

Deutsch, M. (1958). Trust and suspicion. *Journal of Conflict Resolution, 2,* 265–279.

Deutsch, M. (1960). Trust, trustworthiness, and the F-scale. *Journal of Abnormal and Social Psychology, 61,* 138–140.

Deutsch, M. (1973). *The resolution of conflict: Constructive and destructive processes.* New Haven, CT: Yale University Press.

Deutsch, M., & Krauss, R. (1962). Studies of interpersonal bargaining. *Journal of Conflict Resolution, 6,* 52–76.

Duck, S. (Ed.). (1993a). *Individuals in relationships.* Newbury Park, CA: Sage.

Duck, S. (Ed.). (1993b). *Social context and relationships.* Newbury Park, CA: Sage.

Edwards, W. (1954). The theory of decision making. *Psychological Bulletin, 51,* 380–417.

Erikson, E. G. (1963). *Childhood and society.* New York: W. W. Norton.

Erikson, E. G. (1968). *Identity: Youth and crisis.* New York: W. W. Norton.

Fisher, R., Ury, W. L., & Patton, B. M. (1991). *Getting to yes: Negotiating agreement without giving in* (2nd ed.). New York: Penguin.

Flacks, R. (1969). Protest or conform: Some social psychological perspectives on legitimacy. *Journal of Applied Behavioral Science, 5,* 127–150.

Gambetta, D. (1988). *Trust: Making and breaking cooperative relations.* Cambridge, MA: Blackwell.

Gersick, C. (1989). Marking time: Predictable transitions in task groups. *Academy of Management Journal, 32*(2), 274–309.

Gottman, J. M. (1993). The roles of conflict engagement, escalation, and avoidance in marital interaction: A longitudinal view of five types of couples. *Journal of Consulting and Clinical Psychology, 61*(1), 6–15.

Granovetter, M. (1985). Economic action and social structure: The problem of embeddedness. *American Journal of Sociology, 91,* 481–510.

Greenhalgh, L. (in press). Competition in a collaborative context: Toward a new paradigm. In R. Bies, B. H. Sheppard, & R. J. Lewicki (Eds.), *Research on negotiation in organizations* (Vol. 5). Greenwich, CT: JAI Press.

Greenhalgh, L., & Chapman, D. I. (1994a). *The influence of negotiator relationships on the process and outcomes of business transactions.* Unpublished manuscript, Amos Tuck School of Business Administration, Dartmouth College, Hanover, NH.

Greenhalgh, L., & Chapman, D. I. (1994b, March). *Joint decision making: The inseparability of relationships and negotiation.* Paper presented at the Stanford Conference on the Social Context of Negotiation, Stanford Graduate School of Business, Stanford University, Stanford, CA.

Hirschman, A. O. (1984). Against parsimony: Three easy ways of complicating some categories of economic discourse. *American Economic Review, 74,* 88–96.

Holmes, J. G. (1991). Trust and the appraisal process in close relationships. In J. Kingsley (Ed.), *Advances in Personal Relationships, 2,* 57–104.

Hovland, C., Janis, I. L., & Kelley, H. H. (1953). *Communication and persuasion.* New Haven, CT: Yale University Press.

Kahneman, D., Knetsch, J., & Thaler, R. (1986). Fairness as a constant in profit seeking: Entitlements in the market. *The American Economic Review, 76,* 728–741.

Kelley, H. H. (1979). *Personal relationships.* Hillsdale, NJ: Erlbaum.

Kelley, H. H., & Stahelski, A. J. (1970). Social interaction basis of cooperators' and competitors' beliefs about others. *Journal of Personality and Social Psychology, 16,* 190–207.

Kramer, R. M., & Brewer, M. B. (1984). Effects of group identity on resource use in a simulated commons dilemma. *Journal of Personality and Social Psychology, 46,* 1044–1057.

Lewis, J. D., & Weigert, A. (1985). Trust as a social reality. *Social Forces, 63*(4), 967–985.

Lorenz, E. H. (1988). Neither friends nor strangers: Informal networks of subcontracting in French industry. In D. Gambetta (Ed.), *Trust: Making and breaking cooperative relations.* Cambridge, MA: Blackwell.

Neu, D. (1991). Trust, contracting, and the prospectus process. *Accounting, Organization and Society, 16,* 243–256.

Pearce, J. L., Branyiczki, I., & Bakasci, G. A. (1994). *The costs of organizational distrust.* Unpublished manuscript, Graduate School of Management, University of California, Irvine.

Pruitt, D. G. (1981). *Negotiation behavior.* San Diego: Academic Press.

Pruitt, D. G., & Carnevale, P. J. (1993). *Negotiation in social conflict.* Pacific Grove, CA: Brooks/Cole.

Pruitt, D. G., & Kimmel, M. J. (1977). Twenty years of experimental gaming: Critique, synthesis, and suggestions for the future. *Annual Review of Psychology, 28,* 363–392.

Rempel, J. K., Holmes, J. G., & Zanna, M. P. (1985). Trust in close relationships. *Journal of Personality and Social Psychology, 45*(1), 95–112.

Ross, L. (1977). The intuitive psychologist and his shortcomings: Distortions in the attribution process. In L. Berkowitz (Ed.), *Advances in experimental social psychology* (pp. 174–220). San Diego: Academic Press.

Rotter, J. B. (1967). A new scale for the measurement of interpersonal trust. *Journal of Personality, 35,* 651–665.

Rotter, J. B. (1971). Generalized expectancies for interpersonal trust. *American Psychologist, 26*, 443–452.

Sato, K. (1988). Trust and group size in a social dilemma. *Japanese Psychological Research, 30*, 88–93.

Sato, K. (1989). Trust and feedback in a social dilemma. *Japanese Journal of Experimental Social Psychology, 29*, 128–138.

Schlenker, B. R., Helm, B., & Tedeschi, J. T. (1973). The effects of personality and situational variables on behavioral trust. *Journal of Personality and Social Psychology, 25*, 419–427.

Schutz, A. (1967). *A phenomenology of the social world*. Evanston, IL: Northwestern University Press.

Shapiro, D., Sheppard, B. H., & Cheraskin, L. (1992). Business on a handshake. *Negotiation Journal, 8*(4), 365–377.

Shapiro, S. P. (1987). The social control of impersonal trust. *American Journal of Sociology, 93*(3), 623–658.

Sheppard, B. H. (in press). Negotiating in long-term mutually interdependent relationships among relative equals. In R. Bies, B. H. Sheppard, & R. J. Lewicki (Eds.), *Research on negotiation in organizations* (Vol. 5). Greenwich, CT: JAI Press.

Sheppard, B. H., Lewicki, R. J., & Minton, J. (1992). *Organizational justice*. New York: Free Press.

Sherif, M. (1967). *Group conflict and cooperation*. London: Routledge & Kegan Paul.

Tyler, T. (1990). *Why people obey the law: Procedural justice, legitimacy, and compliance*. New Haven, CT: Yale University Press.

Valley, K., Neale, M., & Mannix, B. (in press). Friends, lovers, colleagues, strangers: The effects of relationship on the process and outcome of negotiation. In R. Bies, B. H. Sheppard, & R. J. Lewicki (Eds.), *Research on negotiation in organizations* (Vol. 5). Greenwich, CT: JAI Press.

Williamson, O. E. (1975). *Markets and hierarchies: Analysis and antitrust implications*. New York: Free Press.

Williamson, O. E. (1981). The economics of organization: The transaction cost approach. *American Journal of Sociology, 87*, 548–577.

Worchel, P. (1979). Trust and distrust. In W. G. Austin & S. Worchel (Eds.), *The social psychology of intergroup relations* (pp. 174–187). Belmont, CA: Wadsworth.

Wrightsman, L. S. (1966). Personality and attitudinal correlates of trusting and trustworthy behaviors in a two-person game. *Journal of Personality and Social Psychology, 4*, 328–332.

Wrightsman, L. S. (1972). *Social psychology in the seventies*. Pacific Grove, CA: Brooks/Cole.

Yamagishi, T., & Sato, K. (1986). Motivational bases of the public goods problem. *Journal of Personality and Social Psychology, 50,* 67–73.

Zand, D. (1972). Trust and managerial problem solving. *Administrative Science Quarterly, 17,* 229–239.

Zucker, L. G. (1986). Production of trust: Institutional sources of economic structure, 1840–1920. In B. M. Staw & L. L. Cummings (Eds.), *Research in organizational behavior* (Vol. 8, pp. 53–111). Greenwich, CT: JAI Press.

# 6

· · · · · · · · · · · · · · · · · · · · · · · · · · ·

# Cooperation Within
# a Competitive Context
## Lessons from Worker Cooperatives

### Virginia J. Vanderslice

A significant body of research has demonstrated the beneficial effect of cooperation on productivity, morale, motivation, and effectiveness (Johnson, Maruyama, Johnson, Nelson, & Skon, 1981; Johnson & Johnson, 1982). Yet until recently, workplace cooperation was advocated by relatively few, such as proponents of worker cooperatives (Rothschild-Whitt, 1976, 1979; Adams & Hansen, 1987; Bell, 1988; Blasi, 1988; Jackall & Levin, 1984; Vanderslice, 1988) and worker self-management (Bernstein, 1976; Ellerman, 1975; Gunn, 1984; Vanek, 1975; Whyte & Blasi, 1982). There also had been scattered efforts to develop autonomous work groups in larger companies (Walton, 1975).

Today, the language of cooperation is commonplace in both public and private arenas of the American economy. School districts are restructuring to develop cooperative site-based governance councils. Large corporations are involving workers in cooperative problem-solving groups to improve quality and productivity. Highly participative employee-owned firms such as Springfield Remanufacturing and Reflexite are emerging as serious industry competitors (Case, 1991; Stack, 1992). Cooperation is the conceptual and behavioral basis for current organizational trends such as team-based production, total quality management strategies, many participation and employee involvement initiatives, and new management and leadership paradigms.

Deutsch (1949, p. 20) has conceptualized a cooperative situation "as one in which the goals of the participants are so linked that any participant can gain his goal if, and only if, the others with whom he is linked can attain their goals." Cooperative behavior, then, involves coordination of efforts.

Creating and sustaining cooperation in a work organization, however, is more complicated than establishing interdependent goal structures. Johnson and Johnson (1982) have stated that competitive, cooperative, and individualistic goal structures usually coexist in any group. "What matters is which goal structure dominates group life, not whether any one goal structure is present or absent" (p. 164). Deutsch (1973) also noted that few situations are purely cooperative. To create and sustain effective cooperation, organizations need to understand the factors that threaten its survival as well as the factors that help to promote and sustain it.

In this chapter I examine the dynamics of worker cooperatives in the United States to identify the factors critical to the development and survival of workplace cooperation. Worker cooperatives, interdependently linking members' goals through shared ownership and control, may be the organizational form that most closely meets Deutsch's definition of cooperation. As such, the experience of worker cooperatives may have important implications for organizations that want to promote cooperation but have more narrowly structured goal linkages (for example, the equal distribution of bonuses to individuals on project teams based on the team's success).

## Overview

In the first section of this chapter, I introduce the reader to the key dynamics of cooperation identified by Deutsch. In the second section, data from a selected subset of worker cooperatives are applied to Deutsch's theory of cooperation to delineate the major challenges to cooperation in the American workplace. Based on examples drawn from successful worker cooperatives, a set of factors necessary to sustain effective cooperation in organizations is presented in the third section. The chapter concludes with a brief discussion of the interrelationship among the identified factors affecting cooperation and implications for the future.

The data on which this chapter is based are drawn from a variety of sources. I have studied and provided technical assistance to worker cooperatives and democratically managed organizations—as well as other forms of employee-owned enterprises—for more than twenty years. Some of the examples are drawn from my observations and discussions with members of those organizations over the years. In addition, in-depth interviews were conducted with people from four successful worker cooperatives, three of which have been in existence over ten years. The first is Moosewood, a restaurant in upstate New York that has been collectively owned and operated by its twenty members for nearly twenty years. I describe the structure of Moosewood in much more detail in an earlier paper (Vanderslice, 1988).

The second cooperative is the Center for Community Self-Help, a non-profit organization in Durham, North Carolina, that has provided technical and financial assistance to worker cooperatives for more than ten years. Although technically not a cooperative since no one can own a non-profit organization, the center's nearly fifty employees view it as a cooperative and see themselves as equal members.

The third organization is Cooperative Home Care Associates (CHCA). This enterprise is owned by its more than two hundred workers, who have provided home health care services in New York City for more than ten years. Information about CHCA was supplemented by two documents describing the organization and its history (Dawson & Kreiner, 1993; Surpin & Dawson, 1993).

The fourth worker cooperative is Childspace, a worker-owned and managed child-care organization providing care for infants and preschoolers as well as after-school care for older children. Childspace was established in 1988 and currently employs more than thirty people. Additional information about Childspace was drawn from two articles written by Pitegoff (1993a, 1993b).

I also discuss the Cheeseboard Cooperative in Berkeley, California, relying heavily on an article by Jackall (1984.) The Cheeseboard is a retail store selling cheeses from around the world as well as items such as breads baked on the premises. It had been in existence for more than ten years at the time Jackall's article was written. It is one of the largest cheese stores in its region and at the time employed twenty-two members.

## Deutsch's Theory of Cooperation

Deutsch's theory of cooperation (1949) is built on the central concept that goal interdependence creates a cooperative situation in which people behave supportively of one another. According to Deutsch (1949), when a cooperative situation exists, there are three key dynamics that occur: substitutability, positive cathexis, and inducibility.

### Substitutability

When the actions of each person successfully move other people (whose goals are linked) toward their mutual goal, there is no need for people to repeat each other's actions. Instead, each person can more economically use time and resources by taking different actions that will contribute to moving the group closer to its goal. In this way, cooperative situations encourage specialization, with each person contributing his or her part to move the whole group toward the desired goal (Deutsch, 1949, 1973).

### Positive Cathexis

Deutsch (1949, 1973) reasoned that in a cooperative situation where people's actions support one another, trust and openness among participants results. In such an atmosphere, people develop favorable attitudes toward one another, creating strong friendship ties. This mutual liking helps to sustain the cooperative situation by reinforcing mutually supportive actions even when specific goals change or are frustrated.

### Inducibility

Mutual liking and trust can result in individuals being influenced by one another. It follows that people in a cooperative situation should be able to influence each other more by persuasion than by force. Furthermore, this openness to influence should decrease communication difficulties and create a perception of similarity of attitudes among members (Deutsch, 1949, 1973).

Deutsch (1973) suggested that these same dynamics that are necessary for cooperation also have the potential to cause the deterioration of cooperation. In the next section, evidence from worker cooperatives is examined to determine the extent to which these dynamics have been destructive forces for worker cooperatives. The experience of these cooperatives is also used to delineate other threats to workplace cooperation.

## Threats to Cooperation

To the degree that cooperative dynamics actually undermine cooperation, Deutsch (1973, p. 24) referred to them as "pathologies of cooperation." Along with the positive role each plays in sustaining cooperation, each can also have negative consequences.

### Substitutability

In addition to the efficiencies of time and resources resulting from specialization, Deutsch (1973) theorized that cooperative situations would encourage the development of vested interests. Division of labor would create specialists who would be likely to become more interested in preserving their individual functions than in achieving the overall goals of the cooperative enterprise itself.

This dynamic has been of some concern to cooperatives, particularly as it relates to power. In any organization, cooperative or not, hoarding information or developing and protecting a critical skill is a source of power and influence. Such behaviors create a dependency relationship between the rest of the organization and the individual (Mechanic, 1962). French and Raven (1959) recognized that these behaviors were sources of power based on expertise or control of information.

As opponents of hierarchy, cooperatives in the 1970s and early 1980s typically viewed power equalization as an essential component of their organization (Rothschild-Whitt, 1976, 1979; Deutsch, 1985). Cooperatives were particularly worried about the possibility of power becoming concentrated in a few individuals because of their knowledge or expertise. To minimize expertise-based power discrepancies, many cooperatives instituted job rotation systems (Rothschild-Whitt, 1976). This strategy worked well in low-technology businesses where the skills and knowledge required for different jobs were easy to learn. One Moosewood member commented, "Because we all do everything, no one has a corner on information or opinions in any one area. When it does seem like someone is hoarding particular knowledge, we just confront them."

In businesses where jobs required complex technical skills, however, job rotation has had negative consequences. Members with the most sophisticated skills and knowledge were likely to leave the cooperative organization for other settings where their expertise was more highly valued, both in terms of pay and respect for their hard-earned abilities (Rothschild-Whitt, 1976).

Although worker cooperatives are still concerned about the concentration of power in the hands of a few well-informed individuals, the experience of earlier cooperatives has taught them to balance this concern with the organizational benefits derived from specialization. Accepting the inevitability of differences among people, many cooperatives have developed other strategies to equalize decision-making power, including education, the regular provision of clear and accessible information, and valuing the richness individual perspectives bring to any discussion.

Even if expertise could be eliminated as a potential source of power, it is unlikely that power would be equalized among cooperative members. Moosewood members report that longevity, general experience, high-quality performance, and effort have more often been the sources of individuals' power than has specialized knowledge (Vanderslice, 1988). Jackall (1984) notes that members of the Cheeseboard Cooperative gain power by demonstrating a commitment to the organization. Commitment is seen as a function of how much time and energy an individual gives to the organization.

Finally, having expertise does not necessarily translate into hoarding information. A clear commitment to the concept of cooperation could reasonably be expected to moderate any individual's tendency to fulfill his or her own needs to the detriment of the organization.

The concept of substitutability, then, has raised the issue of expertise-based power dynamics. However, these dynamics seem no more particular to cooperatives than to competitively based organizations, in which it is understood that having a corner on knowledge and information will get you ahead. Overreacting to this potential problem by attempting to eliminate specialization has been costly to some cooperatives. They have lost some of their most talented people and limited their organizational capabilities. Successful cooperatives seem to encourage the development of individual expertise balanced with the sharing of basic information and knowledge necessary to participate effectively in decision making.

## Cathexis

Deutsch (1949, 1973) reasoned that the strong friendship ties resulting from openness and trust in cooperative situations could also result in nepotism and favoritism, which could interfere with task fulfillment and undermine operating rules.

Members of worker cooperatives confirm Deutsch's initial conceptualization of cathexis, since they regularly mention openness, trust, and friendship ties as important elements of their organizations. Personal connections have been an important element in many small worker cooperatives, since many of them draw members from among their friends (Gamson, 1979; Jackall & Crain, 1984; Jackall & Levin, 1984; Rothschild-Whitt, 1979).

On the other hand, neither nepotism nor favoritism are cited as major concerns. Cooperative leaders are careful to avoid any actions that would be viewed as inconsistent with cooperative values of fair treatment. At Childspace, for example, one manager stated, "We are very careful to be sure decisions such as those about cutting people's time are based on a clear set of policies. We need to avoid any perceptions of favoritism."

Strong friendship ties have been the source of other problems for cooperatives that Deutsch did not predict. For example, the sharing of personal viewpoints required by cooperation blurs the traditional separation between personal and work concerns. Jackall (1984) reports that at work Cheeseboard members discuss many interpersonal issues that are not necessarily work related. When conflict occurs in the course of these discussions, interpersonal tensions can disrupt task accomplishment. On the other hand, airing personal difficulties can also result in individuals solving personal problems much more quickly than they would in a traditional work setting. As a result, personal distractions from work can be reduced. One member of Moosewood said, "When I have problems involving my children, I always find support from other members. They even help me out with babysitting."

Other issues related to the strong personal ties of members involve boundaries and norms. Moosewood members have reported that new employees initially may find it difficult to break into the relatively tight friendship circle of long-time members. At Childspace, individuals have found that the close ties that have developed among members have made it difficult to bring in new leadership, as well as to bring in new members. Alternatively, the norm favoring personal connections between members makes it uncomfortable for people who are not interested in becoming close personal friends with other members. These are issues that one rarely has to confront in more traditional work settings.

One other problem that strong personal ties may foster is over-talking issues or decisions in an effort to please everyone and reach a true consensus. Overly long discussions can cause members to become frustrated and disenchanted with cooperation. It is difficult, however, to assess whether this problem results from friendship ties or is the result of undeveloped consensus decision-making skills.

In practice, then, cathexis has been the source of problems for cooperatives, but not the problems that Deutsch originally predicted. The development of strong personal relationships among cooperative members generally has not resulted in nepotism and favoritism, but rather in potentially distracting personal interactions, entry barriers, and overly long decision-making processes. Overall, cooperative members view the openness and trust created by cooperation as much more of an asset than a liability.

## Inducibility

Inducibility, or the readiness to be influenced, is the root of the third pathology of cooperation that Deutsch (1973) predicted. Deutsch reasoned that the willingness to be influenced that grows out of liking might reasonably be expected to result in overconformity. By suppressing differences, this dynamic would have the potential to discourage innovation through a process similar to Janis's concept of groupthink (1972).

Most worker cooperatives are values-based organizations (Rothschild-Whitt, 1979) in which members are expected to adhere to some basic, although often abstract, tenets or principles. These shared beliefs may lead to perceived similarities of attitude. However, dynamics within cooperatives do not support the prediction that members suppress differences of opinion in order to achieve consensus or avoid conflicts. In fact, descriptions of the dynamics in worker cooperatives indicate that overt conflict may be even more common than in more traditional authoritarian organizations, where individuals may be silenced by fear of evaluation or retribution (Jackall, 1983, 1984; Vanderslice, 1988).

A central tenet of cooperative decision-making processes is that each person share his or her opinion or perspective with the group so that the group can benefit from the richness of the diversity that its members bring to the group. The consequence of this principle may be a heightening of differences and public disagreements. On the other hand, people are encouraged to work through their disagreements. Jackall (1984), for example, reported that Cheeseboard members' shared view of the organization as an extended family worked as an integrating mechanism to moderate conflicts that might otherwise have become disruptive.

Sometimes cooperative members don't express their opinions openly. A manager at Childspace noted, "Some newer members tend to be quiet during meetings. They often don't voice their opinions or speak up for quite awhile." However, this manager attributed their silence to a lack of self-confidence, experiences in other work settings where their opinions and ideas were not valued, or lack of experience in being asked to consider issues that in other organizations fall to management. Groupthink was not the issue.

The second destructive dynamic Deutsch predicted in relation to inducibility was that cooperation, by creating norms of agreement, would retard innovation. Providing face value support for this prediction, Moosewood members have described difficulty in getting the group to agree on expansion or diversification (Vanderslice, 1988). However, this problem was not the result of members suppressing conflicting viewpoints. In fact, members had difficulty reaching consensus because they had so many strong and opposing opinions and perspectives.

Regardless of the cause, being slow to change is not necessarily a problem. During their second year in business, members of Childspace decided against an expansion opportunity. They were feeling overwhelmed with the business they already had and were unable to imagine managing even more responsibility. A year later, when the company was more firmly established, an even larger cooperative group did decide to expand the business and bought and renovated a building that became a second child-care site. In retrospect, a manager said, "The group's initial decision not to expand was a good business decision, even though we [the managers] might have made a different decision if we had made the decision ourselves."

## The Central Threat to Cooperation

In his early work on cooperation, Deutsch (1949) noted that cooperation would always coexist with competition. He postulated that a person would behave cooperatively depending on the strength of the pull of alternative paradigms. The experiences of the worker cooperatives reported here indicate that the competitive nature of the United States culture and economy is the central source of threats to sustaining cooperation.

The major institutions that mold the attitudes, behaviors, and values of most Americans teach competition and individualism (Gamson & Levin, 1984; Argyris, 1964). In school, for example, our children are taught skills and values that prepare them for participation in a competitive culture (Bowles & Gintes, 1976; Inkeles & Smith, 1974; Vanek, 1977). These values and behaviors are implicitly accepted by most workers as part of the shared workplace culture. Few of us learn how to be part of a cooperative group, nor do we learn to value outcomes that are tied to group achievement.

When organizations attempt to make cooperation the basis for their operation, they are faced with the task of developing and maintaining a system that runs counter to its cultural context. In fact, cooperatively based organizations in this country, particularly in the late 1970s and early 1980s, were even referred to as "alternative" organizations (Rothschild-Whitt, 1976, 1979).

Worker cooperatives are challenged with the need to generate a common culture and shared set of beliefs among members at the same time they are attempting to meet the demands of the marketplace. Gamson and Levin (1984, p. 220) cited this problem as one of two major reasons that worker cooperatives often are short lived in this country: "The internal requirements for sustaining democratic processes often conflict with the rigors of functioning in a competitive market environment."

In the literature concerned with organizational structure, a similar argument has been made about the relationship between environmental pressures and business structure. In business environments where democratic organizations must interact with enterprises that are more authoritarian in structure, there appears to be a tendency for the democratic organizations to become more hierarchical and less participatory (DiMaggio & Powell, 1983; Pfeffer & Salancik, 1977; Tolbert & Stern, 1991).

## Insulation

The force with which the competitive environment presses against cooperation may be stronger than we generally admit. The strategies and mechanisms developed to address this problem can affect a cooperative organization's success or failure. One obvious strategy for protecting one environment from the influence of an environment with opposing norms and values is to isolate the former from the latter. Deutsch (1985) referred to insulation as the extent to which a cooperative can exist free from the influence of competing paradigms in the broader culture.

In fact, some of the most successful worker cooperatives (that is, those financially viable over time, with continued use of cooperative decision-making processes) have been organizations that have been well insulated from the dominant, noncooperative culture. The most well-known cooperative successes include Mondragon (Gutierrez-Johnson & Whyte, 1977), the Israeli kibbutzim (Rosner, 1982; Whyte & Blasi, 1982), and smaller cooperatively-based communities such as the Oneida Community (Levine & Bunker, 1975). In each of these cases, people have lived and worked together within a system that conscientiously promoted cooperation.

The cooperative work organization has been part of a larger community that includes participants' nonwork lives as well. Deutsch (1985) has contended that in order for people to remain in a cooperative organization, the pull of the organization has to be strong relative to alternatives. Therefore, systems that can better fulfill more of an individual's needs will be better able to retain the commitment of members.

This is not to say that insulation ensures cooperation or democracy. As cults have demonstrated, insulation may, in fact, make it easier for a strong leader to manipulate and control individuals and groups. The point is that insulation makes it much easier to develop and reinforce a set of values, attitudes, and behaviors that differ from those of the predominant culture. Unfortunately, insulation in this culture at this time is very difficult to attain.

In some small American worker cooperatives, the close personal ties of members have created some insulation as individual members provide social and emotional support to one another in a variety of nonwork arenas. Members of both Moosewood and the Cheeseboard have reported socializing together, assisting in the care of each other's children, and providing each other with emotional support (Jackall, 1984; Vanderslice, 1988). However, few worker cooperatives in the United States are part of relatively closed communities that provide worker-owners with services such as banking, health care, education, housing, and so on.

Because they have been unable to sufficiently insulate themselves from the dominant competitive environment, successful worker cooperatives have developed by responding to two related tenets. First, cooperative members need to be realistic about the presses and pulls of the dominant culture as they make structural and policy decisions. Second, substantial resources must be spent developing and maintaining cooperation as the mode of operation, since it is inconsistent with the norms of the dominant culture.

## Key Factors in Sustaining Worker Cooperatives

Observations of the enduring worker cooperatives studied for this chapter indicate there are six interrelated factors that substantially contribute to their continuation. Each factor links back to the two central tenets above. Deutsch (1985) identified four of these factors in an earlier paper: goal interdependence, commitment to cooperative values, education, and networking. Two additional fac-tors—authority and decision-making structures, and strong leader-ship—have emerged from the current analysis as critical. These six factors are important because, together, they address the realities of maintaining cooperation in an inhospitable environment. They provide both the necessary buffer when insulation is unlikely and a practical response to environmental pressures.

### Interdependence

Deutsch (1973) has cited the interdependence of goal attainment, or promotive interdependence, as the defining characteristic of cooperation. The structuring of interdependence is an essential factor in buffering the cooperative situation from its competitive context.

Johnson and Johnson (1982) have suggested that in addition to reward interdependence, task, resource, or role interdependence may also encourage the promotive interdependence necessary for cooperation. However, the central strategy for creating interde-pendence in worker cooperatives is the shared ownership of the organization. When all workers are owners, the success of each indi-vidual is clearly tied to the overall success of the company. With-out this strategy, other sources of interdependence have been insufficient to maintain cooperation.

The legal structure of a cooperative can determine whether an enterprise will remain employee owned, thus preserving the shared economic interest of the employee-owners. Many early worker cooperatives did not adequately protect shared ownership through their legal structure. Ironically, employee ownership often became a victim of its own success. Stock value in successful cooperatives increased so much that when worker-owners left the company, other workers could not afford to purchase their shares at full value. Their only alternative was to sell their shares to outside investors, many of whom were indifferent to notions of cooperation. As nonown-ers, new members did not perceive their interests as interdependent either with those of the worker-owners or with the outside investors. Worker-owned plywood companies were particularly vulnerable to this problem (Gunn, 1984; Zwerdling, 1980).

The destructive force of the dominant culture is more obviously demonstrated by a related structural problem. In some cooperatives, worker-owners have decided not to extend ownership to new hires, creating two classes of workers with conflicting interests rather than interdependent goals (Perry, 1978; Russell, 1985; Zwerdling, 1980). Not surprisingly, the original worker-owners were more interested in improving their own financial situation by gaining a concentra-tion of ownership than they were in the continuation of coopera-tion. This phenomenon has been referred to as worker capitalism (Ellerman, 1975). This problem seems more likely to occur in worker cooperatives that are formed to create or save jobs rather than those formed on the basis of an ideological commitment to cooperation. Having learned this lesson from earlier cooperatives, many cooperatives formed today have legal structures that ensure that all workers—and only workers—are owners, thus perpetuating interdependent goals among members.

## Clarity of the Cooperative Value System

A key factor differentiating successful from unsuccessful cooperatives is how much clarity they have about their cooperative value system and its implementation. Mondragon, the kibbutzim, and religiously-based cooperatives have all been part of larger movements for soli-darity and survival (Gamson & Levin, 1984). In each case, members have had a shared set of "intense experiences and culture on which their democratic values were built" (p. 225).

In contrast, for many worker cooperatives in the United States, cooperation has only been structurally based (defined by stock own-ership and voting rights), rather than values-based. Cooperation has been neither a value rooted in the shared experiences, culture, or beliefs of members nor did it have organizational meaning in terms of values or expectations that defined internal processes or member interactions. Although Rothschild-Whitt (1979) has argued that worker cooperatives are values-based organizations, Gamson and Levin (1984) observed that the shared values that did exist in smaller worker cooperatives often resulted from a rejection of mainstream norms rather than from a shared commitment to a well-defined cooperative ideology. The shared beliefs were mostly comprised of "an abstract acceptance of what is perceived to be their [hierarchy's] opposite: equality, democracy, and freedom of expression" (p. 225).

Without a clear shared agreement about and commitment to a behavioral definition of cooperation, cooperatives have floundered. By confusing cooperation with the necessity to avoid expressions of authority or leadership, along with assumptions that power should be fully equalized among members and refusals to differentially reward or recognize the skills of individual members, worker cooperatives have been unable to function effectively. For example, in cooperatives that avoided expressions of authority, members have been unable or unwilling to put demands on each other or to hold each other accountable, even with regard to behaviors that were destructive (Kreiger, 1979; Case & Taylor, 1979).

Compensation issues exemplify another problem that occurs when cooperation is confused with other ideological issues and when cooperatives ignore the pull of the dominant culture on individuals. Many cooperatives in the 1970s typically paid workers below-market wages (Rothschild-Whitt, 1976, 1979). Workers were expected to trade off compensation for the ideological satisfactions of delivering free or low-cost services to people in need (health clinics, alternative schools), providing better or different products (for example, health foods), or hiring and training people who were unskilled or from low-income backgrounds. Such organizations found that neither the experience of cooperation nor the satisfaction derived from their "good work" was enough to hold members;

members eventually gravitated to jobs they could morally or politically justify while receiving market wages. When an individual has to pay for housing, transportation, food, health care, and education, economic need can outweigh ideology.

A specific example comes from a construction cooperative committed to hiring and training unskilled workers. All worker-owners were paid low wages. The cooperative still made very little profit since it took many more hours to complete a job on the same budget as a company using a skilled workforce. The unintended consequence was that individuals came to this company to get training, then left to take jobs in larger, more traditional construction companies where the wages were far higher (Wessels, personal communication, July 10, 1988). In this case, cooperative members valued higher wages more than whatever degree of empowerment or ideological satisfaction they experienced. As one worker put it, "It is difficult to feel empowered when you're not earning much in a culture that judges value by the size of your paycheck."

In contrast to this example, several of the cooperatives interviewed for this chapter are deeply concerned not only with matching the total compensation packages of more traditional organizations (packages may include health care, child care, housing subsidies, and so on) but also with actually raising the overall compensation for the industry. For both Childspace and Cooperative Home Care Associates, providing decent wages and compensation in industries where people have typically been underpaid is a primary organizational concern. As a result of focused efforts, both cooperatives have been able to provide above-market wages while still fulfilling a commitment to provide jobs and training for relatively unskilled workers.

In each of the successful cooperatives investigated for this chapter, cooperation was a defining organizational characteristic. A strong commitment to clearly defined cooperative values provides an organization with a framework for resolving conflicts and making decisions that support and protect those values. Childspace, for example, from its inception has had a very clear definition of the meaning and implementation of cooperation. Beyond the interdependence created by the organization's legal structure, there is a clear set of expectations about how cooperation will be reflected in the operation of the enterprise. For example, managers are expected to use a participatory style and are evaluated accordingly. People who have been good classroom care givers but who could not interact cooperatively with other staff members have been terminated. Also, cooperative values are taught and reinforced in classrooms.

Similarly, the Center for Community Self-Help is described by one of its managers as being very clear about its core cooperative values and how they define the organization's operating style. Newer members who may not be particularly interested in either cooperation or participating in decision making are required to attend decision-making meetings as part of their jobs. Over time, new members become committed to the same cooperative principles that the core members had firmly established. In this organization, cooperative values have been relied on as a protection against individuals taking too much power. Finally, when rapid growth threatened to remove the majority of employees from decision-making roles, cooperative values were invoked as the defining parameters for developing a matrix structure that maximizes broad-based participation in decision making. The new structure was both efficient for business and maximized participation and cooperation (Schall, personal communication, September 15, 1993).

One reality of existence in the broader U.S. economy is that successful cooperatives have had to integrate their commitment to cooperative values with the economic survival of the business. As the general manager of Women at Work, a cooperatively run painting company in Philadelphia, recently told me, "When I introduce employees to the idea of cooperative interactions and participation in decision making, I always emphasize the ways in which cooperation will have a business payoff. This makes cooperation a compelling business strategy, instead of assuming it is only a moral or stylistic choice" (Brown, personal communication, 1993).

Without combining a moral belief in cooperation with a conviction that cooperation will positively affect the bottom line, it may be difficult to adhere to cooperative principles. Because cooperative behaviors are generally absent from other institutions in the American culture, they usually need more attention and nurturing than do more familiar competitive and individualistic behaviors.

Another challenge that longstanding cooperatives have faced is passing a values commitment from one generation of workers to the next. Many cooperatives have suffered from an inability to maintain the organization's cooperative values as a second or third generation of members takes over (Gillespie, 1981; Russell, 1985; Stern, 1983; Vanderslice, 1986). It is not surprising that most new members join worker cooperatives because of the job, rather than because of a values affinity. When these new members join, they typically have had little exposure to or experience with cooperation. They look to the organization for cues about the company culture, the value system, and appropriate behaviors. Cooperatives that have successfully transferred their value system across generations usually have a well-established cooperative culture and have developed a program through which new members are socialized. A focused program of socialization is necessary to counter the competitive and individualistic norms that people have learned and accepted before they joined the cooperative.

To maintain strong cooperative values, worker cooperatives first need to develop formal behavioral standards and expectations that make abstract principles of cooperation concrete (Gamson & Levin, 1984; Vanek, 1977). Second, members must be held accountable to these standards. Third, these expectations need to be linked to the economic success of the company. Finally, cooperatives must develop strong orientation programs to socialize new members into the value system.

## Strong Leadership

Many cooperatives formed in the 1970s attempted to ensure egalitarianism by opposing the development of strong leadership (Vanderslice, 1988). They confused interdependence with an undifferentiated structure. Without strong leadership, many cooperatives suffered from either covert power struggles or lack of direction.

An organization's leadership is central to establishing and maintaining the organization's culture (Davis, 1984). The leadership role may be even more important in an organization with an internal culture that contrasts with its external environment. Members look to the organization's leadership to understand the particular meaning of cooperation in that setting. Blasi and Whyte (1981) concluded that it is essential for leaders of cooperatives to be able to clearly articulate and justify the values of their organizations.

In most cases where a cooperative organization has been successful over time, there has been a strong leader or leadership core, particularly during the first several years of the organization's existence. Jackall's description (1984, p. 112) of the two Cheeseboard founders is that "they remain the embodiment of the ideals of the group, and, as such, the most important members," even after the collective had been functioning for more than ten years. These founders are "symbols of the group and of its ideals" (p. 112).

Leaders of successful cooperatives share some common characteristics. Effective leaders have industry expertise, business acumen, commitment to a vision of the ideal cooperatively based workplace, and skills to implement and behave consistently with cooperative values. Unfortunately, as many cooperative organizations have discovered, this is not an easy combination to find. To the detriment of organizational stability, many cooperative work organizations have hired and fired a large number of general managers or chief executive officers in their search for someone with the right combination of attributes. When faced with the choice of a leader with one set of strengths or the other, many cooperative organizations have chosen the leader with specific industry knowledge over the leader with a commitment to cooperation. Despite their business or industry expertise, these leaders have rarely been successful if they have an authoritarian operating style. Noncooperative styles have tended to generate internal conflict and resistance that has undermined morale and, consequently, interfered with productivity.

Cooperative Home Care Associates, for example, has experienced two kinds of leaders. One leader had business experience and familiarity with the home health care industry but did not have cooperative experience or commitment. The other had business acumen and both commitment to and experience with cooperation. However, he had only minimal home health care experience. Only the second leader was effective (Dawson & Kreiner, 1993). This experience supports Covey's contention (1990) that organizational leaders' commitment to a clear set of principles—in this case, cooperation—is essential for success. It seems to be the combination of cooperative vision and general business expertise that matters much more than knowledge of or experience in a specific industry sector.

Ironically, the presence of strong successful leaders can create problems for a cooperative by inadvertently generating dependency. Michels (1911) argued that while complex organizations need highly skilled leadership, the presence of such leaders may contribute to the degeneration of democratic decision making. Even when leaders facilitate inclusion, participation, and cooperation, members may still feel dependent on their guidance. The major challenge for leaders of cooperatives is to provide strong leadership for the organization while at the same time encouraging the development of leadership and responsibility throughout the organization. Leaders must provide a clear vision of cooperation as the framework for organizational functioning and yet nurture the development of an evolving organizational vision that is shared by all organizational members. Until such a leader transfers her or his vision and skills to a larger group within the organization, the organization's stability could be seriously jeopardized by the leader's departure.

## Authority and Decision-Making Structure

Participation has often been identified as a dynamic essential to cooperation (Jones, 1979; Lembecke, 1982; Tannenbaum, 1968;

Whyte, 1982). In addition, it has been documented that power differences resulting from differences in status or expertise among members of a cooperative group have resulted in decreased participation by lower-power members (Anderson & Dixon, in press; Mulder, 1971). As discussed earlier, however, attempts to equalize power by minimizing differences in compensation and expertise have had more negative than positive consequences.

Another approach has been to ignore power differences by putting people of different status into cooperative decision-making groups where, theoretically, they all have equal power and authority in making decisions. For example, in some efforts to restructure school governance and localize decision-making power, new governing bodies have been composed of teachers, administrators, parents, and community leaders. These groups have been expected to cooperatively make decisions about education in specific schools. Analyses of the dynamics of these councils indicate that cooperation is affected by dynamics related to people's status outside of the group. Administrators' opinions, for example, carry much more weight than those of low-income parents. Similarly, many teachers are reluctant to publicly disagree with administrators who can fire them (Anderson & Dixon, in press). Bernstein (1976) has suggested that fear of retribution can be mitigated by the creation of an independent judiciary process. This element alone, however, is unlikely to be enough to ensure equalized participation when power differences (beyond reporting authority) are rooted in the external environment.

Successful cooperatives have addressed issues of differential power by accepting the inevitability of differences based on experience, education, and skill and using those differences to enhance cooperation rather than undermine it. The critical factor in this approach is distinguishing when differences in skills, knowledge, and experience are and are not important as the basis for authority.

At Childspace, members have equal power in making ownership-related decisions such as how to use profits, potential expansion, and provision of benefits. In the classrooms, however, the head teachers, who have more knowledge and experience, have final authority, although they are expected to encourage participation from their staff. This model replicates the strategy Carson's Raiders used during World War II. At strategy meetings, all members functioned as equals. During an operation, individuals had specified roles and authority. Ackoff (1981, 1989) uses a similar model in his circular organization, where all managers have policy boards (that only make policy) made up of employees from five different organizational levels.

The structural pattern that has evolved in successful cooperatives is a fairly traditional—but limited—hierarchical management structure that runs the daily business operations. Equal decision-making power is reserved for broad organizational issues such as policy development, allocation of large amounts of company funds, philosophy, and organizational direction. The expected exercise or attribution of authority based on management status is mitigated through ongoing education and sharing of information. Cooperation is also fostered as a behavioral norm about how people are expected to relate to one another and as a management style that favors participation and inclusion. This structure clearly ties cooperative decision making to ownership issues, which are the locus of members' interdependent goals.

## Continuous Education

Education is a major element in all successful cooperative organizations. As Rosen (1987, p. 111) has stated, cooperative organizations need to recognize "the need for continuously recreating the conditions necessary for democracy within the social relations of organizational members." Education is a force that works to counter the influences of the dominant culture that hinder the development and sustenance of alternative ideologies such as cooperation (Friere, 1973).

Education moderates power differences based on knowledge and information. Lipset, Trow, and Coleman (1956) found education to be a critical factor in maintaining union democracy. Education is essential for socializing members in cooperative values and teaching them the skills necessary to behave cooperatively. Through education and experience, members come to learn that cooperative enterprises are significantly different from other organizations to which they have belonged. Education is also one means of developing a stronger and broader leadership core, as well as developing increased job-related skills.

Successful cooperatives provide extensive formal and informal internal education to members in order to develop the knowledge and skills necessary to be confident and effective decision makers as well as to behave cooperatively. More formalized programs usually include education directed at understanding financial information, industry trends, and basic business concepts. Process-oriented programs may focus on developing skills in communication, group problem solving, and group dynamics (Coker & Vanderslice, 1987; Kreiner, 1983; Vanderslice & Leventhal, 1987). Informal education occurs regularly as organization leaders provide adequate background information and fully explain analyses that relate to particular issues under discussion.

Most successful cooperatives also encourage individual development. They may either create internal apprenticeship programs or support external education programs through which interested members can learn job-related skills that will allow them to take on new responsibilities.

### Networking

In his analysis of workplace cooperation, Deutsch (1985) noted that networks provide worker cooperatives the support they cannot expect from the competitive environment in which they exist. Some efforts to create such networks have been successful. For example, the Northeast Ohio Employee Ownership Center has developed a network of more than twenty-five employee-owned companies whose representatives get together several times a year. These networks are not a substitute for insulation, but they have been successful in creating a support system for organizations struggling to implement and maintain cooperation. Through networks, cooperatives have access to technical assistance and forums for discussing common problems and sharing strategies to resolve them.

## Summary

Because worker cooperatives have a legal structure that most closely fits Deutsch's definition of cooperation, I have examined them in this chapter in order to understand what factors pose the greatest threats to cooperation in American organizations and what strategies can be effectively employed to counteract those threats. Deutsch identified many factors that undermine cooperation, including a series of pathologies that arise from the very dynamics that are essential to the cooperative process. The conclusion from my analysis is that the pathologies are much less of a threat to cooperation than another factor: the competitive context within which cooperation must exist in this country. The strength of the competitive and individualistic nature of American culture is reflected in its pull on individuals, even in cooperative settings.

This situation creates two options for worker cooperatives if they are to survive. Either they must be well insulated from the dominant culture or they must develop strategies that provide some insulation at the same time allowing for pragmatic adaptations to the situation. Successful American worker cooperatives have had to follow the latter path.

Without significant insulation, there are six factors that work synergistically to protect cooperatives from the opposing force of the dominant culture, at the same time allowing them to interact with that culture. Careful structuring of interdependent goals is critical. Task and resource interdependence do not seem to be strong enough to ensure ongoing cooperation at the organizational level.

The development of strong commitment to concrete cooperative values is a second essential element for survival. The clarity and strength of this commitment, as well as the skills to carry it out, can be substantially reinforced through two other factors: strong leadership and ongoing educational programs. The internal structuring of authority and decision-making processes needs to reflect cooperative values and to realistically respond to individuals' needs. Finally, networking can provide reinforcement and support for cooperation as well as act as a source of ideas and strategies that help sustain cooperation.

These elements, shared by successful worker cooperatives, have implications for other business organizations in the United States that may wish to function cooperatively. There is no reason to believe that the interrelated strategies and structures developed by worker cooperatives to support cooperation are particular to such organizations. All organizations in the United States exist within the same culture. If anything, more traditional organizations may need to focus even more intently on each of these elements since they are more tightly tied into the dominant culture. Organizations that from their inception have been competitively based may underestimate the power of the dominant competitive cultural forces and find their cooperative efforts unsuccessful if they do not implement a set of deeply integrated changes to support cooperation.

## References

Ackoff, R. L. (1981). *Creating the corporate future*. New York: Wiley.

Ackoff, R. L. (1989). The circular organization: An update. *Executive, 3*(1), 11.

Adams, F., & Hansen, G. (1987). *Putting democracy to work*. Eugene, OR: Hulogosi Communications.

Anderson, G. L., & Dixon, A. (in press). *A socially critical view of the self-managing school*. New York: Falmer Press.

Argyris, C. (1964). *Integrating the individual and the organization*. New York: Wiley.

Bell, D. (1988). *Bringing your employees into the business: An employee ownership handbook for small businesses*. Kent, OH: Kent Popular Press.

Bernstein, P. (1976). *Workplace democratization: Its internal dynamics*. Kent, OH: Kent State University Press.

Blasi, J. (1988). *Employee ownership: Revolution or ripoff?* New York: Ballinger.

Blasi, J., & Whyte, W. (1981). Worker ownership and public policy. *Policy Studies Journal, 10,* 320–337.

Bowles, S., & Gintes, H. (1976). *Schooling in capitalist America.* New York: Basic Books.

Case, J. (1991, January). Collective effort. *Inc.,* pp. 32–43.

Case, J., & Taylor, R. (Eds.). (1979). *Co-ops, communes, and collectives: Experiments in social change in the 1960s and 1970s.* New York: Pantheon.

Coker, C., & Vanderslice, V. J. (1987, Summer). The PACE worker education program. *Worker Co-ops Magazine.*

Covey, S. R. (1990). *Principle-centered leadership.* New York: Summit Books.

Davis, S. (1984). *Managing corporate culture.* New York: Ballinger.

Dawson, S., & Kreiner, S. (1993, January). *Cooperative home care associates: History and lessons.* Paper presented at the Home Care Associates Training Institute.

Deutsch, M. (1949). A theory of cooperation and competition. *Human Relations, 2,* 129–151.

Deutsch, M. (1973). *The resolution of conflict: Constructive and destructive processes.* New Haven, CT: Yale University Press.

Deutsch, M. (1985). *Distributive justice: A social psychological perspective.* New Haven, CT: Yale University Press.

DiMaggio, P., & Powell, W. (1983). The iron cage revisited: Institutional isomorphism and collective rationality in organizational fields. *American Sociological Review, 48,* 147–160.

Ellerman, D. (1975). Capitalism and workers' self-management. In J. Vanek (Ed.), *Self-management* (pp. 145–158). New York: Penguin.

French, J. R. P., Jr., & Raven, B. H. (1959). The bases of social power. In D. Cartwright (Ed.), *Studies in social power* (pp. 150–167). Ann Arbor, MI: Institute for Social Research.

Friere, P. (1973). *Education for critical consciousness.* New York: Continuum.

Gamson, Z. (1979). *Some dilemmas of collective work: The People's Food Cooperative, Ann Arbor, Michigan.* Palo Alto, CA: Center for Economic Studies.

Gamson, Z., & Levin, H. (1984). Obstacles to the survival of democratic workplaces. In R. Jackall & H. Levin (Eds.), *Worker cooperatives in America.* Berkeley: University of California Press.

Gillespie, D. (1981). *Adaptation and the preservation of collectivist democratic organizations.* Paper presented at the American Sociological Association annual meeting, Toronto, Canada.

Gunn, C. (1984). *Worker's self-management in the United States.* Ithaca, NY: Cornell University Press.

Gutierrez-Johnson, A., & Whyte, W. F. (1977). The Mondragon system of worker production cooperatives. *Industrial and Labor Relations Review, 31,* 18–30.

Inkeles, A., & Smith, D. (1974). *Becoming modern.* Cambridge, MA: Harvard University Press.

Jackall, R. (1983). Moral mazes: Bureaucracy and managerial work. *Harvard Business Review, 61,* 118–130.

Jackall, R. (1984). Paradoxes of collective work: A study of the Cheeseboard, Berkeley, California. In R. Jackall & H. Levin (Eds.), *Worker cooperatives in America* (pp. 109–136). Berkeley: University of California Press.

Jackall, R., & Crain, J. (1984). The shape of the small worker cooperative movement. In R. Jackall & H. Levin (Eds.), *Worker cooperatives in America* (pp. 88–108). Berkeley: University of California Press.

Jackall, R., & Levin, H. (Eds.). (1984). *Worker cooperatives in America.* Berkeley: University of California Press.

Janis, I. (1972). *Victims of groupthink.* Boston: Houghton Mifflin.

Johnson, D. W., & Johnson, F. (1982). *Joining together: Group theory and group skills* (2nd ed.). Englewood Cliffs, NJ: Prentice-Hall.

Johnson, D. W., Maruyama, G., Johnson, R. T., Nelson, D., & Skon, L. (1981). Effects of cooperative, competitive, and individualistic goal structures on achievement: A meta-analysis. *Psychological Bulletin, 89,* 47–62.

Jones, D. C. (1979). *Producer cooperatives in the U.S.: An examination and analysis of socioeconomic performance.* Palo Alto, CA: Center for Economic Studies.

Kreiger, S. (1979). *Hip capitalism.* Newbury Park, CA: Sage.

Kreiner, S. (1983). *Design of a worker cooperative education program: The O&O Project as a case study.* Unpublished manuscript, Philadelphia Association of Cooperative Enterprise, Philadelphia.

Lembecke, J. (1982). The workplace democracy movement: A success, but for whom? *Monthly Review, 31,* 52–58.

Levine, M., & Bunker, B. (Eds.). (1975). *Mutual criticism.* Syracuse, NY: Syracuse University Press.

Lipset, S. M., Trow, M., & Coleman, J. (1956). *Union democracy.* New York: Free Press.

Mechanic, D. (1962). Sources of power of lower participants in complex organizations. *Administrative Science Quarterly, 7,* 349–364.

Michels, R. (1911). *Political parties.* New York: Free Press.

Mulder, M. (1971). Power equalization through participation? *Administrative Science Quarterly, 16,* 31–39.

Perry, S. (1978). *San Francisco scavengers: Dirty work and the pride of ownership.* Berkeley: University of California Press.

Pfeffer, J., & Salancik, G. (1977). *External control of organizations*. New York: HarperCollins.

Pitegoff, P. (1993a). Child care enterprise, community development, and work. *Georgetown Law Journal, 81*(1), 1897–1943.

Pitegoff, P. (1993b). Reflections on child care and community development. *Circles: The Buffalo women's journal of law and social policy, 2*, 23–26.

Rosen, M. (1987). Producer cooperatives, education, and the dialectic logic of organization. *Praxis International, 7*(1), 111–124.

Rosner, M. (1982). *Democracy, equality, and change: The kibbutz and social theory*. Darby, PA: Norwood.

Rothschild-Whitt, J. (1976). Problems of democracy. *Working Papers for a New Society, 4*(3), 41–45.

Rothschild-Whitt, J. (1979). The collectivist organization: An alternative to rational-bureaucratic models. *American Sociological Review, 44*, 509–527.

Russell, R. (1985). *Sharing ownership in the workplace*. Ithaca: State University of New York Press.

Stack, J. (1992, June). The great game of business. *Inc.*, pp. 52–62.

Stern, R. (1983). The defense of cooperative values in "alternative" organizations. *Sociologische Gids, 30*, 237–246.

Surpin, R., & Dawson, S. (1993, April). *Quality paraprofessional home health care*. Discussion paper for the United Hospital Fund.

Tannenbaum, A. S. (1968). *Control in organizations*. New York: McGraw-Hill.

Tolbert, P. S., & Stern, R. (1991). Participation and control in law firms. In R. Russell & V. Rus (Eds.), *International handbook of participation in organizations* (Vol. 2, pp. 242–264). Oxford: Oxford University Press.

Vanderslice, V. J. (1986). *Sustaining the cooperative workplace: The effect of generational affiliation on participation and satisfaction*. Unpublished doctoral dissertation, State University of New York, Buffalo.

Vanderslice, V. J. (1988). Separating leadership from leaders: An assessment of the effect of leader and follower roles in organizations. *Human Relations, 41*(9), 677–696.

Vanderslice, V. J., & Leventhal, R. (1987). Employee participation: A game plan for the real world. *Training and Development Journal, 41*(2), 34–35.

Vanek, J. (1975). The worker-managed enterprise as an institution. In J. Vanek (Ed.), *Self-management*. New York: Penguin.

Vanek, J. (1977). Education for the practice of self-management. In Strongforce, Inc., *Democracy in the workplace*. Washington, DC: Strongforce, Inc.

Walton, R. E. (1975). Using social psychology to create a new plant culture. In M. Deutsch & H. Hornstein (Eds.), *Applying social psychology: Implications for research, practice, and training* (pp. 139–156). Hillsdale, N.J.: Erlbaum.

Whyte, W. F. (1982). Restructuring work at Rath Packing. *Employee Ownership*, 1, 4.

Whyte, W., & Blasi, J. (1982). Worker ownership, participation, and control: Toward a theoretical model. *Policy Sciences*, 4, 137–163.

Zwerdling, D. (1980). *Plywood co-ops: Workplace democracy*. New York: Harper-Collins.

# 7

# Social Interdependence
## Cooperative Learning in Education

### David W. Johnson, Roger T. Johnson

Cooperative learning is one of the most important educational innovations of our time. It has permeated all levels of teacher training, from preservice to inservice. Cooperative learning is being used in preschools, elementary and secondary schools, colleges, and adult education programs because of its blend of theory, research, and practice. It is not a strictly American educational phenomenon; it is touted from Finland to New Zealand, from Israel to Japan. What underlies cooperative learning's popularity is that it is based on a well-formulated theory that has been validated by numerous research studies and translated into practical procedures that can be used at any level of education. While this cycle of theory-research-practice is much talked about in the social sciences, there are very few instances in social psychology where it has occurred to the extent it has with cooperative learning.

Four topics are critical in understanding the importance of cooperative learning for education:

1. The theoretical foundation of cooperation (social interdependence theory)
2. Research validating and refining the theory
3. Practical uses of cooperative efforts in education
4. Future prospects of cooperative learning

## Social Interdependence Theory

There are at least three general theoretical perspectives that have guided research on cooperative learning: cognitive developmental, behavioral, and social interdependence.

The *cognitive developmental perspective* is largely based on the theories of Piaget and Vygotsky. Piaget's work begins with the premise that when individuals cooperate, sociocognitive conflict occurs that creates cognitive disequilibrium, which in turn stimulates cognitive development and the ability of individuals to take the perspective of the other. The work of Vygotsky and related theorists is based on the premise that knowledge is social, constructed from cooperative efforts to learn, understand, and solve problems. The *behavioral learning theory perspective* focuses on the impact of group reinforcers and rewards on learning. Skinner focused on group contingencies, Bandura focused on imitation, and Homans—as well as Thibaut and Kelley—focused on the balance of rewards and costs in social exchange among interdependent individuals.

While the cognitive developmental and behavioral orientations have their followings, by far the most important work dealing with cooperation is *social interdependence theory*. Social interdependence exists when individuals share common goals; each individual's outcomes are affected by the actions of the others (Deutsch, 1962; Johnson & Johnson, 1989). Interdependence may be differentiated from social dependence (the outcomes of one person are affected by the actions of a second person, but not vice versa) and social independence (individuals' outcomes are unaffected by each other's actions). There are two types of social interdependence: cooperative and competitive. The absence of social interdependence and dependence results in individualistic efforts. Social interdependence is one of the most fundamental and ubiquitous aspects of being human, affecting all aspects of our lives.

When individuals take action, there are three ways what they do may be related to the actions of others. One's actions may promote the success of others, obstruct the success of others, or not affect the success or failure of others. In other words, individuals may find themselves in one of the following situations (Deutsch, 1949, 1962):

- In a win-lose struggle to see who is best. When a situation is structured competitively, individuals work against each other to achieve a goal that only one or a few can attain. Individuals' goal achievements are negatively correlated; when one person achieves his or her goal, all others with whom he or she is competitively linked fail to achieve their goals.

- Acting individually on their own without interacting with others. When a situation is structured individualistically, individuals work by themselves to accomplish goals unrelated to the goals of others.

- Working together cooperatively to accomplish shared learning goals. When a situation is structured cooperatively, individuals' goal achievements are positively correlated; individuals perceive that they can reach their goals if and only if the others in the group also reach their goals. Thus, individuals seek outcomes that are beneficial to all those with whom they are cooperatively linked.

Theorizing on social interdependence began in the early 1900s, when one of the founders of the Gestalt School of Psychology, Kurt Koffka, proposed that groups were dynamic wholes in which the interdependence among members could vary. One of his colleagues, Kurt Lewin, refined Koffka's notions in the 1920s and 1930s. He believed that the essence of a group is the interdependence among members (created by common goals), which results in the group being a dynamic whole; a change in the state of any member or subgroup changes the state of other elements of the group. Lewin also posited an intrinsic state of tension within group members that motivates movement toward the accomplishment of the desired common goals.

For interdependence to exist, there must be more than one person or entity involved, and the persons or entities must be related so that a change in the state of one causes a change in the state of the others. From the work of Lewin's students and colleagues, such as Ovisankian, Lissner, Mahler, and Lewis, it may be concluded that it is the drive for goal accomplishment that motivates cooperative and competitive behavior.

In the late 1940s, one of Lewin's graduate students, Morton Deutsch, extended Lewin's reasoning about social interdependence and formulated a theory of cooperation and competition (Deutsch, 1949, 1962). Deutsch conceptualized three types of social interdependence: positive, negative, and none. Deutsch's basic premise was that the type of interdependence in a situation determines how individuals interact with each other, which in turn largely determines outcomes. Positive interdependence tends to result in promotive interaction, negative interdependence tends to result in oppositional or contrient interaction, and no interdependence results in an absence of interaction. Depending on whether individuals promote or obstruct each other's goal accomplishments, there is substitutability, cathexis, and inducibility. The relationships between the type of social interdependence and the interaction pattern it elicits is assumed to be bidirectional. Each may cause the other. Deutsch's theory has served as a major conceptual structure for this area of inquiry for the past forty-five years.

Most psychological theories are "soft" in the sense that they lack the cumulative character of scientific knowledge. They tend to be neither corroborated nor refuted. Like General MacArthur, most psychological theories never die but slowly fade away (as people lose interest), without either being widely accepted and built into the larger edifice of well-tested human knowledge or being destroyed by recalcitrant facts and abandoned, perhaps regrettably, as a "nice try."

Deutsch's theory is somewhat of an exception for at least three reasons. First, the theory is well formulated. Second, a considerable body of research has been conducted in the area. Third, social interdependence is important to a wide variety of practitioners. Deutsch's theory, however, has suffered for several reasons:

- The theory was not broadly used to integrate research findings and inspire new research. Much of the research that was conducted was not aimed at directly testing aspects of Deutsch's theory.

- The reviews of existing research were infrequent and did not illuminate what was wrong or inadequate about the theory. Consequently, no serious attempt to disconfirm the theory was mounted.

- The theory was not linked with other theories and integrated into well-tested human knowledge.

- A rival theory of similar magnitude and quality has not been formulated, and the area of inquiry has suffered as a consequence. Although rival theories did exist (for example, formulations by Skinner and Thibaut and Kelley), they were not used to challenge each other but existed side-by-side as parallel theories.

In other words, during the 1950s and 1960s, Deutsch's theory was not refined, enriched, challenged, or crossbred with other theories. There was, however, considerable research being conducted in the area.

## Research on Social Interdependence

The research on social interdependence is notable for the sheer amount of work done, the long history of the work, the wide variety of dependent variables examined, the generalizability and external validity of the work, and the sophistication of the research reviews.

A great deal of research on social interdependence has been conducted over nine decades. Between 1898 and 1989, over 575 experimental and 100 correlational studies were conducted on social interdependence (see Johnson & Johnson, 1989, for a complete listing of these studies). Hundreds of other studies have used social interdependence as the dependent rather than the independent variable. In our own research program at the Cooperative Learning Center at the University of Minnesota over the past twenty-five years we have conducted over 85 studies to refine our understanding of how cooperation works. In terms of sheer quantity of research, social interdependence is one of the most examined aspects of human nature.

A wide variety of dependent variables have been examined in the research on social interdependence. Social interdependence is a generic human phenomenon that affects many different outcomes simultaneously. Researchers have focused on such diverse dependent variables as individual achievement and retention, group and organizational productivity, higher-level reasoning, moral reasoning, achievement motivation, intrinsic motivation, transfer of training and learning, job satisfaction, interpersonal attraction, social support, interpersonal affection and love, attitudes toward diversity, prejudice, self-esteem, personal causation and locus of control, attributions concerning success and failure, psychological health, social competencies, and many others. These numerous outcomes may be subsumed within three broad categories (Johnson & Johnson, 1989): effort to achieve, positive interpersonal relationships, and psychological health.

The research on social interdependence has an external validity and a generalizability rarely found in the social sciences. The more variations in places, people, and procedures the research can withstand and still yield the same findings, the more externally valid the conclusions. The research has been conducted in nine different historical decades. Research subjects have varied as to age, sex, economic class, nationality, and cultural background. A wide variety of research tasks, ways of structuring the types of social interdependence, and measures of the dependent variables have been used. The research has been conducted by many different researchers with markedly different theoretical and practical orientations working in different settings and even in different countries. The diversity of subjects, settings, age levels, and operationalizations of social interdependence and the dependent variables give this work wide generalizability and considerable external validity.

The sophistication of the methodology used to review the research on social interdependence is state-of-the-art. If research is to have impact on theory and practice, it must be summarized and communicated in a complete, objective, impartial, and unbiased way. In an age of information explosion, there is considerable danger that theories will be formulated on small and nonrepresentative samples of available knowledge, thereby resulting in fallacious conclusions that in turn lead to mistaken practices. A quantitative reviewing procedure allows for more definitive and robust conclusions. To establish the current state of knowledge about social interdependence, therefore, we applied the meta-analysis process (Johnson & Johnson, 1989). Meta-analysis is a method of statistically combining the results of a set of independent studies that test the same hypothesis and using inferential statistics to draw conclusions about the overall results of the studies. The essential purpose of meta-analysis is to summarize a set of related research studies so that the size of the effect of the independent variable on the dependent variable is known.

The basic premise of social interdependence theory is that the way interdependence among goals is structured determines how individuals interact, which in turn largely determines outcomes. Research, therefore, has focused on both the interaction patterns found among interdependent individuals and the outcomes resulting from their efforts (see Figure 7.1).

Figure 7.1. Outcomes of Cooperative Efforts.

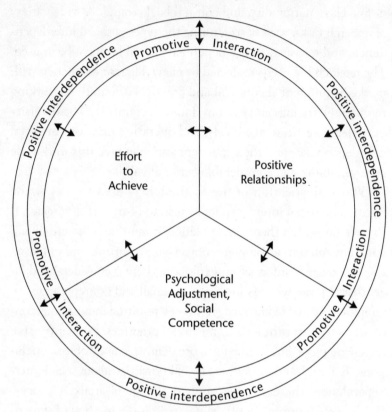

## Interaction Patterns

Positive interdependence creates promotive interaction. Promotive interaction occurs as individuals encourage and facilitate each other's efforts to reach the group's goals (such as maximizing each member's learning). Elsewhere (Johnson & Johnson, 1989) we have shown how group members promote each other's success by:

• Giving and receiving help and assistance (both task related and personal).

• Exchanging resources and information. Group members seek information and other resources from each other, comprehend information accurately and without bias, and make optimal use of the information provided. There are a number of beneficial results from orally explaining, elaborating, and summarizing information and from teaching one's knowledge to others. Explaining and teaching increase the degree to which group members cognitively process and organize information, engage in higher-level reasoning, attain insights, and become personally committed to achieving. Listening critically to the explanations of groupmates provides the opportunity to utilize others' resources.

• Giving and receiving feedback on task work and teamwork behaviors. In cooperative groups, members monitor each other's efforts, give immediate feedback on performance, and, when needed, give each other help and assistance.

• Challenging each other's reasoning. Intellectual controversy promotes curiosity, motivation to learn, reconceptualization of what one knows, higher-quality decision making, greater insight into the problem being considered, and many other important benefits (Johnson & Johnson, 1992).

• Advocating increased efforts to achieve. Encouraging others to achieve increases one's own commitment to do so.

• Mutually influencing each other's reasoning and behavior. Group members actively seek to influence and be influenced by each other. If a member has a better way to complete a task, groupmates usually quickly adopt it.

• Engaging in the interpersonal and small group skills needed for effective teamwork.

• Processing how effectively group members are working together and how the group's effectiveness can be continuously improved.

Negative interdependence typically results in oppositional interaction. Oppositional interaction occurs as individuals discourage and obstruct each other's efforts to achieve. Individuals focus both on increasing their own success and on preventing anyone else from being more successful than they are. No interaction exists when individuals work independently without any interaction or interchange with each other. Individuals focus only on increasing their own success and the efforts of others become irrelevant.

Each of these interaction patterns affects outcomes differently. The outcomes of social interdependence may be organized into three major areas.

### Effort to Achieve

Between 1898 and 1989, researchers conducted over 375 experimental studies on social interdependence and achievement (Johnson & Johnson, 1989). Our meta-analysis of all studies indicates that cooperative learning results in significantly higher achievement and retention than do competitive and individualistic learning (see Table 7.1).

Table 7.1.  Mean Effect Sizes: Impact of Social
Interdependence on Dependent Variables.

|  | Achievement | Interpersonal Attraction | Social Support | Self-Esteem |
|---|---|---|---|---|
| *Total Studies* | | | | |
| Coop versus Comp | 0.67 | 0.67 | 0.62 | 0.58 |
| Coop versus Ind | 0.64 | 0.60 | 0.70 | 0.44 |
| Comp versus Ind | 0.30 | 0.08 | –0.13 | –0.23 |
| *High-Quality Studies* | | | | |
| Coop versus Comp | 0.88 | 0.82 | 0.83 | 0.67 |
| Coop versus Ind | 0.61 | 0.62 | 0.72 | 0.45 |
| Comp versus Ind | 0.07 | 0.27 | –0.13 | –0.25 |
| *Mixed Operations* | | | | |
| Coop versus Comp | 0.40 | 0.46 | 0.45 | 0.33 |
| Coop versus Ind | 0.42 | 0.36 | 0.02 | 0.22 |
| *Pure Operations* | | | | |
| Coop versus Comp | 0.71 | 0.79 | 0.73 | 0.74 |
| Coop versus Ind | 0.65 | 0.66 | 0.77 | 0.51 |

*Note:* Coop = Cooperation, Comp = Competition, Ind = Individualism
*Source:* Johnson and Johnson, 1989. Used by permission.

The more conceptual and complex the task, the more problem solving required, and the more creative the answers need to be, the greater the superiority of cooperative over competitive and individualistic learning. When we examined only the methodologically high-quality studies, the superiority of cooperative over competitive or individualistic efforts was still pronounced.

Some cooperative procedures contained a mixture of cooperative, competitive, and individualistic efforts, while others contained pure cooperation. The original jigsaw procedure (Aronson, 1978), for example, is a combination of resource interdependence and an individualistic reward structure. Teams-Games-Tournaments (DeVries & Edwards, 1974) and Student-Teams-Achievement-Divisions (Slavin, 1986) are mixtures of cooperation and intergroup competition. Team-Assisted-Instruction (Slavin, 1988) is a mixture of individualistic and cooperative learning. When the results of pure and mixed operationalizations of cooperative learning were compared, the pure operationalizations produced higher achievement (Johnson & Johnson, 1989).

Besides higher achievement and greater retention, we have found (Johnson & Johnson, 1989) that cooperation—compared with competitive or individualistic efforts—tends to result in the following:

- Greater willingness to take on difficult tasks and persist, despite difficulties, in working toward goal accomplishment.

- Longer retention of what is learned.

- Increased higher-level reasoning (critical thinking) and meta-cognitive thought. Cooperative efforts promote a greater use of higher-level reasoning strategies and critical thinking than do competitive or individualistic efforts (effect sizes = 0.93 and 0.97 respectively). Even on writing assignments, students working cooperatively show more higher-level thought.

- Better creative thinking (process gain). In cooperative groups, members more frequently generate new ideas, strategies, and solutions than they would on their own.

- Enhanced transfer of learning from one situation to another (group-to-individual transfer). What individuals learn in a group today, they are able to do alone tomorrow.

- More positive attitudes toward the tasks being completed (job satisfaction). Cooperative efforts result in more positive attitudes toward the tasks being completed and greater continuing motivation to complete them. The positive attitudes extend to the work experience and the organization as a whole.

- More time on task. Cooperators spend more time on task than do competitors (effect size = 0.76) or students working individualistically (effect size = 1.17).

Kurt Lewin often stated, "I always found myself unable to think as a single person." Most efforts to achieve are a personal but social process that requires individuals to cooperate and to construct shared understandings and knowledge. Both competitive and individualistic structures, by isolating individuals from each other, tend to depress achievement.

### Positive Interpersonal Relationships

Since 1940, over 180 studies have compared the impact of cooperative, competitive, and individualistic efforts on interpersonal attraction (Johnson & Johnson, 1989). Cooperative efforts, compared with competitive and individualistic experiences, promoted considerably more liking among individuals (see Table 7.1). The effect sizes were higher for high-quality studies and for studies using pure operationalizations of cooperative learning. These positive feelings were found to extend to superiors in the organizational structure. Thus, individuals tend to care more about each other and to be more committed to each other's success and well-being when they work together cooperatively than when they compete to see who is best or work independently from each other.

A major extension of social interdependence theory is social judgment theory, which focuses on relationships among diverse individuals (Johnson & Johnson, 1989). Cooperators tend to like each other not only when they are alike, but also when they are different, for example, in intellectual ability, handicapping conditions, ethnic membership, social class, culture, and gender. Individuals working cooperatively tend to value heterogeneity and diversity more than do individuals working competitively or individualistically. The positive impact of heterogeneity results from a process of acceptance that includes frequent and accurate communication, accurate perspective taking, mutual inducibility (openness to influence), multidimensional views of each other, feelings of psychological acceptance and self-esteem, psychological success, and expectations of rewarding and productive future interaction.

Closely related to the research on the impact of social interdependence on interpersonal relationships is the study of group cohesion (Johnson & F. Johnson, 1994). Generally, the more positive the relationships among group members, the lower the absenteeism, the fewer the members who drop out of the group, and the more likely students will commit effort to achieve educational goals, feel personally responsibility for learning, take on difficult tasks, be motivated to learn, persist in working toward goal achievement, have high morale, be willing to endure pain and frustration on behalf of learning, listen to and be influenced by classmates and teachers, commit to each other's learning and success, and achieve and produce.

In addition, positive peer relationships influence the social and cognitive development of students and such attitudes and behaviors as educational aspirations and staying in school (Johnson & Johnson, 1989). Relationships with peers influence what attitudes and values students adopt: whether students become prosocial or antisocial, learn to see situations from a variety of perspectives,

develop autonomy, have high aspirations for postsecondary education, and learn to cope with adversity and stress.

Besides liking each other, cooperators give and receive considerable social support, in both personal and academic spheres (Johnson & Johnson, 1989). Since the 1940s, over 106 studies comparing
the relative impact of cooperative, competitive, and individualistic
efforts on social support have been conducted. Social support may
be aimed at enhancing another person's success (task-related social
support) or at providing support on a more personal level (personal
social support). Cooperative experience promoted greater task-
oriented and personal social support than did competitive (effect
size = 0.62) or individualistic (effect size = 0.70) experiences. Social
support tends to promote achievement and productivity, physical
health, psychological health, and successful coping with stress and
adversity.

Interpersonal relationships are at the heart of communities.
Learning communities, for example, are based as much on relationships as they are on intellectual discourse. Love of learning and love
of each other are what inspire students (and teachers) to commit
more and more of their energy to their studies. In any classroom,
teachers must reach students' hearts if students are to exert extraordinary efforts to learn. The key to reaching individuals' hearts is
through peer relationships. The more students care about each other
and the more committed they are to each other's success, the harder
each student will work and the more productive students will be.

## Psychological Health

Psychological health is the ability to develop, maintain, and appropriately modify interdependent relationships with others to succeed
in achieving goals (Johnson & Johnson, 1989). To manage social
interdependence, individuals must correctly perceive whether interdependence exists, whether it is positive or negative, be motivated
accordingly, and act in ways consistent with normative expectations for appropriate behavior within the situation. The major
variables related to psychological health studied by researchers

interested in social interdependence are psychological health, self-esteem, perspective-taking ability, social skills, and a variety of related attitudes and values.

A number of studies have been conducted on the relationship between social interdependence and psychological health (Johnson & Johnson, 1989). Working cooperatively with peers and valuing cooperation result in greater psychological health than does competing with peers or working independently. Cooperation is positively related to a number of indices of psychological health, such as emotional maturity, well-adjusted social relations, strong personal identity, ability to cope with adversity, social competencies, and basic trust in and optimism about people. Personal ego strength, self-confidence, independence, and autonomy are all promoted by being involved in cooperative efforts. Individualistic attitudes tend to be related to a number of indices of psychological pathology, such as emotional immaturity, social maladjustment, delinquency, self-alienation, and self-rejection. Competitiveness is related to a mixture of healthy and unhealthy characteristics. Cooperative experiences are not a luxury. They are an absolute necessity for healthy development.

Social interdependence theory has been extended to self-esteem. Self-acceptance is posited to be based on internalizing perceptions that one is known, accepted, and liked as one is; internalizing mutual success; and evaluating oneself favorably in comparison with peers. A process of self-rejection may occur from not wanting to be known, low performance, overgeneralization of self-evaluations, and the disapproval of others. Since the 1950s there have been over eighty studies comparing the relative impact of cooperative, competitive, and individualistic experiences on self-esteem (Johnson & Johnson, 1989). Cooperative experiences promote higher self-esteem than do competitive (effect size = 0.58) or individualistic (effect size = 0.44) experiences. Our research demonstrated that cooperative experiences tend to be related to beliefs that one is intrinsically worthwhile, that others see one in positive ways, that one's attributes compare favorably with those of one's peers, and that one is a capable, competent, and successful person. In cooperative efforts, students realize that they are accurately known, accepted, and liked by one's peers; know that they have contributed to their own, others', and the group's success; and perceive themselves and others in a differentiated and realistic way that allows for multidimensional comparisons based on complementarity of their own and others' abilities. Competitive experiences tend to be related to conditional self-esteem based on whether one wins or loses. Individualistic experiences tend to be related to basic self-rejection.

A number of studies have related cooperative, competitive, and individualistic experiences to perspective-taking ability (the ability to understand how a situation appears to other people) (Johnson & Johnson, 1989). Cooperative experiences tend to increase perspective-taking ability while competitive and individualistic experiences tend to promote egocentrism (being unaware of perspectives other than your own) (effect sizes of 0.61 and 0.44 respectively). Individuals, furthermore, who are part of a cooperative effort learn more social skills and become more socially competent than do persons competing or working individualistically. Finally, it is through cooperative efforts that many of the attitudes and values essential to psychological health (such as self-efficacy) are learned and adopted.

### Everything Affects Everything Else

Deutsch's crude law of social relations (1973) states that the characteristic processes and effects elicited by a given type of social interdependence also tend to elicit that type of social interdependence. Thus, positive interdependence elicits promotive interaction, and promotive interaction tends to elicit positive interdependence. Deutsch's law may also be applied to the three types of outcomes resulting from cooperative experiences.

Each of the outcomes of cooperative efforts (effort to achieve, quality of relationships, and psychological health) influences the others; therefore, they are likely to be found together (Johnson & Johnson, 1989). First, caring and committed friendships come from a sense of mutual accomplishment, mutual pride in joint work, and the bonding that results from joint efforts. The more individuals care about each other, the harder they will work to achieve mutual goals. Second, joint efforts to achieve mutual goals promote higher self-esteem, self-efficacy, personal control, and confidence in one's competencies. The healthier individuals are psychologically, the better able they are to work with others to achieve mutual goals. Third, psychological health is built on the internalization of the caring and respect received from loved ones. Friendships are developmental advantages that promote self-esteem, self-efficacy, and general psychological adjustment. The healthier people are psychologically (that is, free of psychological pathology such as depression, paranoia, anxiety, fear of failure, repressed anger, hopelessness, and meaninglessness), the more caring and committed are their relationships. Since each outcome can induce the others, they are likely to be found together. They are a package, with each outcome a door into all three. Together they induce positive interdependence and promotive interaction.

## Competitive and Individualistic Efforts

The basic social psychological query is, under what conditions are cooperative, competitive, and individualistic efforts effective? Under most conditions, cooperative efforts are more effective than are competitive and individualistic efforts. There is some evidence that on very simple, overlearned, repetitive motor tasks, competition may produce higher achievement than does cooperation (Johnson & Johnson, 1989). It is unclear whether individualistic efforts have any advantage over cooperation.

## Mediating Variables

Cooperation does not work under all conditions. It is only in certain instances that group efforts may be expected to be more productive than individual efforts. Much of our research over the past thirty years has focused on identifying what makes cooperation work. Theoretically, the two essential conditions for cooperation to exist are positive interdependence and promotive interaction (Johnson & Johnson, 1989).

The heart of cooperation is positive interdependence. Group members must believe that they sink or swim together. To be effective, cooperative efforts must be organized around positive goal interdependence, which is established through mutual goals. In order to strengthen positive goal interdependence, joint rewards, divided resources, complementary roles, and a team identity may be used to supplement positive goal interdependence. Without positive interdependence, there is little feeling of responsibility for the group's performance, and interaction has little effect on productivity. The more types of interdependence used in a group, the greater the impact on outcomes. We have also found that resource interdependence without goal interdependence can be counterproductive (Johnson & Johnson, 1989).

An inherent component of positive interdependence is accountability. Group members share responsibility for joint outcomes; therefore, each group member must take personal responsibility for contributing his or her efforts to accomplish the group's goals and for helping other group members do likewise. The stronger the positive interdependence, the greater the personal responsibility felt by group members. The shared responsibility adds the concept of "ought" to members' motivation: one ought to do one's share of the work. Other members ought to contribute their fair share also. Shared responsibility makes it clear that each member will be held accountable for contributing to the group effort by other group members. Individual accountability exists when the performance of each individual member is assessed and the results conveyed to all group members to compare against a standard of performance. It is important that the group knows who needs more assistance, support, and encouragement to complete an assignment. It is also important that group members know they cannot receive a free ride on the work of others.

The second essential element is face-to-face promotive interaction. Once positive interdependence has been established, group members need to interact face-to-face and promote each other's success. Promotive interaction occurs as group members encourage and facilitate each other's efforts to contribute to the accomplishment of the group's goals. Group members give and receive help, exchange resources, give and receive feedback, challenge each other's reasoning, advocate increased efforts to achieve, and mutually influence each other. Promoting each other's success results in group members getting to know each other on a personal as well as professional level.

There are two important aspects of promotive interaction that deserve special attention. The first is social skills. Contributing to the success of a cooperative effort requires that individuals possess interpersonal and small group skills. Placing individuals in a group and telling them to cooperate does not guarantee they will be able to do so effectively; they must be taught the social skills necessary for high-quality collaboration and be motivated to use them. Leadership, decision making, trust building, communication, and conflict management skills must be taught just as purposefully and precisely as task-related skills. Procedures and strategies for teaching students social skills may be found in Johnson (1990, 1993), Johnson and F. Johnson (1994), and Johnson, Johnson, and Holubec (1993).

The second aspect of promotive interaction is group processing. Group processing occurs when members discuss how well they are achieving their goals and maintaining effective working relationships. Cooperative groups need to describe what member actions are helpful and unhelpful and make decisions about what behaviors to continue or change. Such processing enables groups to continuously improve the quality of members' work, facilitates the learning of teamwork skills, ensures that members receive feedback on their participation, and enables groups to focus on group maintenance (Johnson et al., 1993).

The stronger the positive interdependence and sense of personal responsibility, the more intense the promotive interaction—with an emphasis on teamwork skills and group processing—the greater members' efforts to achieve, the more positive the relationships among group members, and the greater members' psychological health.

### Research in Different Cultures

Part of the generalizability of the research on cooperation is due to the diversity of settings in which the research has been conducted. Research on cooperation has been conducted in numerous countries and cultures. In North America (United States, Canada, Mexico), for example, research has been conducted with white, black, Native American, and Hispanic subject populations. In addition, cooperation has been researched in Asia (Japan), Southeast Asia (Australia, New Zealand), the Middle East (Israel), Africa (Nigeria, South Africa), Europe (Greece, Norway, Sweden, Finland, Germany, France, Netherlands, England), and many other countries. Essentially, the findings have been consistent. Higher productivity, more positive relationships, and increased social adjustment and competencies are found in cooperative—as opposed to competitive or individualistic—situations.

The robustness of the research in a wide variety of cultures adds to the validity and generalizability of the theory. The critical research, however, has yet to be conducted. It seems reasonable that different cultures have different definitions of what is cooperative, what is competitive, and where each is appropriate. Within the United States, for example, different Native American tribes have quite different views of cooperation and competition and have different ways of expressing them. Given the hundreds of studies that have established the basic theory of cooperation and competition, there is a need for considerably more research to establish the cultural nuances of how cooperative efforts are conducted.

## Applications in Education

There is a rich and long history of cooperative learning in education. Thousands of years ago, it was written that to understand the Talmud, a student must have a learning partner. As early as the first century, Quintillion argued that students could benefit from teaching one another. The Roman philosopher Seneca advocated cooperative learning through such statements as *qui docet discet* (when you teach, you learn twice). Johann Amos Comenius (1592–1679) believed students would benefit both by teaching and by being taught by other students. In the late 1700s, Joseph Lancaster and Andrew Bell made extensive use of cooperative learning groups in England, and the idea was brought to America when a Lancastrian school was opened in New York City in 1806. Within the common school movement in the United States in the early 1800s, there was a strong emphasis on cooperative learning. In the last three decades of the nineteenth century, Colonel Francis Parker brought to his advocacy of cooperative learning enthusiasm, idealism, practicality, and an intense devotion to freedom, democracy, and individuality in the public schools. Parker's instructional methods of structuring cooperation among students dominated American education through the turn of the century. Following Parker, John Dewey promoted the use of cooperative learning groups as part of his famous project method in instruction (Dewey, 1924). In the late 1930s, however, interpersonal competition began to be emphasized in instruction. Cooperative learning fell into disuse during the 1950s and 1960s as competitive and individualistic learning were seen as new and innovative practices.

The current emphasis on cooperative learning began in the 1960s when social interdependence theory was applied to educational situations (Johnson, 1970; Johnson & Johnson, 1994b). In the mid 1960s, at the University of Minnesota, we began training elementary and secondary teachers, as well as college instructors, in how to use cooperative learning. In the early 1970s, David DeVries and Keith Edwards at Johns Hopkins University (Teams-Games-Tournaments) and Sholmo and Yael Sharan in Israel (group investigation) developed cooperative learning procedures for elementary school students. In the late 1970s, Robert Slavin extended DeVries and Edwards's work by producing modifications of Student-Team-Achievement-Divisions, computer-assisted instruction (Team-

Assisted Instruction), and the jigsaw procedure (Jigsaw II), all for elementary school students. Concurrently, Spencer Kagan (coop-coop, learning structures) and Elizabeth Cohen (groupwork) developed cooperative learning procedures for elementary school students.

The intensive work to develop cooperative learning procedures was based on two different approaches: conceptual and direct. Cooperative learning methods may be classified on a continuum, with conceptual approaches at one end and direct approaches at the other end. Conceptual (or adaptive) approaches (based on nomothetic knowledge) emphasize training teachers in a conceptual understanding of cooperative learning so they can take any lesson with any set of curriculum materials and structure it cooperatively. Direct approaches (based on idiographic knowledge) train teachers how to use a specific activity, lesson, or structure by engaging in a fixed sequence of steps in a lockstep manner. Thus, teachers may be trained to be either instructional engineers or instructional technicians.

In our conceptual approach, educators are trained to use five basic elements of cooperation (positive interdependence, individual accountability, promotive face-to-face interaction, social skills, and group processing) to structure cooperation at two levels: the classroom and the school. In the classroom, cooperative learning should dominate instruction. At the school level, cooperative teams should dominate the work of faculty and staff.

Gaining expertise in using cooperative learning requires an understanding of and ability to implement the elements essential for a cooperative effort. With that understanding, teachers can cooperatively structure any lesson in any subject area with any set of curriculum materials; fine-tune, adapt, and uniquely tailor cooperative learning lessons to their instructional needs, circumstances, subject areas, and students; and diagnose problems some students may have in working together and intervene to increase the effectiveness of the student learning groups. Faculty must carefully structure these basics of cooperation into every lesson. There is a discipline to creating cooperation. The five basic elements underlying effective cooperation are a regimen that, if followed rigorously, will produce the conditions for high effort to achieve, positive relationships, and psychological health.

## Cooperative Learning

There are five ways teachers may use cooperative learning (Johnson et al., 1993). *Formal cooperative learning groups* may last from one class period to the several weeks required to complete a course requirement (such as studying decision making or problem solving, completing a curriculum unit, writing a report, conducting a survey or experiment, reading a chapter or reference book, learning vocabulary, or answering questions at the end of the chapter). Teachers must set objectives, make preinstructional decisions, explain the task and cooperative structure to students, monitor students, intervene to provide task and social skill assistance, evaluate student academic learning, and have students process how well they worked together.

*Informal cooperative learning groups* are temporary, ad hoc groups that last from a few minutes to one class period; they may be used during a lecture, demonstration, or film to focus student attention on the material to be learned; set a mood conducive to learning; help set expectations as to what will be covered in a class session; ensure that students cognitively process the material being taught; and provide closure to an instructional session. *Cooperative base groups* are long-term, heterogeneous cooperative learning groups with stable membership that give the support, help, encouragement, and assistance each member needs to make academic progress (that is, attend class, complete all assignments, learn) and develop cognitively and socially in healthy ways. *Cooperative learning scripts* are standard cooperative procedures for conducting generic, repetitive lessons and managing classroom routines.

Finally, *academic controversy* is the creation of intellectual conflict in a cooperative group by establishing incompatible ideas, information, conclusions, theories, and opinions among members and requiring them to reach an agreement (Johnson & Johnson, 1992). Academic controversy may be created by dividing a formal cooperative learning group of four into two pairs, assigning each pair either the pro or con position on an issue. The pairs then research and prepare their position, present the best case possible, engage in a free-flowing discussion of the issue while trying to persuade their opponents to agree with their position, reverse perspectives by presenting the best case for the opposing position, and drop all advocacy to achieve a synthesis as to the best-reasoned judgment of all four studies on the issue.

When used in combination, these five procedures provide the means for using cooperative learning in most—if not all—instructional situations.

## The Cooperative School

The issue of cooperation among students is part of a larger issue of the organizational structure of schools. The theory and research on social interdependence is as applicable to faculty and staff as it is to students (Johnson & Johnson, 1994a). Teachers, for example, may compete with each other, work individualistically on their own, or work in cooperative teams. The use of cooperation to structure faculty and staff work involves collegial teaching teams, school-based decision making, and faculty meetings.

Just as the heart of the classroom is cooperative learning, the heart of the school is collegial teaching teams (Johnson & Johnson, 1994a). Collegial teaching teams are small cooperative groups in which members work to continuously improve each other's instructional expertise, expertise in using cooperative learning specifically, and success in general. They do so by having members:

1. Provide the help, assistance, support, and encouragement each member needs to gain as high a level of expertise in using cooperative learning procedures as possible

2. Serve as an informal support group for letting off steam and for sharing and discussing problems connected with implementing cooperative learning procedures

3. Serve as a base for teachers experienced in the use of cooperative learning procedures to teach other teachers how to structure and manage lessons cooperatively

4. Create a setting in which camaraderie and shared success occur and are celebrated

Collegial teaching teams are first and foremost safe places where members like to be; where there is support, caring, concern, laughter, camaraderie, and celebration; and where the primary goal of improving each other's competence in using cooperative learning is never obscured. Administrators may also be organized into collegial support groups to increase their administrative expertise and success.

A school-based decision-making program may be created through the use of two types of cooperative teams. First, a task force considers a school problem and proposes a solution to the faculty as a whole. The faculty is then divided into ad hoc decision-making groups and considers whether to accept or modify the proposal. The decisions made by the ad hoc groups are summarized, and the entire faculty then decides on the action to be taken to solve the problem. More specifically, task forces plan and implement solutions to schoolwide issues and problems such as curriculum adoptions and lunchroom behavior. Task forces diagnose a problem, gather data about the causes and extent of the problem, consider a variety of alternative solutions, draw conclusions, and present a recommendation to the faculty as a whole. Ad hoc decision-making groups are used during faculty meetings to involve all staff members in important school decisions. Ad hoc decision-making groups are part of a small group/large group procedure in which staff members listen to a recommendation, are assigned to small groups, meet to consider the recommendation, report their decision to the entire faculty, and then participate with the entire faculty decision on deciding what the course of action should be. The use of these three types of faculty cooperative teams tends to increase teacher productivity, morale, and professional self-esteem.

Faculty meetings represent a microcosm of what administrators think the school should be. If administrators use a competitive or individualistic style in faculty meetings, they have made a powerful statement about the way they want their faculty to teach. The clearest modeling of cooperative procedures in schools may be in faculty meetings and other meetings structured by the school administration. Formal and informal cooperative groups, controversy, cooperative base groups, and repetitive structures can be used in faculty meetings just as they can in the classroom. It is simply a matter of engineering and practice.

## Future Directions

The future of cooperative learning seems bright because of the quality of social interdependence theory, the amount and consistency of the research validating the theory, and the successful application of the theory in classrooms and schools. Given these strengths, it is hard to imagine that cooperative learning would fade away. On the other hand, cooperative learning is much talked about but little used in schools in North America. Perhaps fewer than 10 percent of teachers and professors now use cooperative learning with any frequency or expertise. The promise of cooperative learning lies in continued growth in its strengths and the creation of specific adaptations to current educational issues. A hazard is stagnation in the theorizing, researching, and practical use of cooperative learning.

### Increased Conflict

Growth is based on conflict. There is enough conflict within the area of cooperative learning among theorists, researchers, and practitioners to generate great leaps of growth. First, there is theoretical conflict. The basic assumptions underlying the social interdependence, cognitive developmental, and behavioral learning theories are contradictory and generate different predictions. Social interdependence theory needs to be challenged by the other theories if it is to continue to develop. Theoretical conflicts will potentially keep generating further research for the foreseeable future.

Second, there is ongoing conflict among researchers over the type of studies that need to be conducted. On one side are theory-oriented researchers who argue that studies with high internal validity aimed at validating or disconfirming theory are needed (Johnson & Johnson, 1989). On the other side are evaluators who argue that practical demonstrations of specific cooperative learning strategies and curricula with high external validity are needed (Slavin, 1988).

Third, there is conflict among practitioners as to the effectiveness of different approaches to operationalizing cooperation in classrooms and schools. The direct approach emphasizes highly structured, direct applications of cooperative learning that script both the teachers and students' actions step-by-step. The conceptual approach emphasizes understanding the conceptual structure of cooperation so that teachers may adapt cooperative learning to their specific circumstances. The conflicts among theorists, among researchers, and among practitioners add the promise of growth that will increase the power and relevance of cooperative learning.

## The Future of Social Interdependence Theory

Social interdependence theory needs to be challenged by other theories if it is to continue to develop. The future of social interdependence theory depends on the development of rival theories, the continuation of research to gradually refine and extend the theory, and additional conceptual analysis of social interdependence. As we noted previously, there is considerable potential theoretical conflict between the social interdependence, cognitive developmental, and behavioral learning theories. Presently neither cognitive developmental nor behavioral learning theories are being presented as serious rivals to social interdependence theory. Perhaps the growing interest in cooperation by cognitive psychologists will promote new theorizing. The danger to cooperative learning is the growth of poorly conducted research that does not directly test theory.

Whether or not a rival theory appears, considerable conceptual analysis can be undertaken to refine and advance Deutsch's classic work. Social interdependence is a complex phenomenon, the mediating and dependent variables are complex, and considerable further conceptual analysis needs to be conducted.

## The Future of Research on Social Interdependence

The future of social interdependence research is bright. Much has been done. Much is still left to do. Much will be done. First, the future studies need to include more precise dependent variables that allow comparison with studies in such areas as cognitive psychology and the transfer of learning. Use of these measures will allow the integration of this literature into social interdependence theory. Second, the increasingly widespread use of cooperative learning will result in more and more studies on its successful implementation in schools, colleges, and training programs. Cooperative learning will become a major part of the literature on innovation in education. Third, cooperative procedures will be studied in different settings—such as in units larger than small groups, teams in a wide variety of organizations, and personal and family situations—and will examine such issues as the use of technology in social interdependence and cooperative attempts to solve a wide variety of social problems.

In addition, future studies will increasingly be focused on testing aspects of social interdependence theory. Even though hundreds of studies have been conducted, many of them have not directly tested social interdependence theory and have not clarified the situational conditions limiting and enhancing the effectiveness of cooperative, competitive, and individualistic efforts. We know very little about the conditions under which competitive and individualistic efforts outproduce cooperative ones, create better relationships, and add more to psychological health. What the current evidence indicates is that the conditions under which competitive and individualistic situations promote more positive outcomes are narrow and hard to isolate. Cooperation, compared with competitive and individualistic efforts, promotes the highest levels of a wide variety of outcomes under such a wide variety of conditions that it appears to be a massive main effect. Interaction effects are often more desirable than main effects because interaction effects demonstrate the conditions under which a relationship between the independent and dependent variables does and does not exist. Still, there are reasons why demonstrating a strong main effect is valuable. It is of theoretical interest that the relationship between cooperation and achievement holds across a wide variety of conditions. It is also of practical interest. The consistency and strength of the superiority of cooperation over competitive and individualistic efforts provide security for practitioners. This main effect is dependable.

## The Future of Practical Uses of Social Interdependence Theory

There are a wide variety of cooperative learning procedures and packages promoted for use in classrooms (Johnson et al., 1993). Every year there are more direct strategies and scripts available for teacher use and more curricula packages include cooperative learning as a basic instructional procedure. As cooperative learning has become more popular, the number of people creating direct applications has increased. The number of procedures, techniques, strategies, and scripts available demonstrates the strength of cooperative learning, but there is a danger. The hazard is that cooperative learning may be trivialized by the multitude of techniques that make it easy for teachers to believe that cooperative learning is a set of gimmicks rather than the foundation for all their teaching.

## Specific Adaptations to Current Educational Issues

There are a number of important issues that educators must face in the future. Most such issues result from social forces breaking down positive interdependence in small, personal social systems such as the family, neighborhood, and community, while increasing positive interdependence in large social systems (such as the world). This combination of decreasing positive interdependence at the personal level with increasing positive interdependence at a larger system level places several specific pressures on schools.

## Diversity

There is a long tradition of research on the impact of cooperative, competitive, and individualistic experiences on attitudes toward diverse peers. The research has focused primarily on cross-ethnic and cross-handicap attitudes (see Johnson & Johnson, 1989, for a review of this literature). The diversity of students currently in schools is far greater than it was in the 1960s and 1970s, when the research on ethnic integration and mainstreaming of handicapped children was conducted. Today, it is not all that unusual for a teacher to have students from fifteen different cultures in his or her class. Even common ground such as the same religion is disappearing as immigration increases from Buddhist, Hindu, and Muslim countries. Cooperative learning is a requirement for uniting such diversity and capitalizing on its strengths. Certainly, competitive and individualistic lessons foster disharmony and divisiveness. Adaptations of cooperative learning, however, need to be developed that aim at creating a unifying school culture and promoting an appreciation, respect, and valuing of diversity far beyond anything documented by the current research.

## Technology

The technology of the classroom is rapidly expanding. In the future, educational experiences may be highly influenced by technological teaching aids such as electronic textbooks and networks, distance learning, and multimedia instruction. One of the natural consequences of technology is depersonalization. While the notion of "high-tech, high-touch" is not new, it has yet to be widely implemented in schools. With changing technology in education will come an increasing need for cooperative learning. Cooperative learning will need to be specifically adapted for use with technology.

## Zero Dropout Rate

In today's global economy, everyone—no matter what their job—needs to stay in school their entire career. Not only is graduating from high school a must, students need to be trained and retrained until they retire at age seventy or later. Individuals who drop out of high school—or who stop all education after finishing high school—may have to work for low wages their entire life. While in the 1950s and 1960s, a factory worker could expect to receive higher and higher wages each year, in the 1990s a person who works at McDonalds can expect to earn essentially the same wage forever. The secret for keeping students in school is their relationships with schoolmates and faculty. The more positive and caring a student's relationships, the less likely he or she is to drop out of school. Positive relationships are built through joint cooperative efforts, not through competitive or individualistic experiences.

## Bridging the School-Work Gap

Until recently, the United States economy was based on low-skill, high-wage jobs. These jobs required only strong backs or nimble hands, not knowledge and training. Such jobs are being replaced by jobs requiring considerable academic knowledge, the hands-on skills to do the job, and the ability to work in teams. Even repairing an automobile today (with its microprocessors) requires advanced knowledge of mathematics and physics. One of the advantages of cooperative learning is that it simultaneously increases academic achievement and teaches the interpersonal and small group skills required to be part of a team. Cooperative learning is a bridge between school and work as it educates students in the taskwork and teamwork skills they need to work in the current world economy. This is especially true the more business and industry move to team-based, high-performance organizational structures.

## Values Implicit in Cooperative and Competitive Efforts

There are value systems implicit in cooperative, competitive, and individualistic situations that exist as a hidden curriculum. Competition, for example, focuses students on succeeding at the expense of others and teaches students that there are two types of individuals in the world: winners and losers. Competition is based on negative interdependence, which casts schoolmates as rivals and threats to one's success. Success results from the failures and inadequacies of others. Individualistic efforts emphasize independence and separateness from others. It focuses students on a strict self-centeredness and encourages individuals to ignore the plight of others (who in turn sit back and are indifferent to others' needs). Success results from one's own abilities and efforts only. These value systems are hidden beneath the surface of school life and permeate the social and cognitive development of children, adolescents, and young adults without being delineated, questioned, or challenged.

There is also a value system underlying cooperation. Cooperation emphasizes positive interdependence, which casts schoolmates as friends, colleagues, and collaborators who provide resources to help one succeed. Success results from joint efforts. There is a requirement for being involved, a built-in concern for the common good, a commitment to promoting the success of others, an awareness that one's efforts contribute not only to one's own well-being but to the well-being of others, a responsibility to do one's share of the work (to give an honest day's work for an honest dollar), a mutual identity with others as part of an overall community, a caring for and trust of others, a sense of honor in being trustworthy and a good comrade, a loyalty to one's group and collaborators, a respect for collaborators as individuals regardless of their diversity, an obligation to respond to others' needs with empathy and support, an equality with groupmates regardless of differences (gender, ethnic, cultural, social class, language, ability, and so forth), a sense of fairness in how collaborators are treated, and an obligation to be a good citizen and fulfill one's civic responsibilities.

While cooperation underlies all social systems, it clearly is the underlying theme of democracy in the United States. Cooperation is at the heart of forming a more perfect Union, establishing Justice, ensuring domestic Tranquility, providing for the common defense, promoting the general Welfare, and securing the Blessings of Liberty (capitalization comes from the Constitution of the United States, not from the authors). It is cooperative, not competitive or individualistic, experiences that highlight the self-evident truths that all humans are created equal and are endowed by their Creator with the unalienable rights of Life, Liberty, and the pursuit of Happiness (capitalization comes from the Declaration of Independence, not from the authors). The meaning and importance of these values become apparent in cooperative, not competitive or individualistic, experiences.

There is little discussion of the value systems underlying cooperative, competitive, and individualistic efforts for a number of reasons (for example, the political climate making it risky to do so, the intense emotional conflicts generated by discussions of values, and lack of clear, articulate statements of the values underlying each type of social interdependence). There are problems generated by keeping the value systems implicit, such as an inability to correct misunderstandings and misperceptions. In the future, the values systems underlying cooperative, competitive, and individualistic experiences need to be made explicit so they may be openly discussed, debated, and adopted.

## Creating Learning Communities

There is more to being educated than acquiring academic learning. The school experience is recorded and held in the heart as well as in the head. Cooperative learning will become the teaching method of choice because it addresses important issues beyond academic excellence. These issues include creating a learning community, retaining students, increasing the quality of student life, helping students gain needed interpersonal and small group skills, creating a shared identity among students and faculty, and networking students into caring and supportive relationships. Cooperative learning is especially needed when students are heterogeneous in terms of ethnicity, gender, culture, and achievement. The enemies of school life are isolation, loneliness, anxiety, and failure, which may promote such problems as student suicide, drug abuse, violence, and underachievement. A learning community characterized by personal and academic support is first and foremost created by involving students in cooperative efforts with each other and with faculty.

### Social Development

Changes in the structure of family and community life have left children isolated and without guidance. From being an essential part of the family economic unit (working alongside of parents for forty hours a week or more), many children and adolescents interact with their parents less than one hour a week. From living in small towns where many adults would build relationships with a child, children now live in urban and suburban settings in which neighbors do not know or interact with each other. Children and adolescents suffer more victimizations than do adults, including more conventional crimes (such as assault, robbery, vandalism, theft, rape, homicide), more family violence (such as sibling assault, physical punishment, physical abuse, neglect, psychological maltreatment), and events unique to children (such as family abduction) (Finkelhor & Dziuba-Leatherman, 1994).

Less dramatic—but also important—many homes do not provide children and adolescents with love, support, kindness, sharing, thoughtful conversations, or instructions in manners. With the loss of family and community as sources of support, love, attention, interaction, and socialization, many children and adolescents live in an emotional poverty, without loving and caring relationships, without safety and security, and without guidance.

What is currently missing in educational reform is an emphasis on making schools physically safe places where every student is involved in caring and supportive relationships with peers and faculty and places where students and teachers work together in ways that illuminate the true meaning of decency and civility. Schools underestimate the need for caring, supportive relationships, social skills, and codes of conduct. To make classrooms and schools safe, supportive, and caring places, schools will have to use cooperative (not competitive or individualistic) learning most of the time.

## Psychological Health and Development

In the United States, children, adolescents, and young adults are caught in an epidemic of depression, anxiety, and mental illness (Seligman, 1988). Isolation from peers is especially debilitating for children's psychological health. A few studies have related cooperative, competitive, and individualistic attitudes with various measures of psychological health (see Johnson & Johnson, 1989, for a review of these studies). The more cooperatively oriented a person, the healthier psychologically that person tends to be. The more individualistically oriented the person, the greater the psychological pathology. The more competitive the person, the more complex the mixture of psychological health and illness. The issue of psychological health is of great importance for learning and social and psychological development, but it is largely ignored by educators. In the future, schools may have to confront directly the issue of psychological development and provide the cooperative experiences and social support systems required.

## Achievement

If education becomes a truly rational process, cooperative learning will be the dominant instructional strategy because of its impact on achievement. Sixty percent or more of the student's day should be spent in cooperative learning groups. The amount and consistency of the research ensures the centrality of cooperative learning in instructional procedures.

## Intrinsic Motivation

In the 1860s, Colonel Francis Parker, one of the most persuasive advocates of cooperative learning in the history of the United

States, was fond of saying that there are only two reasons why a student should learn: for the intrinsic joy of increasing his or her competence and for the intrinsic satisfaction of making life better for another person. His rivals spoke of the virtues of extrinsic rewards and incentives. His views still echo today as the debate over intrinsic and extrinsic motivation continues. One of the most interesting aspects of cooperative learning is the intrinsic motivation to achieve that results from positive interdependence and promotive interaction. The use of extrinsic rewards to motivate learning has periodically been attacked as undermining the very processes it is intended to enhance. Kohn (1993) presents a persuasive case that rewards succeed in only one way: obtaining temporary compliance. He concludes that rewards (like punishment) are strikingly ineffective in producing lasting change in attitudes and behavior. Rewards temporarily change what students do without creating any enduring commitment to any value or action. Behavioralists, on the other hand, view rewards and extrinsic motivation as the primary tools of educators. This debate over intrinsic and extrinsic motivation will continue. The more schools try to promote intrinsic motivation in students, the more they will use cooperative learning.

## Effort, Not Ability Orientation

America seems obsessed with the idea that innate ability is the primary determinant of performance. Success in school is viewed as the result of innate ability rather than as the result of effort to learn and succeed (Stevenson & Stigler, 1992). Students are often told not to take math or science courses because they do not have an aptitude for those subjects. Students who are overweight, small, or clumsy are often told not to participate in sports. Students who "have no ear" for music are told not to take choir or band.

The belief that performance is determined primarily by innate ability may reduce the effort students put into their learning. Seventy-one percent of U.S. high school seniors spend one hour or less a night on homework, but 48 percent of them watch three or more hours of television a night. Students take less rigorous classes in order to get higher grades.

The belief that innate ability is the primary determinant of performance seems most congruent with a competitive structure (Johnson & Johnson, 1989). The salient information for determining a subjective probability of success in competition is how one's ability compares with the ability of the other individuals involved (ability focus, self-other comparison). In cooperative situations, the salient information is how hard one and the other group members are going to try and how well members are able to work together effectively (effort focus, self-group comparison). Multiple resources create possibilities that do not exist for any one student. One of the easiest ways to focus students on the relationship between their efforts and their achievement (rather than on their perceptions of their ability) is to ensure students are frequently part of joint efforts to achieve mutual goals.

## Integration of Cognitive and Social Interdependence Processes in Learning

One of the dominant influences in educational psychology during the past twenty years has been cognitive psychology. While cognitive psychologists have primarily been focused on the individual mind, more recent research indicates that critical factors for facilitating learning are requiring students to explain what they are learning to a partner, having the partner monitor this oral recall to detect errors and omissions, and having both elaborate on the information by developing analogies and generating images (for example, Anderson, 1985). O'Donnell and Dansereau (1992) have incorporated such procedures into cooperative learning sequences they label cooperative scripts. The integration of cognitive and social psychological approaches to learning will continue. Cognitive psychologists will include more and more cooperative interaction in their formulations of good teaching practices. It may become increasingly difficult to differentiate between the studies conducted by social interdependence and cognitive theorists.

## Partnership of Cooperation and Conflict

Cooperation and conflict go hand-in-glove; you cannot find one without the other. Cooperation creates conflict, cooperation ends conflict, and cooperation provides the context in which conflicts can be resolved constructively. There are more frequent conflicts and more intense conflicts in cooperative than in competitive or individualistic situations. Frequent and intense conflicts are created by commitment to mutual goals (see the chapter by Raider in this book) and by the relationships among collaborators. The constructive resolution of conflict, furthermore, requires that cooperation be established between adversaries (see Sherif, 1966, on superordinate goals). Deutsch (1973) emphasizes that conflict is resolved more constructively when it occurs in a cooperative context where communication tends to be effective and continual, perceptions of the other party tend to be accurate and constructive, trust tends to exist, and the legitimacy of each other's interests tends to be recognized. Currently, cooperation and conflict are being linked in schools through the establishment of conflict training and peer mediation programs to teach students how to negotiate integrative resolutions to their conflicts of interests (Johnson & Johnson, 1991) and through the use of academic controversy (Johnson & Johnson, 1992).

The increasing violence in our society and schools points toward the need to train every child, adolescent, and young adult in North America (and elsewhere) to resolve conflicts constructively by reaching integrative agreements to their conflicts of interests. The work on integrative negotiations provides a framework for doing so (Pruitt, 1981). As early as the first grade, students may be taught how to negotiate and how to mediate the conflicts of their classmates (Johnson & Johnson, 1994c). A peer mediation program can be established in which every student is taught to negotiate and mediate and takes his or her turn as mediator. In a spiral curriculum, each year the training becomes more complex and detailed until high school graduates have had twelve years of conflict resolution training. While there is considerable discussion of peer mediation programs in schools (especially as a way to reduce violence), there is almost no research demonstrating their effectiveness. This research needs to be expanded considerably in the future.

Conflict is the key for gaining and holding attention in dramatic productions such as plays, movies, and television shows. In a similar way, intellectual conflicts can be used to motivate interest and effort in academic learning. Academic controversy is the creation of intellectual conflict in a cooperative group by establishing incompatible ideas, information, conclusions, theories, and opinions among members and requiring them to reach an agreement (Johnson & Johnson, 1992). Controversy creates intellectual challenges that promote higher-level reasoning, critical thinking, and meta-cognitive thought. The process of controversy consists of the following steps.

1. Students are presented with a problem or decision. They develop an initial conclusion based on categorizing and organizing incomplete information, their limited experiences, and their specific perspective.

2. Students present their conclusion and its rationale to others, thereby engaging in cognitive rehearsal, deepening their understanding of their position, and discovering higher-level reasoning strategies.

3. Students are confronted by other people with different conclusions based on other students' information, experiences, and perspectives.

4. Students become uncertain as to the correctness of their view. A state of conceptual conflict or disequilibrium is aroused.

5. Uncertainty, conceptual conflict, and disequilibrium motivate an active search for more information, new experiences, and a

more adequate cognitive perspective and reasoning process in hopes of resolving the uncertainty. Divergent attention and thought are stimulated.

6. By adapting their cognitive perspective and reasoning through understanding and accommodating the perspective and reasoning of others, students derive a new, reconceptualized, and reorganized conclusion. Novel solutions and decisions are detected that are, on balance, qualitatively better.

The research on the academic use of conflict provides a bridge between social interdependence theory and Piaget's cognitive development theory. It is one of the most promising extensions of cooperative learning and needs to be continued and expanded.

### Teaching for Global Interdependence

To be citizens in a global society, children, adolescents, and young adults need to learn how cooperative systems function and the competencies required to work cooperatively with diverse others (especially the ability to resolve conflicts constructively). Positive interdependence creates both support and vulnerability. Nowhere is that easier to see than on the global level. Individuals, companies, communities, and countries are technologically, economically, ecologically, and politically interdependent. The solution to most problems cannot be achieved by one individual or country alone. The major problems faced by individuals (for example, contamination of the environment, warming of the atmosphere, world hunger, international terrorism, nuclear war) are increasingly ones that cannot be solved by actions taken only at the national level.

There are no longer clear lines between domestic and international problems. The international affairs of one country are the internal affairs of other nations, and vice versa. And when nations and organizations work together to solve mutual or global problems, conflict results. Nations disagree about the nature and cause of the problems, have differing values and goals related to outcomes and means, and disagree on how much each should contribute to the problem-solving efforts. How constructively such conflicts are resolved becomes the central issue for how well positive interdependence is maintained and enhanced. As a result of the rapid increase in global interdependence, schools need to teach all students how to establish cooperation among disparate and diverse individuals with different perspectives and interests and how to resolve the resulting conflicts constructively.

## Barriers to Implementing Cooperative Learning

There are many barriers to change in schools. Three interrelated barriers are the organizational structure of the school, the lack of school districts' commitment to ongoing teacher training, and the lack of teacher commitment to improving instruction and the quality of student life in the school.

The loosely coupled, mass production organizational structure is a formidable opponent to any change in instructional practices, including cooperative learning (Johnson & Johnson, 1994a). Teachers are isolated from each other, function independently, work to achieve vague and ambiguous goals, and are not accountable for being productive or for improving their professional competencies. Until schools change to a team-based, high-performance organizational structure that creates a learning community that nourishes cooperative learning, the status quo of competitive and individualistic learning will be difficult to change.

Very few school districts implement effective training programs for their teachers. A major danger to the long-term use of cooperative learning is that many faculty may implement cooperative learning poorly—on the basis of inadequate training—and become disillusioned. Cooperative learning is a complex instructional procedure that takes considerable time to master. Half-day or even full-day faculty retreats in which entertaining consultants present broad overviews of cooperative learning do not make up a training program. To be effective, staff development on cooperative learning must focus on four factors: (1) initial mastery of cooperative learning procedures during the training sessions, (2) retention of what is learned after the learning session ends, (3) transfer of what is learned in the sessions to the classroom, and (4) long-term maintenance of the learned procedures for years afterwards (Johnson & Johnson, 1994c). To achieve transfer and long-term maintenance, training programs must emphasize:

- Conceptual understanding of the nature of cooperative learning and the basic elements that make it work (rather than an emphasis on preplanned lessons and lockstep procedures)

- Distributed rather than massed training sessions

- Overlearning of cooperative learning procedures (as opposed to broad overviews)

- Actual use of cooperative learning procedures (as opposed to lecturing, describing, and modeling)

- Challenging applications of the cooperative procedures in a variety of contexts and conditions (as opposed to oversimplifying cooperative learning procedures)

Because of the loosely coupled nature of schools and the lack of long-term implementation programs, teachers primarily have to be changed one at a time. Teachers are motivated to change by the conflict between the status quo and the vision of how they want to teach. Creative tension comes from seeing clearly the advantages of cooperative learning and the current reality of competitive and individualistic learning. Anything that clouds the advantages of cooperative learning or that justifies current instructional practices is a barrier to adopting cooperative learning. Without a great deal of personal commitment to good teaching, teachers can be trapped in the status quo (keep doing what you are currently doing). The lure of the status quo is based on at least five factors. The known and familiar provides security. Maintaining the status quo provides freedom from anxiety about lack of competence and failure. Maintaining the status quo avoids short-term failure; to avoid the possibility of failing in attempts to implement a new instructional strategy, many teachers follow the rule of the status quo: *In doubt? Do what you did yesterday. If it is not working, do it twice as hard, twice as fast, and twice as carefully!* Maintaining the status quo provides stability to a teacher's professional identity (changing one's professional practices creates changes in one's professional identity, thereby jeopardizing the security of being what one now is). Finally, maintaining the status quo is easy, as it minimizes the amount of energy and effort required to do one's job.

Cooperative learning is at the heart of a change in teaching paradigms that emphasizes active rather than passive learning (Johnson, Johnson, & Smith, 1991). Ideally, the majority of any class period should be spent in cooperative learning activities that integrate formal and informal cooperative groups, cooperative scripts, academic controversy, and cooperative base groups. But if teachers stay trapped by the lure of the status quo, cooperative learning will be sparsely used as a minor modification of what teachers already do rather than as the dominant instructional method.

Cooperative learning will be adopted much faster and more effectively when schools change to a team-based, high-performance organizational structure, when districts build long-term staff development into the daily pattern of teachers' lives, and when the pride and satisfaction from continuous improvement outweigh the attraction of the status quo.

## Summary

Cooperative learning is one of the best examples in social science of the cycle of theory to research to application to revised theory, new research, and revised practice. Given the quality of the theory, the amount and consistency of the research, and the history of successful use of cooperative learning, whenever the question "What works?" is asked, the first answer is probably cooperative learning. And the answer will get more and more certain in the next few years. Cooperative learning's fundamental grounding in theory and research and its variety of applications ensure that it will increase in importance as an instructional procedure. In addition, social interdependence theory has wide applicability to business and industry, psychotherapy, family life, churches, and all other types of organized efforts.

There is a rich history of theorizing, research, and practice on cooperative efforts. At least three general theoretical perspectives have been proposed: social interdependence, cognitive developmental, and behavioral. Of the three, social interdependence theory is by far the most productive, strategic, powerful, and profound. The research is voluminous. From 1898 to 1989 over 575 experimental and 100 correlational studies were conducted. From these studies it is evident that cooperation, in comparison with competitive and individualistic efforts, promotes higher achievement (as well as retention, higher-level reasoning, creative generation of new ideas, and transfer of learning), more positive and supportive interpersonal relationships (even among heterogeneous individuals), and greater psychological health, social competencies, and self-esteem.

We know more about cooperative learning than we do about lecturing, age grouping, departmentalization, when children should start to read, or the fifty-minute period. We know more about cooperative learning than we do about almost any other aspect of education. What the research indicates is that cooperative learning can be used with some confidence at every grade level, in every subject area, and with any task. The importance of cooperation, furthermore, is seen at the faculty level as well as at the student level. The organizational structure of schools needs to be transformed from a mass production, competitive structure to a team-based, high-performance, cooperative structure. Social interdependence theory is at the heart of such a change.

With the recognition of the effectiveness of cooperative learning, numerous operationalizations of cooperative instructional procedures have occurred. These procedures vary, from conceptual frameworks that empower teachers to implement cooperation in any instructional activity, to direct, lockstep procedures that are easy to learn and use. While cooperative learning is now talked about in every school, however, its use is far less widespread than current educational rhetoric would indicate. Gaining expertise in using cooperative learning is a complex process that takes years of training. Most teachers are not engaging in the effort required to master cooperative learning.

In the future, a number of issues will put additional pressure on schools to adopt cooperative learning, such as increasing diversity, increasing technology, the need to lower the dropout rate, bridging the school-work gap, the need to teach values, the need to attend to the social and psychological development of students, the increased focus on student effort as well as cognitive aspects of learning, the need to address violence and conflict in schools, and pressures to educate students to work in a global economy. To address each of these issues effectively, cooperative learning must be used.

Cooperative learning is based on a profound and strategic theory, and there is substantial research validating its effectiveness. Because of this, there probably will never be a time in the future when cooperative learning is not used in educational programs. Cooperative learning is here to stay.

## References

Anderson, J. (1985). *Cognitive psychology and its implications*. New York: W. H. Freeman.

Aronson, E. (1978). *The jigsaw classroom*. Newbury Park, CA: Sage.

Deutsch, M. (1949). A theory of cooperation and competition. *Human Relations*, 2, 129–151.

Deutsch, M. (1962). Cooperation and trust: Some theoretical notes. In M. R. Jones (Ed.), *Nebraska symposium on motivation* (pp. 275–319). Lincoln: University of Nebraska Press.

Deutsch, M. (1973). *The resolution of conflict.* New Haven, CT: Yale University Press.

DeVries, D., & Edwards, K. (1974). Student teams and learning games: Their effects on cross-race and cross-sex interaction. *Journal of Educational Psychology, 66,* 741–749.

Finkelhor, D., & Dziuba-Leatherman, J. (1994). Victimization of children. *American Psychologist, 49,* 173–183.

Johnson, D. W. (1970). *Social psychology of education.* Troy, MO: Holt, Rinehart & Winston.

Johnson, D. W. (1990). *Human relations and your career* (3rd ed.). Englewood Cliffs, NJ: Prentice-Hall.

Johnson, D. W. (1993). *Reaching out: Interpersonal effectiveness and self-actualization* (5th ed.). Englewood Cliffs, NJ: Prentice-Hall.

Johnson, D. W., & Johnson, F. (1994). *Joining together: Group theory and group skills* (5th ed.). Englewood Cliffs, NJ: Prentice-Hall.

Johnson, D. W., & Johnson, R. T. (1989). *Cooperation and competition: Theory and research.* Edina, MN: Interaction.

Johnson, D. W., & Johnson, R. T. (1991). *Teaching students to be peacemakers.* Edina, MN: Interaction.

Johnson, D. W., & Johnson, R. T. (1992). *Creative controversy: Intellectual challenge in the classroom* (2nd ed.). Edina, MN: Interaction.

Johnson, D. W., & Johnson, R. T. (1994a). *Leading the cooperative school* (2nd ed.). Edina, MN: Interaction.

Johnson, D. W., & Johnson, R. T. (1994b). *Learning together and alone: Cooperative, competitive, and individualistic learning* (4th ed.). Englewood Cliffs, NJ: Prentice-Hall.

Johnson, D. W., & Johnson, R. T. (1994c). Professional development in cooperative learning: Short-term popularity versus long-term effectiveness. *Cooperative Learning, 14,* 52–54.

Johnson, D. W., & Johnson, R. T. (1994d, July). *Teaching students to be peacemakers: Results of five years of research.* Paper presented at the National Association for Mediation in Education Convention, Amherst, MA.

Johnson, D. W., Johnson, R. T., & Holubec, E. (1993). *Circles of learning: Cooperation in the classroom* (3rd ed.). Edina, MN: Interaction.

Johnson, D. W., Johnson, R. T., & Smith, K. (1991). *Active learning: Cooperation in the college classroom.* Edina, MN: Interaction.

Kohn, A. (1993). *Punished by rewards*. Boston: Houghton Mifflin.

O'Donnell, A., & Dansereau, D. (1992). Scripted cooperation in student dyads: A method for analyzing and enhancing academic learning and performance. In R. Hertz-Lazarowitz & N. Miller (Eds.), *Interaction in cooperative groups* (pp. 174–199). New York: Cambridge University Press.

Pruitt, D. (1981). *Negotiation behavior*. San Diego: Academic Press.

Seligman, M. (1988). Boomer blues. *Psychology Today, 22,* 50–55.

Sherif, M. (1966). *In common predicament*. Boston: Houghton Mifflin.

Slavin, R. (1986). *Using student team learning* (3rd ed.). Baltimore, MD: Johns Hopkins University Press.

Slavin, R. (1988, November). Cooperative learning and student achievement. *Educational Leadership*, pp. 7–13.

Stevenson, H., & Stigler, J. (1992). *The learning gap*. New York: Summit.

# Commentary

· · · · · · · · · · · · · · · · · · · · · · · · · · · · · ·

# Cooperation

## The Fragile State

Morton Deutsch

I am delighted by the fine chapters in this part. By nature, I tend to be optimistic, and each chapter challenges pessimistic views I have expressed in some of my writings about the fragility of trust, cooperation, and participative democracy. My most pessimistic statements occur in *Distributive Justice* (1985, p. 244):

> After reviewing the literature on worker participation, worker ownership, worker cooperatives, the kibbutzim, communes, and the like, I am convinced that paradise is not to be found on this earth. I am further persuaded that even the nearest thing to common visions of an earthly utopia—a small, well functioning, worldly, cooperative, egalitarian community—has to work hard and thoughtfully on a continuing basis to preserve its democracy, cooperativeness, and egalitarianism as well as to survive. The inherent tendency of such communities is to break down; it takes sustained effort to prevent this from happening.

The chapter by Lewicki and Bunker is reassuring with regard to the fragility of trust. In their original and brilliant discussion of the developmental stages of trust, they sensibly indicate that the answer to the question about trust's fragility is "it depends," and they indicate what it depends upon. However, I am not sure they answer the question of whether trust and cooperation are more fragile than suspicion and competition (other things being equal). As a result of reading their chapter, my answer would be a bit less dogmatic but nevertheless an affirmation that trust and cooperation are the more fragile states.

My reasoning is quite straightforward and is, I believe, indebted to Heider. Another person can harm you without your consent, but you cannot be benefited without your agreement. Although one can argue that there are exceptions to this statement, it seems to be mainly true.[1] In a two-party relationship, while trust and cooperation can be broken down because of the actions of either party, they can be created or maintained only by the actions of *both* parties. Moreover, there are situations—when the other is competitive and suspicious—in which it is disadvantageous to be cooperative and trusting. In such situations, it is often advantageous to be competitive when the other is cooperative and trusting. Thus, there seems to be an inherent bias in the social world for trust and cooperation to break down more readily rather than to be built up. This bias can be overcome by the types of conditions discussed by Lewicki and Bunker that move trust from its beginning to more advanced stages of development.

Stimulated by Lewicki and Bunker's important analysis, there are two minor theoretical points I wish to make. In a chapter on trust and suspicion written some time ago (1973), I defined trust to include the nonsocial as well as the social. Thus, one can trust that it won't rain, or that the bridge won't collapse, or that there won't be an earthquake in California while one is attending a conference. I think much of Lewicki and Bunker's discussion could readily be adapted to this broader definition by a fuller consideration of how intentionality is a characteristic of people, not of inanimate objects. However, it would pose a problem for their usage of the term *deterrence-based trust* for this first stage, a term that is inappropriate in any case. How does one deter rain? Deterrence has been employed so widely in relation to the Cold War and the nuclear arms race that it has connotations surely unwanted by the authors. Many of us have written about the dangers of an emphasis on deterrence; what looks like deterrence to one side often looks like malevolent, aggressive actions to the other. Mutual deterrence often leads to a vicious cycle, with escalating needs for stronger deterrents. The "trust calculus," if it is to lead to mutual trust, is more apt to be biased toward positive than negative incentives.

The fascinating paper about worker cooperatives by Vanderslice directly confronts the important issue of the survival of workplace cooperatives and what factors contribute to survival. She indicates, as my theory would suggest, that division of labor and specialization of function create difficulties for cooperation. Her emphasis is rightly on power and control problems. She reports that the cooperatives she studied were able to deal with such complications effectively.

However, these are not the only obstacles resulting from substitutability. Substitutability creates problems of communication and loss of unity. If you take any large system—for example, a university (which ideally but rarely is a cooperative system)—the languages of the specialists in each department, as specialization progresses, become less comprehensible to professionals in other areas. Also, each specialist area develops its own goals, which may not be well integrated with the goals of other areas. These problems are more likely, and more difficult to overcome, in larger organizations than in the small ones studied by Vanderslice.

Vanderslice points out some interesting difficulties, which I have not discussed, that close personal ties may cause for cooperatives. There are others, of course, for example, a husband and wife in the same cooperative who get divorced or any two people who come to dislike one another as a result of their interactions outside work. My general point is that the values of *universalism* and of *particularism* are sometimes in conflict in a worker cooperative. A worker who is performing his job poorly (according to general standards) may be kept on because of friendship, his need for the job, or because he is the brother of another cooperative member. As Vanderslice cor-

rectly points out, cooperatives are more apt to survive if they anticipate such difficulties and develop procedures for preventing or
managing them effectively.

I am delighted that Vanderslice has not found evidence of overconformity and lack of innovation in successful cooperatives. As
the important paper by Lewicki and Bunker indicates, there are different stages in the development of trust. Analogously, in the early
stages of the development of worker cooperatives, before mutual
trust is well established, these problems may be more evident. In
any case, for cooperatives to have survived, these pathologies must
have been prevented or managed effectively. Even more important
for survival, as Vanderslice points out, are the abilities to deal with
the difficulties of being a cooperative in a competitive environment.

Vanderslice's identification and discussion of the key factors in
sustaining worker cooperation is a very valuable and original contribution. With some elaboration, it would be an extremely useful
handbook for helping cooperatives ensure their survival. I am persuaded by Vanderslice's happy chapter that cooperatives can survive
with effort, skill, and good luck. It is cheering to have the examples
she provides of such survivors.

David and Roger Johnson have written their usual masterpiece.
Their chapter provides an excellent overview and integration of the
theoretical developments, research, and practical applications
related to cooperation. No one is more qualified to do this than
they. They have been the leaders in developing social interdependence theory, in conducting research as well as integrating the vast
array of research in this area, and in developing educational methods for employing cooperative learning and constructive controversy in the classroom. I feel personally indebted to them for the
wide currency they have given to my ideas in the field of education.

In their extensive theoretical and empirical work, they have
done much to detail the specific processes by which promotive
interdependence gives rise to promotive interactions, and how such
interactions have positive effects on student achievement, interpersonal relations, and psychological health. This is a major intel-

lectual achievement, enabling more systematic theoretical analysis and research on the social and cognitive mediating processes through which promotive interaction has such powerful, positive effects.

I am so much in agreement with the main thrust of the Johnsons' chapter that I have no desire to carp about any of its details. However, I note that they are even more optimistic than I am about the benefits of cooperation. They do not discuss such matters as its potential pathologies, its occasional failures, the conditions under which it is not applicable, the types of people who have difficulty in functioning well in cooperative groups, and so on. It is not that they do not recognize, for example, that the skills involved in teaching cooperative learning well are only acquired with considerable effort and time. Nor would they deny that in a competitive society, it takes much experience for people to acquire the knowledge, attitudes, and skill required to be effective cooperative members of the various groups to which they belong. The Johnsons rightly stress the many benefits to be derived from cooperation, but they do not emphasize sufficiently their realization of how much persistent, intelligent effort is required to develop and sustain effective cooperation. The Johnsons and I would surely agree that the effort is very worthwhile. They have exemplified such sustained effort in their own highly productive careers.

## Note

1. One could, for example, assert that the inner self of the person is not harmed unless it accepts, in some measure, the responsibility for being harmed. Analogously, one could reason that people can experience an increased sense of well-being without any recognition of how it occurred.

## References

Deutsch, M. (1973). *The resolution of conflict: Constructive and destructive processes*. New Haven, CT: Yale University Press.

Deutsch, M. (1985). *Distributive justice: A social psychological perspective*. New Haven, CT: Yale University Press.

# Part III

. . . . . . . . . . . . . . . . . . . . . . . . . . . . . . . .

## Justice

# 8

# Equity, Equality, and Need

## Three Faces of Social Justice

### Robert Folger, Blair H. Sheppard, Robert T. Buttram

For many years justice research centered on equity (Adams, 1965). Equitable outcome distributions reward people in proportion to their inputs at a constant rate of exchange (equivalent outcome/input ratio) across people. One of Morton Deutsch's classic articles (1975), however, helped usher in the modern trend of considering other conceptions of justice. Deutsch wrote that equity "is only one of the many values which may underlie a given system of justice" (p. 137). He noted two other principles of distributive justice in particular: need and equality. Since then, the list of justice principles has grown. Following Thibaut and Walker's distinction (1975) between distributive and procedural justice, for example, Leventhal (1980) described seven procedural justice principles, and Tyler and Lind (1992) have recently articulated three alternatives. The list is growing. New principles of justice seem to sprout like weeds in a garden (see Greenberg, 1987; Lind & Tyler, 1988).

Greenberg's recent survey (1990) of this literature noted a burgeoning terminological and conceptual confusion. We think some of this confusion has occurred because justice concepts have accumulated inductively from research. For example, research shows that the practice of giving explanations influences perceived fairness. Grouping types of explanations together—for example, as excuses versus justifications (Bies, 1987)—can yield new categories without necessarily emphasizing the functions such practices serve. Deutsch instead adopted a functionalist orientation based on a priori theorizing about the purposes of justice. We think functionalist theorizing can reduce conceptual clutter.

We follow Deutsch's lead in claiming that principles of justice reduce to a small but rich set of ideas about the functional requirements of social life. In terms of "societal functioning" (1975, p. 140), Deutsch related equity, equality, and need to three crucial but divergent social goals: the tendency "for economically-oriented groups . . . to use the principle of equity, for solidarity-oriented groups to use the principle of equality, and for caring-oriented groups to use the principle of need as the basic value . . . of distributive justice" (p. 147). Thus equity, equality, and need are prominent outcroppings on the justice landscape not as principles endorsed for their own sake (that is, not because of value intrinsic to the shape of an outcome distribution per se) but because of the social goals such distributions presumably help accomplish. Each distributive principle is an outward manifestation of a separate, underlying functional goal, a norm endorsed because it fosters desirable conditions of social life (Deutsch's insight).

We think one of Deutsch's chief contributions was to identify three requirements of social institutions as systems: sufficient economic productivity, adequate solidarity among its members, and the nurturing of those members to at least some minimal extent (1975). At this institutional level of analysis, he indicated how distributive justice principles facilitate what social systems must do to survive and to maintain a capacity for effectiveness. We address this level of analysis first.

We then show how the same line of reasoning can apply at two additional levels of analysis. In contrast to the *institutional* level that we associate with Deutsch, we will examine levels we call *individual* and *interpersonal*. Some of what we say about these levels probably overlaps with themes either implicit or explicit in the rich text of Deutsch's article (1975). Because three key ways of thinking about justice emerge in similar form at each level of analysis, we also affirm the value of Deutsch's functionalist orientation toward the study of justice.

After showing how each level exposes three similar functions of justice, we discuss why these three functions are so prominent. We also extend Deutsch's approach to indicate how procedural justice can parallel the three norms of distributive justice. The remainder of our chapter then raises questions about the co-occurrence of the three ways to think about justice. That discussion strays farthest from one reading of Deutsch's position, which tends to emphasize the separate application of each principle (for example, associating each distribution rule with a different primary goal for a group). We focus on situations in which more than one way of thinking about justice might receive serious consideration, as more than one functional goal presses for attention at the same time. We think that addressing such issues extends Deutsch's original formulation in new and potentially fruitful directions.

## The Societal/Institutional Perspective

For a society or organization to function effectively, three central activities need to occur (Sheppard, Lewicki, & Minton, 1992): keeping members, producing efficiently and effectively, and sustaining the well-being of the members. (We use the term *organization* to mean all manner of social organization that has some production requirement for the organization to survive.) Without members, a social institution cannot exist. Without efficient and effective production, it cannot compete. Without their essential needs met, members will focus on those unmet needs and not on the institution's purposes. Deutsch's three distributive justice principles arise from these three essential ingredients of organization:

1. Relative *equality* of distribution validates people's feelings of full-fledged membership in a cohesive unit, whereas gross

inequality can fractionate the organization (in essence, making it more than one unit, with sub-unit members who do not feel fully included in the whole).

2. *Equity* can foster the motivation to produce. Without rewards based on productivity, the motivation for productivity may lag.

3. Distribution of resources according to *need* ensures that the essential needs of all societal and organizational members are met.

For Deutsch, the principles of equity, equality, and need address the question, "Under what conditions do societies or organizations function best?" This question focuses on social units at the institutional level (for example, a society or an organization as a whole). A leader of a country or a corporate chief executive officer (CEO) is the person most likely to adopt such a broad overall corporate or societal view. Anyone preoccupied with the concerns of an individual societal member or with a relationship between a few members would be less likely to focus on the lofty goals of ensuring that the society maintains its solidarity, produces effectively, and meets the essential needs of all societal members. These functions are important in the abstract but are not likely to direct the day-to-day activities of most societal members. Thus, it is important to consider how the perspective of the architects of societies and organizations matches those of the individual members of that society.

Do individuals who evaluate the fairness of outcomes adopt goals that reflect the perspective of the CEO, or the president, or the constitutional author? Do people adopt the view of Jefferson or Gandhi or Lenin or Susan B. Anthony or Jack Welch, or do they have other more personally relevant considerations in mind? We contend that a complete explanation of the psychology of social justice requires both a more individual and also a specifically interpersonal perspective to explain more completely the means through which justice principles are invoked and applied. In the next two sections of the chapter, we consider justice first from the perspective of individual identity and then from the perspective that people are likely to adopt when thinking about their interpersonal relationships. People obviously might have concerns about the effective functioning of society or their own organization, but concerns about justice can also arise at other levels of analysis. Our discussion tries to show that surprisingly similar principles evolve from each point of view. We contend that personal identity and interpersonal relations serve as the micro underpinnings of justice notions operating at the more encompassing macro levels of organizational or societal units.

## The Individual Perspective

Folger and Buttram (1993) adopt a functional approach to the micro level of justice for individuals. They propose that three conceptions of justice at the individual level of analysis help accommodate different ways of thinking about who people are and what they have done. Justice at the micro level involves how to treat a given person. Few, if any, questions about the fair way to treat someone can be answered without knowing something about the person. What should be known to ensure fair treatment? Folger and Buttram classify what should be known into three categories that match functions served by equity, equality, and need.

The nature of what should be known to meet a person's needs, for example, tends to be rather idiosyncratic. To address a person's needs out of caring concern for that person and a desire to nurture the person, certain characteristics unique to that person come into play (for example, highly personalized reactions to deprivation or harm, such as when people with the same disease require different treatments because of idiosyncratic allergic reactions to certain medications). In contrast, granting everyone equal treatment does not require any personalized or individuated information at all, only the type of general information that identifies the set of people meant by "everyone" (such as every person in a serving line, for the sake of serving equal food portions). Equitable treatment means treatment commensurate with an individual's relative position on some appropriate dimension of inputs (for example, contributions to an exchange). Such graded criteria reflect yet a third category of information potentially available about individuals and relevant to their fair treatment, namely information differentiating individuals using measures such as more/less that are often objectively ascertainable, perhaps even from measures with ratio-scale properties (for example, different amounts of money contributed by two people).

Folger and Buttram (1993) called this model the S-A-N framework. S, A, and N stand for the first letters of three key words in the following statement about aspects of a person's identity: each person is in certain respects like Some other people, like All other people, like No other person (a paraphrase of Kluckhohn & Murray, 1953, p. 53). This statement in essence identifies three quite fundamental ways of describing people.

Social evaluations often differentiate in some-versus-other fashion along a continuum, such as accomplishment. Many of us want recognition indicating how we are like SOME people, namely those admired because their deeds have yielded worthwhile consequences, and not like others (the less meritorious). This desire probably reflects a healthy avoidance of the learned helplessness that would result if we could not perceive any consequences of our actions. We want our actions to have consequences; we want to reap returns as "outcomes" from our "inputs" of action. For example, efforts directed toward productive performance, or toward other contributions judged worthwhile by society or a given exchange partner, ought to warrant a commensurate payoff. Obviously this description fits the classic definition of justice as *equity*, common since Aristotle (see Adams, 1965).

For other purposes, however, people instead prefer to be treated just like everyone else (ALL others) in a given set; treatment is based not on what they have done, but on who they are (see Linton, 1936, for the distinction between achieved and ascribed statuses). In the broadest grouping, we want to be treated exactly like all others who are human, just because we are also human. This parallels the norm of *equal* distributions, where everyone receives the same outcome. A group sharing outcomes equally may also do so because each person in the group is a member of the group in good standing (for example, equal bonuses given to members of a team that makes the playoffs).

Finally, there are respects in which each of us craves the uniqueness associated with our own individual identities, to be treated like NO other person. We want certain outcomes to be particularized and personalized, for example, the love we expect from a parent or a spouse, who knows more about our idiosyncratic needs than anyone else and who has genuine concern about our well-being. Outcome criteria for fair treatment often focus on special *needs* when this individualized orientation dominates.

In sum, an analysis at the individual level (the description of a given person's identity) yields the same principles of justice as an analysis at the macro, impersonal level of the firm or social system. Equity, equality, and need apply at both levels. A third level of analysis also reveals the same three modes of thinking about justice, and we turn to it next.

## The Interpersonal Perspective

There is an intermediate point between the self and the organization or the society. As Fiske (1991) argues, social relations are the elemental pieces of social structure through which individuals come to form social units, including larger systems such as organizations and societies. Considering justice from the perspective of interpersonal relations is especially valuable because relationships are the bridge between self and organization. Relationships are the building blocks of larger social structures, such as organizations, economies, and societies. Individual identity and institutionalized social architecture meet in relationships.

Relationships take on characteristic patterns. Some, such as kinship or close friendship, typically show empathic concern and understanding. Others lack a close emotional bond, such as impersonal commercial transactions (which, when handled by computer, may involve two people who do not even know one another's identities). Still others seem to lie somewhere in between the two extremes: neither completely informal and highly personalized nor entirely depersonalized and formalized. Many associations of various kinds, for instance, have some formally structured aspects (for example, a hierarchy of authority) and yet also require a degree of cooperation and interdependence among members that encourages a sense of camaraderie and cohesiveness, as well as a relatively harmonious tone to most interactions.

Fiske exhaustively reviewed the literature on relationships from sociology (for example, Durkheim, 1933; Weber, 1915/1946; Tonnies, 1888/1935; Buber, 1923/1987; Blau, 1964), anthropology (for example, Polanyi, 1957; Malinowski, 1961; Sahlins, 1965; Udy, 1959), psychology (for example, Piaget, 1973; Krech & Crutchfield, 1965; Leary, 1957; Clark & Mills, 1979), and theology (Ricoeur, 1967). Fiske's conclusions about fundamental relationship forms roughly match our preceding discussion of the fundamental functions of justice at the institutional and individual levels. Fiske's analysis diverges from ours somewhat in that he identifies four fundamental forms of interpersonal relationships compared to our three fundamental functions of justice. However, as we describe below, we believe this apparent lack of correspondence results primarily from a minor difference in emphasis and perspective.

Fiske argues for the existence of four elemental forms of human relationships—communal sharing, authority ranking, equality matching, and market pricing—defined as follows:

> Communal Sharing is a relation of unity, community, . . .
> and kindness, typically enacted among close kin.
> Authority Ranking is a relationship of asymmetric differences, commonly exhibited in a hierarchical ordering

of statuses and precedence, often accompanied by the exercise of command and complementary displays of deference and respect. Equality Matching is a one-to-one correspondence relationship in which people are distinct but equal, as manifested in . . . equal share distributions or identical contributions, . . . and turn taking. Market Pricing is based on an (intermodal) metric of value by which people compare different commodities and calculate exchange and cost/benefit ratios [1991, p. ix].

These four forms surface repeatedly in writings on human relationships and have been used in anthropological research on a diverse set of peoples. Fiske's assertion about the pervasiveness and importance of these four forms of human relationships is not a modest one, but it speaks to this chapter's argument that thoughts about justice cluster into only a few basic patterns, reflecting characteristic types of concerns and functional goals that emerge with consistent similarity across multiple levels of analysis. Fiske writes, "My hypothesis is that these models are *fundamental* . . . [as] the lowest or most basic-level 'grammars' for social relations. Further, the models are *general*, giving order to most forms of social interaction, thought, and affect. They are *elementary*, in the sense that they are the basic constituents for all higher-order social forms. It is also my hypothesis that they are *universal*, being the basis for social relations among all people in all cultures and the essential foundation for cross-cultural understanding and intercultural engagement" (1991, p. 25, italics in original).

The development of a child's sense of justice provides an illustration of the very general, elementary, and universal nature of these relational models. Although we use this simple example, it can in no way capture the full range of evidence found in Fiske's book.

Infants seem to experience a parent as an extension of themselves. The relationship is built on caring, unity between parent and child, and fulfilling the child's *needs* (communal sharing). This type of relationship does not have to exist between parent and child. Sometimes it exists between siblings who relish feeding one another their own food, disregarding who gets how much. Parents may worry about hygiene at such times, but the siblings' sense of fairness seems to entail freely sharing until the other is satisfied.

Of course, before very long a child encounters authority, in the form of a father or mother whose role has now expanded beyond caregiving to include rule setting: establishing boundaries, admonishing bad behavior, and encouraging good behavior. The child begins to perceive parental preferences as dominant (authority ranking). Justice amounts to obedience.

Still later the child begins to engage peers or siblings as distinct beings. Initial exchanges between children generally entail parallel play or joint play. In both instances the rules of engagement most typically entail reciprocity as *equalized* sharing—the same amounts, closely similar objects—or turn taking (equality matching).

Eventually, however, children begin to seek things from people who are not family, friends, or neighbors but strangers possessing desirable objects. Stores, restaurants, miniature golf places, and videogame halls need some mechanism of exchange that permits the child to make reasonable choices based on some sense of equivalence or relative comparison across domains. Money is introduced to permit the purchase of goods and to allow comparison of unlike things on a single dimension of currency (market pricing). A Big Mac is worth 6 video games, as its price is $1.50 and a videogame is worth 25 cents. Such comparisons allow for exchanges across very unlike things. One of the authors' eldest son's first experience with market pricing came through his desire to purchase a Supernintendo system with his allowance. He was able to count the money and knew just what he was giving up to buy the system.

These examples briefly illustrate how three of Fiske's relational types align with need (community sharing), equality (equality matching), and equity (market pricing) as distribution principles. We will discuss authority ranking subsequently, in connection with procedural justice.

Thus, in summary, three different levels of analysis yield the same justice principles. Notably, the parallel is constructed from arguments about what is elemental, or fundamental, at each level. Organizations could not function if the three social goals of member retention, productivity, and member well-being were not met. Aspects of individual identity function to indicate the extent to which a person is like some others, like all others, or like no other person—fundamental distinctions at this lowest level of analysis. Similarly, at the interpersonal level, Fiske's arguments and evidence suggest that his relational forms are universal and elemental. These results—parallel for each set of derived justice norms—indicate a remarkable consistency across three distinct levels of analysis regarding fundamental aspects of social life.

This consistency is not inconsequential. We suspect that each of the three justice norms articulated by Deutsch taps not only a critical social goal but also a fundamental social form conjointly reflected at the level of social identity, relationships, and organization. In other words, each level exposes three primary clusters of thought about the nature of social life. Assuming that parallels across three levels do, indeed, reflect something very basic about social concerns, we suggest that the three core images of justice— as primary mental models of fairness in social life—tend to exhibit a key property that we discuss next.

## Parallel Foundations for Procedural Justice

If three distinctively parallel ways of thinking about justice emerge across a range of analytic levels (from micro to macro), other prominent principles of justice should also derive from those same fundamental ways of approaching the requirements of social life. Although we do not try to illustrate how all principles of justice might represent a special case of one of these three primary forms, we examine procedural justice as an example. Our discussion up to this point has focused on distributive justice. The same ways of thinking about the requirements of social life, however, also underlie procedural justice considerations. Procedural rules are said to be important if they in and of themselves address the social functions delineated by Deutsch, the relational types delineated by Fiske, and the descriptive terms for social identity outlined by Folger and Buttram.

Consider, for example, three principles of procedural justice identified by Tyler and Lind (1992): neutrality, standing, and trust. *Neutrality* entails "an unbiased decisionmaker who is honest and who uses appropriate factual information to make decisions" (p. 831). Neutrality evokes images of accurate, effective, and efficient design processes for maximizing economic productivity at the institutional level, where such authorities occupy administrative positions. Similar to Leventhal's emphasis (1980) on accuracy, consistency, and bias suppression as three essential criteria of procedural fairness, the neutrality concept is also a procedural equivalent to the exchange function of currency or money. An unbiased, universal procedure permits fair comparison across all people and situations, just as money can constitute a universal and neutral medium of exchange (see Fiske's relational model of market pricing). Finally, note the role of neutrality in delineating deservingness, that is, for deciding fairly the appropriate differentiations among one aspect of people's social identities (the performance or accomplishment-based aspect of achieved status). When a person is treated like some other people, the process used to make that determination should be unbiased and neutral. The authority implementing such a process should be dedicated to ensuring a level playing field of competition for achieved status. Only under such conditions will people feel comfortable about being differentiated in the first place, because the distinction of some versus others should reflect genuine aspects of personal identity (one's own individual qualities) rather than extraneous features of the differentiating mechanism itself.

The conceptual basis for *standing* assumes that people value their status within a group and use their treatment by an authority as an indication of whether their status as members has been affirmed. For example, "if people are treated rudely, they know that the authority they are dealing with regards them as having low status within the group" (Tyler & Lind, 1992, p. 831). Such consideration affects feelings of belongingness to a social group, organization, or society. Treatment reflecting low standing or non-standing undermines feelings of membership.

Finally, "trust involves the belief that the intentions of third parties (that is, authorities) are benevolent, that they desire to treat people in a fair and reasonable way" (Tyler & Lind, 1992, p. 831). Operationally, trust includes asking whether the authority took the viewpoint of interested parties into account, tried to be fair to them, and took account of their needs. If one believes that authorities are concerned with the members' well-being and needs, then it is possible to engage the broader social system's purposes.

In a sense, therefore, Tyler and Lind's model is a relatively direct translation of Deutsch's functional notions about outcomes to the realm of procedures. Procedures address the functioning of social life as much as do the outcomes produced by those procedures. Procedures can grant people a secure sense of ascribed status, such as the rights and privileges of full membership in some group or citizenship in a society (standing); that assurance of "like all others" at the individual level also fits procedural forms of equality matching at the interpersonal level (for example, turn taking) and aids solidarity at the macro level of institutional functioning. Similarly, procedures can assure people of reasonable decisions (neutrality) for all three levels of analysis (that is, decisions relevant to individual differentiation, market pricing, and economic maximization). Procedures can also help ensure that groups and societies do not lose members through deprivation and that individuals can expect consideration of their interests and needs even if it means making exceptions to some rule (trust).

Note, therefore, a difference between outcomes and processes: the latter do not always function to provide material well-being immediately as to provide a sense of psychological well-being now as a stand-in for the prospects of material well-being later. The assurances of good procedures—assurances about trust, neutrality, and standing—function more as symbolic outcomes than as tangible outcomes. The neutrality that is one of the key assurances of a reasonable decision-making procedure, for example, has an inherent rationality desirable as an end in itself, which differs somewhat from the rational precision of an equitable distribution. In the latter case, "rationality" refers literally to the "ratio" of outcomes to inputs; in the former, to the reasonableness of a process's administration, in contrast with arbitrary and capricious decision-making formats.

## Authority Relations

There is one non-parallelism across the three levels of analysis; Fiske adds authority ranking as a fourth elemental form of social relations. We can accommodate this new form with the others as follows: the fourth form implies differences in the authority to resolve issues of social relations, including issues pertaining to the other three forms. Note that according to Tyler and Lind's logic, authorities as problem solvers should resolve such issues by attending to procedural aspects of fairness. Authority ranking is fair, therefore, when the authority acts to ensure trust, neutrality, and standing. Perhaps there are even tendencies for authorities to consider different criteria more or less important within a given social form. Thus, kin-group leaders might be most concerned with trust, whereas union leaders might care more about standing and leaders in business might value neutrality.

Standing is an especially interesting criterion, as under the notions of authority ranking it takes on a somewhat revised meaning. Standing, to Tyler and Lind, entails consideration for people as equal members of a social group or organization. In Fiske's terms, standing means to act so as to ensure the existing authority ranking. Standing as a member of a social group or organization need not mean standing as an equal member, but standing relative to one's rank. This points to a slight paradox in the relatively egalitarian notions of Tyler and Lind. Authority ranking demands differences in rank, and thus differences in standing. To act as an authority to ensure equality of membership is somewhat contradictory. A resolution is that in some ways we are all equal, such as all being equal before the law, but in other ways certain preferences dominate over others. Thus, a monarch needs to abide by the law he or she established or the law has no merit, but the monarch sets law nonetheless. Parents may have the capacity to establish a principle for determining what television channel will be watched at a given point in time, but loathed be the parent who violates that principle for his or her own benefit. It is often for such reasons that households have more than one television.

Finally, we mention yet another possible way to incorporate aspects of authority ranking into our overall approach. We begin with some comments related to an issue raised by Deutsch (1975), namely, the scope of justice. Note that equality is the sole principle that does not differentiate people, whereas need entails one type of basis for differentiating and equity another. Whenever equality applies, however, the lack of differentiation it stipulates has a feature related to what Deutsch called the scope conditions of justice. Whereas a justice principle itself specifies things such as the amounts or proportions people are to receive (and according to what criteria), its scope involves specifying to whom the principle applies. Equality means that everyone receives the same thing, but who counts as "everyone"? Everyone in the same group, of course, but how big is the group? A family? An organization? All the citizens of a society? Or all members of the human race? What about animals?

Delimiting the scope of a justice principle—the range of people to whom it applies—means creating a category into which those people fit. Others, outside the scope of application, constitute a separate category. In that sense, Fiske's model of equality matching contains within it the logical source of conditions necessary for the rise of authority ranking. One way of thinking about what it means to treat everyone within a given group all the same, in other words, is to distinguish all of them from some other group of people—who themselves would also be treated exactly the same within their own group, although not necessarily the same as those in the first group. Equality matching applies logically only within groups (the scope condition), not between or among groups. It is perfectly consistent with the sameness of treatment given to all members of the same group, however, that a rank order could exist regarding the respective differences in treatment for each group. The hierarchical structure of a rank ordering is in turn perfectly consistent with the development of lines of authority (that is, differential status by rank along with prestige, influence, and the like). Although the implications of this approach need to be worked out in greater detail, we think this line of argument at least shows that addressing authority ranking as a separable set of issues need not be incompatible with the thrust of our message in this chapter.

## Implications

In this section we briefly outline some areas for further exploration. We try mostly to raise new questions rather than to provide definitive answers. We group issues into two complementary clusters. The first includes new sources of conflict: previously ignored or less well-appreciated ways in which people come to disagree about what's fair. The second cluster suggests some ways to resolve those disputes about fairness, capitalizing on approaches exposed by our discussion and otherwise likely to have been overlooked.

### Sources of Disagreement and Conflict Flare-Ups

The ubiquity of the three ways to think about justice suggests also their coexistence as conflicting standards. Three lenses for viewing justice issues are often quite readily at hand. A person might easily shift back and forth, using first one and then another way of framing concerns about fairness. Each frame of reference, of course, evokes its own standards of fairness, and the standards often compete as conflicting values.

These alternative standards might exist as land mines just beneath conscious awareness (that is, each frame of reference is not always salient). People might not necessarily be conscious about three ways of thinking about fairness simultaneously, comparing each fairness standard with others to contemplate the different consequences each might entail. The three might remain at all times potentially accessible, however, perhaps in latent form, until suddenly elicited or made salient by some cue. Whereas an employee might be thinking about equitable pay most of the time, for example, sudden knowledge of the company's flagrant disregard for employee health—perhaps after hearing about a co-worker's cancer—might trigger conscious awareness of need as a standard for caring about the well-being of individual employees.

When justice issues have been framed one way and then another comes to mind, ways of thinking about justice can have conflicting implications. If reasons for dividing resources equitably have dominated a discussion, for example, greater cognitive conflict occurs once some compelling reasons for considering equal sharing are introduced to the discussion. If three underlying ways of thinking about fairness always exist in a latent state, ready to be evoked in a sudden flash of insight or because of some new cuing stimulus suddenly introduced or made salient in a situation, then the grounds for disputes about fairness are indeed numerous.

Such an outlook emphasizes diversity rather than uniformity of opinion. We assume that each person might, on at least some occasions, be entirely capable of altering his or her evaluative judgments about fairness quite rapidly, perhaps several times in succession. If that is true for any given individual at the intrapersonal or intrapsychic level of cognitive conflict (that is, thinking first one way and then the next, weighing alternatives against one another), then bringing two or more people together multiplies the sources of conflict and the probability of its occurrence.

The tone of this discussion, of course, departs from one of Deutsch's themes (1975). Recall that Deutsch argued that if a group has a dominant goal (for example, productivity or harmonious solidarity), a dominant value of fairness would tend to emerge (equity or equality, respectively). We instead focus on situations where the members of a group disagree as to what's fair and what's not. We have discovered that discussions about fair pay generate such disagreements in our classes, especially as regards paying the members of an interdependent work team (also verified with laboratory data by Folger, Kass, Grzelak, & Januc, 1993). On the one hand, equity tends to be favored by those who think it fosters individual initiative and thus overall productivity (as well as discouraging free rider effects). On the other hand, attention to need or equality tends to be favored by those who think that only those norms will encourage the degree of cooperative interdependence necessary for successful group performance. Thus, even with a common dominant goal of productivity for both sets of people, they disagree about which norm of fairness will contribute best to the accomplishment of that goal.

Deutsch's suggestions clearly have a kernel of truth that is both important and enlightening. Many times a single norm of justice will dominate almost everyone's thinking in a given situation. We simply focus on another possibility worthy of investigation: that there are more grounds for disagreeing about what's fair than past discussions in the literature have implied (for an exception, see Sheppard et al., 1992). Perhaps stable situations and isolated groups with a long history of well-established customs produce monolithic views of justice quite readily, but conditions of instability—such as organizational change—more often create ambiguity and hence the potential for viewing justice through any of several lenses. Justice, being in the eye of the beholder, shares with perception the quality of displaying unique interactions between the viewer and the viewed. Just as some visual displays will be perceived the same by virtually all viewers (for example, light waves at a certain frequency seen as red except by the color-blind), some situations will typically yield widespread consensus about what's fair; just as other visual displays will appear different to different viewers and can even transform from moment to moment for the same viewer (for example, drawings of reversible staircases), the perception of fairness can vary both across and within persons.

Justice studies could benefit from contingency models that specify when a multiple-value view is more likely than a single-value view. Neglected possibilities include multiple justice standards even with the same relationship and the same resource. Some illustrations come from Cosmides and Toomby's evolutionary model (1992) of the propensity for humans to notice exploitation and unfulfilled obligations. For instance, they speculate (based partly on anthropological evidence) that greater variance in food supplies evokes greater preference for equal sharing, whereas food under more direct control of causal contingencies (less dependent on chance, fortuitous factors) tends to be allocated by norms of deserved equity. Two groups living under otherwise similar circumstances would have different distributive preferences if the variability of a given food source differed. Similarly, the same groups might distribute one food based on a norm of equal sharing (for example, meat gathered by hunters on an unpredictable basis) and yet distribute another food (for example, garden vegetables) on an entirely different basis—such as restricting access to close family members who contribute to the garden's maintenance.

We conclude this part of our discussion with two observations. First, recall that the three faces of justice are discernible across levels of analysis. Multiple cues thus exist for forms of fairness, increasing the likelihood that further approaches to justice will emerge with each additional person evaluating a given situation. Under such circumstances, any source of instability will also heighten conflicts about fairness—and stable situations in organizations are becoming increasingly rare. Global competitiveness, downsizings and restructurings in connection with mergers or acquisitions, conversion of work processes into team-based formats because of emphases such as Total Quality Management, and a host of other factors make today's organizations hotbeds of transformational change (for example, teams and other interdependencies undermine the dominance of equity as the norm considered essential for organizational productivity). Under such conditions, lack of consensus about fairness seems likely to be the rule rather than the exception (Cobb, Folger, & Wooten, in press; Cobb, Wooten, & Folger, in press). As multinational corporations bring employees from different cultures together to work with one another, yet another source of disagreement about fairness is introduced. For example, the post-communist countries of Eastern and Central Europe obviously have a collectivist history that makes them more sympathetic to egalitarian and need-based norms, and many parts of the world place a much greater emphasis on relationships, in comparison with the tendency toward impersonality that has dominated economic life in the United States.

A second observation: our discussion about the three faces of justice has called attention not only to three different levels of analysis from which those "faces" might emerge, but also to two dimensions that can reveal the three faces: outcomes and processes. Once again, the possibility of multiple sources from which concerns about justice might arise translates into multiple reasons why disagreements about justice might occur. Specifically, people can disagree not only about outcome norms but also about process norms. Thinking about outcomes, one person might choose a single dominant value (for example, a preference for equity). Meanwhile, having instead focused attention on processes, another person in the same situation might instead choose a different dominant value (for example, a concern about equal status or standing among members of a group, where all are entitled to the same rights and privileges as full-fledged members).

Other sources of disagreement might arise from conflict about norms of process. Consider first the norm of consistency in relation to Tyler and Lind's discussion of neutrality as a process concern. Consistency in evaluation processes, such as in performance appraisal methods, might seem desirable both from management's institutional perspective (rewarding meritorious contributions appropriately to motivate productivity by consistently applied incentives) and from the employee's perspective (receiving equitable rewards as verification of being better than "some" others who are less deserving). If an evaluation process or a given evaluator is neutral in the sense of introducing neither systematic error (for example, biases such as favoritism) nor random error (for example, whimsical, arbitrary, capricious decisions), then results over time and across evaluated persons should display consistent patterns. Such results would indicate a uniform neutrality, as if the same algorithm had been applied consistently.

Now think about a competing process norm for justice: flexibility. Some people might be more interested in authorities' having discretionary say-so rather than following a fixed algorithm like a cook with a recipe (using exact and precise measures, never deviating from amounts specified). In other words, the process norms of neutrality and trust (Tyler and Lind's terms for consistency versus flexibility, respectively) can conflict with one another. Someone who wants consistency might disagree with someone who feels that fair processes take individual differences and unique circumstances into account and allow discretionary action.

This theme differs markedly from the predominant tone of the procedural justice literature, which emphasizes the "fair process effect" (see Folger, 1977): so long as fair procedures are used, diffuse support for a system can be maintained despite whatever bad outcomes people might receive. That is, much of the emphasis has been on the potential for procedurally fair methods to reduce the amount of conflict. In contrast, we note that disagreements can occur because of alternative mental models about what constitutes a fair process. Such disputes can arise because each of two values is a desirable property of procedures, yet those two values seem to have contradictory implications—as when the value of consistency conflicts with the value of flexibility. Rather than choosing between the lesser of two evils, a person in this case might feel forced to choose between two competing positive values. Further theorizing and research need to be directed to identifying such dilemmas and how they are resolved.

## Possible Resolutions of Multiple-Value Dilemmas

In this section we speculate about creative approaches for taking into account seemingly contradictory or conflicting orientations toward justice. We focus on policies that use a single norm for determining outcomes (for example, equity), which ignores potential conflict over alternative ways to think about justice. We suggest that to mitigate this potential shortcoming, the implementation of a policy should take alternatives into account. Our variations on this theme draw from the concept of *interactional justice* (Bies, 1987; Tyler & Bies, 1990), which refers to the conduct of authorities as they take specific actions when administering a policy's implementation. Managers' actions and the tone or style of implementing a policy, for example, can vary in the timing with which decisions are implemented, the manner in which they are explained, and whether authorities' actions display qualities such as consideration, understanding, and sympathy toward those adversely affected. Those aspects of implementation give authorities opportunities to indicate their support for additional, supplemental justice values that might seem absent from the initial decision about the policy itself. A policy might dictate using equity criteria such as performance appraisal ratings to determine which workers are laid off, for example, but alternative principles of justice could dominate the implementation process.

Research has demonstrated that both the victims and the survivors of layoffs only sometimes turn their negative feelings into hostility toward management as the source of layoffs. Reduced hostility occurs if management's process of policy implementation seems fair (for example, giving timely notice, providing sincere and adequate explanations); when such fairness is lacking, hostility rises with the perceived adversity of the layoff (for example, Brockner, Konovsky, Cooper-Schneider, Folger, Martin, & Bies, 1994). This line of research at times has revealed striking examples of what might otherwise seem like relatively trivial implementation factors, except that they prove to have powerful impact as sources of process justice or injustice. A common complaint about implementation at the end of the fiscal and calendar year (when termination logically coincides with a transition point in annual cycles), for example, is the cruelty of layoffs during the holiday season of November and December. Inflicting pain during times that should be filled with pleasure (for example, on someone's birthday) seems callous and unfeeling, yet lack of attention to such procedural matters as timing seems the norm rather than the rule. Layoff implementation procedures require as much attention as the justice norms regarding the layoff decision itself.

A colleague recently described to one of us a layoff implementation that allowed personalized timing to accommodate individual need (D. Rousseau, personal communication, January 1994). She consulted with a firm that had conducted a large layoff. Employees were told that they would be laid off during 1994. Each employee, however, was allowed to choose the day when he or she would have employment terminated. We think this creative approach reflects attention to each person's own unique needs and circumstances. It is an extension of the "help yourself" idea typifying Fiske's description of communal sharing, such as the manner in which people serve themselves to their own individually sized portions of food during ritual meals that emphasize the communal sharing relationship model.

Apologies illustrate a second form of interactional justice during implementation that supplements the justice norms addressed during decision making. The act of apologizing or expressing remorse can be part of the process that authorities enact when implementing decisions. By supplementing an equity norm used in making a decision, an apology potentially adds a dimension of fairness that might otherwise be missing, thereby restoring balance to a three-legged stool. If the three legs of justice described in this chapter conflict during decision making and result in the use of a single justice principle, that can mean a potential imbalance analogous to a stool with only one leg. In order for apologies to supply the type of balance that would be gained from adding the other two legs to the stool, the apologies should address the two remaining types of concerns. Therefore, we next discuss a distinction between two possible functions of apologies.

To understand one of the two key functions that apologies can serve, consider first that the absence of an apology can convey a perception that the harmed victim is less than human, not even worthy of common civility and courtesy. The presence or absence of remorse symbolically communicates, respectively, either "I am willing to treat you as another human being, equally worthy of dignity and respect" or "I treat you with contempt, too far beneath me in status to dignify with acts of common courtesy or simple decency: you are subhuman, a worm, unworthy of any regard from me." The difference between these two messages explains moral outrage about the lack of an apology. Not to receive an apology puts someone outside the category of "all other" human beings, ostracized and disenfranchised from equal dignity and respect. Lack of remorse, therefore, can be classified as a process injustice parallel to the distributive injustice of violating equality (it also ignores the concerns of Fiske's equality-matching model and the S-A-N principle that people are in certain respects all alike).

As an apology, saying "I'm sorry" does not communicate explicitly what the speaker is sorry about. Not all apologies intend to convey the message we described above: remorse about one's conduct and an attempt to seek forgiveness from the victim of one's wrongdoing, or at least to acknowledge the right of all victims to hear whether the harm doer feels any shame or remorse. Some acts of apology instead focus on expressing sympathy about the other person's suffering (for example, "I'm sorry you are hurting" as a way of indicating that your unhappiness makes me unhappy, too). This type seems to illustrate a process-related instance of concern for another's personal well-being, parallel to the distributive norm of need (and to Fiske's communal sharing model, as well as to the "like no other" facet of the S-A-N approach).

If intended to convey concern, this type of sorrow is prone to be personalized and individuated. It should stem from anguish because of knowledge about the particular person who is suffering and specific aspects of his or her situation. Furthermore, it should be an act of genuine caring, illustrating the well-intentioned motives of benevolence that Tyler and Lind associated with their "trust" as a process term for authority's conduct. Notice, for example, that on occasion a person's request for an apology seems not to insist on well-meaning intent; the person demanding an apology may even go so far as to say "I don't care whether you mean it or not, but I'm not dropping this matter until you at least *say* you're sorry." This seems like a demand for dignity or for equal status, consistent with Tyler and Lind's notion of standing. In contrast, when the other person's expression of sorrow really means the person feels bad because the victim feels bad, then the harm doer has empathetically identified with the other person's unique situation (more like the Tyler and Lind category of trust).

Does it help to link two functions of apologizing with two forms of justice? For now, the idea is speculative. Our tripartite approach did help raise the question, however, in contrast with single-value approaches that overlook the totality of justice concerns and multiple ways to address them.

Finally, let us revisit the conflict of consistency versus flexibility and exceptions. We suspect that when perfect consistency means no exceptions, people eventually become less willing to enforce the rules. For example, both employees and management might agree that for punishable infractions of legitimate work rules (for example, safety violations that jeopardize lives), an equitable disciplinary philosophy is "let the punishment fit the crime." At first blush, the corresponding procedural requirement might seem to be absolute consistency: rules applied with neutrality rather than favoritism should produce consistently equitable disciplinary decisions. Small safety violations might incur only small fines, for example, whereas severe infractions might justify suspension without pay or even immediate firing.

Unfortunately, no code can cover all potentialities. A manager trying to enforce disciplinary rules will, sooner or later, encounter a situation that doesn't quite fit any known set of guidelines. An employee might be technically in violation of official policy, for example, but the manager knows that the employee really acted with justifiable good cause, exercising sound judgment and violating the technicality for a very good reason. But what if no exception can be made in such cases? Rather than punishing across a broad range of punishable behaviors, managers might avoid discipline or succumb to biases such as leniency and the central-tendency error of outcomes only at a mid-range level. Too much consistency, that is, might lead consistently to all outcomes being clustered together.

If so, granting managers more discretionary authority to make exceptions could contribute to greater equity rather than less, provided that the basis for making exceptions would still affirm process-related ideals compatible with equity. Consider the relationship between the ideal of neutrality and equitable outcomes: a genuinely neutral decision maker's consistency derives from avoiding both systematic bias (for example, favoritism) and random error (for example, capricious, arbitrary decisions). When exceptions seem called for and can be justified by good reasons, therefore, the basis for making the exception is principled: it stems from principle rather than from biases such as favoritism, and the use of a principle means that the decision is not arbitrary or capricious (that is, it is understandable and meaningful rather than the result of unknown, chaotic forces).

We hope readers have found our chapter provocative for one reason if no other: we have ventured into some uncharted territory. An expanded framework that hopes to do "justice" to the three aspects of fairness Deutsch identified—equity, equality, and need (in the somewhat reinterpreted manner we have used)—will have a lot of ground to cover if it is to live up to that potential. The prospective benefits of eventually covering such ground seem worth the considerable effort this venture will surely require. We have only too briefly tried to suggest what look like "sightings of promise" in two key arenas: new ways in which justice seems more problematic than ever before, and new ways in which considering justice as a multifaceted phenomenon might yield creative approaches for even the most problematic dilemmas of fair treatment. With a tip of the hat to Mort Deutsch, we want to close by simply saying thanks for giving us so much to think about.

## References

Adams, J. S. (1965). Inequity in social exchange. In L. Berkowitz (Ed.), *Advances in experimental social psychology* (Vol. 2, pp. 267–299). San Diego: Academic Press.

Bies, R. J. (1987). The predicament of injustice: The management of moral outrage. In L. L. Cummings & B. M. Staw (Eds.), *Research in organizational behavior.* (Vol. 9, pp. 289–319). Greenwich, CT: JAI Press.

Blau, P. (1964). *Exchange and power in social life.* New York: Wiley.

Brockner, J., Konovsky, M., Cooper-Schneider, R., Folger, R., Martin, C. L., & Bies, R. J. (1994). The interactive effects of procedural justice and outcome negativity on the victims and survivors of job loss. *Academy of Management Journal, 37,* 397–409.

Buber, M. (1987). *I and thou.* (R. G. Smith, Trans.). New York: Macmillan. (Original work published 1923)

Clark, M. S., & Mills, J. (1979). Interpersonal attraction in exchange and communal relationships. *Journal of Personality and Social Psychology, 37,* 12–24.

Cobb, A. T., Folger, R., & Wooten, K. (in press). The role justice plays in organizational change. *Public Administration Quarterly.*

Cobb, A. T., Wooten, K. C., & Folger, R. (in press). The role of justice in organizational development. In R. Woodman (Ed.), *Research in organizational development*. Greenwich, CT: JAI Press.

Cosmides, L., & Toomby, J. (1992). Cognitive adaptations for social exchange. In J. H. Barkow, L. Cosmides, & J. Toomby (Eds.), *The adapted mind: Evolutionary psychology and the generation of culture* (pp. 163–228). New York: Oxford University Press.

Deutsch, M. (1975). Equity, equality, and need: What determines which value will be used as the basis of distributive justice? *Journal of Social Issues, 31*, 137–149.

Durkheim, E. (1933). *The division of labor in society*. New York: Macmillan.

Fiske, A. P. (1991). *Structures of social life: The four elementary forms of human relations*. New York: Free Press.

Folger, R. (1977). Distributive and procedural justice: Combined impact of "voice" and improvement on experienced inequity. *Journal of Personality and Social Psychology, 35*, 108–119.

Folger, R., & Buttram, R. T. (1993). *What does it mean to be fair? A framework for capturing the multiple facets of fairness*. Unpublished manuscript, Tulane University, A. B. Freeman School of Business, New Orleans, LA.

Folger, R., Kass, E., Grzelak, J., & Januc, J. (1993). [Decisions about distribution norms for work teams.] Unpublished raw data.

Greenberg, J. (1987). A taxonomy of organizational justice theories. *Academy of Management Review, 12*, 9–22.

Greenberg, J. (1990). Organizational justice: Yesterday, today, tomorrow. *Journal of Management, 16*, 399–432.

Kluckhohn, C., & Murray, H. A. (1953). Personality formation: The determinants. In C. Kluckhohn, H. A. Murray, & D. M. Schneider (Eds.), *Personality in nature, society, and culture* (pp. 53–70). New York: Knopf.

Krech, D., & Crutchfield, R. S. (1965). *Elements of psychology*. New York: Knopf.

Leary, T. F. (1957). *Interpersonal diagnosis of personality: A functional theory and methodology for personality evaluation*. New York: Ronald Cress.

Leventhal, G. S. (1980). What should be done with equity theory? New approaches to the study of fairness in social relationships. In K. J. Gergen, M. S. Greenberg, & R. H. Willis (Eds.), *Social exchange: Advances in theory and research*. New York: Plenum.

Lind, E. A., & Tyler, T. R. (1988). *The social psychology of procedural justice*. New York: Plenum.

Linton, R. (1936). *The study of man*. East Norwalk, CT: Appleton & Lange.

Malinowski, B. (1961). *The dynamics of culture change: An inquiry into race relations in Africa*. New Haven, CT: Yale University Press.

Piaget, J. (1973). *The child and reality: Problems of genetic psychology*. New York: Grossman.

Polanyi, M. (1957). *The great transformation: The political and economic origins of our time*. Troy, MO: Holt, Rinehart & Winston.

Ricoeur, P. (1967). *The symbolism of evil*. (E. Buchanan, Trans.). Boston: Beacon Press.

Sahlins, M. (1965). On the sociology of primitive exchange. In M. Banton (Ed.), *The relevance of models for social anthropology*. (Association of Social Anthropologists, Monograph 1.) (pp. 139–236). London: Tavistock.

Sheppard, B. H., Lewicki, R. J., & Minton, J. W. (1992). *Organizational justice: The search for fairness in the workplace*. New York: Lexington.

Thibaut, J., & Walker, L. (1975). *Procedural justice: A psychological analysis*. Hillsdale, NJ: Erlbaum.

Tonnies, F. (1935). *Community and society*. (C. P. Loomis, Trans.). Oxford: Transaction. (Original work published 1888)

Tyler, T. R., & Bies, R. J. (1990). Beyond formal procedures: The interpersonal context of procedural justice. In J. S. Carroll (Ed.), *Applied psychology and organizational settings* (pp. 77–98). Hillsdale, NJ: Erlbaum.

Tyler, T. R., & Lind, E. A. (1992). A relational model of authority in groups. In M. P. Zanna (Ed.), *Advances in experimental social psychology* (Vol. 25, pp. 115–192). San Diego: Academic Press.

Udy, S. H. (1959). *Organization of work: A comparative analysis of production among nonindustrial peoples*. New Haven, CT: Human Relations Area Files Press.

Weber, M. (1946). The social psychology of the world religions. In H. Gerth & C. W. Mills (Eds. and Trans.), *From Max Weber: Essays in sociology* (pp. 267–301). New York: Oxford University Press. (Original work published 1915)

# Tradeoffs in Justice Principles
## Definitions of Fairness

## Tom R. Tyler, Maura A. Belliveau

During a speech at the 1985 meeting of the Society for Experimental Social Psychology in Evanston, Illinois, Morton Deutsch noted that when he began his research career he had not originally intended to study issues of social justice. His work began with an effort to explore the dynamics of conflict and cooperation in interracial housing projects. However, in the course of that work, he found that the social conflict he was examining was expressed by those involved in social justice terms. People invoked principles of justice and injustice to explain their satisfaction or dissatisfaction with their state, and those feelings of social justice and injustice shaped people's behavioral reactions to their experiences. In other words, issues of justice were the medium through which people framed, discussed, and reacted to issues of social conflict. Hence, social justice became the inevitable focus of a social scientist interested in the realities of intergroup conflict and cooperation.

Deutsch's work not only suggests that issues of cooperation and conflict are framed in terms of justice. It further argues that the principles of justice people use when framing their reactions to social interactions are shaped by the structure of the conflict situation. Deutsch suggests that the nature of the interdependence among the parties to a relationship influences their cognitive, motivational, and moral orientations toward the interaction (1982).

These orientations (people's "goals" in the interaction), in turn, influence which justice principles people apply to the interaction.

Until recently, research on social justice has generally focused on judgments of distributive fairness and the consequences of perceived distributive injustice. Judgments of justice or injustice have been shown to influence feelings of satisfaction and dissatisfaction, as well as commitment and loyalty, and to impact a wide variety of behaviors, including both negative actions—such as joining extremist groups or rioting (Crosby, 1976)—and positive actions—such as rule following and voluntary decision acceptance (Tyler, 1990). In contrast to this predominant focus on the consequences of injustice, Deutsch has been concerned with the antecedents of injustice. He has examined the origins of the justice concerns that arise in the course of social interaction.

Deutsch's concern with the antecedents of injustice is reflected in his classic paper on the use of equity, equality, and need as justice principles (1975). Deutsch argues that the nature of social justice judgments is influenced by the goals of the parties affected. For example, he suggests that "in cooperative relations in which economic productivity is a primary goal, equity rather than equality or need will be the dominant principle of distributive justice" (p. 143).

The suggestion that interaction goals shape the importance accorded to different principles of justice has been widely confirmed in social justice research. Studies suggest that the importance of productivity as a goal in social interaction is linked to the importance of equity as a justice principle, while the importance of positive interpersonal relations is linked to the importance of equality and need (Austin, 1980; Barrett-Howard & Tyler, 1986; Benton, 1971; Curtis, 1979; Elliott & Meeker, 1984, 1986; Foa & Stein, 1980; Greenberg, 1979a, 1979b, 1983; Lamm, Kayser, & Schwinger, 1982; Lamm & Schwinger, 1980; Leventhal, 1976; Leventhal, Michaels, & Sanford, 1972; Mikula, 1980; Mikula & Schwinger, 1978; Mitchell, Tetlock, Mellers, & Ordonez, 1993; Morgan & Sawyer, 1967, 1979; Murphy-Berman, Berman, Singh, Pachauri, &

Kumar, 1984; Notz & Starke, 1987; Okun, 1975; Peterson, 1975; Prentice & Crosby, 1987; Sampson, 1975; Schwinger, 1980, 1986; Shapiro, 1975; Stake, 1983).

Deutsch has further argued that interaction goals are shaped by the underlying structure of the interdependence among the parties to an interaction (1982). Deutsch develops a typology of situations that vary along four dimensions: cooperative or competitive orientation, equal versus unequal power, task versus socioemotional orientation, and formal versus informal setting. He hypothesizes that variations along these dimensions shape the cognitive, motivational, and moral orientations of the people in a given situation. This suggestion has been supported by the work of Barrett-Howard and Tyler (1986), who experimentally varied the structure of interdependence along the four dimensions identified by Deutsch. They found that the variations influenced both people's goals in the interaction and the justice principles they used.

A key contribution of Deutsch's analysis is the recognition that many goals might potentially be important within social interaction, with their relative importance varying across settings. Two types of goals have been recognized as particularly central: task goals and socioemotional goals. When dealing with others, people are instrumentally oriented, seeking to obtain certain outcomes for themselves. They have tasks they want to accomplish, resources they want to gain. In addition, people are concerned about developing and maintaining positive, cooperative, beneficial social relations with others.

Using practicing managers as allocators, Meindl (1989) examined the role of goals and relationships between workers in determining the use of distributive principles. While managers tended toward equity in their overall allocations, Meindl found a significant effect for the interaction of values and interdependence, demonstrating that managers' perceptions of the appropriateness of equity or equality were affected by both goals in the interaction and the relational context.

Deutsch's work is an important corrective to the overattention to task goals, which developed through the dominance of equity theory as an area of social justice research during the 1960s and 1970s. Equity theory made many important contributions to our understanding of social justice through work on the effect of variations in how people are paid, but it heightened attention to situations in which productivity and efficiency were the primary interaction orientation. In fact, researchers generalized from this type of setting to propose equity as an overall principle governing social interaction (Walster, Walster, & Berscheid, 1978).

The recognition that there are multiple goals in social interaction—with their importance varying across settings and multiple justice principles arising from them—suggests a more complex model of social justice than one based on any single principle of justice. It suggests that attention must be fixed on the nature of the relationship among different interaction goals and different justice principles.

## Equity/Equality Tradeoffs

Perhaps the most interesting idea to emerge from the literature on the relationship among interaction goals is the idea of tradeoffs (Bowie, 1971; McConnell, 1987; Okun, 1975). The literature suggests that there is a tradeoff between the use of equity and equality. The assumption is that equity promotes productivity but harms social harmony. The use of equality, on the other hand, promotes social harmony at the expense of productivity. Consequently, authorities must balance these different principles when making allocation decisions.

This conclusion has been derived from a paradigm that, for the most part, *assumes* that distributive justice principles affect productivity or social harmony, rather than proving the existence of this causal link. While people believe that group harmony is related to group performance (Guzzo, Wagner, Maguire, Herr & Hawley,

1986), these beliefs constitute implicit theories, not empirically proven truths. Furthermore, this assertion denies a possible positive relationship between task and socioemotional goals. While organizational researchers have not found that the happy group is necessarily a productive group, it may be that the productive group is the happy group. From this perspective, principles that support task achievement may indirectly support group harmony.

Two related questions within distributive justice research remain. Are distributive justice tradeoffs a necessary part of social interactions? Must justice principles support only one goal: group harmony or productivity?

Deutsch (1985, 1987, 1989) questions the assumption that the use of equity is especially likely to promote productivity. He presents experimental data suggesting that equality can also promote productivity. If so, then there is no necessary tradeoff between the goal of productivity and the use of equality as a reward principle.

Deutsch's efforts to deal with concerns about the tradeoff between equality and equity fall within the distributive justice framework for understanding social interaction. His approach is based on the assumption that both task and socioemotional goals must be met through the fair distribution of rewards but that differing principles of distributive justice are judged fair within different situations.

Deutsch's work resulted in social psychologists' efforts to understand the nature of the tradeoffs among varying principles of distributive justice that people make in the course of their social interactions. However, most efforts have generally been confined within the framework of outcomes. More recently, social psychologists' efforts have extended beyond the outcomes of reward distribution to the procedures decision makers use and their enactment of those procedures. We believe that it is through such a conceptual expansion that a more complete understanding of people's connections to others can be most effectively reached.

# A Procedural Approach to Interaction Goals

We propose incorporating issues of distributive and procedural justice into a single conceptual framework through which the relationship between interaction goals and justice concerns can be examined.

The centrality of socioemotional feelings of loyalty, commitment, and legitimacy to procedures (Tyler and Lind, 1992) suggests that it is important to broaden the discussion of goal tradeoffs to include a consideration of procedural issues. Traditional treatments of social justice assume that both task and socioemotional concerns must be addressed within a distributive justice framework. Hence, the need for tradeoffs. However, it is possible that a broader framework, which includes attention to issues of both distributive and procedural justice, could provide an alternative way of thinking about the relationship between goals and justice principles.

Using a more general social justice framework suggests the possibility that the core goals of meeting task objectives and maintaining positive interpersonal relations can be met by differential effects of distributive and procedural justice. In particular, decision-making procedures might be used to maintain a favorable socioemotional climate, while task goals are met through the use of distributive principles in the allocation of resources (Tyler, 1991).

# Theoretical and Empirical Development of Procedural Justice

During the past decade, the field of social justice research has been broadened by increased attention to issues of procedural justice. Building on the pioneering work of Thibaut and Walker (1975) and Leventhal (1976), researchers have demonstrated that people are concerned about the fairness of decision-making procedures, in addition to being concerned about the fairness of outcomes (see Lind and Tyler, 1988, for a review of research).

An especially striking aspect of procedural justice findings is that procedural justice has a particularly strong influence on loyalty and commitment to groups and organizations (Tyler & Lind, 1992). While both the fairness of outcomes (distributive justice) and of the decision-making process (procedural justice) influence people's personal satisfaction, procedural justice influences reactions to authorities and organizations more powerfully than outcome-based measures. Allocation and dispute resolution are key to people's feelings about groups (loyalty, commitment) and group authorities (for example, their legitimacy), and their behavioral responses to rules (voluntary compliance) and situations in which prosocial actions are beneficial but not prescribed (organizational citizenship behavior). This is true in work settings (Alexander & Ruderman, 1987; Folger & Konovsky, 1989), political organizations (Tyler & Caine, 1981; Tyler, Rasinski, & McGraw, 1985), and legal contexts (Tyler, 1990).

The most recent developments in procedural justice research indicate that procedural fairness judgments are not simply based on characteristics of the procedures themselves but on their enactment as well (Lind & Tyler, 1988; Tyler, 1989, 1991, 1994; Tyler & Lind, 1992). Individuals attend to the interpersonal treatment they receive from decision makers, and their judgments of procedural fairness flow from their perceptions that they have been treated honestly, openly, and with consideration (Tyler, 1988). A recent managerial simulation demonstrates that these dimensions of fairness behavior affect both perceptions of a decision maker's effectiveness and people's group commitment (Belliveau & Tyler, 1993).

## Applying the Integrated Justice Framework

If distributive justice were responsive only to issues of efficiency, that would not necessarily mean that equity should be used as the primary principle of distributive justice. Critiques such as Deutsch's suggest that the effects of different principles of distributive justice need to be explored. To some extent, that exploration has occurred. However, it should include dimensions of procedures (both objective features of procedures, such as whether they allow evidence presentation, and characteristics of their enactment, such as whether people are treated with respect when they present evidence) as well as variations in distributive principles. Such an integrated approach need not involve the assumption of tradeoffs between the goals of enhancing productivity and efficiency and the need to maintain positive interpersonal relations.

An example of this social justice strategy can be found in the work of Brockner, DeWitt, Grover, and Reed (1990) on coping with job layoffs. They demonstrate that managers can mitigate the effects of layoffs on the survivors who remain in the work setting by providing accounts of the reasons why layoffs are necessary and of the procedures through which they occur (that is, by demonstrating the use of a fair procedure). In this case, the decisions necessary for the efficiency of the company (that is, the decision to lay off workers) could be made without a focus on socioemotional issues, while socioemotional concerns are addressed through the approach taken to making and implementing those decisions.

Experienced managers already recognize the importance of using fair procedures in decision making. Tyler and Griffin (1991) interviewed experienced managers and administrators and found that they regarded the use of fair procedures as more central to issues of interpersonal relations than fair decisions. Hence, managers may already be sensitive to this approach to effectively meeting task and socioemotional goals.

In summary, there is substantial support for the suggestion that procedural issues dominate socioemotional concerns. What is less clear at this time is whether efficiency and productivity are linked to issues of distributive justice, rather than to procedural justice. If not, then perhaps distributive justice issues ought to be regarded as secondary to efficiency and productivity. At this time, however, such a conclusion is not warranted, since there is little empirical research on the relative influence of distributive and procedural justice on efficiency and productivity.

The work of Deutsch has been crucial to the development of the field of social justice because Deutsch stepped behind the occurrence or nonoccurrence of feelings of injustice to ask how those feelings are shaped by the structures within which people interact and the resulting goals. This focus on the antecedents of justice offers great promise as a mechanism for integrating the generally distinct literatures on the consequences of distributive and procedural justice.

## Why Does a Procedural Justice Strategy Work?

The model of justice underlying Deutsch's writings is rooted in theories of social exchange. Social exchange theories suggest that people's goals in social interactions are primarily linked to their concerns over material resources. People want to develop methods of effectively exchanging resources, and they develop justice principles as one approach to managing social interactions. For example, Deutsch argues that justice principles only develop and apply within the framework of productive exchange relationships (1985).

The social exchange framework has not only influenced theories of distributive justice. The procedural justice model articulated by Thibaut and Walker (1975) is also based on a social exchange model of social interaction. It suggests that people are primarily concerned with maintaining direct or indirect control over their outcomes in interactions with others. Such control allows them to maximize their gain in interactions, thereby acquiring desired resources.

Lind and Tyler (1988) propose an alternative—the group-value model—to the resource-oriented models that have been built on a social exchange base. They suggest that people are interested in two issues. The first is their estimates of their long-term interests. People recognize that they cannot always receive what they want. Sometimes they must defer to the needs of other group members.

But they are concerned about whether they will receive reasonable levels of outcomes in the long run. They assess this likelihood by examining the fairness of group decision-making procedures, believing that if decisions are made fairly, then, over time, they will receive just outcomes. These concerns are instrumental, but they differ from the short-term instrumentalities emphasized by control models (Thibaut & Walker, 1975). This long-term view of outcomes is consistent with social exchange perspectives.

The second issue of concern in the group-value model is personal identity. Group-value theory suggests that people are interested in having a favorable self-identity and that they use information in interactions with others to shape their sense of identity. In other words, in addition to the goal of resource acquisition, people have the goal of identity affirmation.

Tyler and Lind (1992) suggest that such concerns about identity affirmation lead people to focus on relational issues when dealing with others. Three relational issues are important: the belief that procedures are neutral, the belief that others are trustworthy, and the recognition of personal standing by others through respectful, dignified, treatment (that is, status recognition) (see Tyler, 1989; Tyler and Lind, 1992). Each of these conveys information to people about their position within the relationship or organization involved in the interaction. These relational issues have been linked directly to evaluations of procedural fairness (Tyler, 1989).

Tyler (1994) demonstrates that the relational concerns outlined are, in fact, a distinct second justice motive, which differs from the resource concerns that develop from social exchange models. He demonstrates that there are two distinct justice motives: one resource based, the other relational in character. Resource concerns influence assessments of distributive justice; relational concerns influence assessments of both distributive and procedural justice. In other words, procedural justice judgments are purely relational in character.

This finding suggests that the ability of procedural justice to facilitate the attainment of task and socioemotional objectives develops out of the connection of procedural justice to relational concerns. Since relational concerns are distinct—not linked to resource issues—they can be dealt with separately from the questions of resource distribution, which are central to models of distributive justice.

The suggestion that people are concerned about their feelings of self-worth is in accord with other suggestions that people try to develop and maintain positive views about themselves. In his theory of self-affirmation, Steele (1988) suggests that people make both cognitive and behavioral adjustments in an effort to avoid information that is potentially injurious to their feelings about themselves. Similarly, Tesser (1988) proposes a self-evaluation maintenance model, which suggests that people actively behave in ways designed to enhance their self-evaluations.

These theories reflect a dramatic change in the conceptualization of the relationship between individuals and others. They recognize that people are concerned about their sense of self and use feedback from others to help define self-identity. Hence, people's connections with others are linked to issues of identity, in addition to concerns about resource exchange.

## Why Are There Identity Concerns in Social Interaction?

Research in the area of social cognition suggests that people have good reasons for being concerned that interactions with both the world and with others in the world may pose a threat to their sense of self. People typically believe that they are more cognitively capable than they actually are (Taylor & Brown, 1988) and that they are better able to control events than they actually are (Crocker, 1982; Langer, 1975).

The exaggerated feelings of competence people have about themselves influence their dealings with others (Tyler & Hastie,

1991). Because of a tendency to exaggerate their contributions to interactions and their value to others, people often receive feedback that is inconsistent with their sense of self. For example, people give themselves more credit for success than they should. This means that there is a persistent tension within interactions, with people feeling that they deserve more than they get.

People's expectations are often dashed by reality (Tyler & Hastie, 1991). In dealing with the material world, people often find that their exaggerated evaluations of their competence are unsustainable. A person in the midst of a traffic accident discovers that his driving ability is not as good as he imagined and that he should have worn his seat belt; a motorcyclist finds that she cannot avoid a collision and that she should have worn her helmet; a crime victim realizes that he should have considered where to walk at night. Similarly, social reality dashes people's expectations. People are not able to deliver the persuasive communication that changes others; they do not receive the acclaim and material rewards they feel their achievements merit. It is in the cauldron of social interaction, where people's hopes are often unmet, that issues of social justice become central to loyalty and commitment to groups.

Allocations by principles of equity, equality, and need are essentially a direct assault on feelings about the self because of biases in individual perceptions of inputs and needs. Because the use of equity links rewards to evaluations of relative competence and the value of one's contributions, it provides feedback about how one's self is viewed by others. It directly confronts people with evidence that others do not share their view about the magnitude of their contributions to group interactions. Equality, in contrast, provides similar feedback when individuals feel that their inputs are independent, identifiable, and subject to reward. Needs are subject to distortion, and decisions incongruent with an individual's expectations based on perceived needs may be even more damaging to self-evaluations. Needs are fundamentally more intrinsic and reflect vulnerabilities, whereas inputs can be viewed as voluntary contributions to a group that reflect a person's capabilities. Each of these distribution principles hinges on perceived entitlements, which will inevitably reveal a discrepancy between people's estimations of their own value and the feedback they receive from others.

In each transaction, an individual's outcome expectations can be violated. The favorability of each outcome is clear. Individuals face greater difficulty in assessing their overall outcomes. Discerning both one's absolute and relative treatment is a more complex and uncertain overall calculation.

Procedural justice provides an alternative model for managing allocation because it provides a way to affirm people's sense of self-worth. Treatment with dignity and respect indicates to individuals that they are valued by others, reaffirming their sense of self. This interpersonal affirmation of the self is distinct from the resources that people gain or lose in interactions with others.

This suggestion has dramatic implications for alternative ways to handle the problems of pursuing task and socioemotional goals in interpersonal settings. In general, the perspective we are outlining suggests the need to design procedures that reaffirm people's sense of self and self-worth as a way of maintaining their sense of positive identity.

One way to define procedures is to provide an alternative way to reaffirm people's status. The work of Weisenfeld, Brockner, and Martin (1993) provides a provocative example of this approach to self-affirmation. They suggest that job layoffs are a potential threat to positive feelings among both those laid off and survivors who empathize with those who are laid off. Layoffs generally have a negative effect on the commitment of survivors to the organization. However, this decrement in commitment does not occur if survivors have their self-worth reaffirmed in an unrelated way.

The suggestion that an unrelated reaffirmation of personal worth can maintain commitment to an organization is supported by the findings of studies of third-party dispute resolution (Tyler & Lind, 1992). These studies find that interpersonal treatment—treatment with respect and dignity—has a positive effect on people's feelings when dealing with third parties. Such treatment reaffirms people's personal status, as communicated by others.

Another possible approach is to define the issue involved as irrelevant to the self—to block vulnerability. For example, in presenting a task to female and minority subjects, Steele (1993) informed his female subjects that men—and his minority subjects that whites—typically do better on the task. If women and minorities think their performance on a task reflects on their abilities, their performance is inhibited. If, however, they are told that their performance says nothing about their abilities, they perform at a higher level. Similarly, bad outcomes that are due to external circumstances, not to personal failures, should have reduced negative implications for the self.

Why does equity threaten the self? As has been noted, equity defines judgments as evaluations of the self and of self-worth. Instead of blocking vulnerability, it heightens it.

## How this Approach Differs from Distributive Justice Research

Deutsch's view of the psychological dynamics underlying concerns about social justice is shaped by social exchange theory. Deutsch suggests that people are primarily interested in developing and maintaining profitable exchange relationships with people and groups. They are therefore motivated to balance the two key aspects of such interactions: task goals and socioemotional goals. The effort to balance task and socioemotional goals can be seen in the form of the bargainer's dilemma. Negotiators seeking gain for themselves engage in "tough" bargaining tactics designed to maximize personal gain from interactions. Their behavior is constrained, however, by their desire to maintain the interaction for purposes of mutual gain and not drive the other party away. Hence, the task goal of maximizing gain must be balanced against the socioemotional goal of maintaining the relationship (Rubin & Brown, 1975).

A similar balancing effort underlies efforts to trade off between the justice principles of equity, equality, and need. As in bargaining, the socioemotional concerns that are the focus of attention are important because they allow interactions to continue.

In the identity model that underlies relational models of procedural justice, socioemotional concerns are of an entirely different type. People are focused on the information they receive from others about themselves. People are seeking to create and maintain a positive self-image. They use information from interactions with others to do so.

We are not arguing that people are necessarily always interested in their social bond to others. In fact, studies suggest that in short-term, transient, relationships (Tyler & Dawes, 1993) or at the beginning of social interactions before social bonds have been established, behavioral decisions are more strongly instrumentally based (Tyler, Huo, & Lind, 1993). However, once involved in interactions with others and allowed to make social bonds, people focus on the implications of the behavior of others for their self-concept. For example, when choosing whether to be involved in mediation, people focus on their estimates of their control in mediation. However, when evaluating mediation sessions after they occur, people react to relational issues.

## Deutsch's Contribution to Justice Research

Deutsch recognized that people's concerns about social justice do not appear out of nowhere. Instead, they develop out of the goals people have in their social interactions, and their form is responsive to the nature of those interactions. This recognition that interaction goals are an essential antecedent shaping justice principles is crucial to understanding the psychological dynamics of social justice.

Our analysis accepts Deutsch's insight that interaction goals define the nature of justice concerns. Research has supported Deutsch's suggestion that social exchange models, which focus on people's resource concerns, explain distributive justice effects. However, procedural justice effects, which are socioemotional in character (impacting commitment, loyalty, and evaluations of authorities and rules), are better explained by identity-based relational models of justice.

Our integrated model suggests that people's resource goals are linked to their concerns about both distributive and procedural justice. Identity affirmation goals are linked to concerns about procedural justice. Hence, a framework encompassing both forms of justice provides an alternate model for describing people's concerns in their relationships with others.

Our reframing of the traditional equity versus equality tradeoff is not simply an academic issue of definitions. As we have noted, it opens up a new window on the concerns that underlie people's socioemotional connections with others. Through procedures that do not threaten—or that affirm—people's sense of self and self-identity, people are provided with a basis for continued commitment and loyalty to relationships and groups that is distinct from their reactions to the allocation of resources.

## Importance of Social Justice Research

The promise of social justice research lies in its hopeful implications for the ability of both social groups and individuals to bridge differences in interests and values. While Americans, accustomed to living within a stable society, may not regard social unrest as a realistic issue for concern, recent events in nations such as the former Yugoslavia and the former Soviet Union dramatically illustrate the fragility of social order and the potential for societies to break apart into warring factions through intergroup and interpersonal conflict. The ability of groups or individuals to manage differences and maintain positive social bonds and productive interactions should not be taken for granted.

Instrumental models of the person suggest a fairly grim vision of intergroup life, with individuals and the groups to which they belong struggling to gain as much as possible for themselves and putting constant pressure both on those with whom they interact and on social authorities to provide them with desired outcomes. In the current struggles over cuts in the national budget, for example, leaders are haunted by a vision of special interest groups that evaluate budget cuts solely in terms of what they gain or lose. In struggles over policy issues ranging from abortion to affirmative action, authorities are similarly worried about the effect of making policies that go against the values and interests of some social groups.

Social justice research suggests that there are mechanisms to deal with conflicts over interests and values. To some appreciable extent, people are willing to defer to decisions they do not agree with and that do not favor them because they evaluate those decisions against criteria of fairness, rather than in terms of self-interest. This important insight, articulated by Deutsch in the context of distributive justice research, has become a more general implication of the literatures on both distributive and procedural justice. Both literatures have amply demonstrated that people's feelings and their actions are shaped by their judgments about what is fair.

However, for justice principles to be an effective bridge across interests and values, it is not enough for people to agree that justice is important. It is also essential that people share some consensus on how justice is defined. In the case of procedural justice, for example, it would be of little value for people to share the willingness to accept a fairly made decision if there were not a decision-making procedure that was commonly accepted as fair.

Deutsch's early work on the antecedents of justice is crucial to the issue of consensus. To the extent that people in different situations are led by those situations to have different goals and to use different principles of justice to evaluate procedures and outcomes, then consensus about justice will be difficult to obtain. In the context of distributive justice, Deutsch (1975) articulates broad principles of consensus on how justice should be defined, for example, the importance of equity in management settings, equality in political and legal settings. It is also clear, however, that such a consensus is not total; the structure of interdependence influences goals, and goals influence the definition of justice (Barrett-Howard & Tyler, 1986). A similar conclusion also emerges from more recent research on procedural justice (Tyler, 1988). Hence, elements of both consensus and diversity are found in the definition of justice.

America is moving toward increasing diversity in the values and cultural backgrounds of its citizens and is developing an ethnically diverse workforce, one that also includes more female participation. These increases in diversity suggest that consensus in definitions of justice will become more and more central to the ability of the legal and political system, as well as work organizations, to function effectively. Further research on this question is clearly needed, and Deutsch's examination of the antecedents of views on justice provides an important framework for guiding that research.

## The Psychology of Justice

Another aspect of theories of social justice involves psychological models of social justice, that is, efforts to explain why people care about justice. While this was addressed by Deutsch in terms of theories of social exchange, more recent theories of justice have given greater weight to the identity aspects of people's relationship to groups.

Moving from a resource-based to an identity-based view of injustice makes it clear that the occurrence of injustice carries important symbolic messages for its victims—implications about their status in society that influence feelings of self-worth and self-esteem. Such concerns are articulated in the *Brown v. Board of Education* decision, where the United States Supreme Court focused on the psychological harm to self-esteem from the stigma of inferiority conveyed by segregation. Similarly, requiring people to sit in the back of a bus is an important symbol of procedural injustice (bias, nonneutrality) and an indication of inferior social status.

More recent are issues of gender discrimination and the wage gap between men and women. While economists and sociologists might argue that women should not be concerned about a 7 percent wage differential, such a differential—regardless of its tangible implications for the distribution of resources—carries an important symbolic meaning of both distributive and procedural inequality.

A focus on the relational aspects of procedural justice makes the symbolic meaning of injustice clear. When a minority group member is beaten or insulted by the police or when a woman receives a haphazard performance review or feedback based on criteria linked to her "femininity," they are not simply denied desired resources or subjected to real physical harm; they are demeaned and humiliated as people, and their feelings of self-worth and self-esteem suffer accordingly.

An identity-based model of justice shows why the motives or intentions of others are so central to evaluations of justice. When organizations create formal procedures, such as appeals mechanisms, but those within the organizations believe that those mechanisms do not reflect a benevolent motive, then those formal structures of fairness have little impact (Bies & Tyler, 1993). Conversely, many informal mechanisms for allocation and dispute resolution—for example, mediation—are judged to be fair if they are enacted in ways that communicate dignity, respect, and trustworthy motives on the part of others.

Beyond communicating a message about access to resources, procedures communicate messages about a person's status within society. Hence, social justice concerns arise not just as a way to regulate and mediate people's social exchanges of resources; they also convey important messages about self-worth and self-esteem.

# References

Alexander, S., & Ruderman, A. (1987). The role of procedural and distributive justice in organizational behavior. *Social Justice Research, 1*, 177–198.

Austin, W. G. (1980). Friendship and fairness: Effects of type of relationship and task performance on choice of distribution rule. *Personality and Social Psychology Bulletin, 6*, 402–407.

Barrett-Howard, E., & Tyler, T. R. (1986). Procedural justice as a criterion in allocation decisions. *Journal of Personality and Social Psychology, 50*, 296–304.

Belliveau, M. A., & Tyler, T. R. (1993, August). *The effect of bargainer fairness behavior and self-interest seeking on individual and group attitudes and outcomes: Do nice guys finish last?* Paper presented at the annual meeting of the Academy of Management, Atlanta, GA.

Benton, A. A. (1971). Productivity, distributive justice, and bargaining among children. *Journal of Personality and Social Psychology, 18*, 68–78.

Bies, R. J., & Tyler, T. R. (1993). The litigation mentality in organizations: A test of alternative psychological explanations. *Organization Science, 4*, 352–366.

Bowie, N. E. (1971). *Towards a new theory of distributive justice.* Amherst: University of Massachusetts Press.

Brockner, J., DeWitt, R., Grover, S., & Reed, T. (1990). When it is especially important to explain why: Factors affecting the relationship between managers' explanations of a layoff and survivors' reactions to the layoff. *Journal of Experimental Social Psychology, 26*, 389–407.

Crocker, J. (1982). Biased questions in judgment of covariance studies. *Personality and Social Psychology Bulletin, 8*, 214–220.

Crosby, F. (1976). A model of egoistic relative deprivation. *Psychological Review, 83*, 85–113.

Curtis, R. (1979). The effects of knowledge of self-interest and social relationship upon the use of equity, utilitarian, and Rawlsian principles of allocation. *European Journal of Social Psychology, 9*, 165–175.

Deutsch, M. (1975). Equity, equality, and need: What determines which value will be used as the basis of distributive justice? *Journal of Social Issues, 31*, 137–149.

Deutsch, M. (1982). Interdependence and psychological orientation. In V. J. Derlega & J. L. Grzelak (Eds.), *Cooperation and helping behavior: Theories and research* (pp. 15–42). San Diego: Academic Press.

Deutsch, M. (1985). *Distributive justice: A social psychological perspective.* New Haven, CT: Yale University Press.

Deutsch, M. (1987). Experimental studies of the effects of different systems of distributive justice. In J. C. Masters & W. P. Smith (Eds.), *Social comparison, social justice, and relative deprivation*. Hillsdale, NJ: Erlbaum.

Deutsch, M. (1989). Equality and economic efficiency: Is there a tradeoff? In N. Eisenberg, J. Reykowski, & E. Staub (Eds.), *Social and moral values* (pp. 139–153). Hillsdale, NJ: Erlbaum.

Elliott, G. C., & Meeker, B. F. (1984). Modifiers of the equity effect: Group outcome and causes for individual performance. *Journal of Personality and Social Psychology, 46,* 586–597.

Elliott, G. C., & Meeker, B. F. (1986). Achieving fairness in the face of competing concerns: The different effects of individual and group characteristics. *Journal of Personality and Social Psychology, 50,* 754–760.

Foa, U. G., & Stein, G. (1980). Rules of distributive justice: Institution and resource influences. *Academic Psychology Bulletin, 2,* 89–94.

Folger, R., & Konovsky, M. (1989). Effects of procedural and distributive justice on reactions to pay raise decisions. *Academy of Management Journal, 32,* 115–130.

Greenberg, J. (1979a). Group versus individual equity judgments: Is there a polarization effect? *Journal of Experimental Social Psychology, 15,* 504–512.

Greenberg, J. (1979b). Protestant ethic endorsement and the fairness of equity inputs. *Journal of Research in Personality, 13,* 81–90.

Greenberg, J. (1983). Self-image versus impression management in adherence to distributive justice standards. *Journal of Personality and Social Psychology, 44,* 5–19.

Guzzo, R. A., Wagner, D. B., Maguire, E., Herr, B., & Hawley, C. (1986). Implicit theories and evaluation of group process and performance. *Organizational Behavior and Human Decision Processes, 37,* 279–295.

Lamm, H., Kayser, E., & Schwinger, T. (1982). Justice norms and determinants of allocation and negotiation behavior. In M. Irle (Ed.), *Studies in decision making* (pp. 359–410). New York: de Gruyter.

Lamm, H., & Schwinger, T. (1980). Norms concerning distributive justice. *Social Psychology Quarterly, 43,* 425–429.

Langer, E. J. (1975). The illusion of control. *Journal of Personality and Social Psychology, 32,* 311–328.

Leventhal, G. S. (1976). The distribution of rewards and resources in groups and organizations. *Advances in Experimental Social Psychology, 9,* 91–131.

Leventhal, G. S., Michaels, J. W., & Sanford, C. (1972). Inequity and interpersonal conflict: Reward allocation and secrecy about rewards as methods of preventing conflict. *Journal of Personality and Social Psychology, 23,* 88–102.

Lind, E. A., & Tyler, T. R. (1988). *The social psychology of procedural justice*. New York: Plenum.

McConnell, C. R. (1987). *Economics*. New York: McGraw-Hill.

Meindl, J. (1989). Managing to be fair: An exploration of values, motives, and leadership. *Administrative Science Quarterly, 34,* 252–276.

Mikula, G. (1980). On the role of justice in allocation decisions. In G. Mikula (Ed.), *Justice and social interaction* (pp. 127–166). New York: Springer-Verlag.

Mikula, G., & Schwinger, T. (1978). Intermember relations and reward allocation. In H. Brandstatter, J. H. Davis, & H. Schuler (Eds.), *Dynamics of group decisions* (pp. 229–250). Newbury Park, CA: Sage.

Mitchell, G., Tetlock, P. E., Mellers, B. A., & Ordonez, L. D. (1993). Judgments of social justice: Compromises between equality and efficiency. *Journal of Personality and Social Psychology, 65,* 629–639.

Morgan, W. R., & Sawyer, J. (1967). Bargaining, expectations, and the preference for equality over equity. *Journal of Personality and Social Psychology, 6,* 139–149.

Morgan, W. R., & Sawyer, J. (1979). Equality, equity, and procedural justice in social exchange. *Social Psychology Quarterly, 42,* 71–75.

Murphy-Berman, V., Berman, J. J., Singh, P., Pachauri, A., & Kumar, P. (1984). Factors affecting allocation to needy and meritorious recipients. *Journal of Personality and Social Psychology, 46,* 1267–1272.

Notz, W., & Starke, F. (1987). Arbitration and distributive justice: Equity or equality? *Journal of Applied Psychology, 72,* 359–365.

Okun, A. M. (1975). *Equality and efficiency: The big tradeoff*. Washington, DC: Brookings.

Peterson, C. C. (1975). Distributive justice within and outside the family. *Journal of Psychology, 90,* 123–127.

Prentice, D. A., & Crosby, F. (1987). The importance of context for assessing deservingness. In J. C. Masters & W. P. Smith (Eds.), *Social comparison, social justice, and relative deprivation* (pp. 165–182). Hillsdale, NJ: Erlbaum.

Rubin, J. Z., & Brown, B. R. (1975). *The social psychology of bargaining and negotiation*. San Diego: Academic Press.

Sampson, E. E. (1975). On justice as equality. *Journal of Social Issues, 31,* 45–64.

Schwinger, T. (1980). Just allocation of goods: Decisions among three principles. In G. Mikula (Ed.), *Justice and social interaction* (pp. 95–126). New York: Springer-Verlag.

Schwinger, T. (1986). The need principle of distributive justice. In H. B. Bierhoff, R. L. Cohen, & J. Greenberg (Eds.), *Justice in social relations* (pp. 211–226). New York: Plenum.

Shapiro, E. G. (1975). The effect of expectations of future interaction on reward allocations in dyads: Equity versus equality. *Journal of Personality and Social Psychology, 31,* 873–880.

Stake, J. E. (1983). Factors in reward distribution: Allocator motive, gender, and Protestant ethic endorsement. *Journal of Personality and Social Psychology, 44,* 410–418.

Steele, C. M. (1988). The psychology of self-affirmation: Sustaining the integrity of the self. *Advances in Experimental Social Psychology, 21,* 261–302.

Steele, C. M. (1993, August). *Social stigma and the schooling and career outcomes of women and black Americans.* Paper presented at the annual meeting of the Academy of Management, Atlanta, GA.

Taylor, S. E., & Brown, J. D. (1988). Illusion and well-being: A social psychological perspective on mental health. *Psychological Bulletin, 103,* 193–210.

Tesser, A. (1988). Toward a self-evaluation maintenance model of social behavior. *Advances in Experimental Social Psychology, 21,* 181–227.

Thibaut, J., & Walker, L. (1975). *Procedural justice.* Hillsdale, NJ: Erlbaum.

Tyler, T. R. (1988). What is procedural justice? Criteria used by citizens to assess the fairness of legal procedures. *Law and Society Review, 22,* 301–355.

Tyler, T. R. (1989). The psychology of procedural justice: A test of the group-value model. *Journal of Personality and Social Psychology, 57,* 333–344.

Tyler, T. R. (1990). *Why people obey the law.* New Haven, CT: Yale University Press.

Tyler, T. R. (1991). Using procedures to justify outcomes: Testing the viability of a procedural justice strategy for managing conflict and allocating resources in work groups. *Basic and Applied Social Psychology, 12,* 259–279.

Tyler, T. R. (1994). *Psychological models of the justice motive: The antecedents of distributive and procedural justice. Journal of Personality and Social Psychology, 67,* 850–863.

Tyler, T. R., & Caine, A. (1981). The role of distributional and procedural fairness in the endorsement of formal leaders. *Journal of Personality and Social Psychology, 41,* 642–655.

Tyler, T. R., & Dawes, R. (1993). Justice in organized groups: Comparing the self-interest and social identity perspectives. In B. Mellers (Ed.), *Distributive justice.* New York: Cambridge University Press.

Tyler, T. R., & Griffin, E. (1991). The influence of decision makers' goals on their concerns about procedural justice. *Journal of Applied Social Psychology, 21,* 1629–1658.

Tyler, T. R., & Hastie, R. (1991). The social consequences of cognitive illusions. *Research on negotiations in organizations* (Vol. 3). Greenwich, CT: JAI Press.

Tyler, T. R., Huo, Y., & Lind, E. A. (1993). *Preferring, choosing, and evaluating dispute resolution procedures: The psychological antecedents of feelings and choices.* Unpublished manuscript, University of California, Berkeley.

Tyler, T. R., & Lind, E. A. (1992). A relational model of authority in groups. In M. Zanna (Ed.), *Advances in experimental social psychology* (Vol. 25). San Diego: Academic Press.

Tyler, T. R., Rasinski, K., & McGraw, K. (1985). The influence of perceived injustice on support for political authorities. *Journal of Applied Social Psychology, 15,* 700–725.

Walster, E., Walster, G. W., & Berscheid, E. (1978). *Equity: Theory and research.* Needham Heights, MA: Allyn & Bacon.

Weisenfeld, B., Brockner, J., & Martin, C. (1993). *Survivors' reactions to job layoffs: A self-affirmation analysis.* Paper presented at the annual meeting of the Academy of Management, Atlanta, GA.

# 10

# Perceived (In)Justice

## Freeing the Compliant Victim

## Michelle Fine, L. Mun Wong

In this manner, Hester Prynne came to have a part to perform in the world. With her native energy of character, and rare capacity, it could not entirely cast her off, although it had set a mark upon her, more intolerable to a woman's heart than that which branded the brow of Cain. In all her intercourse with society, however, there was nothing that made her feel as if she belonged to it. Every gesture, every word, and even the silence of those with whom she came in contact, implied, and often expressed, that she was banished, and as much alone as if she inhabited another sphere, or communicated with the common nature by other organs and sense than the rest of human kind. She stood apart from mortal interests, yet close beside them, like a ghost that revisits the familiar fireside, and can no longer make itself seen or felt [Hawthorne, 1978, p. 109].

We begin with Hester Prynne, a young woman marked by a scarlet letter, exiled from her community for moral transgression. As she stood in the town square, separated from community, she gained vision, empathy, and voice. Surveying closely the politics and social embroidery of injustice, she saw and testified to the hypocrisy, secrets, and lies that bound her town together. Though she had rarely seen injustice from the inside, looking from without, her eyes opened wide to a tapestry of social violence.

Perspectives and positions influence how we see justice and injustice. With Prynne in mind, we wander into the social psychological literatures, desperately seeking an answer to the question posed by Barbara Bunker and Jeff Rubin in the introduction to this book: Why do so many "victims" see justice in circumstances others would consider unjust?

This chapter is organized to unravel the shifting social psychological dynamics operating in situations that might be considered unjust. We first review what social psychology has said about "victims'" reactions, by distinguishing between the conditions under which individuals "see" injustice and the conditions under which groups bring a "grievance" against injustice, in their own critical voices. We end with an invitation for social psychological analyses of institutional ideologies and practices through which social injustices have been justified, resistances dampened, and critique exported.

This chapter is written in the intellectual legacy of Morton Deutsch. Mort has been a most significant teacher for Michelle, and I coauthor this essay with a talented graduate student, L. Mun Wong. Across four generations of students of injustice, including Kurt Lewin before Mort, we mine the theories and methods of social psychology to probe and provoke questions of social consciousness and injustice, and we press on with the next generation of questions surrounding the stubborn structures, ideologies, and practices of social injustice. Those of you who know Mort will understand that we only hope this chapter can elicit that twinkle in his dancing eyes.

## Seeing Injustice

Imagine a conversation between Hester Prynne and Mort Deutsch.

Deutsch writes, "The victim is less likely than the victimizer to lose his sensitivity to injustice because he is the one who is experiencing the negative consequences due to the injustice. He is also less likely to feel committed to the official definitions and indoctrinations because of his lack of participation in creating them" (1985, p. 24).

In these quotes, wisdom emanates from the exported margins of society. The wisdom of critique comes from the marginality of vision and the deprivation of power. For the purposes of this chapter, the term *victim* refers to members of "disadvantaged groups" who suffer "outcome disparities" or adverse treatment, even if they "come to believe they are personally entitled to less than . . . members of more advantaged groups" (Major, 1994, p. 313).

Like our invented conversational partners, sociologist Dorothy Smith (1987) and political scientist Nancy Hartsock (1983) also argue that those who are most oppressed and subjugated see most clearly the silhouettes of social injustice. Within social psychology, Deutsch (1985) has argued that victims are more sensitive than victimizers or nonvictims to the nuances of injustice and are more likely to see that dominants control social institutions and sanction forms of injustice to benefit themselves. With confirming evidence from a laboratory experiment, Fine (1980) reports that victims see and name injustice more readily than do nonvictims. But this popular understanding, that victims have greater insights into injustice, has been widely disputed by recent social psychological studies investigating job discrimination, battered women, abortion, and sexual harassment. Under conditions that outsiders might consider unjust, social psychologists repeatedly report that victims see themselves as individually well treated and free from injustice, even if they acknowledge that their groups are disadvantaged.

In her study of working women and employment discrimination, for instance, Faye Crosby (1982) surveyed a group of young, well-educated, white suburbanites in Newton, Massachusetts, about their jobs, views on employment opportunities and equity for women, and domestic arrangements. Crosby found that white men and women did not differ in their sense of being targets of discrimination, even though white women objectively earned less than white men. When the women were asked about the general conditions for white women, however, they were more likely than men to express discomfort and apprehension. Crosby terms this discrepancy between a woman's awareness of gender-related job discrimination and her apparent lack of sensitivity to her own disadvantage as "the denial of personal discrimination."

Surprised by her results, Crosby has continued to refine and document this phenomenon in diverse samples (Crosby, Pufall, Snyder, O'Connell, & Whalen, 1989; Clayton & Crosby, 1992). In most cases, a pattern emerges; individuals report dissatisfaction and discrimination for the general conditions of their groups but fail to identify themselves as victims of discrimination. Similar findings have been reported in samples of Canadian working women (Hafer & Olson, 1989), Francophones (Guimond & Dube-Simard, 1983), and white gay men and lesbians (Birt & Dion, 1987). This seeming paradox is also found among black MBAs in the United States (Ford, 1988) and black lesbians (Mays & Cochran, 1987, reported in Clayton & Crosby, 1992).

Within the employment discrimination literature, Brenda Major and her colleagues (Major, 1987, 1989; Major & Konar, 1984; Major, McFarlin, & Ganon, 1984), in a series of surveys and experimental studies, document a similar finding. Women's sense of financial entitlement appears consistently to be lower than men's. Women generally allocate fewer rewards to themselves. When assigned lower job-related rewards, women are generally just as satisfied with their jobs and pay as men. Likewise Janice Steil (in press) concludes that women report a lower sense of entitlement at home. Despite evidence that women shoulder more responsibility for child care, perform more domestic chores and carry more socioemotional domestic work, they do not express these inequities as grievances or injustices.

The inability or refusal of individual adults to see or voice personal injustice extends beyond work and heterosexual relations. In the social psychological literature, it is reported that health-related victims are also unlikely to characterize their circumstances as unjust. Women with breast cancer "cognitively de-victimize" (Taylor, Wood, & Lichtman, 1983, p. 28), develop a stronger sense of self (Taylor, 1983), and invent multiple coping strategies to positively control the situation (Collins, Taylor, & Skokan, 1990). Equity theorists have argued that in order to justify or restore equity, victims distort reality, convince themselves that victimization has brought benefits, or believe that their victimizer deserves the benefits she or he has accrued (Walster, Berscheid, & Walster, 1976). In this way, Janoff-Bulman (1979) finds that rape survivors cope best when they adopt behavioral self-blame strategies to deflect fears about the uncontrollable nature of future rapes (also Wortman, 1976).

Thus, a substantial body of research has investigated the individual effects of victimization (for good summaries of research on victimization, see Wortman, 1983; see Collins et al., 1990, for an attempt to integrate these two sets of literature). Some studies document a range of negative consequences, such as fear, anxiety, depression, and difficulties in maintaining a view of the self as meaningful and a sense of purpose in daily interactions (Janoff-Bulman & Frieze; 1983). Others document positive consequences. Taylor (1991), for instance, talks about the power and resilience of the mind to create positive illusions to mask the pain and sufferings that result from victimization: "The brain is a remarkable organ and never more so than when it is actively seeking to turn a disastrous event into one that is less tragic or even beneficial. . . . Viewed in one light, a situation may look to be quite dire and unenviable, yet viewed in another, one may appear to be quite fortunate. Systematic and selective perceptions and evaluations help 'victims' to minimize their victimization by focusing on beneficial qualities of the situation" (p. 167).

Taylor documents positive reappraisals of one's social condition, gains in self-knowledge, and mastery over one's life. When an assumptive world is destroyed, victims may regain control by rebuilding its content or by engaging in cognitive processes that select out damaging information (Janoff-Bulman & Frieze, 1983; Janoff-Bulman, 1979). One might conclude from this review of the social psychology of victimization that substantial evidence exists of what Karl Marx described as "false consciousness." Some victims, as a class, fail to realize that they are being discriminated against and exploited. They appear unable or unwilling to identify with or act within their own interests. This accusation has been leveled at women of the upper class (Ostrander, 1984), women of the New Right (Klatch, 1987), black conservatives (West, 1993), and anti-choice women activists (Ginsburg, 1989). But when researchers investigate *why* adults hold such paradoxical positions, we hear less that they are deluded and more that they are operating through complex, often contradictory, consciousness and surviving in institutions trying to make them see justice where little prevails (Asch & Fine, 1988; Condor, 1986; Dolnick, 1993; Katz & Burt, 1988; Klatch, 1987).

The following reflection on an interview conducted by Mun reveals how smoothly we, as researchers, can underhear the nuanced narratives of informants. (The names have been changed to protect the anonymity of our interviewees.)

### Fieldnotes: 3 June 1993

I was late for the interview and as I rushed into the restaurant, I find Jamal with a white man; unshaven, untidily dressed, and staring at her without speaking a word. I was startled by the presence of this man. Jamal (a 22 year old self-identified Palestinian Muslim woman who wears a "cover") sensing my discomfort, quickly assured me that he is leaving soon. I was relieved and immediately asked for a more private space where we could conduct the interview. We found a booth in the corner and after being served by the waitress, Jamal asked me "Is he looking at us?" I said no . . . she gave a sign of relief and the look of annoyance and panic was gone. I inquired about this man and she told me that Jim was one of the instructors in her college. He has followed her, called her a couple of times at home and even leased an apartment from her parents' building. But she continued to inform me that he has also inspired her and helped her with a book that she has been working on, giving her encouragement and support. And finally, she said, "Without his help, I would not have gotten a B+ for inorganic chemistry." I held off from pursuing this incident since I reasoned that I would get to this case when I interviewed her. Meanwhile, I looked over and found Jim stealing glimpses of Jamal as we were chatting away. . . .

### 8 June 1993, School Courtyard

We were sitting in the school courtyard and trying to complete the remainder of the interview, and Jim walks towards us from a distance. I said to Jamal, "Jim is coming over." She looked irritated and annoyed, asked me not to pay any attention to him. She kept asking me whether he is approaching. I replied in the affirmative, she slightly bent her head forward, trying to conceal herself from Jim. He walked by us and she said in relief, "Maybe he did not see me" . . . I guess not. . . .

[When I asked Jamal why she has not brought up Jim in her discussion of violence]

Jim? Why? . . . Because of Jim to me, [pause by interviewee] never harassed me, I can handle him. . . . I don't consider that harassment. . . . I would drop kick him if he come next to me, you see. . . . But me . . . I can handle myself. I don't consider that harassment . . . Now (I: But he is your professor?) Exactly and he is my tutor, so maybe he is doing this because he cares about me and he is my teacher . . . that is why I cannot jump to a conclusion and I won't jump to a conclusion but he does like to follow me . . . if he comes next to me, I would drop

> kick his ass. . . . I will take care of him like no other
> women took care of him in his life . . . let's put it this
> way . . . the two balls he has, I cut and find out what he
> is . . . that is why I don't consider that harassment . . .
> because you didn't mess with me, that is why I don't con-
> sider that harassment.

Neither Jamal's situation nor her analysis are unique. Brodkey and Fine (1988) have written about white middle-class graduate students who have been sexually harassed by their professors. In a qualitative review of well over one hundred sexual harassment narratives, Brodkey and Fine noticed that women who experienced sexual harassment from faculty adopted, with stunning regularity, a clinical and scientized narrative about their victimizers' roles and motives. These women volunteered reasons, offered excuses, and, more often than not, justified their harassers' behaviors. The women worked hard to understand faculty behaviors, while numbing their own consequences. Rosemarie Roberts (1993) reports similar findings with a racially mixed sample of women and men undergraduates from New York City; students work hard to absolve men of accountability in cases of sexual harassment, seeking explanations, instead, in the woman/victim's behaviors.

Jamal, in contrast, was a poor Palestinian woman who grew up in the streets of Jersey City. Unlike the graduate students who placed mind over body, her approach to survival was to own her body and fend off any possible attacks from Jim. She refuses to abandon her body to a privileged scientific discourse that abstracts women's experiences. Mind and body are used jointly to understand, to protect herself, and still to account for the victimizer.

Jamal's narrative is a challenge to social psychological theorizing. She navigates across choppy waters of contradictions and paradoxical justifications. Gramsci (1971), Du Bois (1903), Collins (1991), and Matsuda (1990) would frame Jamal's story by explaining that social institutions help shape—but also split—the consciousness of subordinates. Subordinates, they argue, draw from two conflicting conceptions of the world. One is the "official" story; the other bubbles up from oppressed people's lived experiences. These conflicts are played out in what Terry Eagleton (1991) has termed the "performative contradiction" between what one says and what one tacitly reveals in behavior. Jamal's story begins to make more sense.

Jamal grew up in a household where mothers, sisters, and wives were abused by their spouses. She harshly condemns her father's actions and strongly disapproves of her brothers' abuse and serial marriages. Yet she identifies with her father and male "street" friends. They have saved her from the merciless hands of her brothers and the streets of Jersey City. She attributes her fortunate escapes from patriarchy to her own efforts and shrewdness, and to some of the very men who also assault. When her mother and sisters have been beaten, Jamal blames them for remaining in their relationships and not fleeing. When Jim harassed her, she felt that she was in control of her emotions, and therefore was not victimized. If he crosses a yet unspecified boundary, however, she promises that she will protect herself.

Jamal denies her (gendered) injustice and voices a critical analysis of culture-based injustice (race, class, nationality). Instead of casting Jamal as a woman in denial, it is important to understand how she constructs a paradoxical stance that allows her to criticize, internalize, deny, and identify, simultaneously, with and against oppressive conditions.

In sum, we take the position that victims are better judges than nonvictims and victimizers of social injustice. Victims who are sentenced to the margins of society don't always—but can—articulate critically, with sharpness of vision and perceptions of hypocrisy (Bumiller, 1988; hooks, 1991; Merry, 1985). As individuals, they may be less acute in their judgments than when they identify with a collective. In either case, they surveil the politics of injustice (Foucault, 1980), in the legacy of Hester Prynne, fingering opportunities to reveal oppressive acts committed by social institutions and conventions (Rollins, 1985). But in institutions where ideologies and practices of individualism prevail, rarely will victims bring grievances through official and sanctioned procedures (Bumiller, 1988). The silencing features of institutional life guarantee a yawning space between seeing injustice and publicly grieving it. This space is a political and structural one; it is not merely psychological.

## Grieving Injustice

Over twenty years ago, Albert Hirschman authored a text on responses to injustice. He distinguished between three institutional options—exit, voice, and loyalty—when he wrote, "My principal point—and puzzlement—is easily stated: exit has been accorded an extraordinary privileged position in the American tradition, but then, suddenly, it is wholly proscribed, sometimes for better, sometimes for worse. . . . Why raise your voice in contradiction and get yourself into trouble as long as you can always remove yourself entirely from any given environment should it become unpleasant?" (1970, p. 108). And yet two pages later Hirschman answers his own question: "Exit is bound to be unsatisfactory and unsuccessful, even from the point of view of the individuals who practice it. The point is familiar . . . this unsatisfactory process of individual mobility" (p. 110).

In studies of "real world" injustices, social psychologists rarely measure institutional exit, although we regularly document low rates of grievance or "voice." Sexual harassment cases are among the best documented, if nongrieved, events of social injustice. Stephanie Riger (1991, pp. 497, 498) reports that:

> Despite the high rates found in surveys found in sexual harassment of women, few complaints are pursued through official grievance procedures. Dzeich and Weiner (1984) concluded, after reviewing survey find-

ings, that 20 percent to 30 percent of female college students experience sexual harassment. Yet academic institutions averaged only 4.3 complaints each during the 1982–83 academic year. . . . Although victims of all forms of discrimination are reluctant to pursue grievances, women, who are most likely to be victims of sexual harassment, are especially disinclined to pursue sexual harassment grievances for at least two reasons. First the interpretation in policies of what constitutes harassment may not reflect women's viewpoints, and their complaints may not be seen as valid. Second, the procedures in some policies that are designed to resolve disputes may be inimical to women because they are not compatible with the way that many women view conflict resolution. Gender bias in policies, rather than absence of harassment or lack of assertiveness on the part of victims, produces low numbers of complaints.

Linda Brodkey and Michelle Fine, in their analysis of sexual harassment narratives by female graduate students, found evidence much like Riger's. Brodkey and Fine report similarly high ratios of harassment to low rates of grievance. While harassment was reported by over 70 percent of respondents, grievances were filed by under 10 percent. Graduate students said they worried about retaliation, loss of professional reputation, and further victimization in the grievance process. Most refused official remedies or what Hirschman might call "voice." However, these women were not resigned, accepting, or loyal. Many were furious. Few, however, were prepared to take on the men or the institution and sacrifice their professional lives. Brodkey and Fine learned that the number of official grievances does not reflect the incidence of harassment; the two may actually be inversely related in an institutional climate that sanctions harassment.

Recognizing the paucity of studies, and acts, of individual grievance, we searched the literature for studies of collective public protests and uncovered Emily Abel's work (1981) on faculty women who have brought class-action discrimination lawsuits against their universities. Abel asserts that two conditions must precede the lodging of a public complaint. First, there must be a collective basis for the discrimination, that is, the faculty women quilted their individual stories together into a gendered pattern of nontenuring and promotion. Second, individualistic beliefs in meritocracy must be unraveled and challenged before individuals can join a protest. For these women, bringing a grievance in the academy involved "challenging the meritocracy . . . call[ing] into question a system that rewarded them in the past" (p. 512). Reviewing the literatures on protest, we found much evidence to confirm Abel's analysis. Whereas a sense of collective identity facilitates the public critique of social injustice, a belief in individualistic meritocracy is inhibitive.

In *Falling from Grace* (1988), Katherine Newman examines how women and men make sense of the injustice of downward mobility, using dislocated managers, the air traffic controllers' (PATCO) walkout, and blue collar workers from closed factories and mines. Strong bonds among the air traffic controllers not only incited their collective protest but buffered the adverse psychological impact of their downward mobility. Newman writes, "The strikers have formed an enduring national community even though they have moved into other occupations. It is a community born of collective struggle and defeat, but one whose solidarity continues to cloak each individual with the knowledge that he or she is not alone" (1988, p. 155).

The PATCO men were "brothers in a moral protest, rather than individual victims of impersonal rejections, [who] found self-respect in their loss, a redemption that was not available to downwardly mobile managers" (p. 155). In contrast, the unemployed managers were steeped in meritocratic individualism. They faced a much lonelier shattering of their world view and endured, typically alone, "the crushing self-blame that an ethic of individualism inspires" (p. 234). A similar analysis surfaces in Newman's more recent study (1993) of the *Declining Fortunes* of contemporary baby boomers. Documenting two generations of individualists, Newman witnesses how both the postwar generation and their offspring attribute economic success or failure to individual fortitude, or its absence. Actively rejecting larger economic and historic factors as relevant to their personal trajectories, baby boomers embrace individualism and are thereby unable and unwilling to attribute their current plight to the economic climate. Their parents, too, attribute their personal prosperity and wealth to individual actions and self-styled hard work, ignoring the opportunities made available through the postwar economy and government programs. Newman writes: "When [they] reminisce about who they are, about what their experience represents in the national panorama, this exciting, optimistic sense of upward movement is not what they recall. . . . Most especially the hand of government [is extracted] from the moral tales they tell about how they became the prosperous citizens they are" (1993, p. 89).

These two generations are cloaked in individualism, camouflaging economic and political conditions that surround their respective good and ill fortunes. Retreating into a psychological discourse of individual traits, effort, and perseverance, neither generation has access to a collective analysis, critical consciousness, or an image of shared protest. Seeing injustice, and grieving injustice, are rendered virtually impossible by the fog of meritocratic individualism.

We return then to the findings of Crosby, Majors, and others, who suggest that individuals recognize and name group-level discrimination with greater acuity than they do instances of personal discrimination. We add, now, the finding of Taylor, Wright, Moghaddam, and Lalonde (1990) that experimental subjects are less likely to pursue individual protests than they are collective protests in the face of institutional exclusion. And we conclude that, given the institutional muzzling of protest and nurturing of beliefs in meritocratic individualism, it is unlikely that individual acts of injustice will provoke high levels of outrage and protest. A more likely outcome is alienation. Bumiller writes, "The metaphor of the mask of the victim represents the concept of alienation. The . . . true self is separated from an alien persona. . . . Alienated persons feel no sense of interconnectedness as they play their social roles. . . . This stifles a sense of conflict; those who perceive discrimination do not extrapolate from their experience to a sense of social harm. They often fail to see their daily mistreatment as part of a larger struggle" (1988, p. 62).

Individuals may name publicly and act publicly against injustice primarily when they are in relationships and in communities affected by injustice. There is certainly abundant evidence to suggest that this is the case for poor and working-class women (Ackelsberg, 1988; Gilkes, 1988; Lykes, 1986). Those who experience individual inequities may not see clearly or name them unequivocally as injustices because seeing injustice requires a sense of collectivity—inaccessible to most—an undoing of meritocratic beliefs—threatening to many—and something else to believe in— a tall order. If we believe, as social psychologist Faye Crosby implores us to believe, that public complaint is a good thing, then we must understand the institutional conditions under which it is likely to be displayed and the institutional conditions that muzzle it (1993). (See also Henry Mintzberg (1983) on "professional bureaucracies" as institutional structures in contexts such as universities, in which professional entrepreneurs are sufficiently isolated so that they do not and cannot organize as a collective.)

If, for instance, group identity is a necessary foundation for collective protest, then contemporary theoretical and empirical murmurs about the erosion of collective identities—seen in the recent works of Cameron McCarthy (1993) on "nonsynchronic relations," Stuart Hall (1991) on "fluid identities," and Howard Winant on "hybridity"—should give us pause. With the flourishing of multiculturalism, the fragmentation of once intact and nostalgic communities, the proliferation of multiple consciousness, border cross-ings, and postmodern identities, the grounds for collective identity, and thereby for collective protest, may be shifting like sands out from under (Giroux, 1992).

To illustrate: when Cameron McCarthy introduces "nonsyn-chrony," he is challenging the belief that similarly situated "indi-viduals or groups, in their relation to economic, political and cultural institutions . . . [essentially] share identical consciousness and express the same interests, needs, or desires at the same point in time" (1993, p. 338). McCarthy's work advances critical race the-ory substantially when he shifts focus from individuals to institu-tions. McCarthy contends that institutions establish dynamics of competition, exploitation, domination, and cultural selection that pit "same-class" individuals against each other. Persons with pre-sumably shared bases of identity are often placed at competitive cross-purposes. Solidarity, collective consciousness, and protest are thereby rendered unlikely (Kwong, 1992; Kim, 1993; Omi & Winant, 1993). Instead, alienation and intragroup conflict flourish.

If these readings of poststructural theory and of social psycho-logical empiricism are roughly correct—that collective identity is a necessary precondition for social critique and protest (Crosby, 1993) and that social movements/identities are today broadening beyond narrow, essentialist bases of group membership (West, 1993)—then the political space from which collective identities, critical con-sciousness, and social protest will arise is up for intellectual grabs (see Louise Lamphere, 1992, for a discussion of a movement of polit-ical coalescing beyond essentialism and nationalism). This does not mean that pain, protest, and outrage are out of vogue; this does not mean that acceptance of injustice, passivity, or silence prevail. This does mean, however, that the sites for collective identities and protest are pivoting, as are the arenas through which resistances are likely to be expressed. Political scientist James Scott (1988) has sug-gested that analysts of injustice stop looking for evidence of resis-tance and protest in statistics on the use of official and sanctioned grievance procedures. He entices researchers to look, and listen, instead, to the whispers of survivors narrating their lives. While many victims may publicly sound timid, Scott argues that within their "hidden transcripts of resistance" lies profound social critique. Voices of protest and outrage may be institutionally appropriated and then misheard or represented by dominants and social scientists as self-blame, denial, or loyalty. Our empirical documentation may inadvertently serve to represent as normative (and deserved) existing structures of inequity.

Scott's theorizing suggests that the production of performative denial is an institutional and ideological accomplishment, not a psychological state. Denial and the absence of grievance may reveal more about institutions and ideologies than about individuals. Scott contends, and some of our own empirical data confirms this, that institutions that produce injustice also produce organizational dynamics that muzzle protest. Some of these organizations also, presumably, worry that their workers, students, or other subordinates aren't sufficiently "empowered" to protest. They then may hire social scientists who, inadvertently, reinforce the sense that the problem lies in the individuals who aren't sufficiently assertive to protest or who don't realize their disadvantage. While we argue that Scott underestimates the internalization of institutional hegemony, we agree that institutions are clever at fixing the gaze on individuals and away from institutional policies, practices, and hierarchies (Fine, Guinier, Balin, Bartow, & Satchel, 1993). We turn now to qualitative analyses of voices of resistance to eavesdrop on the layers of protest, denial, and conflict embedded in victims' narratives of injustice.

## Hidden Transcripts

As noted above, if we take the literature on public acts of grievance at face value, it's disappointing, at least to those of us who valorize protest or are voracious consumers of outrage. If, however, we assume that the absence of grievance reveals a delicate sequence of institutionally constructed provocation, surveillance, and inhibition, then we can probe the contradictory layers of resistance, denial, struggle, and justification voiced by victims and wander behind the seeming denial of injustice.

In the intellectual spirit of John Gaventa, James Scott contends that social scientists, organizers, and advocates have looked for evidence of social protest in too narrow a set of places. Quite critical of notions like false consciousness, "total institutions" (Goffman, 1961), or the presumed "success" of hegemony, Scott urges a distinction between public transcripts of domination and compliance and those hidden transcripts of resistance that constitute a "zone of constant struggle between dominants and subordinates . . . not a solid wall" (1988, p. 14). Demanding an "interrogation of power," he contends that "it is more accurate to consider subordinate classes less constrained at the level of thought and ideology, since they can in secluded settings peak with comparative safety [but] more constrained at the level of political action and struggle, where the daily exercise of power sharply limits the options available to them. To put it crudely, it would ordinarily be suicide for serfs to set about to murder their lords and abolish the seigniorial regimes; it is however plausible for them to imagine and talk about such aspirations providing they are discreet about it" (p. 91) (see also Kaminstein, 1988; Rollins, 1985).

If we believe that institutions incite, surveil, and export voices of social critique (Hirschman, 1970), then behind "victims' masks" (Bumiller, 1988), which may appear to be silent, expressionless, denying, or accepting, can be found "hidden transcripts of resistance."

We review three studies that seek to investigate how victims "make sense" of and narrate their circumstances. We take as our focus high school dropouts (Fine, 1991), women heroin addicts (Friedman, Marisa, & Johnson, in press), and incest survivors

(Genovese, 1993), individuals all marked with twentieth-century scarlet letters. We analyze closely their whispers and public performances; we analyze critically how social institutions—schools, methadone clinics, and families—both provoke and expel critique, in ways that paradoxically produce victims who appear anesthetized, compliant, satisfied, or silent about social injustice but who are, instead, deeply wounded, usually conflicted, and profoundly critical. Dropouts, women heroin addicts, and incest survivors are typically portrayed as duped, depressed, and passive victims. Having pried open the "social space of dissident subcultures" (Scott, 1988), we often hear well-articulated commentary on social and institutional practices that alienate, marginalize, and purge.

Michelle Fine (1991), in *Framing Dropouts*, questions the popular portrait of urban dropouts as victims or perpetrators, both characterized by psychologists as unmotivated, depressed, or unintelligent. Fine found, instead, that low-income urban dropouts were significantly more critical of racial and economic injustices, significantly less conforming, and significantly less depressed (using Beck's inventory) than a comparison sample of students who stayed in school. Low-income high school dropouts had academic standing equal to their persisting peers, but in open-ended interviews, they narrated prophetic doubts about the value of high school education to them, questioning the avowed relationship of hard work to economic outcomes. Persisting students were far less challenging, far more compliant, and statistically more depressed.

Likewise, in a study of twenty-five white, middle- and upper-class women recovering from heroin addiction, Friedman et al. (in press) present the narratives of elite white women who adamantly rejected what they saw as their class-based gender prescriptions—to be obedient, subservient, selfless, and low in feelings of self-worth. These women resisted traditional feminine expectations reinforced by family members and by peers.

But while we listen to the adolescents and young adults who dropped out voicing critique and enacting frightening, if oddly

courageous, forms of resistance, we worry about the adverse consequences that tumble out of their hidden transcripts. By dropping
out, for instance, these young adults thought they were taking control of their lives. Yet, as Fine writes, "their very lives, self-conscious
critique, or even naive questions pierce the fragile veneer of equal
opportunity, [but they] typically pay a price. Their critique may be
banished, suppressed, or declared 'wrong' on a standardized test.
They may be sent off to a psychologist for assistance, classified as
insubordinate, seen as cause for a suspension, or labeled . . . as a student with special needs" (1991, p. 61).

Eventually, the dropouts paid a big price socially and economically. Likewise, the women heroin addicts who abandoned their
privileged backgrounds and lifestyles, who turned to heroin as a way
to "transcend" restrictive expectations. They testify that they challenged gender domination through their heroin use to "help them
feel better"—by offering strength, self-worth, and feelings of invin-
cibility—and to enable them to "take control" of their lives. Heroin,
like dropping out, gave them a space for critique, a way out of
classed, gendered stereotypes.

But these women, like the dropouts, soon began to realize the
enormous price they paid for their critique and for their acts of resistance. Dropouts couldn't get work; drugs were controlling the lives
of these heroin addicts. Stealing, providing sexual services, and performing stereotypically feminine jobs to support their habits, they
began to see the heroin subculture as a mirror of the dominant culture, devaluing and relegating women to low status.

From the narratives of adult female incest survivors collected by
Toni Genovese (1993), we hear another set of victims, this time
young women who tried to talk within their institutions of injustice.
These survivors delivered stories, as children and as adults, about
incest *to* their families, schools, and communities. But unlike the
dropouts and heroin addicts, who delivered critique self-consciously
through opposition and troublemaking, Genovese found that most
of the women in her sample tried to talk gently. Nonetheless, to a

woman, each experienced a profound silencing, which echoed through a familywide refusal to know. Their words and memories were contested. Their grievances and screams for help were reconstituted. When these survivors confided in their mothers, Genovese found, they were usually ignored or accused of ruining their mothers' lives and destroying their families. No wonder, then, that so many adult survivors "choose" silence. No denial. No acceptance. No more talk.

Seventeen-year-old dropouts were full of possibilities, motivation, and energy. But by age twenty-one, dropouts had turned their critique inward. By age twenty-one, they blamed themselves, not schools, racism, or labor conditions, for their personal failures. Like Newman's managers and baby boomers, the dropouts eventually punished themselves through a language of regrets and individualistic self-blame. Anger and depression filled those spaces where critical collective consciousness might have flourished.

Similarly, the women heroin addicts who "successfully" moved into methadone clinics ultimately shifted their ideologies, critique, and consciousness to relocate the source of "the problem" within themselves. Clinics prescribe such a shift; each woman is encouraged to redefine herself as a victim of her own pathological disposition in order for "successful recovery" to take place. Critical assessments of the dominant culture melted away, while attempts to contain these women by the medical profession were abundant (see also Rains, 1971).

From these three examples, victims do not appear to be poor judges or hesitant articulators of social injustice. Sometimes clearly and sometimes vaguely, they see institutional conditions that incite and those that inhibit their sense of injustice. These high school dropouts, women heroin users, and incest survivors critique, rebel, drop out of, and sometimes become loyal to institutions that betray them, leading to self-blaming in their narrated autobiographies. These victims journey through Hirschman's three options and navigate a chronology of critique. In the beginning, within institutions they experienced as oppressive, they were fundamentally unwilling to display loyalty. They all tried voice, through registers available to and invented by them. Eventually, they all exited.

In these three cases, we find young men and women with intimate knowledge of injustice, enacting strong and troubling acts of resistance. And in all three cases, these young women and men were institutionally betrayed. Twice. First, in the original voicing of their critique of schooling and labor, high school dropouts were silenced and exported out of high schools. The women heroin users were exploited by husbands and male drug addicts, and medicalized for their transgressions. The incest survivors' pleas were systematically appropriated, if not gagged with family handkerchiefs.

Second, after they exited their schools, homes, and communities, many of these high school dropouts, women heroin addicts, and incest survivors realized that their resistances fundamentally reproduced their worst fears. For some, their early social critique turned inward. For most, a sullen silence settled in. Framing this excursion as denial artificially simplifies the chronology of critique these young women and men tried to navigate. Even while we acknowledge that they, too, contribute to their own impoverished circumstances, it is incumbent on social scientists to track how institutions protect themselves from accusations of injustice and create tunnels of blame back to individuals most disadvantaged.

With deep complexity, social institutions eventually render most victims mute, but not naive. The dropouts, women heroin users, and incest survivors, though differentially situated at the margins of race, class, and gender, were all unable to sustain critical talk against their "home" institutions. Their biographies of critique and grievance allow us to see that institutions create conditions in which injustices brew and are contested, resisted, or accepted. As social psychologists, we have spent much time focusing on who sees and who grieves injustice (Fine, 1980) but rarely on revealing the powerful subtexts of resistance, on tracking the rich and troubling biographies of critical consciousness, or on illuminating those features of institutional life that make inequities seem fair, natural, and deserved. We turn now to institutions to understand how they are implicated in producing what sounds like denial of injustice.

## Institutionalizing Injustice

Pierre Bourdieu (1991) invokes the word *institution* as if it were a verb: "The act of institution is an act of magic" (p. 119). . . . "An act of communication, but of a particular kind: it signifies to someone what his identity is, but in a way that both expresses it to him and imposes it on him by expressing it in front of everyone and thus informing him in an authoritative manner of what he is and what he must be" (p. 121). This is also one of the functions of the act of institution: to discourage permanently any attempt to cross the line, to transgress, desert, or quit.

To understand this institutional magic, we present what we thought would be a simple gender equity analysis of the University of Pennsylvania Law School (Fine et al., 1993). This case study reveals how institutional policies and practices ensure and normalize the production of gender and race stratification, amidst ideologies of diversity and gender and race neutrality. This institution makes magic, as Bourdieu attests. A few "winners" flourish, while many "losers" flounder. Everyone learns her or his place in the hierarchy. Believers, ranging from agnostics to zealots, are socialized over three years into the almost uninterruptable culture of meritocratic individualism. As professional socialization succeeds and becomes reflected in students' identities, possibilities for critical consciousness and collective protest evaporate (see Scott Turow, 1988, on this point).

In "Becoming Gentlemen: The Education of Women at the University of Pennsylvania Law School," Fine et al. (1993) describe preliminary research by and about women law students at the University of Pennsylvania Law School, a typical, if elite, law school stratified deeply along gender lines. Our data base draws from stu-

dents enrolled at the law school between 1987 and 19
includes academic performance data from 981 students, self-reported
survey data from 366 students, written narratives from 100 students,
and group-level interview data of approximately 60 women and
men students. According to our data, the educational strategies of
the law school create and legitimate inequity cast as merit and yield
adverse consequences for women, all while being touted as gender
neutral.

Four major findings deserve mention. First, our study showed
strong attitudinal differences between women and men in year one.
That is, the first-year women were far more critical than first-year
men of the social status quo, of legal education, of sexism and
racism. By their third year, however, women law students were no
more or less critical than their third-year male peers, and far less
critical than their first-year female counterparts. A disproportion-
ate number of the women we studied entered law school with an
explicit commitment to public interest law (33 percent of first-year
women versus 8 percent of men). Two years later, however, women
and men held equivalent corporate ambitions; few were interested
in public interest work (of third-year students, only 7 percent of
women and 7 percent of men were interested in public interest law).
By year three, men and women were statistically indistinguishable
on all measures except for levels of "emotional distress," where
women "won."

Second, we found that despite identical entry-level credentials
for men and women, an academic performance differential was set
in place in the first year of law school and maintained by gender
over the next two years. By the end of their first year in law school,
the men were three times more likely than the women to be in the
top 10 percent of their class. After year two and again after year
three, men were two times more likely to be in the top 10 percent.
In a pattern established firmly in the first year, and maintained
thereafter, women receive relatively lower grades, have lower class
rank, and earn fewer honors.

Third, many women were deeply alienated from the Socratic method of classroom instruction, which is the dominant pedagogy for almost all first-year instruction. Women self-reported much higher rates of silence and lower rates of class participation than did men for all three years of law school. Our data suggest that many women do not "engage" with this methodology. It makes them feel strange, alienated, and "delegitimated." They "disidentify" (Steele, 1992), with some complaining that they can no longer recognize their former selves. One woman described herself as an alienated "social male." "Law school is the most bizarre place I have ever been. . . . [First year] was like a frightening out-of-body experience. Lots of women agree with me. I have no words to say what I feel. My voice from that year is gone." Another young woman narrates the embodiment of hierarchy, and a sense of personal deficit: "For me the damage is done; it's in me. I will never be the same."

Fourth, we collected evidence of substantial economic consequences for women who graduate from law school after experiencing what they describe as a crisis of identity. These women graduate with less competitive academic credentials, are not represented equally within the law school's academic and social hierarchies, and are less successful in securing prestigious or desirable jobs after graduation.

*Is this a case of institutional injustice—or not?* We spent much time listening to varied interpretations of the data from university colleagues. There was, initially, substantial resistance to a gender-based interpretation. Over time, however, many law school faculty were willing to concede that there was such a story to tell. Some were not very alarmed. The point of law school, they contended, is to produce, shape, and promote, through meritocracy, a particular type of legal thinker who is competitive, adversarial, and ruthless. This person values logic over emotion and neutrality over commitments; he or she supports individual rights over community interests. To these faculty members, our data confirm who is likely to be the best and the brightest, who is the most able "produce" for law firms, which are, presumably, the law school's "clients." For these faculty, these are not data of injustice. They are evidence of meritocratic streamlining.

As Howie Winant (1993) argues, however, the identities and stratifications created and then legitimated within the law school "operate as a cover for deep inequalities, for what Balibar calls the 'theme of hierarchy,' and as justification for racist practices of all kinds" (p. 175). No one raised the possibilities of reimagining the law school to be more cooperative, flatter, less hierarchical, but still intellectually and professionally engaging (see Vanderslice, in this book). These were considered oxymoronic.

The law school study at Penn may be the Aesopian example of institutions that incubate social identities and ideologies in the name of "merit." Gramsci has argued that the real work of domination lies not in coercion, but in hegemony—convincing people to believe in, work for, and defend the very systems that threaten their livelihoods and steal their souls. This law school not only produces few winners and many losers; it generates and educates through an ideology that justifies as natural and deserving grossly differential patterns of winning. "Winners"—in this case, disproportionately white males—see their outcomes as largely due to intellect, hard work, and talent. "Losers"—in this case, women initially fired up by a powerful critique of law school, the law, and broader social inequities—come to learn their place in the hierarchy and to justify its structures. Women (and men) learn not to transgress, desert, or quit. No exit, little voice, and no protest. Becoming a professional means being socialized into individualism and meritocracy, and away from collective struggles, thereby inhibiting critique. As Bourdieu cleverly notes, this is magic. But is it denial?

In such institutional contexts, "seeing" or "naming" injustice doubles as an act of personal vulnerability and institutional disloyalty. From white women or students of color, such naming is typically heard as "sour grapes." Subtly it moves underground or perverts into "stress," emotional amnesia, physical health problems, or dropping out. Opportunities for critically examining institutional practices, or for nurturing collective consciousness, are limited. As institutional denial of injustice swells, collective consciousness shrivels. And, needless to say, few use the official grievance procedures to protest. To do so would be to suggest this is aberrant behavior, and it appears far more typically institutionalized and accepted than that.

## De-Meaning Denial

What are the roots of those democratic social movements that both enlarge the opportunities of participation and enhance people's abilities to participate in the public world? [Evans & Boyte, 1986, p. viii].

This chapter makes the case for social research on the institutional practices that incite, and then inhibit, critical collective consciousness of social injustice. Inviting us all to crawl behind the discomforting findings of "denial" of personal injustice, we use our last pages to press for a bold, activist, research project on social injustice, undertaken in the spirit of Sara Evans and Harry Boyte. This project has four parts. First, we invite lots of fine-grained analyses of those institutional policies and practices that create and justify social hierarchies. which emerge as natural or deserved. Second, we solicit a rigorous, qualitative archiving of the hidden transcripts of resistance that are muzzled, muttered, or even shouted "irrationally" within and outside these institutions, masquerading as denial or paranoia. Third, we look forward to critical examinations of "neutral" ideologies that perpetuate injustice and mothball social institutions against accusations of injustice (for example, merit, which protects gender and race stratification; the recently popularized False Memory Syndrome, which serves to invalidate the claims of women speaking out about incest; the recent policy of allowing lesbians and gays to serve in the military as long as they "don't tell"). Fourth, we need social psychological studies of collective consciousness and protests as they nest within what Sara Evans and Harry Boyte (1986) call "free spaces"—places where safe and critical talk can percolate and be hatched into transformative social possibilities. Evans and Boyte detail with broad and delicious strokes how such spaces can be constructed, how to keep them democratic and moral, and how fragile they can be—especially if "invaded" by social scientists (1986). And yet we imagine action research, in the spirit of Kurt Lewin, that would enrich the connective tissues of such spaces, and we encourage such work.

A social psychological project confined, primarily, to studying laboratory-created responses to individual injustices or to assessing victims' uses of official grievance procedures at a single point in time can tell us only very partial stories about social injustice, victimization, and privilege (see Fine, 1980, for an example of such problematic work). This chapter, instead, proposes a smorgasbord for understanding protest. Our imagined project invites social psychologists to analyze injustice over time in schools, families, communities, the House of Representatives, corporations, courts . . . and perhaps even to nurture the conditions for free spaces to flourish. In such spaces, the very categories we seek to understand, the very discourses we assume unproblematic, the very institutions we inhabit, and the very grievance procedures we have helped to create can be critically examined and transformed. An activist project for a social psychology of injustice awaits. If we don't pursue it, we might very well ask, Who is denying?

## References

Abel, E. (1981). Collective protest and the meritocracy: Faculty women and sex discrimination lawsuits. *Feminist Studies, 7*(3), 505–537.

Ackelsberg, M. (1988). Communities, resistance, and women's activism. In A. Bookman & S. Morgan (Eds.), *Women and the politics of empowerment* (pp. 297–313). Philadelphia: Temple University Press.

Asch, A., & Fine, M. (1988). Introduction: Beyond pedestals. In M. Fine & A. Asch (Eds.), *Women with disabilities* (pp. 1–37). Philadelphia: Temple University Press.

Birt, C. M., & Dion, K. L. (1987). Relative deprivation theory and responses to discrimination in gay male and lesbian sample. *British Journal of Social Psychology, 26*, 139–145.

Bourdieu, P. (1991). *Language and symbolic power*. Cambridge, MA: Harvard University Press.

Brodkey, L., & Fine, M. (1988). Presence of mind in the absence of body. *Journal of Education, 170*, 84–99.

Bumiller, K. (1988). *The civil rights society*. Baltimore, MD: John Hopkins University Press.

Clayton, S. D., & Crosby, F. J. (1992). *Justice, gender, and affirmative action*. Ann Arbor: University of Michigan Press.

Collins, P. H. (1991). *Black feminist thought*. New York: Routledge.

Collins, R. L., Taylor, S. E., & Skokan, L. A. (1990). A better world or a shattered vision? Changes in life perspectives following victimization. *Social Cognition, 8*(3), 263–285.

Condor, S. (1986). Sex role beliefs and "traditional" women: Feminist and intergroup perspectives. In S. Wilkinson (Ed.), *Feminist social psychology* (pp. 97–118). Philadelphia: Open University Press.

Crosby, F. J. (1982). *Relative deprivation and working women*. New York: Oxford University Press.

Crosby, F. J. (1984). The denial of personal discrimination. *American Behavioral Scientist, 27*(3), 371–386.

Crosby, F. J. (1993). Why complain? *Journal of Social Issues, 49*(1), 169–184.

Crosby, F. J., Pufall, A., Snyder, R., O'Connell, M., & Whalen, P. (1989). The denial of personal disadvantage among you and me, and all the other ostriches. In M. Crawford & M. Gentry (Eds.), *Gender and thought* (pp. 79–99). New York: Springer-Verlag.

Deutsch, M. (1985). *Distributive justice: A social psychological perspective*. New Haven, CT: Yale University Press.

Dolnick, E. (1993). Deaf as culture. *Atlantic Monthly, 27*(3), 37–51.

Du Bois, W.E.B. (1903). *Souls of black folk*. Chicago: A. C. McClurg.

Eagleton, T. (1991). *Ideology*. New York: Verso.

Evans, S., & Boyte, H. (1986). *Free spaces*. Chicago: University of Chicago Press.

Fine, M. (1980). *Options to injustice*. Unpublished doctoral dissertation, Teachers College, Columbia University, New York.

Fine, M. (1991). *Framing dropouts: Notes on the politics of an urban high school*. Albany: State University of New York.

Fine, M., Guinier, L., Balin, J., Bartow, A., & Satchel, D. (1993). Becoming gentlemen: The education of women at the University of Pennsylvania Law School. *University of Pennsylvania Law Review, 141*(6), 1001–1082.

Fine, M., & Weis, L. (1993). [Reconciling voices of hope and despair]. Unpublished raw data.

Foucault, M. (1980). *The history of sexuality* (Vol. 1). New York: Vintage.

Friedman, J., Marisa, A., & Johnson, D. P. (in press). Women and heroin: The path of resistance and its consequences. *Gender & Society.*

Genovese, T. (1993, February). *Disclosing abuse: Silence and telling.* Paper presented at the 14th Ethnography in Education Forum, Philadelphia.

Gilkes, C. (1988). Building in many places: Multiple commitments and ideologies in Black women's community work. In A. Bookman & S. Morgan (Eds.), *Women and the politics of empowerment* (pp. 53–76). Philadelphia: Temple University Press.

Ginsburg, F. D. (1989). *Contested lives: The abortion debate in an American community.* Berkeley: University of California Press.

Giroux, H. (1992). *Border crossings.* New York: Routledge.

Goffman, E. (1961). *Asylums.* New York: Doubleday.

Gramsci, A. (1971). *Selections from prison notebooks.* New York: International.

Guimond, S., & Dube-Simard, L. (1983). Relation deprivation theory and the Quebec nationalist movement: The cognition-emotion distinction and the personal-group deprivation issue. *Journal of Personality and Social Psychology, 44*(3), 526–535.

Hafer, C. L., & Olson, J. M. (1989). Beliefs in a just world and reactions to personal deprivation. *Journal of Personality, 57,* 799–823.

Hall, S. (1991, Fall). Identity and difference. *Radical America,* 9–22.

Hartsock, N. (1983). *Money, sex, and power.* White Plains, NY: Longman.

Hawthorne, N. (1978). *The scarlet letter* (2nd ed.). New York: W. W. Norton.

Hirschman, A. O. (1970). *Exit, voice, and loyalty.* Cambridge, MA: Harvard University Press.

hooks, b. (1991). *Yearning.* Boston: South End Press.

Janoff-Bulman, R. (1979). Characterological versus behavioral self-blame: Inquiries into depression and rape. *Journal of Personality and Social Psychology, 37*(10), 1798–1809.

Janoff-Bulman, R., & Frieze, I. H. (1983). A theoretical perspective for understanding reactions to victimization. *Journal of Social Issues, 39*(2), 1–17.

Kaminstein, D. S. (1988, Fall). Toxic talk. *Social Policy,* pp. 5–10.

Katz, B. L., & Burt, M. R. (1988). Self-blame in recovery from rape. In A. W. Burgess (Ed.), *Rape and sexual assault II.* New York: Garland Press.

Kim, E. (1993). Home is where the han is: A Korean-American perspective on the Los Angeles upheavals. In R. Gooding-Williams (Ed.), *Reading Rodney King—Reading urban uprising* (pp. 215–235). New York: Routledge.

Klatch, R. E. (1987). *Women of the new right.* Philadelphia: Temple University Press.

Kwong, P. (1992, June). The first multicultural riots. *Village Voice*, pp. 29–32.

Lamphere, L. (1992). *Structuring diversity*. Chicago: University of Chicago Press.

Lykes, M. (1986). *The will to resist: Preservation of self and culture in Guatemala*. Paper presented at the Latin American Studies Association Meeting, Boston.

Lykes, M. (1988). Dialogue with Guatemalan Indian women: Critical perspectives on constructing collaborative research. In R. Unger (Ed.), *Representations: Social constructions of gender*. Ann Arbor: University of Michigan Press.

McCarthy, C. (1993). Beyond the poverty of theory in race relations: Nonsynchrony and social difference in education. In L. Weis & M. Fine (Eds.), *Beyond silenced voices*. Albany: State University of New York Press.

Major, B. (1987). Gender, justice, and the psychology of entitlement. In P. Shaver & C. Hendrick (Eds.), *Review of personality and social psychology* (Vol. 7). Newbury Park, CA: Sage.

Major, B. (1989). Gender differences in comparisons and entitlement: Implications for comparable worth. *Journal of Social Issues*, 45(4), 99–115.

Major, B. (1994). From social inequality to personal entitlement: The role of social comparisons, legitimacy appraisals, and group membership. *Advances in Experimental Social Psychology*, 26, 293–355.

Major, B., & Konar, E. (1984). An investigation of sex differences in pay expectations and their possible causes. *Academy of Management Journal*, 27, 777–792.

Major, B., McFarlin, D., & Ganon, D. (1984). Overworked and underpaid: On the nature of gender differences in personal entitlement. *Journal of Personality and Social Psychology*, 47, 399–412.

Matsuda, M. J. (1990). Pragmatism modified and the false consciousness problem. *Southern California Law Review*, 63, 1763–1782.

Merry, S. (1985). Concepts of law and justice among working class Americans: Ideology as culture. *Legal Studies Forum*, 9, 59–67.

Mintzberg, H. (1983). *Power in and around organizations*. Englewood Cliffs, NJ: Prentice-Hall.

Newman, K. (1988). *Falling from grace*. New York: Vintage.

Newman, K. (1993). *Declining fortunes*. New York: Basic Books.

Omi, M., & Winant, H. (1993). The Los Angeles "race riot" and contemporary U.S. politics. In R. Gooding-Williams (Ed.), *Reading Rodney King—Reading urban uprising* (pp. 97–116). New York: Routledge.

Ostrander, S. A. (1984). *Women of the upper class*. Philadelphia: Temple University Press.

Rains, P. M. (1971). *Becoming an unwed mother*. Hawthorne, NY: Aldine.

Riger, S. (1991). Gender dilemmas in sexual harassment policies and procedures. *American Psychologist*, 46(5), 497–505.

Roberts, R. (1993). *Sexual harassment in a college setting: Attributions of and about men and women*. Unpublished manuscript.

Rollins, J. (1985). *Between women*. Philadelphia: Temple University Press.

Scott, J. (1988). *Domination and the arts of resistance*. New Haven, CT: Yale University Press.

Smith, D. (1987). *The everyday world as problematic: A feminist sociology*. Boston: Northeastern Press.

Steele, C. (1992, April). Race and the schooling of black Americans. *Atlantic Monthly*, pp. 68–78.

Steil, J. (in press). Marital equality: Benefits and barriers. In M. Lerner & G. Mikula (Eds.), *Entitlement and the affectional bond*. New York: Plenum.

Taylor, D., Wright, S., Moghaddam, F., & Lalonde, R. (1990). The personal/group discrimination discrepancy. *Personality and Social Psychology Bulletin*, 16(2), 254–262.

Taylor, S. E. (1983). Adjustment to threatening events. *American Psychologist*, 38, 1161–1173.

Taylor, S. E. (1991). *Positive illusions*. New York: Basic Books.

Taylor, S. E., Wood, J. V., & Lichtman, R. R. (1983). It could be worse: Selective evaluation as a response to victimization. *Journal of Social Issues*, 39, 19–40.

Turow, S. (1988). *One l*. New York: Farrar, Straus & Giroux.

Walster, E., Berscheid, E., & Walster, G. W. (1976). New directions in equity research. In L. Berkowitz & E. Walster (Eds.), *Advances in experimental social psychology*. San Diego: Academic Press.

West, C. (1993). *Race matters*. Boston: Beacon Press.

Winant, H. (1993). Amazing race: Recent writing on racial politics and theory. *Socialist Review*, 23(2), 161–183.

Wortman, C. B. (1976). Causal attributions and personal control. In J. H. Harvey, W. J. Ickes, & R. F. Kidd (Eds.), *New directions in attribution research* (Vol. 1). Hillsdale, NJ: Erlbaum.

Wortman, C. B. (1983). Coping with victimization. *Journal of Social Issues*, 39(2), 195–221.

# 11

# Drawing the Line

## Social Categorization, Moral Exclusion, and the Scope of Justice

### Susan Opotow

How can genocides occur? What social psychological processes permit ordinary, decent people to harm others? Recent instances of widespread harm include the Third Reich's genocide policy (Lifton, 1986), the My Lai massacre (Kelman & Hamilton, 1989), and the institutionalization of political violence in the Third World (Sloan & Montero, 1990; Zwi & Ugalde, 1989). To better understand how such extreme harm doing can occur and how people are able to perpetrate or condone it, I examine ordinary psychological processes that can induce people to perceive others as eligible for harmful treatment.

## The Scope of Justice

Each of us has a psychological boundary for fairness, the *scope of justice* or *moral community*, within which concerns with justice and moral rules govern our conduct. A narrow scope of justice constricts the set of situations in which justice concerns are applicable (Deutsch, 1974, 1985; Opotow, 1990c; Staub, 1987, 1990).

For social categories inside our scope of justice, concerns about deserving and fair treatment are salient. We perceive harm that befalls them as lamentable or outrageous. For social categories outside the scope of justice, the concepts of deserving and fair treatment do not apply and can seem irrelevant. We can perceive those outside as nonentities, undeserving, or expendable. Harm that befalls them does not prompt the concern, remorse, or outrage that occurs when those inside the scope of justice are harmed. *Moral exclusion* occurs when we exclude groups or individuals from the scope of justice. As a consequence of such exclusion, moral values and rules that apply in relations with insiders are not applicable, permitting moral justifications—even jubilation—for harm that befalls outsiders.

Our scope of justice is a fundamental psychosocial orientation toward others that underlies many social judgments and behavior. Walzer (1983, p. 31) asserts its primacy in his claim that "the primary good we distribute to one another is membership in some human community." Topics in psychology relevant to the scope of justice include altruism, aggression, prejudice, discrimination, stigma, enemy images, conflict, cooperation, competition, obedience to authority, justice, and victimization. The construct *scope of justice* links these topics and has been enriched by research on each of these facets of moral exclusion.

### Bases of Exclusion

Social categories that have been excluded from the scope of justice and have experienced harm as a result include people who are women, aged, black, Jewish, prisoners of conscience, slaves, children, or retarded. This sampling of excluded social categories indicates the wide variation in criteria for inclusion, such as ideology, skin color, age, and cognitive capacity. Any social or physical characteristic can serve as the basis for social differentiation and moral valuation. Religious identity has been a powerful basis for moral exclusion and persecution throughout human history. Skin color, a neutral physical characteristic, is another conspicuous basis for social categorization that generates discriminatory treatment against those whose skin color differs from the "norm" (Archer, 1985; Tajfel, 1978).

This sampling of excluded social categories suggests the kinds of harm that can befall those who are excluded from the protections of community membership, including abrogation of rights, denial of economic opportunities, and physical exclusion through institutionalization. Tajfel (1982, pp. 486–487) describes how social categorizations in World War II led to the abrogation of rights and, ultimately, the destruction of millions of people that required no justifications: "The 'marking off' from the rest of the population . . . applied to uncounted numbers of Russians, Poles, Gypsies, Jews (German or not), mentally retarded, and many other categories of human beings. They were not so much marked off from the rest of the population, as from their definition of being human, and all that this entails. It is not that attributions of some kind or another were made about the motives of all those people. *No attributions needed to be made at all*, no more than attributions are made about insects subjected to a DDT treatment" [italics in original].

The persecution of heretics, Jews, and lepers during the Middle Ages was ostensibly justified by "stigmatizing" characteristics— heretical views, sinister practices, and moral afflictions—that disqualified each group from community membership. Although each group had particular stigmatizing characteristics associated with it, all three groups were perceived as physically and morally loathsome, frightening, and capable of polluting society. All three groups were essentially treated the same way: "They were required to advertise in their dress the segregation from society at large which was institutionalized by imprisoning heretics and confining lepers to lazar houses or villages and Jews to their increasingly strictly defined residential quarters in cities. In all three cases exclusion from the community extended to civil rights, denying access to public courts and office, security of property during life and disposal of it after death" (Moore, 1987, p. 66).

Physical separation of excluded groups from the community was not only achieved by confinement to strictly defined quarters but also by prohibitions on association. Those who sheltered or defended heretics, for example, were excluded from community privileges and protections: "All who gave them any help would not be eligible to give evidence or seek redress in the courts, and nobody would have any dealings with them, either socially or in business" (Moore, 1987, p. 24). Similarly, in World War II, sheltering or feeding Jews was punishable by death in Nazi-occupied areas (Hallie, 1979).

## Mild and Severe Exclusion

Notorious instances of exclusion that occurred during widespread state-sanctioned actions—such as the African slave trade and the events of the Middle Ages and the Third Reich—are psychologically similar to more ordinary instances of exclusion that occur today when some social categories are perceived as outside the scope of justice and are harmed by deprivation of resources and dignity. Groups excluded from the scope of justice in contemporary society experience discrimination in such spheres as education (Fine, 1990), housing (Danielson, 1976), and employment (Clayton & Crosby, 1992).

Severe instances of exclusion differ from everyday, milder instances in their scope and severity, but mild and severe instances of exclusion share some psychological orientations toward those excluded: (1) the excluded are perceived as psychologically distant; (2) the community feels no sense of moral obligation toward them; (3) the excluded are viewed as nonentities, expendable, or undeserving; and (4) the community approves procedures and outcomes for them that would not be acceptable for those inside the scope of justice.

Consistent with Deutsch's contention (1973, p. 365) in his "Crude Law" that "the characteristic processes and effects elicited by a given type of relationship tend also to elicit that type of social relationship," it appears reasonable to propose a bidirectional causal relationship between these psychological orientations and exclusion. That is, just as exclusion elicits these orientations, the orientations also engender exclusion. The abject condition of those degraded by exclusion serves to justify their degrading treatment.

## Recognizing Injustice

We tend to believe that social conventions of the present are fairer and more humane than those of the barbarous past, when blatant inhumanities were condoned. Yet each society has limits to its liberalism and ignores or legitimizes its own injustices. Because the injustices of any society are based on shared social perceptions and conventions, they are "institutionalized, invisible, and accepted as if inevitable" (Fine, 1990, p. 9). For example, it is easier to recognize exclusionary attitudes toward women apparent in clitoridectomy—female genital mutilation—than in the high rate of violent victimization toward women in our society (Sorenson & Bowie, 1994). As a society's mores undergo change, injustices of previous discriminatory practices become apparent. For example, at present there is greater awareness of the exclusionary attitudes that have led to sexual harassment and the location of environmental hazards in communities of color.

Psychologically, it is comfortable to perceive those who exclude and harm others as evil or demented, but we each have boundaries for justice. Our moral obligations are stronger toward those who are close to us and weaker toward those who are psychologically distant. For example, when the media report on suffering and deaths that are inflicted by totalitarian regimes or that result from intranational conflicts (although the quantity of this attention can vary considerably [Goodman, 1992]), such as in Cambodia, El Salvador, Nicaragua, Peru, Liberia, the former Yugoslavia, and Rwanda, we often fail—as a nation, as communities, and as individuals—to provide aid or help resolve the conflict. Rationalizations for inaction include the futility of doing much of use, not knowing where to start, and insufficient knowledge about the politics of the situation.

Closer to home, Blackman (1993, p. 19) observes that poor women, particularly those who have perpetrated family violence, have been excluded from both society and psychological scholarship: "We, middle-class Whites mostly, have not simply failed to see and to know these women. We have deliberately turned away so as not to see these taboo acts that we might imagine at desperate moments but would never enact. We have kept our distance affirmatively, defensively, and perhaps, even, self-righteously." In reality, we each have limited time and resources; yet how we structure our time and expend those resources reveals our moral priorities and the social categories that fall outside our scope of justice.

Our capacity for justice appears to be finite. Just to consider justice has a cost in energy and resources. This cost is likely to be higher when conflict escalates and resource scarcity increases (Leventhal, 1979; Staub, 1989; Staub & Rosenthal, 1994). Exclusion could be an adaptive defense that simplifies our lives and conserves time, energy, and resources.

## Empirical Research

Experimental and qualitative research I conducted examined some of the social psychological conditions that modify the scope of justice in everyday life. This research focused on approaches to understanding the nature, antecedents, and consequences of the scope of justice.

### Background

Experimental research I conducted examined the role of three hypothesized antecedents—utility, similarity, and conflict severity—on the scope of justice and on attitudinal consequences of inclusion and exclusion. (See Opotow, 1987, 1993a, for an overview of the literature and methods.) This research, like many justice studies, utilized an allocation decision to examine justice beliefs. Participants read of a conflict of interest between people and a beetle for a parcel of land, made an allocation decision concerning the parcel, and answered questions that revealed the justice beliefs associated with their decision.

The beetle served as a target to examine the scope of justice for several practical reasons. First, utilizing a beetle maximized the range of responses and eliminated problems with social desirability. While it is acceptable to advocate protection or extermination of a beetle, this range of responses would be unacceptable for human groups or more familiar animals. Second, people know very little about beetles (Kellert, 1984), making it possible to fabricate experimental manipulations for utility (a "beneficial" versus a "harmful" beetle) and similarity (a beetle "similar" to people versus a beetle "dissimilar" to people). Third, utilizing the beetle maximized the inequality in social status and the psychological distance between stakeholders in the conflict. Finally, utilizing the beetle provided useful data on the protection of unpopular but useful animals (Opotow, 1993a, 1993b).

Qualitative research I conducted utilized interviews about actual interpersonal conflicts that junior high school students had experienced with peers. Analyses of these narratives examined social cognitions associated with inclusion in and exclusion from the scope of justice. Adolescents' interpersonal conflicts served as a vehicle for understanding how ordinary events modify people's scope of justice and for examining correlates of inclusion and exclusion. In contrast to the experimental study, this investigation provided an opportunity to examine the scope of justice in the context of relationships among equals. (See Opotow 1990a, 1991, 1992, for details on methods.)

## What is the Scope of Justice?

Precisely what is the scope of justice? To identify the components of this construct, dependent measures in the experimental "beetle" study assessed a variety of beliefs based on the justice literature (Austin & Hatfield, 1980; Cohen & Greenburg, 1982; Deutsch, 1982; Lerner, 1980; Mikula, 1980; Nader, 1975; Rawls, 1971; Staub, 1979; Walzer, 1983). Principal components analysis of dependent measures yielded a reliable scope of justice scale (Opotow, 1987, 1993a) consisting of three items: (1) belief that considerations of fairness apply to another, (2) willingness to make sacrifices to foster another's well-being, and (3) willingness to allocate a share of community resources to another.

Qualitative research on adolescents' peer conflicts utilized these three items derived from the experimental beetle study in interviews that asked participants whether an adversary in an interpersonal conflict was someone entitled to fair treatment, someone they were willing to help, and someone to whom they would loan money (Opotow, 1990a). Junior high school students' responses yielded eight combinations of "yes" and "no" responses. Most responses clustered into only three combinations: (1) all affirmative or inside the scope of justice, (2) all negative or outside the scope of justice, and (3) a mixture of "yes" and "no" responses or "conditional exclusion" in which participants would *not* care if their adversary were treated unfairly, would *not* loan money to their adversary, but *would* be willing to help.

This clustering of responses suggests that the scope of justice is a continuous rather than a dichotomous construct. It also suggests that a prosocial orientation modulates inclusion and exclusion, at least in the context of an interpersonal conflict among peers. It would be interesting to know if responses to these three items in the context of adolescents' peer conflicts would cluster the same way in other kinds of interpersonal relationships (such as among unequals) and in other social contexts (such as intergroup conflict). It is possible that as conflicts become more distant from oneself (such as across the globe), other scope of justice items might instead modulate inclusion and exclusion.

### What are the Antecedents and Consequences of the Scope of Justice?

My experimental and qualitative research has also investigated plausible antecedents and consequences of the scope of justice based on theory and research on social categorization (Lerner & Whitehead, 1980; Tajfel, 1978), interpersonal attraction (Byrne, 1971), cooperation, competition, and conflict (Calabresi & Bobbitt, 1978;

Coser, 1956; Deutsch, 1973, 1985; Leventhal, 1979), and ethno-centrism (Brewer, 1979; LeVine & Campbell, 1972). The following describes research findings based on analyses of variance and path analyses that clarify the relationship between the scope of justice and its hypothesized antecedents—utility, similarity, and conflict severity—as well as the effect of these antecedents and the scope of justice on a hypothesized consequence of inclusion: willingness to engage in concrete protective actions.

## Utility

Returning to my experimental study, manipulations induced subjects to view the beetle's utility to people as "beneficial" or as "harmful." Statistical analyses indicated that utility influenced the scope of justice in two ways. First, utility predicted inclusion. A beetle perceived as beneficial was more likely to be included in the scope of justice than a beetle perceived as harmful. Second, an interaction between utility and conflict indicated that, in comparison with low conflict, high conflict reduced the scope of justice more precipitously when the beetle was perceived as beneficial than when it was perceived as harmful (Opotow, 1987, 1993a). Path analyses indicated that utility had a direct and stronger relationship with a consequence of the scope of justice—willingness to take concrete protective actions—than it did with the scope of justice (Opotow, 1993b). This finding suggests that when utility is salient and a social category is perceived as beneficial, its protection may be a more important concern than its inclusion in the scope of justice. Utility focuses attention on self-interest; while protective actions might further self-interest, inclusion might not.

## Similarity

The relationship between similarity and the scope of justice is less straightforward and quite intriguing. Experimental manipulations in the beetle study induced subjects to view the beetle as "similar" or "dissimilar" to people. Statistical analyses indicated that, contrary to expectations, similarity did not predict inclusion in the scope of justice. However, a key item in the scope of justice scale—the belief that considerations of fairness apply—predicted inclusion in an interesting interaction with conflict. In low conflict, participants who perceived the beetle as similar were more likely to believe that considerations of fairness applied than participants who perceived the beetle as dissimilar, as expected. In high conflict, this effect was reversed: participants who perceived the beetle as *dissimilar* were more likely to believe that considerations of fairness applied than did participants who perceived the beetle as similar. Open-ended responses indicated that in low conflict, participants were concerned with fairness and rights, but in high conflict, they mentioned self-interest and practical considerations.

A principal components analysis of the items measuring similarity and utility in the beetle study indicated that similarity was composed of two distinct dimensions: *complexity* (comprising the items "complex," "similar," and "developed") and *intelligence* (comprising the items "intelligent," "inventive," "aware," and "consciously alert"). Path analyses that differentiated between these two dimensions yielded distinctly different justice outcomes. Complexity predicted inclusion in the scope of justice but had no effect on a consequence of inclusion: willingness to take protective actions. Intelligence predicted exclusion from the scope of justice and, mediated by scope of justice, unwillingness to take protective actions (Opotow, 1994).

These contradictory findings explain why similarity had no effect on the scope of justice when entered as a unitary construct and offer evidence that similarity is a multidimensional construct with distinct justice and behavioral outcomes for each dimension. The findings also suggest that while intelligence can be perceived as an asset in those close to us or in low-conflict situations, it can pose a threat in relations with those who are unfamiliar or psychologically distant or when resource scarcity increases.

My qualitative research on adolescents' peer conflicts also investigated the relationship between similarity and the scope of justice. Analyses of adolescents' narratives found a more straightforward relationship between similarity and inclusion: the greater the number of similarities participants discerned between themselves and an adversary, the more likely they were to include that adversary within their scope of justice. The number of dissimilarities and a similarity/dissimilarity ratio were not associated with inclusion or exclusion. This suggests that similarity has an additive effect on inclusion. It also suggests that when multiple similarities foster inclusion, dissimilarities may be perceived as inconsequential or even as an asset that complements one's deficiencies with another's proficiencies.

The finding that similarity engenders inclusion is consistent with the literature on attraction and affiliative behavior (Byrne, 1969, 1971). However, in contrast to that literature, which emphasized attitudinal similarities, the junior high school students in the qualitative research mentioned nonattitudinal similarities such as physical traits, temperament, behavior, and social relationships (for example, "we are both sentimental," "we have long hair, we're both chubby, we both know English, we're both smart," "we were brought up in the same kind of families"). These examples suggest that attitudinal similarities might be inferred from more concrete and observable traits. Perhaps there is a developmental component to this finding, suggesting that with increasing age or intellectual sophistication, assessments of similarity based on concrete attributes give way to assessments of similarity based on attitudes. It would be interesting to know how nonattitudinal and attitudinal attributes influence each other and the basis for similarity judgments across developmental stages.

### Conflict Severity

My experimental research using the beetle found a strong and straightforward relationship between conflict severity and scope of justice. Increasing conflict severity predicted exclusion from the scope of justice (see Opotow, 1987, 1993a, for details). Analyses of qualitative data offer insight into how conflict modifies the scope of justice.

Junior high school participants in the qualitative research were more likely to describe an adversary as excluded from their scope of justice in two kinds of conflicts: (1) those that involved actual physical contact (rather than threats of contact or an emotional or mannered verbal exchange) and (2) those that participants reported they "won" (rather than conflicts in which the opponent won, both won, or no one won).

The finding that physical contact reduced the scope of justice is interesting for several reasons. First, most participants reported that their own aggressive behavior equaled that of their adversary, suggesting that physical contact was reciprocated. Second, participants reported that a heated verbal exchange could result in long-lasting harm to self-esteem and confidence in a way that physical contact did not. Third, physical contact is a heterogeneous category that included slaps and kicks. Consistent with research on victimization in schools (Garofalo, Siegel, & Laub, 1987), physical contact mostly described brief scuffles that resulted in little, if any, injury.

The heterogeneity of the physical contact category suggests that physical contact may have a potent symbolic significance that alters social cognitions concerning what is going on and who is the adversary. An adversary's physical actions may offer concrete evidence that a conflict is more severe than previously thought or that an adversary is a different kind of person than previously thought—a person who is more aggressive, has worse judgment, or lacks personal restraint. It can be unsettling or painful to learn that an adversary—often a friend or a classmate—is willing to dispense with a personal relationship to champion an immediate issue that can appear trivial or result from unconfirmed or scanty evidence. Consistent with Lerner's assertion (1981) that the dynamics of an encounter serve to organize social experiences, physical contact in a conflict is a salient dynamic that can trigger a reorganization of social cognitions about persons and situations. It can lead conflict participants to reassess the severity of a situation, and it can lead to an adversary's exclusion from the scope of justice.

The second kind of conflict that led to exclusion from the scope of justice were those that junior high school participants in the study reported they won. The relationship between defeating an adversary and excluding that adversary from the scope of justice suggests that the sense of power engendered by conquest facilitates victim derogation. In the most violent conflict episode in the qualitative data, a young man described what he did to an adversary *after* he won a conflict: "I choked him; I threw him in the garbage, spit at him" (Opotow, 1990a, p. 8). The effect of conquest on exclusion is evident in wars when victorious troops desecrate people and property. The finding that victory fosters adversary derogation and narrows the scope of justice is disturbing because four times more study participants reported they won the conflict than reported that their opponent won, suggesting that perceiving oneself as victorious may be a common cognitive bias.

Two kinds of conflicts concluded with constructive outcomes that preserved the relationship between disputants: those that were brief in duration and those in which junior high school participants were able to take an adversary's perspective. Most participants in brief conflicts—those lasting minutes or hours—reported that their relationship with their adversary survived the conflict; participants in protracted conflicts—those lasting days, weeks, or months— reported that formerly positive relationships with a peer had not survived the conflict. This findings suggest that a social psychological process occurs over time that tears apart the relationship, gradually widening the psychological distance between people enough to sever their connection and the perception that they belong in the same moral community. A young woman describes this process: "We sort of got back together after that but it wasn't quite the same. It was just a little less, you know, 'buddy,' you know. There were certain little things she would do. Like sometimes she would ignore me a little bit and that would really get me mad. And then I would start thinking about it and then my opinion of her sort of lessened. And it was just that kind of thing all the way through" (Opotow, 1991, p. 8).

The second correlate of a constructive conflict outcome—ability to take an adversary's perspective—indicates that junior high school participants who could respond to the question "Could you imagine what your opponent was thinking?" with plausible thoughts concerning the specific situation at hand had conflicts that differed in several important ways from those of participants who could not: the conflicts were less aggressive, they concluded with reconciliation, and the relationship with the adversary remained positive after the conflict (Opotow, 1992). Acknowledging another's perspective may limit the scope of one's own entitlements by placing another's needs and rights in a position to be considered. This, in turn, makes it difficult to view the other as a nonentity, expendable, undeserving, and outside the community in which moral rules, values, and considerations of fairness apply.

In sum, both the experimental and qualitative data from the two studies I have described indicate that aspects of utility, similarity, and conflict modify the scope of justice. These data raise an intriguing question: what social and psychological conditions sufficiently restructure social relations to modify the scope of justice? We have seen how conflict can change relationships, stimulate new social perceptions, and prompt a reconfiguration of the moral community. In the next section, I examine characteristics of social conflict that can provoke these changes.

## Changing the Justice Status Quo

Conflicts are effective change agents because they emphasize areas of divergence in relationships. They emphasize divergent norms among disputants that can trigger and intensify conflict. They also can emphasize incompatibilities in dispositions that were previously undetected or unimportant. The process of exclusion can be gradual, so that over time, psychological distance increases sufficiently to allow identification of the adversary as belonging to a different social category than oneself, a category outside the scope of justice. A young woman's comment captures this social recategorization: "The way she talks to people—Oh God! I can't understand how I could have ever been friends with *that*" (Opotow, 1991, p. 8).

Realizing that a conflict exists begins a process of recategorization. Junior high school participants in the qualitative study identified the cause of conflict as their adversary's unexpected, inappropriate behavior that contrasted with their own patently reasonable behavior and interpersonal expectations (Opotow, 1991). Their self-serving perceptions and judgments magnified an adversary's imperfections (see Judd, 1978) and induced the students to see their adversary as a different kind of person than before the conflict. As a consequence of such destabilization of an interpersonal relationship, participants perceived former friends as frightening, untrustworthy, immoral, and having bad or false values, similar to perceptions of enemies (see Holt & Silverstein, 1989; Volkan, 1985; White, 1984) or of outgroups in ethnocentric conflict (see Brewer, 1979; LeVine & Campbell, 1972).

Do particular kinds of conflicts give rise to exclusion and socially sanctioned harm? Deutsch (1973) identifies many kinds of conflict. Conflicts are constructive when participants experience satisfaction with the outcomes and believe that they have gained; conflicts are destructive when participants experience dissatisfaction with the outcomes and believe they have lost. Among destructive conflicts, Deutsch's description of escalating conflicts matches research findings on the effect of conflict on exclusion. Escalating conflicts are those characterized by competitive processes, misperception, biased perception, and commitment to maintaining the conflict out of pressures for cognitive and social consistency. Consistent with Walzer's assertion (1983) that denial of community membership results in the tyranny of insiders over outsiders and begins "the first of a long train of abuses" (p. 62), escalating conflicts often focus on issues of power and control.

### Rise of the Persecuting Society

In an historical analysis of social factors that gave rise to the persecuting society of the Middle Ages, Moore (1987) argues that ruthless attempts to consolidate power intensified the persecution of groups already at the margins of society. Efforts to change the power balance, exert control, and create societal arrangements that favored princely, centralized power required persecutory mechanisms that controlled the populace while persecuting marginalized groups.

Based on Douglas's work (1966) on the protection of societal boundaries in the Congo, Moore argues that persecution in the Middle Ages was most intensely directed at groups whose functions or value in society gave them greater importance than their status would suggest. "Fear of pollution" by groups possessing ostensibly stigmatizing characteristics, Moore argues, "is the fear that the privileged feel of those at whose expense their privilege is enjoyed" (1987, p. 101). Persecution emerged during this period of political transition because the essential functions of low-status groups impeded the consolidation of political power. In this case, exclusion had a political urgency even though it may have been economically counterproductive. Hilberg (1961) provides a modern-day instance of an economically counterproductive—but politically expedient—policy in the Third Reich's liquidation of the Jews, which drained resources that could have been more productively spent on military efforts.

Once the persecutory procedures of the inquisitions of the Middle Ages were in place, they were applied in other situations and to other groups of people, including groups defined especially for the purpose of persecution and for abstract crimes not committed against anyone. Such persecutory mechanisms, Moore asserts, could later be found in witch hunts of the sixteenth and seventeenth centuries and in totalitarian regimes of the twentieth century. Political violence in Central and South America over the past two decades is another example (Ugalde & Vega, 1989).

The marked intensification of persecution during a period of centralizing and consolidating power in the Middle Ages suggests that in struggles for power, tensions between central and marginal groups can spur exclusion (Tyler & Lind, 1990). This explains why targets of exclusion do not tend to be the equal, worthy opponents of principled competition (Deutsch, 1982) but instead are often groups at the margins of society. Consider these examples of excluded groups: Jews, lepers, and heretics during the Middle Ages; witches in sixteenth- and seventeenth-century Europe and nineteenth-century America; Jews, Gypsies, and homosexuals in the Third Reich; and the HIV-positive and homeless people today.

## Implications for Theory and Research

Applied to the scope of justice, Moore's analysis suggests that in conflicts that grow out of struggles to acquire and consolidate power, tensions between the opposite poles of utility and similarity can engender exclusion. That is, groups or individuals likely to be excluded from the scope of justice are those perceived as simultaneously beneficial and harmful and as simultaneously similar and dissimilar.

We can discern the dynamics of persecution described by Moore in contemporary intergroup relations between advantaged and disadvantaged groups. For example, social categories defined by gender or ethnic identity, such as women and people of color, are beneficial because they perform essential societal functions; at the same time, they are harmful because their low status and undercompensation can engender suspicion and guilt or can spark social unrest. Women, for example, perform essential functions in the family (Steil & Weltman, 1991) and community while occupying lower status than men and receiving lower compensation in employment (Kim, 1989).

Moore's analysis recalls Ambivalence-Amplification Theory (Katz, Wackenhut, & Glass, 1986), which holds that ambivalence arises from feelings of aversion and hostility and—at the same time—sympathy and compassion toward stigmatized groups. Citing studies over the past four decades that found that white Americans held ambivalent attitudes toward African Americans, Katz et al. propose that ambivalent attitudes toward stigmatized groups produce psychological discomfort, arising from cognitive inconsistency, that threatens self-esteem and core values. This results in "response amplification" (p. 105), more extreme positive or negative behavior directed at stigmatized persons. Response amplification is consistent with excessively negative attitudes and harmful behavior directed at those who are excluded from the scope of justice.

To create an analog for the social realities that give rise to exclusion from the scope of justice, theoretical models and research designs need to incorporate the tensions in conflicts that spark exclusion. Moore's analysis of the evolution of a persecuting society and Ambivalence-Amplification Theory suggest that research designs that induce subjects to orient themselves to only one pole of the utility and similarity dimensions might be too simplistic to capture the dynamics of exclusion. The next phase of research on moral exclusion should test the hypothesis that exclusion occurs when both poles of the utility and similarity dimensions are potent and in conflict. Such testing can occur through research designs in which subjects are induced to perceive a target as being simultaneously beneficial and harmful and as being simultaneously similar and dissimilar with respect to the target's complexity and intelligence. Future research should also compare the effects of these tensions for targets of exclusion that are perceived as having central and marginal group status.

## Conclusions

What do analyses of milder instances of exclusion from the scope of justice suggest about the social psychological origins of genocides? They suggest that gradually and sometimes unsuspectingly, coopted by conflicts (even minor ones) over power and control, people can cast out social categories that possess "stigmatizing" characteristics that disqualify them from the care, protection, and justice distributed to those inside the scope of justice. Conflicts that spur exclusion are not only political attempts to change the balance of power in international, intergroup, and interpersonal relationships; the conflicts are also psychological, concerning opposing orientations toward those we exclude: those who benefit as well as harm us and those who are similar but whose similarity is insufficient or frightening. Over time, harms and dissimilarities eclipse benefits and similarities, gradually moving marginal groups outside the scope of justice and loosening moral restraints against harming them.

Exclusion gains momentum in a process of mutual influence between individual perceptions and societal conventions. Individuals internalize prevailing societal arrangements, reshape their perceptions of marginalized groups, and reconfigure their moral community. The attitudes and behaviors of individuals reshape the societal arrangements, redefine group entitlements, and narrow the scope of justice. The interaction between individuals and society is evident when psychopathic individuals attack members of social categories they abhor. Their obviously flawed moral justifications that they are rooting out evil are not very different from state-inflicted harm that occurs in widespread violations of human rights. The institutionalization of exclusion, such as racism and religious fanaticism, is far more virulent and dangerous than the individual manifestation because harm occurs on a vast scale and over a longer period of time. However, moral exclusion can engender widespread harm within a society only when people individually reshape their perceptions of marginalized groups and cast them out of their scope of justice.

These analyses suggest that we can interrupt this cycle of exclusion and harm doing when we strive to take the perspective of others during conflict, to resolve conflicts quickly before they escalate out of control, and to seek solutions that integrate the concerns and interests of all parties rather than adopt a win-lose orientation toward the conflict. The analyses also suggest the importance of resisting perceptual changes that view some social categories as increasingly harmful, dissimilar, and outside the boundary in which concerns about justice govern conduct.

This chapter has sketched out some of the social psychological processes that lead people to see others as outside the scope of justice. There is still a great deal to learn about this important topic, with far-reaching implications for social justice in the world and in our own lives.

## References

Archer, D. (1985). Social deviance. In G. Lindzey & E. Aronson (Eds.), *The handbook of social psychology* (3rd ed., Vol. 2, pp. 743–804). New York: Random House.

Austin, W., & Hatfield, E. (1980). Equity theory, power, and social justice. In G. Mikula (Ed.), *Justice and social interaction* (pp. 25–61). New York: Springer-Verlag.

Blackman, J. (1993, August). *At the frontier: In pursuit of justice for women*. Paper presented at the annual meeting of the American Psychological Association, Toronto.

Brewer, M. B. (1979). The role of ethnocentrism in intergroup conflict. In W. G. Austin & S. Worchel (Eds.), *The social psychology of intergroup relations*. Pacific Grove, CA: Brooks/Cole.

Byrne, D. (1969). Attitudes and attractions. In L. Berkowitz (Ed.), *Advances in experimental social psychology* (pp. 36–89). San Diego: Academic Press.

Byrne, D. (1971). *The attraction paradigm*. San Diego: Academic Press.

Calabresi, G., & Bobbitt, P. (1978). *Tragic choices*. New York: W. W. Norton.

Clayton, S. D., & Crosby, F. J. (1992). *Justice, gender, and affirmative action*. Ann Arbor: University of Michigan Press.

Cohen, R. L., & Greenberg, J. (1982). The justice concept in social psychology. In J. Greenberg & R. L. Cohen (Eds.), *Equity and justice in social behavior*. San Diego: Academic Press.

Coser, L. (1956). *The functions of social conflict*. New York: Free Press.

Danielson, M. N. (1976). *The politics of exclusion*. New York: Columbia University Press.

Deutsch, M. (1973). *The resolution of conflict: Constructive and destructive processes*. New Haven, CT: Yale University Press.

Deutsch, M. (1974). Awakening the sense of injustice. In M. Lerner & M. Ross (Eds.), *The quest for justice: Myth, reality, ideal* (pp. 19–42). Toronto: Holt, Rinehart & Winston.

Deutsch, M. (1982). Interdependence and psychological orientation. In V. J. Derlega & J. L. Grzelak (Eds.), *Cooperation and helping behavior: Theories and research* (pp. 15–42). San Diego: Academic Press.

Deutsch, M. (1985). *Distributive justice: A social psychological perspective.* New Haven, CT: Yale University Press.

Douglas, M. (1966). *Purity and danger.* London: London University Press.

Fine, M. (1990). "The public" in public schools: The social construction/ constriction of moral communities. *Journal of Social Issues, 46*(1), 107–119.

Garofalo, J., Siegel, L., & Laub, J. (1987). School-related victimizations among adolescents: An analysis of National Crime Survey (NCS) narratives. *Journal of Quantitative Criminology, 3*(4), 321–338.

Goodman, W. (1992, September 2). Why it took TV so long to focus on the Somalis. *The New York Times,* p. C18.

Hallie, P. (1979). *Lest innocent blood be shed: The story of the village of Le Chambon and how goodness happened there.* New York: HarperCollins.

Hilberg, R. (1961). *The destruction of the European Jews.* Chicago: Quadrangle.

Holt, R. R., & Silverstein, B. (1989). The image of the enemy: U.S. views of the Soviet Union [Special issue]. *Journal of Social Issues, 45*(2).

Judd, C. M. (1978). Cognitive effects of attitude and conflict resolution. *Journal of Conflict Resolution, 22,* 483–498.

Katz, I., Wackenhut, J., & Glass, D. C. (1986). An ambivalence-amplification theory of behavior toward the stigmatized. In S. Worchel & W. G. Austin (Eds.), *Psychology of intergroup relations* (2nd ed., pp. 103–117). Chicago: Nelson-Hall.

Kellert, S. R. (1984). *Attitudes toward invertebrates.* Unpublished manuscript, Yale University, New Haven, CT.

Kelman, H. C., & Hamilton, V. L. (1989). *Crimes of obedience.* New Haven, CT: Yale University Press.

Kim, M. (1989). Gender bias in compensation structures: A case study of its historical basis and persistence. *Journal of Social Issues, 45*(4), 39–49.

Lerner, M. J. (1980). *The belief in a just world.* New York: Plenum.

Lerner, M. J. (1981). The justice motive in human relations: Some thoughts on what we know and need to know about justice. In M. J. Lerner & S. C. Lerner (Eds.), *The justice motive in social behavior: Adapting to times of scarcity and change.* New York: Plenum.

Lerner, M. J., & Whitehead, L. A. (1980). Procedural justice viewed in the context of justice motive theory. In G. Mikula (Ed.), *Justice and social interaction* (pp. 219–256). New York: Springer-Verlag.

Leventhal, G. S. (1979). Effects of external conflict on resource allocation and fairness within groups and organizations. In W. G. Austin & S. Worchel

(Eds.), *The social psychology of intergroup relations*. Pacific Grove, CA: Brooks/Cole.

LeVine, R. A., & Campbell, D. T. (1972). *Ethnocentrism: Theories of conflict, ethnic attitude, and group behavior*. New York: Wiley.

Lifton, R. J. (1986). *The Nazi doctors*. New York: Basic Books.

Mikula, G. (Ed.). (1980). *Justice and social interaction*. New York: Springer-Verlag.

Moore, R. I. (1987). *The formation of a persecuting society*. Cambridge, MA: Blackwell.

Nader, L. (1975). Forums for justice: A cross-cultural perspective. *Journal of Social Issues, 31*(3), 151–170.

Opotow, S. V. (1987). Limits of fairness: An experimental examination of antecedents of the scope of justice. *Dissertation Abstracts International, 48* (08B), 2500. (University Microfilms No. 87-24072)

Opotow, S. (1990a, August). *Justice beliefs in adolescents' interpersonal conflicts with peers*. Paper presented at the annual meeting of the American Psychological Association, Boston.

Opotow, S. (Ed.). (1990b). Moral exclusion and injustice [Special issue]. *Journal of Social Issues, 46*(1).

Opotow, S. (1990c). Moral exclusion and injustice: An introduction. *Journal of Social Issues, 46*(1), 1–20.

Opotow, S. (1991, August). *Social cognitions and moral judgments in adolescents' aversive exchanges with peers*. Paper presented at the annual meeting of the American Psychological Association, San Francisco.

Opotow, S. (1992, August). *Pluralism and nonviolence*. Paper presented at the annual meeting of the American Psychological Association, Washington, DC.

Opotow, S. (1993a). Animals and the scope of justice. *Journal of Social Issues, 49*(1), 71–85.

Opotow, S. (1993b, August). Predicting protection: The scope of justice and environmental attitudes. Paper presented at the annual meeting of the American Psychological Association, Toronto.

Opotow, S. (1994). Predicting protection: Scope of justice and the natural world. *Journal of Social Issues, 50*(3), 49–63.

Rawls, J. (1971). *A theory of justice*. Cambridge, MA: Harvard University Press.

Sloan, T. S., & Montero, M. (Eds). (1990). Psychology for the third world [Special issue]. *Journal of Social Issues, 46*(3).

Sorenson, S. B., & Bowie, P. (1994). Girls and young women. In L. Eron, J. Gentry, & P. Schlegel (Eds.), *Reason to hope: A psychosocial perspective on violence and youth* (pp. 167–176). Washington, DC: American Psychological Association.

Staub, E. (1979). *Positive social behavior and morality: Socialization and development* (Vol. 2). San Diego: Academic Press.

Staub, E. (1987). *Moral exclusion and extreme destructiveness: Personal goal theory, differential evaluation, moral equilibration, and steps along the continuum of destruction.* Paper presented at the annual meeting of the American Psychological Association, New York.

Staub, E. (1989). *The roots of evil: Origins of genocide and other group violence.* New York: Cambridge University Press.

Staub, E. (1990). Moral exclusion, personal goal theory, and extreme destructiveness. *Journal of Social Issues, 46*(1), 47–64.

Staub, E., & Rosenthal, L. H. (1994). Mob violence: Cultural-societal sources, instigators, group processes, and participants. In L. Eron, J. Gentry, & P. Schlegel (Eds.), *Reason to hope: A psychosocial perspective on violence and youth* (pp. 281–313). Washington, DC: American Psychological Association.

Steil, J. M. & Weltman, K. (1991). Marital inequality: The importance of resources, personal attributes, and social norms on career valuing and the allocation of domestic responsibilities. *Sex Roles, 24,* 161–179.

Tajfel, H. (1978). *Differentiation between social groups: Studies in the social psychology of intergroup relations* (European Monograph in Social Psychology, No. 14). London: Academic Press.

Tajfel, H. (1982). Instrumentality, identity, and social comparison. In H. Tajfel (Ed.), *Social identity and intergroup relations.* New York: Cambridge University Press.

Tyler, T. R., & Lind, E. A. (1990). Intrinsic versus community-based justice models: When does group membership matter? *Journal of Social Issues, 46*(1), 83–94.

Ugalde, A. & Vega, R. R. (1989). Review essay: State terrorism, torture, and health in the Southern Cone. *Social Science and Medicine, 28,* 759–765.

Volkan, V. D. (1985). The need to have enemies and allies: A developmental approach. *Political Psychology, 6,* 219–247.

Walzer, M. (1983). *Spheres of justice: A defense of pluralism and equality.* New York: Basic Books.

White, R. K. (1984). *Fearful warriors: A psychological profile of U.S.-Soviet relations.* New York: Free Press.

Zwi A., & Ugalde, A., (Eds.). (1989). Political victimization in the Third World [Special issue]. *Social Science and Medicine, 28*(7).

# Commentary

• • • • • • • • • • • • • • • • • • • • • • • • • • • • • • •

# Justice

## Why We Need a New Moral Philosophy

### Morton Deutsch

One of my earliest memories focuses on injustice. I was about three-and-a-half years old. We were all staying at a resort in the Catskills, and a counselor organized a game of softball for the older kids (the six-to-eight-year-olds). I was excluded from it because I was too young and was asked to stay on the side. I was very mad, and when a foul ball was hit near me, I recall picking it up, running with it, and then throwing it as far as I could in a direction away from the players.

I have always had a passionate feeling about injustice and being excluded. I was the youngest of four sons and, having skipped grades several times, I was the youngest in my classes throughout my school years. In many situations, I was excluded or was the underdog. As a result, I developed a strong identification with and empathy for the downtrodden in the world. When I was exposed to Marxist thinking at college (The City College of New York) during the Depression, I evolved a conceptual framework for thinking systematically about injustice and a political orientation for changing society so as to reduce injustices.

I am delighted that all of the excellent chapters in this part combine serious thought and passion about injustice. I now offer some reflection about each of them.

The chapter by Folger, Sheppard, and Buttram delights my theoretical persona. It is intellectually elegant and a substantial contribution to the social psychology of justice. Not only does it generalize some ideas with which I have been associated but it also develops an expanded new framework for thinking about both theoretical and practical issues in this area. In response to this chapter, I offer two comments: one about the meaning of equality and the other about the conflict between equality and equity norms of justice.

The S-A-N framework is useful in emphasizing that the recognition of individuality is an important aspect of justice (at least in Western societies). However, I would question their statement that an *equal* distribution implies that everyone receives the *same* outcome. As I have stated elsewhere (1985), it is important to recognize the difference between egalitarianism and pseudoegalitarianism. The emphasis in egalitarianism is equality, not sameness. Advocates of equality and egalitarianism are primarily opposed to *invidious* distinctions among individuals or groups but do not assume that all distinctions are invidious. (See Deutsch, 1985, pp. 41–43, for a more detailed statement.) The insistence on treating people identically, without regard to circumstance, is pseudoegalitarianism, which often masks basic doubts or ambivalence about commitment to egalitarian values. In experimental research, same treatment is often the most convenient or only way of operationalizing equality, but in everyday life, *equal treatment* is often not *same treatment*. It is not equal treatment, for example, to require all students to take an identical intelligence test in Spanish whether or not they are proficient in Spanish.

In their excellent discussion, Folger, Sheppard, and Buttram rightly emphasize the many possible conflicts that can arise among the different norms of justice. One particular conflict has been much discussed in the social science literature: that between equity and equality, that is, between economic efficiency and solidarity. As Tyler and Belliveau note, economists commonly assume that there is a tradeoff between equality and efficiency. However, research studies by my students and myself (Deutsch, 1985) indicate that this is not necessarily so and that equality may lead to greater efficiency when successful work requires cooperation. The norm of equity often induces a competitive orientation that interferes with effective cooperation.

However, I confess that my thinking is somewhat muddled about the psychological orientations associated with task-oriented or economic social relations, in contrast with those that are socioemotional or solidarity-oriented in character. On the one hand, I have indicated that each of these two types of relations gives rise to distinctive cognitive, motivational, and moral orientations that do not seem compatible. On the other hand, common sense, as well as research, would suggest that the best functioning groups, in terms of productivity as well as satisfaction, are those high in both task and socioemotional orientations. Years ago, Freed Bales suggested that groups—and also families—resolve this dilemma by having separate task and socioemotional leaders. I am inclined to take his suggestion one step further and propose that every effective group member has internalized both orientations and is able to bring to bear the relevant orientation at the appropriate occasion. I know that when negotiating with a car salesman, I am able to bring into play an entirely different psychological orientation than the one I have in my interactions with my grandchildren.

In light of their apt summary of my work in the first part of their chapter, I am puzzled by Tyler and Belliveau's characterization of my approach to social justice as being rooted in theories of social exchange. As I indicated in my book *Distributive Justice*, when I started to read the literature on the social psychology of justice, I was appalled by the narrowness of the dominant approach in this area: the economic or social exchange model underlying equity theory. My approach is more broadly conceived. It is, as Folger, Sheppard, and Buttram state, a functionalist approach in which economic values, although important, are only one of many types of values with which a system of justice is concerned.

I am very sympathetic to Tyler and Belliveau's basic themes. First is their emphasis on personal identity as one of the important values in a system of justice; their emphasis is on self- and social esteem rather than on such other aspects of personal identity as gender, occupation, and race. Second, they stress the importance of procedural justice in affecting self-esteem. Third, they indicate the significance of whether one is treated fairly and with respect in determining one's commitment and loyalty to relationships and groups.

There is little doubt that most scholars would agree with the authors' theses and be grateful, as I am, for a more explicit articulation of these views. However, I do differ with their opinion that distributive justice is concerned with the distribution of commodities or instrumental values while procedural justice is more specifically related to personal identity. Teachers, parents, authorities, and peers frequently distribute evaluations, praise, and criticism that bear on self-esteem. And, as every parent knows, the distribution of commodities to their children (for example, pieces of chocolate cake at the dinner table) may have profound implications for self-esteem. Quite commonly, the distribution of resources has symbolic value relating to social and self-esteem that may be more significant than the substantive value of the resources. This is not to deny that respectful treatment by the person or group making the distribution may ameliorate some of the negative effects on those who receive relatively little of the substance or value being distributed.

Although I have written little about procedural justice as such, I have stressed its importance, even going so far as to suggest that it is "a key aspect of distributive justice, and it is reasonable to believe that the sense of injustice is more often aroused by complaints about the procedures involved in a distributive process than about the distributive values governing it" (1985, p. 35). From my current perspective, there is a two-way relation between procedural and distributive justice. Under the general heading of procedural justice, I would include such processes as decision-making procedures, the assignment of personnel to roles in the decision-making and distribution processes, the styling and timing of the distribution, the rules or criteria employed to represent the distributive values, and the measurement procedures used to implement the criteria. It is evident that the values employed in a distribution as well as the actual distribution of any particular distributive value can be very much affected by the various facets of procedural justice. Similarly, the various facets of procedural justice can be distributed in different ways depending on what canons of distributive justice are employed. Thus, who should participate in the decision-making process? Those who are most expert, those who are most representative of the group, or those who are most affected by the decision? Similar questions can be raised about each of the facets of procedural justice.

Much of practical politics is concerned with distribution issues related to procedural justice. If one's political group can influence the decision-making procedures, the personnel, the rules and measurement procedures, and so on, it can affect the outcomes (such as income, security, education, status, and health, as well as self-esteem) that will be distributed to one's group relative to other groups. Unfortunately, there appears to be a self-fulfilling prophecy operating such that if one has little hope of being treated justly and one's self-esteem is low, one is unlikely to engage in the political activities that might give rise to a more just society. Nevertheless, as Nelson Mandela has demonstrated, a charismatic leader can provide a positive example of the hope, determination, and psychological strength that is able to break through the vicious cycle of despair created by systematic injustice.

Michelle Fine is one of the most creative, challenging, and socially responsive of my former students. She is well described by the phrase that I used to characterize Kurt Lewin (Deutsch, 1992, p. 31): "tough-minded and tender-hearted." As her chapter indicates, she has the intellectual toughness to challenge the scientism of much of social science by using a methodology in her research that many would consider unorthodox and a lyric writing style that is suffused with humane values rather than the antiseptic manner of much academic prose.

The chapter by Fine and Wong focuses on an important question: why do victims of injustice often not "voice" their complaints or "exit" from their situations of injustice despite their awareness of being unfairly treated? The authors conclude that the institutional muzzling of protest (through biased or insensitive grievance procedures, retaliation, the potential damage to one's reputation and career, and so on) and the lack of better alternatives, combined with culturally indoctrinated beliefs in meritocratic individualism, are more likely to lead to alienation than high levels of overt outrage and protest. They emphasize that the ideology of meritocratic individualism inhibits the formation of a collective identity among those subjected to injustice by encouraging a focus on individuals, rather than on institutional policies, practices, and hierarchies. (I would use the phrase *meritocratic and competitive individualism* as a more inclusive label for the issues they discuss.)

Any social scientist whose ideas have been influenced by Marxist thought, as mine were, will have no difficulty accepting the validity of the perspective offered by Fine and Wong and will be delighted by their detailed analyses and vivid illustrations of their thesis. I strongly endorse their call for an activist project for a social psychology of justice.

I note one point in their chapter that has provoked further thought. As the authors indicate, acceptance of the ideology of meritocratic individualism can lead to self-blame. On the other hand, its rejection can contribute to the development of an awareness of oppression by societal and institutional polices and practices. The sense of being a victim, unable to exert any control over one's fate, can induce one to be alienated and to drop out, with ultimately harmful consequences, as illustrated by Fine and Wong in their description of school dropouts and women heroin addicts. I suggest that it can also lead to the *role* of being a victim, with such secondary gratifications as feeling superior to the oppressors and having an excuse for one's personal failings. Ideally, instead of dropping out or adopting the victim role, the downtrodden would develop a positive collective identity and seek to change institutional policies and practices.

However, even when this seems hopeless, the individual need not revert to the role of victim. Within the context of a society and institutions that largely determine the fate of different categories of people, there is still sufficient slack in the system to permit meritocratic individualism to work to some degree for some individuals. This produces a dilemma: the "success" of some individual members of a category of people who are objects of discrimination "proves" to those in power that racism and sexism do not exist; the lack of success of others "proves" that the unsuccessful people are inherently incapable of succeeding. This dilemma need not be accepted by people who belong to groups who are subjected to discrimination. The slack in the system can be used not only to achieve individual success but also to forge a positive collective identity with increased resources to challenge the system of injustice. However, those who are successful despite the prevailing systemic injustices must retain their psychological identities as a member of the collective and not allow themselves to be seduced into believing that the lack of success of others in their group is due to a lack of individual merit.

Susan Opotow's important paper is concerned with a question of profound significance: under what conditions do we see others as not entitled to the just treatment to which members of our moral community are normally entitled? Her rich discussion illustrates some of the horrors of moral exclusion as well as some of the conditions that give rise to it. I shall not summarize her conclusions but will instead comment on two side issues in her paper: the use of beetles in her experimental study and her statement that our capacity for justice appears to be finite.

It was a very original and thought-provoking innovation to study the conditions under which beetles would be included or excluded from the moral community of the human subjects who participated in her experiment. However, in thinking about my own relations with beetles, it occurred to me that there is an ambiguity in some of her discussion, as well as in that of other scholars in this area. For example, Melvin Lerner (1980), in his discussion of the "just world" hypothesis, does not specify its limits of applicability. Are people motivated to treat all others justly or only those who are included in one's moral community? Similarly, Opotow does not make a sharp distinction between being *excluded* and *not being included* in one's moral community. Prior to reading Albert Schweitzer, I had not excluded beetles from my moral community; I simply had never thought to include them or even that they were relevant to it.

The category "not included" contains more than those who are excluded. Exclusion is a more active process. The odious actions that Opotow describes toward heretics, Jews, lepers, and other stigmatized groups were *persecutions,* not merely omissions of willingness to help others in distress. It is true that if I do not include beetles in my moral community, I am freer to take actions that disregard their well-being and that may even harm them inadvertently, but I am not likely to persecute them and feel justified in doing so.

As individuals, communities, and nations, we often fail to respond to others in distress. This is not necessarily because they are excluded from our moral community but rather because they are not included. We do not seek to harm them or justify their distress— unless we feel guilty because we are not able to help them. As Opotow indicates, psychological distance makes us feel little obligation to treat "remote" others the way we treat those who are psychologically close. Implicitly she poses a key question: in an increasingly interdependent and hugely populated world, how can we develop a psychological sense of closeness toward those with whom we have no personal contact? How can we think globally but act locally? This is a vital topic insufficiently addressed by social scientists.

Opotow indicates our capacity for justice appears to be finite. If we were to be global in our inclusiveness and seek to respond to all those who need help—those in Rwanda, Sudan, Bosnia, Haiti, the oppressed, the poor, the homeless, the sick, and so on—we would be overwhelmed. All of us face moral dilemmas because of our finite capacity to respond helpfully to the many injustices we see in the world. Some people react to the discomfort produced by such dilemmas by constricting their sense of injustice and by employing various defense mechanisms to ward off the feelings of rage, guilt, or helplessness induced by their limited capacity to respond effectively to injustice. Hopefully, there are many others, including Susan Opotow, who maintain a lively awareness of injustice as they seek to expand their own, as well as their society's, capacity to respond constructively to injustice. My own tendency, for example, when faced with an endless number of homeless beggars on the streets of New York, is to limit my direct giving to small amounts of money to several individuals in my immediate neighborhood, to give substantial amounts to groups who are active and effective in providing assistance to the homeless, and to support legislation and social action to eliminate homelessness. Nevertheless, I feel that my tactical and strategic moral choices, even in this one area, do not have a solid intellectual foundation. My sense is that we are in desperate need of good thinking by moral philosophers and social scientists to aid us in making the difficult moral choices that we continuously face as our awareness of injustices increases.

### References

Deutsch, M. (1985). *Distributive justice: A social psychological perspective*. New Haven, CT: Yale University Press.

Deutsch, M. (1992). Kurt Lewin: The tough-minded and tender-hearted scientist. *Journal of Social Issues, 48*, 31–44.

Lerner, M. (1980). *The belief in a just world: A fundamental delusion*. New York: Plenum.

# 12

· · · · · · · · · · · · · · · · · · · · · · · · · · · · ·

# In Response

## Discussion and Conclusions

### Jeffrey Z. Rubin, Barbara Benedict Bunker

W hen we began this project, provoked by the many important contributions of our mentor Morton Deutsch, we had little idea of the directions our work would take. Our initial discussions with Mort, usually over a cup of coffee or a meal—like any self-respecting New Yorker, Mort prefers to mix his intellectual work with a modest repast—turned to some of the leading edge questions in the domains of conflict, cooperation, and justice. Based on our conversations, the two of us, as editors, recruited authors to address a subset of the many questions for future theory and research that Mort helped us to identify.

And there we expected our work to end. Authors would reflect on the latest problems and possibilities and express their observations in writing, Mort would comment on each substantive part of the project, and we would have our book. Instead, we find ourselves stimulated to make various observations and comments on each of the chapters in this collection; indeed, we find ourselves with comments on Mort Deutsch's own comments. This concluding chapter, then, continues the dialogue begun in this book.

## Conflict

The first chapter in this section, by Rubin and Levinger, was designed to address the question of whether, and to what extent, conflict principles can be generalized from one setting to the next. While interpersonal, intergroup, interorganizational, and international conflicts have generally been assumed to be fundamentally alike, this chapter examines this assumption more closely. Focusing on the similarities and differences between interpersonal and international conflict, in particular, the authors conclude: first, the differences are nontrivial; second, the differences help explain why conflicts in the international arena tend to be so much more dangerous than their interpersonal cousins; and third, the areas of similarity between interpersonal and international conflict help point the way toward possibilities for conflict reduction in the international arena.

The chapter by Rubin and Levinger represents not so much a theoretical statement as a taxonomy, a checklist of dimensions that can be used to encode the essential features of conflicts at *any* level. Or so the authors would have us believe. And yet, embedded in their analysis are several assumptions that require clarification.

First, the authors apparently believe that one can construct a conflict continuum, stretching from interpersonal at one end to international at the other. Like most conflict analysts, Rubin and Levinger seem to assume that conflicts that take place at intermediary points on this continuum are similar to those at the extremes. But they may not be. Group and organizational conflicts may actually be governed by a rather different set of principles, and these principles may then be lost in the game of moving between continua endpoints. Perhaps the interpersonal and international really *do* have more in common with each other than with either the group or organizational levels. Similarly, note that the very use of a continuum implies a *linear* relationship among the different levels of conflict. Perhaps a curvilinear arrangement better fits these relations. For example, a linear continuum would seem to imply that the simplest of the conflict arrangements is the interpersonal, with intergroup and interorganizational conflicts being of moderate complexity, and the most complex being the international. But perhaps this is not really the case.

Second, the authors, like almost all of their conflict research colleagues, seem to assume that the way to play the conceptual game of generalization is by working from apparently simpler levels of analysis to their more complex counterparts. Start with analysis of interpersonal conflict, then move from this to lessons (theoretical or applied) for international relations. But why not deliberately create a *gedankenexperiment* in which one plays the reverse game? Begin with the international level; work from case analyses of notorious international exchanges, for example, and see what lessons would be implied for the interpersonal level. If scholars really are justified in generalizing from one level to the other, shouldn't it be possible to posit a transitivity rule, allowing us to move from international to interpersonal levels as readily as we do the reverse? Perhaps when scholars try to play this little game they will find that things are not quite as transitive as they seem.

Finally, a second *gedankenexperiment* comes to mind in the context of generalization across levels of analysis. Why not assume that the four major conflict levels are actually entirely different from one another? In his chapter on the cultural limits of generalizability of conflict theory, elsewhere in the part on conflict, Guy Olivier Faure argues that one way to free oneself from the dominating, polarizing effect of North American conflict theory is to start de novo; in effect, we would work our way out from within different cultures, in this way devising theories of conflict that are guaranteed not to be a copy of, or a reaction to, a dominating American perspective. Analogously, why not assume that different levels of conflict reside in different universes? Let us study each universe, aware of the others, but trying as best we can to resist the temptation to move from one level to another.

The second chapter in this part, by Guy Olivier Faure, addresses the extent to which conflict formulations are generalizable from one society or culture to the next. In some sense, the question posed here is equivalent to that addressed by Rubin and Levinger: both chapters examine the question of generalizability, either across levels of analysis or across cultures. But where Rubin and Levinger argue that generalizability *is* possible, albeit tempered by certain key areas of dissimilarity between interpersonal and international conflict, Faure is more circumspect. He highlights the limitations of current conflict theory. Politely but insistently, the author concludes that conflict theory is largely a creation of Western social science (United States social science, in particular). This has had two important consequences. First, conflict theorists have assumed that the same principles apply in one cultural setting as in another. This may not be the case at all. Second, the American perspective has been so dominant that approaches emerging from other cultures have been trapped in the American view—either by emulating it or by reacting to it—rather than finding a voice of their own.

To this assertion we would expect our mentor to respond politely but firmly: "poppycock." As Mort notes in his responsive commentary to the conflict section, it is his hope that our field can develop constructs and specify the relations among them so they are applicable across cultures and time. We suspect that this is more than a mere statement of hope for the field. Mort probably does believe that a set of conflict constructs has emerged that can be generalized from one culture to the next. And Faure, we suspect, would demur.

As do we, at least in part. While we believe that certain constructs—especially those describing structural relations, such as "cooperation," "competition," "interdependence," and so on—really are the same from one culture to the next, there may be at least as many concepts that do not lend themselves to generalization across culture. Included in this latter listing are some rather prominent constructs, including "conflict," "negotiation," and "trust," to name but a few.

Regarding the construct of "conflict," Faure observes the differences among French, American, and Chinese views—and clearly one could take this cultural differentiation much further. "Negotiation," in turn, is generally regarded in the West as an acceptable means of working out a solution to a presenting problem through the give-and-take of offers. While there may be disagreement over the nature of the process at work—some focus on compromise while others focus on joint problem solving—there is no disagreement about the ultimate goal of the process: agreement. Yet in other cultures we have visited over the years, it is common to regard negotiation as tantamount to surrender, the result that obtains when one is unable to get what one wants through the usual means: force. Finally, consider the construct of "trust," which is the focus of the chapter by Roy Lewicki and Barbara Bunker, in the section in the book on cooperation. While our mentor, Mort, would no doubt argue for the generalizability of this construct, and Lewicki and Bunker would add their assent (although perhaps qualified by the particular kind of trust invoked), we wonder about those cultures where trust has no meaning at all—simply because there is no concept of "trust."

There may thus be broad generalizability in the case of many concepts but not in the case of many others. The challenge is to sort out those constructs that truly are sufficiently robust to allow cultural transfer from those that are not. Next, we would want to know what it is that differentiates the generalizable constructs from their less robust counterparts. In making the case for the development of a truly universal theory of conflict, Faure argues (at least a bit) for the necessity of starting over. If we are to shake off the overdetermining effects of American social science, he implies, it will be necessary to consider beginning again. While such an approach has the virtue of cleanliness, it has the decided disadvantage of discarding the decades of solid thinking in American social science. It is for this reason that we are particularly pleased to see that Faure offers a variety of other methodological and conceptual approaches to the further development of a more truly universal conceptualization of conflict.

The third chapter in the conflict section, by Dean Pruitt and

Paul Olczak, addresses the issue of intractable conflict. In our luncheon conversations with Mort Deutsch, he argued for the importance of better understanding those conflicts that simply do not lend themselves to the usual forms of settlement or resolution. In their essay, the authors respond to this challenge by presenting one of the first thoughtful explorations of intractable conflict. They argue that intractable conflicts (both in the interpersonal and international domains) are characterized by perturbations among five key elements: motivation, affect, cognition, behavior, and environment—their MACBE model. Under conditions of intractable conflict, they assert, all five elements are affected in some way; as a system, a change in any element effects changes in each of the others. Moreover, if intractable conflict is to be ameliorated, changes must be effected in one or more of these five components. Pruitt and Olczak propose a sequence of seven steps (or "modules") toward this end.

As an early and ambitious attempt to sharpen our understanding of intractable conflict, this chapter offers many creative insights, even as it raises more questions than it can possibly answer. And this is exactly as it should be. Here, then, are a few of the ideas that the Pruitt and Olczak chapter has sparked for us.

First, we are struck by the authors' skillful application of ideas drawn from one body of literature (on marital conflict) for another (international conflict). In our experience, some of the richest insights are derived in precisely this way, by developing cross-cutting observations from one field or discipline for another. In this regard, we find interesting the resemblance between the authors' motivation-driven analysis of ways out of intractable conflict (recall the importance of "ripeness" in their formulation) and the organizational change literature. The observations of Pruitt and Olczak are very similar to those of Schein and Bennis (1965), who describe how dissatisfaction with one's own behavior is the critical ingredient in individual change. In order to bring about organizational change, it is necessary to orchestrate three elements: dissatisfaction (D) with current organizational functioning, a vision (V) of the direction in which one wants the organization to go, and first steps (F), which represent a way of moving in the desired direction (Beckhard & Harris, 1987). These must be greater than the predictable resistance (R) that any giving up of the status quo involves. The relationship among these elements is a multiplicative one (D x V x F > R), indicating that all are necessary if organization change is to result. And to repeat, one can easily see the resemblance between this traditional model of organization change and the present analysis of intractable conflict.

Second, we find Pruitt and Olczak's analysis of the concept of "ripeness" in conflict settlement unusually insightful. Others have surely written about this motivational state over the years, but these authors bring special insight to the discussion. Of special interest is their distinction between unilateral and bilateral ripeness, where previous analysts have almost always assumed ripeness to be of the latter sort. Thus, a conflict is ripe for resolution or settlement when the parties to the dispute are (jointly) ready to take it seriously, to solve the problem confronting them. But what if only one side regards the conflict as ripe, while the other is rather far from such a motivational state? What does one do then? While the Pruitt and Olczak chapter does not offer specific answers to the question of unequal ripeness, it surely does raise a whole new set of questions.

At the same time, the authors' very focus on individual psychological states has perhaps led Pruitt and Olczak to say less than they might have about the interactive, dynamic qualities of intractable conflict. What may start out as a set of individual psychological states eventually ends up as a self-reinforcing system in which perceptions have been transformed into new, unpleasant realities. As Deutsch observes in his own comments on their essay, after a while, it is not a distortion or a misperception for each side to see the other as having malevolent intentions; the conflict process has made the perceptions become reality. Each side has become the other's worst nightmare. Or to frame this point most generally, perhaps the most interesting things to happen in an intractable conflict are to be found not among a listing of individual properties or attributes but as part of the *interaction* among the antagonists. While the authors do, indeed, discuss various interactive processes in their provocative chapter, these circles and spirals require continuing attention. The imagery of a spiral is that of a vortex or eddy, drawing ever increasing energy from its surroundings, gathering momentum as it goes. Such imagery can only be evoked when one part of an escalated interpersonal system plays off against another.

A third point brought home by Pruitt and Olczak concerns the key difference between moderately and heavily escalated conflict systems. Almost lost in the midst of their ambitious chapter is an interesting thesis: namely, that moderate escalation requires changes in only one or two of the MACBE elements, whereas intractable conflict invokes all five. To the extent that the authors are correct in their assessment, this suggests the necessity of a multifaceted attack on escalated conflict; since all five elements are interrelated in a complex system, all five must be taken into account in any intervention.

One final observation: while both the five-element MACBE model and the seven-step sequence of modules for combating intractable conflict offer much room for reflection, they also leave us slightly dissatisfied, with a sense that things don't quite fit together on the same conceptual continuum. In the case of the MACBE model, E (environment) and B (behavior) seem rather different—as conceptual elements—from the first three: M (motivation), A (affect), and C (cognition). Moreover, it strikes us that much of the most interesting psychological material is assigned by default to the category of environment; what variable of social psychological interest would *not* go there? Regarding the seven modules for addressing intractable conflict, we find the authors' list an interesting one—but also a list with items that don't quite seem to belong together. Lowering one side's aspirations, for example, is an important precondition for inducing the kind of ripeness that is necessary. But how does this condition square with a second module in their approach, namely, conflict training? Somehow, conditions and procedures don't quite belong in the same conceptual basket.

The final chapter in the conflict section takes up the matter of conflict resolution training, alluded to by Pruitt and Olczak, and looks closely at the current uses, successes, and failures of such conflict training. More broadly, Ellen Raider addresses the translation of our cumulative knowledge about conflict and its resolution into relevant and usable strategies for social change. While the author acknowledges the place of negotiation and mediation training, her primary focus is on conflict resolution training in schools. How can we help teachers impart conflict resolution skills to their students? And what are these skills, exactly? In her focus on applications of conflict resolution training to the educational system, Raider's chapter forms a natural bridge with the chapter on cooperative learning training programs by David and Roger Johnson (in the section on cooperation).

Raider advances a ten-step model for teaching negotiation at the secondary school level. As she points out, the success of such an approach assumes some degree of participant willingness to act cooperatively toward one another. Yet, as both she and Mort Deutsch point out, classrooms and even teachers are often very encouraging of competition—and resistant to cooperative alternatives. The problems of moving people from a competitive to a more cooperative outlook (a problem that forms the core of the cooperation section) is key to Raider's efforts to describe a successful system for promoting conflict resolution skills. You can lead a horse to water, but you can't make it drink. And you can propose a sophisticated and exciting conflict resolution curriculum, but unless the gatekeepers (administrators, teachers) and end users (students) themselves are ready to embrace the possibilities that such a curriculum has to offer, training programs are likely to fail.

It is hard enough to shift an individual's outlook from competition (or individualism) to cooperation. Far more difficult is the task of shifting the perspective of an organizational system such as the

one represented by our educational institutions. More than a workshop of a few days is necessary, Raider points out, especially if participants are to be given the necessary opportunity to learn,
practice, and internalize new behaviors. And while Raider describes
in detail a program that is designed to coach and help participants
internalize the things they have learned, we wonder if this is sufficient. Theorists of organizational culture change (Deal & Kennedy,
1982; Schein, 1985) would probably observe that training individuals without simultaneous intervention to change the culture in
which such individuals act may attenuate the beneficial effects of
training. Unless the institutional culture changes, how much coun-
tercultural behavior will individuals be able to sustain?

At the same time, it is also clear that Raider appreciates the
importance of the national and ethnic differences addressed in
Faure's chapter. But where Faure points out the impact of culture
on the meaning of concepts, Raider focuses on cultural differences
in learning style, as well as the need to adapt interventions to different cultural learning preferences. It is quite possible that understanding the cultural meaning of some of the concepts analyzed by
Faure would enable more effective delivery of the very training that
Raider advocates.

One other observation is in order regarding the Raider chapter
on conflict resolution training, and it is provoked by Mort Deutsch's
own commentary. While he is correct in observing the appalling
lack of research on the various aspects of such training, there actually *is* a growing body of knowledge about the nature of effective
training. Kirkpatrick (1983), for example, outlines a four-level
framework for evaluating the effectiveness of training regimens:
Level 1: measures of participant reaction to the program; Level 2:
measures based on participant behavior both before and after a
training regimen; Level 3: measures of transfer of the training to the
participant's work setting; and Level 4: measures of how the training regimen actually affected the system's output or products, for
example, profit, waste, production, quality of work accomplished.

The higher the level at which one is operating, the more confident the change agent can be that the training regimen in question is having the desired effects on the organization. Perhaps this sort of crude classification system could be applied to the conflict resolution training field, as we continue our efforts to understand different ways of instilling (and knowing whether we have instilled) new conflict skills.

Before leaving the conflict section, we have two broad comments, stimulated both by the authors and by Deutsch's thoughtful responsive commentary. First, we are struck by the continuing importance of what might be called the unit of analysis problem. How should one best conceive of conflict: in individual, dyadic, or broader systemic terms? Rubin and Levinger's analysis of similarities and differences between interpersonal and international conflict seems largely driven by a dyadic perspective; power asymmetry, for example, is an attribute of the conflicting parties, not of one individual. But this dyadic perspective may have built-in limitations, as when the authors turn their attention to the settlement of conflict, arguing that there are a limited number of different approaches; their analysis, however, leaves no room for the possibility that one side may be ready to settle conflict through one approach (say, negotiation), while the other may be more inclined to capitulate, withdraw, or call on the services of an outside intervenor.

While the Faure chapter, in its focus on broad concepts of conflict, is not particularly hamstrung by the issue of unit of analysis, Pruitt and Olczak, as well as Raider, circle around this issue—albeit in somewhat different fashion than Rubin and Levinger. Thus, Pruitt and Olczak take a largely individualistic perspective; as already observed, such a perspective makes it difficult to engage fully the dyadic and dynamic features that attend the development of intractable conflict. Raider's perspective includes both the individual and interpersonal levels of analysis (as in the relationship between teacher and student, trainer and participant); but what of the broader institutional culture in which such training occurs?

While Raider certainly does acknowledge the importance of this broader template, relatively little of her analysis takes such contextual considerations into account.

Conflict theory rides on the back of the analytic units from which it is derived. Each unit brings something to the conceptual enterprise, while also leaving other possible gains behind. Needed, we believe, are multiple perspectives—individual, dyadic, group, institutional, and cultural—where these perspectives may at times offer contradictory insights. At least as often, however, we believe that the use of multiple conceptual lenses will likely enhance our ability to understand the nature and resolution of conflict.

Our second comment concerns Mort Deutsch's distinction between "grandiose" and "picayune" theorists. Picayune theorists do not generalize beyond the data, so their generalizations are very limited. Grandiose theorists—and Mort identifies himself as one—are trying to develop ideas that apply from cave people to space people, across cultures and across levels of analysis. Given Deutsch's distinction, who among us would deliberately choose to identify ourselves as a picayune theorist? All picayune theorists, please stand up and be recognized!

But beyond the fact that almost all of us, as social scientists, presume to be grandiose in our theoretical ambitions (leaving to others the necessary work of tracing out the picayune implications and details of our grand work), there are two broader implications that bear on the study of conflict. First, if one truly accepted the possibility of a grand (grandiose) theory of conflict, one with generalizability across lines of culture and levels of analysis, this would likely result in our smoothing over the differences in approach, assumption, and perspective that sharpen our overall theory. Pruitt and Olczak have enriched their analysis of intractable conflict immensely by building on the writings about conflict-intensified marital relationships. And Faure's analysis of cultural differences in the understanding of concepts in conflict theory is immensely enriched by his very search for (what others might regard as picayune) differences rather than areas of grand overlap and homogeneity. It is the attention to differences, as well as similarities, that makes for the richest theory.

Second, in the area of conflict studies, one can see the yin and yang of both tendencies. In its earliest days, the conflict field was characterized by the presence of multiple disciplines, each operating in ignorance of the others, devising narrow theories in the absence of a broader formulation. Over the last several decades, the conflict field has moved in the direction of grandiosity, taking strength and comfort from the view that conflicts at different levels, in different cultures, and at different points along the theory-practice continuum are fundamentally alike. While this view is certainly appealing, we have argued that such a perspective papers over differences in perspective that may be most instructive.

No doubt, *both* conceptual perspectives—integration and differentiation, lumping and splitting, theorizing that is grandiose and that which is picayune—are necessary. Theory building requires both halves, and these must work not in competition but in collaboration with each other.

## Cooperation

Even before he began writing in earnest on the topic of conflict, Mort Deutsch wrote about the causes and consequences of cooperation and competition; indeed, this was the topic of his dissertation research in the late 1940s. In the years since, Mort and others have written extensively about various aspects of the original formulation, with particular interest in the effects of cooperation on a broad range of outcomes.

In his comments on the three chapters in this section of the book, our mentor reminds readers of the fragility of cooperation. Citing a passage from a 1985 publication, he notes that the inherent tendency of cooperative communities is to break down. The three chapters in this part see things differently. Each, in its own way, takes up the case for trust, cooperation, and promotive interdependence and argues for the (surprising) robustness of the phenomenon in question. Mort may have doubts about the stability and staying power of cooperation, but his students, friends, and colleagues clearly are more optimistic.

While each chapter tackles a different topic, all end up building on Mort's original theory of cooperation (and competition). Roy Lewicki and Barbara Bunker examine the nature of trust, which is a key concept in cooperation theory. Cooperation, notes Mort Deutsch, has three distinct effects: substitutability, positive cathexis, and inducibility. The second chapter, by Virginia Vanderslice, takes each of these three effects and examines them in the context of worker cooperatives. The chapter by David Johnson and Roger Johnson offers a comprehensive review of the research evidence concerning the effects of cooperation and then examines the specific effectiveness of training programs.

The first of the three chapters, by Lewicki and Bunker, lays out a stage model of trust, and this alone constitutes an important contribution to the literature. For too long, theorists have regarded trust as a largely monolithic construct and have thrown a disparate assortment of issues pertaining to trust into a single conceptual basket. The authors depart from this narrow view of trust in the model they outline.

Lewicki and Bunker argue that the easiest and earliest form of trust is one based on deterrence, or, more broadly, what the authors refer to as *calculus-based trust* (CBT). This early form of trust occurs when people do what they say because of the consequences of doing anything else. When one has enough information about others to understand them and to predict accurately their likely behavior, another stage of trust is reached: *knowledge-based trust* (KBT). This form of trust de-emphasizes interpersonal control by sanctions and emphasizes control via predictability. Finally, there's *identification-based trust* (IBT), which is based on a full internalization of the other party's desires and intentions. These three types of trust are usually understood and ordered such that one must first experience calculus-based trust (CBT) before moving on to knowledge-based trust (KBT), with identification-based trust (IBT) coming only after that.

The chapter by Lewicki and Bunker offers a clear and sensible answer to their central question: "Is trust fragile?" Their answer is that it depends on the kind of trust invoked. Trust violations are not simple unilinear events; the phenomenon of a violation differs at different stages. In CBT, for example, safeguards (sanctions) are such that violations bring predictable responses, probably without self-esteem implications. In KBT, a violation means my information was faulty or my perception inaccurate, or that this was an externally caused, one-time-only event. But in IBT, much more is involved in a violation, namely, vulnerability. The authors have thus made a start at moving from gross generalization (trust is fragile) to specifying when it is—and perhaps when it is not so fragile at all.

Still, there are questions to which this chapter gives rise, questions that invite continuing attention by interested scholars. First, if it is true, as Lewicki and Bunker argue, that one first experiences CBT, then KBT, and finally IBT, how explain the trust an infant has for his or her parent or a puppy for its master? Is this really a matter of calculus? Or is the child perhaps simply born with a degree of basic trust in the world, believing the world to be a kind and gentle place—unless or until proven otherwise? Perhaps the resting state is one of trust, rather than distrust or suspicion, with this state modified based on subsequent experience. The authors write that at the beginning of relationships, trust is very fragile, for there is no history to count on. Are they not assuming that distrust is the resting state, the status quo, with trust being the result of a departure from this initial experience? But is this really true of infants and puppies? Don't they come into this world full of trust, with the expectation that they will be looked after, tended to, cared for?

Second, and consistent with our observations about several of the chapters in the conflict section, Lewicki and Bunker advance a model that is largely unilateral in nature. Their trust model focuses on the conditions under which person A comes to trust B, but what about trusting relationships? One can understand such relationships as the simple combination of A trusting B and B trusting A, or one can argue instead that something *relational* has emerged that is qualitatively different than some additive property. A's trust of B may cause B to trust A in return, which increases A's trust, and so on. Where does such an interactive and dynamic perspective on trust fit into the authors' model? The answer, perhaps, is that it doesn't fit into the current framework but has a place in future iterations of the model.

Third, after combing through the intricacies of their trust model, the question remains: what happened to the role of affect? The model is frankly cognitive in nature and has set aside (at least temporarily) the more traditional view of trust as an affective state in which people care enough about others that they are willing to put their welfare (or that of individuals they care about) in the others' hands. If trust is reduced to a matter of predictability, then what are the limits of the concept of trust? Does it make sense for me to trust your intention to kill me? Does it make sense for me to trust your ability to behave in antisocial ways? What's happened to the element of caring that is so commonly associated with the concept of trust?

One final observation about the Lewicki and Bunker chapter seems in order. Although the authors have developed their model of trust with interpersonal settings in mind, it is interesting to consider how their model applies in settings that are rather different. In the international arena, for example, one can see all three forms of trust emerging, and in very much the sequence the authors posit. Thus, first is the trust based on some calculation of rewards and punishments; in the Middle East, the Palestinians and Israelis have long understood the harm (and potential benefit) the other side could inflict on them, and their trust could thus be reasonably described as calculus based. Second, there emerges the trust that comes from knowledge of another's pattern of behavior; in the Middle East, each side has come to know the other's moves so well over the years that a kind of knowledge-based trust has inevitably emerged. Finally, in the instance of identification—the last stage in the development of trust—witness the Oslo accords of September 1993, where trust resulted from Palestinians and Israelis coming to believe in the existence of a certain core of shared values and assumptions about peace in the region and about each other's core identity.

Virginia Vanderslice's chapter, the second one in the section on cooperation, offers a splendid counterpart to the Johnson and Johnson chapter (which follows), while making a number of valuable contributions in its own right. Where the Johnson brothers present a detailed excursion through the literature on cooperative interdependence, Vanderslice offers a textured account of cooperative interdependence as it operates in a real and important practical setting: worker cooperatives. In this chapter, we come to understand how cooperatives function, where they have succeeded and failed, and what opportunities and dangers they face in the future.

After a review of Mort Deutsch's theory of cooperation, Vanderslice examines each of the three so-called pathologies of cooperation (as described by Deutsch), using cooperatives in the United States as applied laboratories in which to test the theory. The author's overall assessment appears to run along the following lines: yes, cooperation *can* and *does* have problematic consequences, at least when people become overly cooperative. However, on the basis of an analysis of four cooperatives, these problems are less extreme than Mort would have us believe, and each can be countered through appropriate measures.

One potential problem resulting from undue cooperation is the development of vested interests, where people develop specialized functions and begin to lose sight of the big picture. In response, Vanderslice proposes the introduction of an incentive system that rewards performance; employees in cooperatives are thereby encouraged to focus on what they do and the quality of their performance, rather than the position they happen to occupy.

A second potential problem is that of nepotism or favoritism: cooperators may come to believe that only others like themselves, living inside the organizational tent, are worth caring about. In this regard, the author wisely points to the value of setting standards that apply to everyone and developing policies that are fair. As with the problem of vested interests, if ways can be found to judge performance based not on the position you happen to occupy or whom your friends happen to be, this should have the effect of objectifying the basis of evaluation.

A third potential problem in excessively cooperative systems is that of inducibility, meaning that cooperators are so eager to be helpful (and to not get in the way) that they bend over backward to do whatever the group appears to want them to do; as a result, group members may suppress personal doubts about the wisdom of some courses of action. Vanderslice does not find this to be a problem in the cooperatives she has evaluated. Indeed, she argues that employees in such cooperatives are more likely than their traditional counterparts to express dissenting views, as necessary.

The central threat to cooperatives (and more generally, to cooperative arrangements of all kinds) stems from the competitive nature of the United States culture and economy. Few Americans learn how to be part of a cooperative group or to value outcomes that are tied to group achievement. What Vanderslice is discussing here, of course, is closely akin to the Johnsons' account of the problem with cooperative approaches: namely, that they are difficult to implant, take too long to master, and run counter to the prevailing culture. Vanderslice has thus documented the importance of the Johnsons' assertion in the context of cooperatives.

Another point: we find Vanderslice's discussion of factors that can be used to help sustain cooperatives to be particularly valuable. This is so not only because of what she has to say about cooperatives but because of the implications for cooperative arrangements more generally. In theory, each of the factors she advances could be used in *any* cooperative arrangement, including the cooperative learning environment advocated by the Johnsons. Her advice concerning the problem of insulation (the need to protect cooperators from external attack), for example, suggests a model of education in which at least some classrooms are best taken out of the mainstream and deliberately isolated. And when Vanderslice raises the issue of compensation of cooperative employees (observing a disturbing tendency to pay workers below market wages, presumably on the grounds that it is so much more pleasant to work in a cooperative environment), her suggested solution (higher wages) makes perfect sense in the context of cooperative learning. Unless we pay teachers a decent wage, it will be all but impossible to create a learning environment in which they are willing to work to instill norms of cooperation.

One final observation is in order. Vanderslice's comments about the importance of education in cooperatives is reminiscent of Senge's idea (1990) of a "learning organization," an institution that is capable of ongoing change based on learning from its own experience. This idea, currently very popular in business circles, is indicative of the movement in United States organizations toward recognition of the need to retrain workers, to educate them to business realities so that they can be full partners in decision making for the larger enterprise. Senge's ideas have been criticized on the grounds that they lack practicality. Organizations need to learn, but how exactly can they go about doing this? Based on the Vanderslice essay, it looks like cooperatives are ahead of the pack in this regard. Perhaps social interdependence fosters norms that encourage an organizational capacity to learn.

The last chapter in this section, by David and Roger Johnson, stands as a powerful antidote to those who would preach the virtues of competition or rugged individualism. The authors offer an extensive overview of the research on the effects (and effectiveness) of cooperation, as observed in the laboratory, in the workplace, and in educational settings. As they point out, it is difficult to find an area of social psychological inquiry that has received closer scrutiny than cooperation. This is probably so for two different reasons. First, the original theory of cooperation and competition is framed in such a way that it has allowed researchers to examine its implications. Second, because of the obvious applied significance of social interdependence theory—in interpersonal relations, in the workplace, in school—the theory has generated enormous interest among practitioners. And no one has studied this bridge between theory and practice or helped make the principles of cooperation more user friendly in different settings than the Johnsons. David and Roger Johnson also happen to be brothers, which offers additional evidence in support of the possibilities of cooperation, even among such unlikely candidates as siblings!

The story the Johnson brothers have to tell is ultimately a tale with a simple message: cooperation works. It works more often, more ubiquitously, and more powerfully than we commonly assume. However, their story also leaves us wondering if things aren't just a bit more complex than would appear.

First, can cooperation and cooperative learning really serve as all things to all people? Is there really a simple, single elixir of cooperativeness that, like one of those old-fashioned patent medicines, can cure all aches and pains? What, we are left to ponder, are the potential or actual costs of a cooperative learning approach? Reading between the lines, it would appear that one such cost is time. The Johnsons imply that it takes a very long time—perhaps even a lifetime—to truly master the intricacies of cooperative learning. If so, then it is more important than ever to find some shorthand version that can be taught more quickly. Doing so would no doubt address the issue, raised by the authors, of why cooperative approaches have not been more widely accepted in the classroom.

Second, what has happened to the concept of individualism in the Johnsons' analysis? Perhaps, in advancing the strongest case possible for the virtues of cooperation, the authors have neglected some of the variants on Deutsch's three motivational orientations—cooperation, competition, individualism—that paint a more complex picture. Consider, for example, the meaning of the concept of enlightened self-interest in negotiation. According to this perspective, my objective as a negotiator should be to do the very best I can, enlightened by awareness of our interdependence. Because it is the case in negotiation that I can only get what I want if you allow me to, I need you. It is not that I like or dislike you, regard you as friend or adversary. The simple fact is that I need you in order to do well. For that reason, it will be necessary that you, the person at the other side of the table, also be able to do (at least acceptably) well.

Enlightened self-interest is neither individualism, cooperation, nor competition. It is a blend of individualism informed by interdependence. And while mixtures such as this do not find their way into the Johnsons' treatise on cooperation, we believe they have a place in a variety of applied settings. This raises the broader question: what is the best fit among cooperation, individualism, and competition? If one could design a situation to optimize energy and work flow, as well as personal growth, would one want to create a situation of cooperative interdependence only? The answer, we suspect, is no. It may be that some competition is energizing (at the intergroup level, this is certainly the case). Competition also challenges individuals to do their very best even when they compete against themselves, as in some sports. Any good thing, even cooperation, when taken to an extreme, may become a bad thing. We need to know more about creative mixtures of various motivational orientations, searching for the proper place and circumstances in which these mixtures can bring out the very best in people.

A third issue for further thought stems from the authors' characterization of cooperative learning and positive interdependence as ideal states, replete with numerous virtues and untold opportunities. And yet, we know the world out there often is a harsh place, full of rugged individualism, dog-eat-dog competitiveness. How can one reconcile cooperativeness as an ideal state with the demands and constraints of reality? Assuming that the Johnsons and their colleagues are eventually successful in implanting norms of cooperativeness in youngsters, how will this prepare them for the world of adulthood? How can one begin to create more cooperative patterns of interdependence—whether at home, in school, or on the job—without at the same time influencing the surrounding milieu to be more accepting of such an orientation?

More broadly, there may be a disconnect between the values inculcated in school and those that find acceptance in the world of work. In Japan, for example, the educational system is notoriously competitive, separating out only the very best and brightest for advanced training. Yet the Japanese work environment is alleged to be extremely cooperative, with consensus building regarded as a cardinal norm. How to reconcile these mismatches between childhood and the world of adulthood?

Before concluding our commentary on the cooperation section, we have a few more general observations about the three chapters. One of the things uniting all three is a shared belief in the possibilities of trust and cooperation. While none of the authors directly tackles the robustness of cooperation, each seems to believe in it. This enthusiasm for cooperation notwithstanding, we are left wondering if our mentor, Mort Deutsch, isn't right to be a bit skeptical. First, it takes two sides to develop a cooperative relationship, but only one sufficiently determined fool to make a mess of things. Cooperation may thus be a fragile state to establish because there must be some element of shared understanding and perspective; in the absence of such shared views, the relationship will deteriorate rapidly into one of individualism or competition. Second, to truly instill or implant cooperation, one must do more than change patterns of interdependence. One must also pay attention to the surrounding context. Cooperatives will have trouble surviving in the competitive work culture of the United States, writes Vanderslice, unless they can find some way of either changing the dominant culture (an impossibility) or isolating themselves sufficiently. And cooperative learning will continue to have trouble gaining acceptance, acknowledge the Johnsons, unless and until the larger educational system of which cooperative learning is a part comes to be more accepting of cooperation as a value system.

The second comment concerns the matter of stages, a topic always near and dear to the hearts of psychologists. Each of the three chapters proposes a developmental process that individuals, groups, and organizations must undertake if they are to achieve cooperation. The nature of these processes is spelled out by the authors in only rudimentary fashion, however. Perhaps one of the keys to instilling greater acceptance of cooperation, then, is to be found in the principles of stage theory. Perhaps what each of the contributors to this section is implicitly telling us is that only a graduated approach will do. Trust is acquired in stages; worker cooperatives have to move through several stages (as Mort Deutsch observes in his comments) before gaining broad acceptance, and cooperative regimens of all sorts must first obtain a toehold before their gains can be consolidated. We are left wondering whether the next round of research and theory in this area should not focus on the signposts along the road to broad-based acceptance of cooperation, and the steps that must be taken to advance from one of these signposts to the next.

## Justice

Every once in a while a paper appears with eventual influence that far exceeds its author's expectations. Surely this must be the case with Mort Deutsch's 1975 article in the *Journal of Social Issues*. In the space of twelve brief pages, our mentor threw out a challenge to the architects of equity theory, a formulation that had emerged as dominant both in economics and in parts of social psychology. Equity theory argued that people wish to be compensated in proportion to the resources they bring with them to an enterprise;

hence, the ratio of input to output should be equivalent from one person to the next. But, argued Deutsch, there are other justice motives apart from equity. In particular, one must pay attention to the circumstances that lead people to be motivated by equality and by need.

The four chapters in the concluding section of the book use Mort's stunningly influential paper as a springboard to move in new and exciting directions. Folger, Sheppard, and Buttram discuss how to reconcile or bridge the potential conflicts that arise among the three faces of social justice: equity, equality, and need. Similarly, the chapter by Tyler and Belliveau examines the trade-offs that arise among the three justice principles, although the authors carry the analysis in a strikingly different direction. If each of these chapters regards the search for justice as a motivational state, then Fine and Wong instead treat justice as a state; their chapter studies the situational conditions that conspire to induce conditions of injustice or instead lead people to feel that they have been justly treated. Finally, Opotow backs away from justice analysis and raises the broad question: who counts? Who is worthy of being regarded as a candidate for justice, anyway?

The chapter by Rob Folger, Blair Sheppard, and Robert Buttram is a tribute to Mort Deutsch's 1975 article on the three justice motives of equity, equality, and need. Institutional pursuit of sufficient economic productivity is driven by equity, the issue of adequate solidarity of group or organizational members is driven by the justice motive of equality, while the nurturing of those members to at least some minimal extent is driven by the justice principle of need. But Deutsch has primarily characterized the justice principles that operate in an institutional context; one of the contributions of the Folger, Sheppard, and Buttram chapter is to translate and extend this analysis into both interpersonal and individual settings.

The authors outline an S-A-N framework for understanding key elements in interpersonal relations. People, they say, are motivated by the need to feel that in certain ways they are like Some other people, like All others, and like No other person (that is, they are treated idiosyncratically). The wish to feel that one is being treated like all others taps into the motive of equality; the wish to feel that one is treated like some others ties into equity; while the wish to be treated in special ways relates to the principle of need. We are struck, in the S-A-N model, by the tension between using standards (such as equity and equality) in order to determine the outcomes one should receive and the wish at the same time to feel distinctive and special along the way. This potential tension is addressed, albeit in different ways, in the subsequent chapters by Tyler and Belliveau and by Fine and Wong.

If equity, equality, and need bear on the issue of *distributive* justice (the distribution of outcomes), then Folger, Sheppard, and Buttram advance three principles (building on the work of Tyler and Lind, 1992) that bear on the matter of *procedural* justice (concerning the *way* in which justice is meted out by a decision maker, quite independent of the outcomes obtained). These three principles are neutrality, standing, and trust. The first of these decision-maker attributes, neutrality, reflects honesty and lack of bias. It corresponds in a rough way to the justice principle of equality, inasmuch as it presumes that we will be treated in like fashion by the decision maker in question. Standing refers to the sense that one's place in a hierarchical structure is taken into account, and it relates to the justice principle of equity. Finally, trust involves the belief that a decision maker is treating people in a fair and reasonable way, and it corresponds in a rough way to the principle of need.

It can thus be seen that one of the chief contributions of the chapter by Folger, Sheppard, and Buttram is to extend Mort Deutsch's 1975 tripartite analysis of justice principles in two directions: first, from institutional to interpersonal and individual levels, and second (much as Tyler and Belliveau do in their own way), from distributive to procedural justice issues. In extending Mort's ideas in these ways, the authors have, in effect, pointed to the power and parsimony of these ideas. No wonder they conclude their essay with a tip of the hat to Mort Deutsch.

At one point in their ambitious chapter, Folger, Sheppard, and

Buttram suggest that the three justice principles may coexist as conflicting standards. In thus asserting the conflicting nature of the equity, equality, and need justice principles, the authors are very much in keeping with the writing of many theorists working in the justice area. Indeed, the tension among these principles is acknowledged in the next chapter, by Tyler and Belliveau, and these authors cite others who, in turn, have been interested in the conflicting push and pull of equity, equality, and need.

But why, exactly, must these three principles be conceived as oppositional? Why cannot the three coincide and function in a syntonic way? As but one small example, consider the situation in which two people have equal claims to a single orange. (Negotiation aficionados will recognize this orange story from Fisher, Ury, and Patton, 1991.) Each individual is equally thirsty and has exactly the same opportunity—or lack thereof—to quench his or her thirst in other ways. Moreover, each has worked just as hard as the other and hence is equally deserving of the reward afforded by a piece of orange. The principle of equality would call for the two to divide the orange 50–50. But the principle of equity would also call for a 50–50 split. And since they are equally needy, the last principle (need) would similarly lead to an even division of the orange.

In this simple illustration, the three principles are not in conflict at all. Rather, they are operating in a perfectly complementary way, pointing all the more clearly toward what Schelling (1960) would call a prominent solution. An even division of the orange fairly jumps off the page as the solution of choice, inasmuch as all three norms point in exactly the same direction.

While we realize that it is useful—for theory development purposes—to assume a conflict among the three standards of equity, equality, and need, it does seem that future analysts might do well to consider some of the ways and circumstances in which justice standards converge rather than conflict. Indeed, in his comments on the chapter by Folger, Sheppard, and Buttram, Mort Deutsch acknowledges Freed Bales's early research on group functioning, where it was observed that all task groups seem to require the services both of a task specialist (who moves the group toward completion of its work) and a socioemotional leader (who pays attention to interpersonal relations). The importance of both productivity and satisfaction goals, Mort continues, invites the speculation that in any truly effective group, its members have internalized both productivity and satisfaction standards—and know how and when to call on each. In other words, an effectively functioning group should be able to integrate the different standards of both distributive and procedural justice, to blend these into a harmonious package.

One final observation provoked by Folger, Sheppard, and Buttram. The authors point to the possible tension between two norms commonly applied in judgments of fairness. One is the norm of consistency: evaluate and treat everyone the same way, applying the same standard. The other is the norm of flexibility: people in positions of authority should be able to have the discretion to respond to individual needs and preferences, rather than having to apply a fixed algorithm across the board. Perhaps the way to reconcile this apparent tension between consistency and flexibility is by positing an ideal world in which standards of justice are applied consistently to *others* but flexibly to *us*. In other words (and this theme is echoed in several of the other chapters in the justice section), we may privately be in favor of a double standard, one that judges others according to a single, consistent metric, while giving us the benefit of the doubt whenever possible.

The thesis of the second chapter, by Tom Tyler and Maura Belliveau, is that issues of procedural justice may ultimately be more important than distributive concerns. As important as it is to get the outcomes one aspires to, it may be even more important to feel valued, to have a sense of personal gratification, to have one's core identity confirmed. As evidence in support of this view, Tyler and Belliveau report research in which decision makers regarded the use of fair procedures as more central to issues of interpersonal relations than making fair decisions.

This is a provocative thesis. Think of it: what matters ultimately is not the outcomes one achieves but how one is made to feel along the way. And yet we are worried about the possible ideological danger inherent in such a perspective. Instead of paying workers a decent wage, would it suffice to persuade them that they are valued, respected, even loved by management and that they should be pleased to be part of their particular organization? It is not that the Tyler and Belliveau thesis is wrong, we believe, but that it is potentially dangerous. Rather than change the reward structure so that people end up getting what they deserve, institutions can instead fiddle with variables that have an impact on one's sense of fair play.

We are reminded here of a parallel approach currently found in various business organizations. Many companies are introducing programs to empower workers, to give workers both more control and more responsibility in their work life. When programs are accompanied by some kind of profit sharing, so that workers who participate more actively obtain a greater share of available profit, the system works fine. But some organizations are introducing structures that push for continuous improvement, like self-managing teams, without real recognition that the pay structure needs to reflect new roles and responsibilities. Ultimately, participants in these arrangements may cry foul.

Elsewhere, Tyler and Belliveau observe that there is a persistent tension within interactions, with people feeling that they deserve more than they get. This echoes our own observation on the tension between standards of consistency and flexibility. No matter what standard of justice is applied, it may be that we tend to feel undervalued and undercompensated. Indeed, as Tyler and Belliveau go on to point out, the very application of principles of equity, equality, and need may be experienced as a direct assault on feelings about the self. Any justice principle may leave us feeling undervalued, as if we've gotten something from the system not because of our idiosyncratic specialness but because of some rule! Institutions and groups promulgate rules and impose standards as a way of creating a level playing field. From the individual's perspective, however, the very imposition of such principles risks getting him or her lost in the maze of rules. What we want, above all else, is special treatment.

One final observation concerning the Tyler and Belliveau chapter is in order. They close with a brief but impassioned commentary on injustice as a motivating force. It is when people are deprived of the things they aspire to, write the authors, that their feelings of self-worth and self-esteem suffer. We find ourselves wondering, yet again, whether there may not be some principle of asymmetry in operation here: perhaps when it comes to matters of perceived injustice, Tyler and Belliveau are right to assert that people ultimately chafe at the sense of not being treated respectfully. However, when it comes to matters of justice, perhaps people lean more toward distributive principles and the attainment of coveted resources. To put this point another way, perhaps we are upwardly mobile when it comes to obtaining resources (wanting our fair share, and then some) but turn inward and lick our personal wounds when we experience ourselves as having been treated unjustly. When things are going well, we are less concerned with identity issues and more concerned with our share of the resource pie. But when things are going poorly, identity concerns come to the fore, provoked by an acute sense of all that we have been denied.

The third chapter in the justice section, by Michelle Fine and L. Mun Wong, contrasts well with the first two. Where Folger, Sheppard, and Buttram, as well as Tyler and Belliveau, argue that justice is a motivational state and a personal need, Fine and Wong argue from the perspective that justice and injustice are creatures of societal structure and institutional abuse. If the first two chapters discuss the ways in which the search for principles of justice informs both the distribution of outcomes and the procedures that govern interpersonal relations, Fine and Wong are concerned instead with the vicelike grip of social structure (what Mort Deutsch refers to in his comments as "institutional muzzling").

Early in this powerfully written contribution, the authors use the illustration of Hester Prynne to indicate the value of occupying marginal positions in social interaction. We entirely agree. Marginality allows the individual to stand apart, to gain the perspective that comes from being perched at the edge of events, able to peer into multiple worlds from his or her special place. Because of their ability to occupy multiple statuses, to have access (even temporarily) to multiple groups, to see the world through multiple lenses, marginal individuals are important sources of insight. They also can serve as gatekeepers to social influence and social change. For example, if you hope to influence management to change its policy on a set of issues, you may wish to begin by seeking out the assistance of someone who once was (but no longer is) a member of management; this person will know who to talk to, how to construct an influence strategy, and so on. And if you, as an American business executive, are about to negotiate with the Chinese, you may wish to begin by talking with a Chinese who has lived in both cultures, who can help you understand some of the issues and perspectives you will want to take into account.

Marginality thus confers access to differing, often conflicting, sources of information. *Being* marginal, however, is another story, especially if one is not marginal by choice. It's one thing to be able to move from one group to another, gaining acceptance in each, able to move away and enjoy one's marginal status for as long as one chooses. And it's another matter entirely to be forced into marginality, to be stripped of one's proper place in a group because one is simply not right or acceptable in some way. The chapter by Fine and Wong is primarily concerned with these latter folk, the true victims of injustice.

As the authors write, those who are most oppressed and subjugated see most clearly the silhouettes of social injustice. And yet the authors also observe that victims frequently see themselves as well treated, even if they acknowledge that their groups are disadvantaged. How, then, to explain this paradox, the idea that others in one's group are being badly treated while you yourself have been singled out for special care? The answer, we suspect, fits with the Tyler and Belliveau view that we tend to distort our perceptions of justice in ways that either favor or harm us relative to the treatment of others. If we see ourselves as deserving of special treatment, while belonging to a group that is being treated poorly, then we will constantly be on the lookout for cues that allow us to think that we are different from the rest of the pack. Part of the reason that many Jews ended up trapped in Nazi Germany is that, while they acknowledged the miserable treatment that Jews were being subjected to elsewhere, they concluded that this did not apply to them. They were special Jews.

It is this subjective sense that principles of justice (or injustice) apply differently to others than to oneself that plays right into the hands of institutional coercion. As Fine and Wong write, institutions are clever at producing a focus on individuals and away from institutional policies and practices. Yes, institutions are very good at knowing how to buy individual collaboration through the judicious application of reward. For example, when you go to request a pay raise, you are told that there are limited funds in the budget this year. But you are told that *you are an exception* to the rule and will be granted a special raise anyway. The net effect is likely to be one of co-optation. Your need to feel different and especially deserving has made it possible for you to be bought off by the organization.

Elsewhere, Fine and Wong note that while a sense of collective identity facilitates the public critique of social injustice, a belief in individualistic meritocracy inhibits it. Again, if we believe we are individually favored by those around us, this will buy off our passion for disruption and social reform. The challenge is to find some way to create a collective identity, a sense of *we*-ness that swamps the perhaps more dominant (at least in our culture) sense of *I*-ness. This is very much what Mort Deutsch is saying in his responsive commentary, when he writes that those who are successful despite injustices must retain their psychological identities as members of the collective and not allow themselves to be seduced into believing that the lack of success of others in their group is due to a lack of individual merit. Looping back to the Tyler and Belliveau chapter, we are left wondering whether the posited dominance of needs for self-esteem and identity confirmation over the achievement of successful outcomes does not leave us all a bit too vulnerable to the subtleties of institutional abuse through the administration of selective reward.

The concluding chapter in this section, by Susan Opotow, examines justice issues from a strikingly different angle. Where the first two chapters evaluated the role of different justice motives and the third analyzed the role of institutional constraints on justice, Opotow expands the canvas to consider one of the core justice issues: namely, who is entitled to just treatment, and who exists outside this charmed circle?

In deciding who counts, Opotow argues that people look for excuses to exclude others from moral consideration. This one doesn't count because she's different. That one is food (for example, beef, lamb) so it doesn't have rights. This one feels differently than we do about death (for example, the American view of the Vietcong during the Vietnam War). That one doesn't feel pain and suffering the way we do. And so forth. Opotow's chapter highlights the same self-serving biases that have emerged in each of the justice section. "All animals are equal," says one of the pigs in George Orwell's *Animal Farm*, "but some animals are more equal than others." You should be subjected to standards of justice; I deserve special treatment. You don't deserve to be considered for just treatment at all; I certainly do. In this way, we too often tend to differentiate ourselves from others, and in ways that allow us to look away from others' misery.

In a similar vein, Opotow points out that we tend to regard social conventions of the present as more humane and fair than those of the barbarous past when blatant inhumanities were condoned. In other words, we tend to regard people from past eras as somehow more primitive than we are today. They were simple, but we are complex. They were rigid and dogmatic in their outlook, but we are subtle, flexible, and differentiated in our thinking. More broadly, one can see, yet again, the powerful tendency to skew perceptions of others vis-à-vis ourselves in a self-serving fashion. Whether it is people from one culture peering out at members of another culture and concluding that their values are not only different but lesser than their own, or members of one race, gender, or sexual orientation encountering someone different than themselves, the underlying process appears to be very much the same.

A potentially interesting and important illustration of the all-too-human tendency to create boundaries of moral inclusion and exclusion can be seen in the wave of "political correctness" (PC) that is currently sweeping some circles in the United States. In the name of being more open and tolerant of diverse perspectives, the PC movement insists that there are right ways of thinking and wrong ways (not unlike the cultural revolution in the People's Republic of China some years ago). For example, if you fail to distinguish between Native Americans and individuals from the nation of India—referring to both simply as Indians—you are showing your insensitivity to an important distinction. To be insensitive in this way is, in turn, to become unworthy of inclusion in a group of open-minded, politically correct people. Thus, in the name of openness and tolerance of diversity, the PC movement has come to impose its own special rules of inclusion and exclusion.

More broadly, this leaves us wondering whether it isn't in the very nature of social movements of all kinds—or, indeed, in the very nature of the human condition—to create a sense of we-ness and they-ness. Social psychologists have long understood the power of even minimal social cues in leading people to differentiate themselves from those around them. After all, if everyone and everything were to be included for consideration, how would differentiation ever occur? Like stereotyping, rules of moral inclusion and exclusion help us to simplify our cognitive and psychological environment, making it easier for us to distinguish between those who are acceptable and those who are not.

In his responsive commentary, Mort Deutsch observes the distinction between being excluded and not being included. Exclusion, he points out, is a more active process. This raises for us the broader issue of what may be called the resting state in justice decisions. Are people included unless and until rules for exclusion are derived? Or is it possibly the reverse, namely, that people are excluded unless reasons can be found for inclusion? Opotow seems to assume that the former principle applies, but we wonder under what circumstances the latter occurs. Country clubs, universities, fraternities, and countless other associations and organizations seem to proceed from the view that other people (strangers) are excluded from consideration (moral and otherwise) unless special conditions pertain, as when an individual is allowed access to the inner sanctum. We find ourselves wondering what sort of theory of moral justice would develop if one proceeded from automatic exclusion to inclusion, rather than the other way around.

Elsewhere in the paper, Opotow comments that our capacity for justice appears to be finite. Although Mort Deutsch seems to accept this assertion as valid, we would demur. Why not assume that an orientation toward moral justice makes it that much more likely that one will apply standards of moral justice in other settings and circumstances? Just as we typically assume that there are no limits to the love we can feel toward others, why not assume that justice functions in much the same way? It is often said that truly learning how to love makes it possible to love more widely and wisely. Perhaps the same applies to behaving in moral ways toward others. In any event, we see no reason to posit some innate human limitation in our capacity to experience a sense of justice.

One final comment on the Opotow chapter. The author raises a valuable question: how can we interrupt the cycle of exclusion and harm doing? Her answers include learning to take the perspective of others during conflict, resolving conflicts quickly—before they can escalate out of control—and seeking solutions that integrate the concerns and interests of the parties involved. But there are other possibilities as well. As Johnson and Johnson, as well as Vanderslice, indicate, it may be possible to help interrupt the cycle of exclusion by enhancing a sense of positive interdependence. Also, what about the possibility of introducing an external enemy, thereby redefining the boundaries of one's own group so as to include others who were heretofore excluded? The list continues, and we would encourage scholars interested in the topic to turn their attention more systematically to the issue of breaking the cycle of moral exclusion.

To summarize our musings on these four justice section chapters, we were struck with our mentor's revelation about the origins of his own interest in justice. As a young child, excluded from a softball game, Mort Deutsch came to understand the painful experience of exclusion, of not counting, of being the victim of (as he experienced it) deliberate injustice. Each of these chapters explores this agenda further, each in its own way. Opotow tries to understand why people are excluded. Fine and Wong explore the role of institutions in manipulating people according to their own agenda. Tyler and Belliveau, as well as Folger, Sheppard, and Buttram, build on Mort's earlier and influential writings to understand better how, why, and when different standards of justice are applied.

Finally, we are struck by the parallelism among the four chapters in their emphasis on what can be crudely called issues of asymmetry. We see others differently than we see ourselves; on this, all the authors seem to agree. We believe in justice, but especially for us. And we believe in the importance of standards, except when we're the object of them. Then we insist on special treatment. It is this human tendency to regard issues of justice in this asymmetric way that brings a very human face to the checks and balances of more unabashedly economic formulations. Such formulations can take us only so far. It is left to the students of human behavior to understand why justice is ultimately judged with so subjective a yardstick.

## Conclusions

Having commented on each of the book's contributions, we close with a few observations about the themes that have bubbled up in this concluding chapter. These themes apply with equal pertinence to the topics of conflict, cooperation, and justice, and we briefly comment on each.

One broad conceptual issue discussed here concerns the unit of analysis problem. Is it the individual, the relationship, or the larger social system that is, or should be, the object of research interest? Different theoretical frameworks emerge, depending on which conceptual unit of analysis is chosen. A theory of intractable conflict, trust, or procedural justice will look very different when the individual decision maker is the unit of analysis or when it is instead the interactive relationship. This is surely not a new issue in social psychology, but the chapters in this book are a reminder of the continuing attention this issue deserves.

Second, we have had reason to comment on Mort Deutsch's distinction between grandiose and picayune theory in the social sciences. While we respect our mentor's preference for the grander, more conceptually ambitious formulations, we have argued that both forms of intellectual inquiry are necessary if theory is to be advanced. Lumpers get lost in the stars without their splitter counterparts, while splitters are in danger in disappearing in a welter of detail without the visionary inclinations of their lumper brethren. Both perspectives are necessary, whether one is developing theories of conflict, cooperation, or justice. Again, while we acknowledge that this is certainly far from a new issue, the chapters in this book attest to the importance of maintaining a balance between integrating and differentiating perspectives. And if a balance cannot conveniently be maintained, then turn taking can be a fun way to keep both ends of the theory development continuum in motion.

A third conceptual theme concerns what we have called the issue of asymmetry. This is our tendency to regard others differently than ourselves, to expect others to be held to a different standard than we (wish to) hold ourselves. Social psychologists have been writing about selective perception for years, but these chapters have brought home yet again the power of this cognitive process.

Fourth, although dealing with topics that could invite some measure of intellectual despair (conflict, cooperation and competition, and justice), the chapters have been surprisingly upbeat throughout. Mort Deutsch's reservations about the fragility of cooperation and trust notwithstanding (we would add justice to the list), the authors have been optimistic in their expectations that good will triumph over bad, justice over its darker counterpart, and constructive conflict resolution over its destructive sibling.

Finally, we have been impressed by the importance of grounding efforts at social change in a broader context. Cooperative learning and work arrangements will have a hard time surviving unless the surrounding educational or work environment is appropriately supportive. And efforts to make people feel like they are being treated justly will ultimately fail unless there are structural changes that corroborate this heightened sense of procedural justice. It should perhaps not be surprising that a group of (largely) social psychologists have reinvented the importance of ground in relation to figure, but we find it interesting that so many of the chapters in this collection have pivoted around the importance of understanding the larger context in which social change takes place.

And so we come to the end of this book's intellectual journey. Begun several years ago, with three-way conversations in New York restaurants, this enterprise comes to a close. Our mentor, Morton Deutsch, has been a guiding intellectual presence in our two lives and in the lives of his other students, his many colleagues, his many admirers and critics. His work has a life of its own, and Mort's ideas will continue to provoke, comfort, and persuade for many generations to come. Rather than echo his work here, we have tried to honor it and our mentor by prodding our colleagues to push differing lines of inquiry just a step or two beyond where we have come to at present. Possibly, some days or months hence, you the reader may find yourself intrigued by one of the observations found here and as a result decide to go back for yourself to Mort's many important writings. If you find yourself challenging these ideas, turning them in new and intriguing ways, then you will have brought great pleasure to the two of us and a twinkle to Mort's eyes. Thank you for joining with us in this adventure.

## References

Beckhard, R., & Harris, R. (1987). *Organizational transitions*. Reading, MA: Addison-Wesley.

Deal, T. E., & Kennedy, A. A. (1982). *Corporate cultures*. Reading, MA: Addison-Wesley.

Deutsch, M. (1975). Equity, equality, and need: What determines which value will be used as the basis of distributive justice? *Journal of Social Issues, 31*, 137–149.

Fisher, R., Ury, W. L., & Patton, B. M. (1991). *Getting to yes: Negotiating agreement without giving in* (2nd ed.). New York: Penguin.

Kirkpatrick, D. A. (1983). *A practical guide for supervisory training and development* (2nd ed.). Reading, MA: Addison-Wesley.

Schein, E. H. (1985). *Organizational culture and leadership*. San Francisco: Jossey-Bass.

Schein, E. H., & Bennis, W. G. (1965). *Personal and organizational change through group methods: The laboratory approach*. New York: Wiley.

Schelling, T. C. (1960). *The strategy of conflict*. Cambridge, MA: Harvard University Press.

Senge, P. M. (1990). *The fifth discipline: The art and practice of the learning organization*. New York: Doubleday.

Tyler, T. R., & Lind, E. A. (1992). A relational model of authority in groups. In M. P. Zanna (Ed.), *Advances in experimental social psychology* (Vol. 25, pp. 115–192). San Diego: Academic Press.

# Name Index

• • • • • • • • • • • • • • • • • • • • • • • • • • • • •

# Subject Index

## A

Abrogation of rights, 349

Academic controversy, teaching, 99–100, 213, 227–228, 243–244, 338

Acceptance therapy, 78

Accountability, group member, 222

Achievement and social interdependence, 214–216, 239, 304

Action effects on others, 206–207

Adolescents, 238–239, 240–241; peer conflicts research on, 353–354, 356–357, 358–360; urban dropout, 331–335

*Adult Conflict Resolution*, 102

Adult training. *See* Conflict resolution training

Adversaries. *See* Information; Perception

Affect, ambivalence and amplification of, 115, 363–364, 407, 412

Agents, trusted, 151–153, 160

Aggression: culture-bound views of, 42–43; physical, 358–359; scope of justice and severity of, 358–359. *See also* Power; Warfare

Agreements: conflict resolution, 26, 111, 242–243; enforceability of, 26, 31, 34–35; win-win, 67

Air traffic controllers (PATCO), 326–327

Alienation, 328, 338, 376

Allocation, distributive justice, 54, 279, 301, 352, 374–375; procedural justice and, 303–304

Alternative organizations, 185, 190

Altruism, 379

Ambivalence-Amplification Theory, 363–364

America. *See* Latin America; United States

Analysis approach to conflict, 74–77, 80–81, 86, 115; before negotiation, 83. *See also* Conflict

Anger, 74, 77, 87 n. 2, 162

Animals, justice for, 353

Antagonists, perceptions of, 28–29, 31, 361–363, 387–388

Antecedents: of conflict, 21–22, 33, 42–43; of conflict resolution, 72; of justice, 299, 305–306, 307, 354–360

Apologies and justice, 283–285

Arab cultures, 43, 44–45

Arbitration. *See* Mediation

Asia. *See* China; Japan

Aspirations. *See* Goals (aspirations); Interdependence, promotive

Assertiveness training, 74

Association for Supervision and Curriculum Development (ASCD), 102